PHILOSOPHICAL AND IDEOLOGICAL VOICES IN EDUCATION

Related Titles of Interest

Current Issues and Trends in Education
Jerry Aldridge & Renitta Goldman
ISBN: 0-321-07978-7

Impact Teaching: Ideas and Strategies for Teachers to Maximize Student Learning
Richard Howell Allen
ISBN: 0-205-33414-8

The Way Schools Work: A Sociological Analysis of Education, Third Edition
Kathleen Bennett de Marrais & Margaret LeCompte
ISBN: 0-8013-1956-0

New Teacher's Performance-Based Guide to Culturally Diverse Classrooms
Timothy R. Blair
ISBN: 0-205-38206-1

How to Develop a Professional Portfolio: A Manual for Teachers, Third Edition
Dorothy M. Campbell, Pamela Bondi Cignetti, Beverly J. Melenyzer, Diane H. Nettles, & Richard M. Wyman
ISBN: 0-205-39341-1

Researching Teaching: Exploring Teacher Development through Reflexive Inquiry
Ardra L. Cole & J. Gary Knowles
ISBN: 0-205-18076-0

Developing a Professional Teaching Portfolio: A Guide for Educators
Patricia Costantino & Marie De Lorenzo
ISBN: 0-205-32955-1

The Moral Stake in Education: Contested Premises and Practices
Joan F. Goodman & Howard Lesnick
ISBN: 0-321-02340-4

Historical Documents in American Education
Tony W. Johnson & Ronald Reed
ISBN: 0-801-33314-8

College Division
ALLYN AND BACON
75 Arlington Street, Suite 300
Boston, MA 02116
www.ablongman.com

PHILOSOPHICAL AND IDEOLOGICAL VOICES IN EDUCATION

GERALD L. GUTEK

Professor Emeritus
Loyola University Chicago

Boston ■ New York ■ San Francisco
Mexico City ■ Montreal ■ Toronto ■ London ■ Madrid ■ Munich ■ Paris
Hong Kong ■ Singapore ■ Tokyo ■ Cape Town ■ Sydney

Executive Editor: *Stephen D. Dragin*
Senior Editorial Assistant: *Barbara Strickland*
Senior Marketing Manager: *Tara Whorf*
Editorial-Production Administrator: *Annette Joseph*
Editorial-Production Service and Electronic Composition: *Stratford Publishing Services*
Composition Buyer: *Linda Cox*
Manufacturing Buyer: *Andrew Turso*
Cover Administrator: *Kristina Mose-Libon*

For related titles and support materials, visit our online catalog at
www.ablongman.com.

Between the time Website information is gathered and then published, it is not unusual for
some sites to have closed. Also, the transcription of URLs can result in typographical errors.
The publisher would appreciate notification where these errors occur so that they may be
corrected in subsequent editions.

Library of Congress Cataloging-in-Publication Data

Gutek, Gerald Lee.
    Philosophical and ideological voices in education / Gerald L. Gutek.
      p.   cm.
    Includes bibliographical references and index.
    ISBN 0-205-36018-1
    1. Education—Philosophy.   I. Title.

  LB14.7.G88 2004
  370'.1—dc21   2003051879

Printed in the United States of America

10 9 8 7 6 5 4 3   HAM 08 07 06 05 04

For my grandson, Charles Milford Jordan III, "Mills,"
and his parents, Jennifer and Charles Jordan

CONTENTS

■ ■ ■ ■ ■

CHAPTER THREE
Realism   35

CHAPTER FOUR
Theistic Realism (Thomism)   53

CHAPTER FIVE
Pragmatism   70

CHAPTER SIX
Existentialism   86

CHAPTER SEVEN
Philosophical Analysis   107

CHAPTER EIGHT
Postmodernism   121

PART II   IDEOLOGIES AND EDUCATION

CHAPTER NINE
Ideology and Education   142

xii CONTENTS

CHAPTER TWELVE
Conservatism   197

CHAPTER THIRTEEN
Marxism   215

CHAPTER SIXTEEN
Essentialism, Basic Education, and Standards   263

CHAPTER SEVENTEEN
Perennialism   279

CHAPTER EIGHTEEN
Progressivism   294

PREFACE

Philosophical and Ideological Voices in Education is intended for use in the Cultural Foundations of Education, especially in the philosophy and ideology of education. The book is divided into three parts: Part I—Philosophies of Education; Part II—Ideologies and Education; Part III—Theories of Education.

Part I introduces the subject of philosophy of education and examines the following philosophies: Idealism, Realism, Theistic Realism or Thomism, Pragmatism, Existentialism, Philosophical or Language Analysis, and Postmodernism. Idealism, Realism, and Theistic Realism are considered more traditional philosophies, resting on a foundation of metaphysics. Existentialism, Pragmatism, Philosophical Analysis, and Postmodernism are more recently developed philosophies that reject metaphysics. They emphasize areas such as epistemology, language, or social relationships, rather than metaphysics.

Part II examines the relationship between ideology and education. It seeks to define and clarify the nature of ideology, a term frequently used but loosely examined in educational discourse. Part II also discusses the nature of ideology in relation to Liberalism, Conservatism, Marxism, and Liberation Pedagogy. Liberalism and Conservatism are two highly visible and influential ideologies that command a large number of adherents in American society and politics. The implications for educational policy and legislation are emphasized in the discussion of Liberalism and Conservatism. Marxism is examined primarily as a tool of analysis that continues to influence educational thinking, especially among Postmodernists and Critical Theorists. Although its precise location as a philosophy, ideology, or theory is subject to debate, I have located Paulo Freire's Liberation Pedagogy within the section of the book that deals with ideologies. This is because of Freire's belief that all education is grounded in ideology.

Part III examines theory and education in general, and then discusses Essentialism, Perennialism, Progressivism, and Critical Theory as four theories of education. Although somewhat similar, Essentialism and Perennialism are shown to have different philosophical origins. Perennialism's affinities with Aristotelian Realism and Thomism are emphasized as a key area of difference. Progressivism is treated in relationship to Pragmatism and Liberalism. Critical Theory is discussed in terms of its relationship to Postmodernism and Liberation Pedagogy.

RELATIONSHIP OF THE PARTS

The three main subjects of the book—philosophies, ideologies, and theories—are examined as related themes that often intersect in educational ideas. Part I, on philosophy and education, establishes the broad perimeters of the field and indicates the orientation of each of the philosophies to metaphysics, epistemology, axiology, and logic. Each of these areas is then related to education, schooling, curriculum, and instruction. Part II, on ideology, points out that while ideologies are different from philosophies, they often draw on or derive some of their principles from philosophy. Part III, on theory, makes a further relationship to the preceding parts by indicating that some theories borrow principles and terminology from philosophy and ideology.

CHAPTER HEADINGS AND SECTIONS

In writing the book, I did not deliberately strive to make each chapter parallel in its sections and headings. Rather, I let the subject lead me to the important points I thought should be made. However, there is a pattern throughout the book, in that each chapter includes the following:

- Definitions of the philosophy, ideology, or theory.
- A placement of the philosophy, ideology, or theory in its history, and in relation to its major contributors.
- An answer to the question: Why study the philosophy, ideology, or theory?
- A discussion of the major principles and educational implications of the philosophy, ideology, or theory.

PRIMARY SOURCE SELECTIONS

The primary source selections are intended to illuminate and give greater depth to the particular philosophy, ideology, or theory being discussed. Whenever possible, primary sources have been selected to illustrate the views of founding figures, such as Plato for Idealism, Aristotle for Realism, and Mill for Liberalism, for example. Other selections deal directly with educational issues or represent contemporary points of view. A feature of the primary source selections is the focusing questions that precede each selection. They are designed to guide the reader through the particular selection.

OTHER PEDAGOGICAL FEATURES

Among the book's pedagogical features are Discussion Questions, Inquiry and Research Projects, Internet Resources, and Suggestions for Further Reading.

In addition, boxes highlight and summarize key points for the philosophies, ideologies, and theories examined. In my classes I frequently use such summary boxes to reiterate important points. As I wrote the book, I decided to incorporate them into the text.

ACKNOWLEDGMENTS

I want to thank Steven I. Miller, my colleague in Foundations of Education at Loyola University, for his advice on some of the sections of the book.

My thanks go to Steven Dragin, my editor at Allyn and Bacon, for his encouragement and support as the manuscript was developed, reviewed, and revised.

My wife, Patricia, has always been a patient listener as I discussed the book's problems and progress. My appreciation also goes to my daughter, Laura Lee Swiatek, a third-grade teacher, and my son-in-law, Charles Jordan, a former social science secondary teacher, who gave me their insights about the relationship of theory to practice.

CHAPTER ONE

PHILOSOPHY AND EDUCATION

This book is written for students in professional programs in teacher education—for those planning to become teachers, and for teachers in the early stages of their careers. It is intended to connect the urgent problems teachers face each day to the important issues that concern them over their entire careers as educators. An urgent problem must be solved immediately, often with a quick response. An important issue is one that will affect a teacher throughout her or his career. Many of the urgent problems relate to classroom management, dealing with the school as part of a larger educational system, and relationships among students, colleagues, supervisors, and parents. The important problems are those that deal with one's purpose as an educator, one's mission as a teacher, and one's relationship to the world of knowledge and to society and its problems. In discussing how to differentiate between the urgent and the important, I talked with a secondary school teacher of social studies. He identified the following as urgent matters he had to deal with every day as a teacher:

1. Taking class attendance (every class, every day, each week, for an entire semester or year) and considering the amount of time this takes and how it adds up during the academic semester or year.
2. Posting assignments for each school day. While following a course syllabus, he found it necessary to pinpoint and post assignments for the students.
3. Completing the various administrative tasks mandated as part of the school system. For example, completing an assignment sheet for homebound students who were ill; completing special education student evaluation forms, with attention to increased mainstreaming of special education students in general classes; meeting with colleagues to discuss joint teaching strategies and articulation between classes; filling out forms to check out a TV or VCR, or reserve a class period in the library.

While the teacher regarded these urgent matters as necessary within the school system, he felt that they often interfered with matters he knew were more important. Among the important matters he identified were: researching and understanding a new book or a new concept that he was preparing to teach to students and relating it to a larger body of knowledge; being prepared to discuss and interpret an important current event and relate it to the broader national and world scene; finding ways to determine how students were reacting to an area of knowledge, or to a new idea or concept. These more important concerns dealt with questions such as: What is knowledge? What is the relationship of events to the larger world? What does something mean? These important questions were those related to philosophy of education—to the questions: What is reality? What is true? How do we know? What does it mean? These are the questions that will be examined in this book as we proceed through philosophy and ideology of education and a consideration of educational theories.

Significant and persistent questions are present throughout a teacher's career: Why did I become and why do I remain a teacher? What am I doing as a teacher and does it make a difference? How do my actions and behavior as a teacher affect my students, not only today, but throughout their lives? What is the meaning and purpose of educating another person? What do I teach and why do I teach it?

When reflected upon, the urgent and immediate everyday concerns lead to larger and more enduring perspectives. The significant and important issues are philosophical in that they examine how teachers establish what they believe is true or false, good or evil, right or wrong, beautiful or ugly. The philosophical examination of what makes something significant provides an opportunity to reflect on the urgent and the important and to study their relationship to each other.

Many students in teacher education programs and teachers in their early careers are often so preoccupied with urgent problems that they tend to defer the truly important matters for a future they hope will be less hectic and less hurried. They often approach philosophy of education as a subject that is remote from the urgent problems of the contemporary classroom. In contrast, many experienced teachers who have dealt with the urgent but everyday problems of motivating students, planning lessons, managing classrooms, and assessing students' progress want to probe more deeply into the larger questions of education and to construct a perspective on their lives as professional educators.

In this book, I want to bridge the gap between the urgent and the important concerns by providing a philosophical, ideological, and theoretical context that helps to put them into perspective. Such a perspective allows the teacher to stand back from the immediate issues and to see how they relates to a career in education.

Philosophy of education examines questions of: What is the meaning and purpose of education? Why, and how, do teachers educate people? What difference does education make for individuals and for society? These questions cannot be answered by true–false or multiple choice tests. These questions are points of departure to teachers' significant concerns. Just as our life journey is one of a growing perspective into our relationships to the world, its peoples, cultures, and societies, our study of philosophy, ideology, and theory of education challenges us to develop our own answers to these questions and to create our own philosophies of education.

WHAT IS EDUCATION?

If a teacher is asked, "What do you do as a teacher?" the most obvious and direct answer is likely to be, "I educate students."

While we can agree that teachers educate students, we can ask other questions: What do you mean by education? What are you doing when you educate someone? While the questions are direct, the answers are neither easy nor simple. For example, do the following responses really answer the question: What do you mean by education?

- I teach students to read, write, compute, and use a computer.
- I teach students to be economically productive persons and good citizens.
- I teach students to appreciate art, literature, music, and drama.
- I teach students the skills needed in industry and business.
- I teach students to be critical thinkers and problem-solvers.

If, like good students, we go to the dictionary to find the meaning of the word *education*, we will find the following:

1. The act or process of educating or being educated.
2. The act or process of providing a person with the knowledge, skill, competence, or usually desirable qualities of behavior or character by a formal course of study, instruction, or training.
3. A conditioning, strengthening, or disciplining of the mind or faculties.[1]

Although the dictionary points us toward an answer, it does not tell us what kind of knowledge, skill, competence, or desirable qualities of behavior are to be provided. It is this consideration of "what kind of" or "whatness" that brings us to philosophy of education. When we deal with philosophical questions, we are concerned with the most general concerns about what is true, what is good, and what is beautiful to all, not only some, of us. At this juncture, we become involved with philosophy's four major subdivisions:

- **Metaphysics,** the study of what is ultimately real and what really exists; it deals with essence, that which remains after all else is gone or that which is essential to existence. Closely related to metaphysics is *cosmology*, speculation about the universe's origin and structure.

- **Epistemology,** examining issues of knowing, deals with how we acquire knowledge, what we can know, and how we can explain or justify what we claim to know. How do we know what we know? Is knowledge empirical; that is, is it based on or derived from sensory experience? Or is knowledge acquired by the mind, through reasoning alone? Or is knowledge revealed to us by God?

- **Axiology** deals with issues relating to values in ethics (what is morally right or wrong) and aesthetics (what is beautiful). **Ethics** examines moral truth and action. Those who believe in objective values claim that morality is universally and eternally valid. Subjectivists, in contrast, see values arising from personal tastes, feelings, or preferences in particular situations or circumstances. Utilitarians claim that what is valuable brings the greatest good to the greatest number of people. Rejecting universal moral standards, cultural relativists hold that right and wrong depend on what people do in particular contexts and situations at different times. **Aesthetics** considers art and beauty in its most general terms. It seeks to answer such questions as: What is beauty? How do we evaluate works of art? Are aesthetic judgments personal or public, subjective or objective?

■ **Logic** deals with the rules of, or how we organize, our reasoning. It examines the validity of arguments. *Deductive logic* is reasoning that moves from a general statement or principle to a particular point or specific example. *Inductive logic* is reasoning that moves from the specific or particular to more general conclusions.

Metaphysics, Knowledge, and Curriculum

We now look at what education is, in light of the divisions of philosophy. What is the knowledge that teachers seek to provide to students? Many teachers impart knowledge in such subjects as English, history, chemistry, or mathematics, for example. In so doing, they seek to convey to students a body of knowledge that they believe is true and worth knowing. However, beyond the teaching of a subject, lie the questions: What is real? What is true? What is of most worth and value? Consider the following questions: What is most real about you as a person? How do you define yourself? How have others defined you?

School curriculum does not include everything there is to know; it includes some, but not all, areas of knowledge. It includes those subjects curriculum makers have decided are worthwhile for people to learn. It excludes what they judge to be harmful to persons and to society. The act of selecting some area of knowledge, but not others, leads to the metaphysical question: What is truly and essentially real? What is in the curriculum is determined by how the question is answered. The follow-

SUBDIVISIONS OF PHILOSOPHY

- **Metaphysics:** Speculations about the nature of ultimate reality. What is real?
- **Epistemology:** Knowledge and knowing. How do we know what we know?
- **Axiology:** Values—the "shoulds" and "oughts" of our lives. What and why do we value a thing, action, or relationship?
- **Ethics:** A subdivision of axiology, deals with issues of good and bad, right and wrong. What makes an action good or bad or right or wrong?
- **Aesthetics:** A subdivison of axiology, deals with issues of beauty. What makes something beautiful or ugly?
- **Logic:** The rules or procedures of correct thinking. Are we thinking correctly, in a logical manner? Logic is further divided into *deductive logic*, from the general to the specific, and *inductive*, from the specific to the general.

ing chapters consider how various philosophies answer the question: What is real? A useful strategy in dealing with metaphysics, knowledge, and curriculum is to ask yourself, and then record your response to the question: What do you believe are the real areas of knowledge that should be included in the curriculum? Then, as you read further, return to your answer and either confirm or revise it. As you do this, you will be creating your philosophy of education.

A Caveat About Metaphysics.   Some of the early chapters in this book examine the more traditional philosophies of Idealism, Realism, and Theistic Realism (or Thomism), that are grounded in metaphysics—speculation about ultimate reality. However, other philosophies, such as Existentialism, Pragmatism, Philosophical Analysis, and Postmodernism are nonmetaphysical or even antimetaphysical in that they reject such speculation as meaningless, unverifiable, or historical constructions used to give one class or group control over others. Philosophical Analysis, for example, would place metaphysical statements in the category of those that cannot possibly be proved or disproved by empirical means. These nonmetaphysical positions argue that modern philosophy's challenge is to free it from its earlier metaphysical past. (More distinctions about metaphysical and nonmetaphysical philosophies will be made in later chapters.)

Epistemology, Knowing, and Methodology

With metaphysics, we considered what it is that we know. What is it that is truly real? Now we ask how we know what we believe is knowledge. Here the concern is with the general process of knowing. How do we arrive at our concepts and ideas about reality? Ask yourself how you know what you know. What do you believe is the most authoritative, true, and valuable way of knowing? It is possible to give several answers to these questions, such as I know because I:

- Receive information through my senses—sight from my eyes, sound from my ears, smell from my nose, and touch or feeling from my fingers.
- Believe God has revealed truth to us in the Bible.
- Found it on the Internet.
- Consider all reasonable people would believe it to be true.
- Believe it is scientifically valid.
- Just believe it is true in my heart.
- Have been taught skills and knowledge by my parents, teachers, and professors.
- Found it in a book in the library.

The above are only a few of the responses to the question of how you know. Also, note that the sources of our knowing rely on different kinds of authorities. Which of these authorities is most creditable? To begin our study of epistemology, we can consider some of the responses above in terms of the authority and process of knowing. Those who rely on their senses believe that knowledge comes from outside us through a process of sensation. Those who believe in the authority of a sacred book or text, such as the Bible or the Koran, believe knowledge is revealed by God. Those who consider that we can use reason to gain knowledge emphasize human rationality—the power to make deductions about reality. Then there are those who believe knowledge lies somewhere inside of us—in our minds—and that we can bring it to consciousness through introspection or meditation. Still others look to an authority figure—a scientist or a scholar—to investigate and do research on a topic and make some conclusions about it.

At this point, we still have not said with certitude how we know, but we raise the question for further inquiry. As you did with the topic of metaphysics, reflect on, examine, and record what you believe about how we know. As you read the subsequent chapters, return to what you have written and either confirm or revise it.

Just as metaphysics relates to curriculum, connections can be made between epistemology and methodology of instruction. Conceptions of how humans know relate to how to teach. The following frequently used teaching strategies are mentioned in terms of their relationship to epistemology:

- Reading and discussing an assigned book in any subject assumes the authors possess some authoritative knowledge that is worth studying.
- Using the Socratic method to stimulate students to bring their ideas to consciousness assumes that they possess some kind of interior knowledge.
- Doing a laboratory experiment to test a chemical reaction assumes that we can use our senses to measure a result.
- Having pupils organize objects and items into animals, vegetables, and minerals implies that our minds can classify these objects into related categories.
- Using a constructivist design in which students construct their beliefs about reality involves using the senses and experience.

The various methods of instruction identified above suggest that a relationship exists between our beliefs about knowledge and knowing, and how we teach our students to know. If we believe knowledge is already present in the mind, then methods of teaching will seek to draw forth that knowledge. If we believe that knowledge is derived through the senses, then teaching methods will emphasize sensory learning. If we believe that knowledge comes from some kind of authority, then we will use the evidence that authority provides to form our beliefs about reality.

Axiology, Values, and Character

In this section we examine axiology, the subdivision of philosophy that examines values in ethics and aesthetics. Ethics concerns issues of moral right and wrong and aesthetics examines how judgments are made about what is beautiful or ugly. Education, in any society, seeks to develop a particular kind of character that exhibits preferred behaviors. For example, there is a strong movement for character education in American schools. While character formation has long been an educational concern, the questions remain: What kind of character? What kind of ethical behavior is preferred?

The world's major religions—Christianity, Judaism, Islam, Hinduism, and Buddhism—all prescribe behavior that is prized as good and proscribe that which is bad.

Nations, too, have general codes of what constitutes good citizenship. Value-bearing language carries with it the prescription—should or ought—and the proscription—should not or ought not. Consider the following commonplace statements that have been part of your education and remain in your students' education. You should:

- Honor your mother and father.
- Respect authority.
- Take turns.
- Tell the truth.
- Respect private property.
- Protect the environment.
- Resolve disputes in a nonviolent way.
- Not break the law or damage property.
- Not stereotype or discriminate against individuals because of race, religion, gender, or ethnicity.

The above statements point to a certain kind of character that is preferred in America, and in many other societies. The major ethical questions, like those of metaphysics and epistemology, are based on our philosophy. Are there universal and timeless principles of good and right? Are the values carried by these principles found in all societies at all times? Or are values relative to different cultures? Do they express what some people prefer at a given time in a given place?

Aesthetics examines how we determine what is beautiful or ugly, and how we decide what is harmonious or discordant. Education in literature and poetry and the fine arts—music, art, drama, and dance—are those aspects of education that aim to cultivate aesthetic appreciation and creation. It acquaints us with the great works of art—books, paintings, music, and drama. Aesthetics asks the question: What is it about these works of art that make them worthy of inclusion in the curriculum? What criterion of beauty do they meet or fail to meet? Are these works beautiful because they reflect and represent some universal qualities of the human experience? Or are they beautiful because they exemplify the modes of art that are popular at a particular time and place? What is better, classical or popular art? How do we go about teaching art appreciation in its various forms—literary, musical, dramatic, cinematic, and so on? Does appreciation depend on what a person likes or are there standards beyond personal preferences?

Aesthetic creation refers to how we express ourselves by creating beauty in art, music, dance, painting, sculpture, writing, and other similar pursuits. Singing, dancing, painting, playing music, working with clay, cutting paper designs, and drawing begin in preschool, kindergarten, and the primary grades and extend upward in more sophisticated kinds of artistic expression in secondary and higher education. These artistic activities continue as an important part of adult and continuing education programs. The same questions about universality and cultural relativism we asked about aesthetic appreciation also apply to aesthetic expression.

Aesthetic judgment is also important in the more general sense in that it examines what makes a culture and society beautiful and harmonious. The ancient Greeks, for example, regarded the city-state, or *polis*, to be the center of their lives. Its public buildings, city squares such as the *agora*, temples, such as Athens' Parthenon, and their art forms, were important elements in their education. For the ancient Greeks, *paideia* referred to the total education or upbringing in the culture as well as more formal schooling. To the extent that the city-state was beautiful and harmonious, these aesthetic qualities had strong possibilities for shaping the Greek citizen as a harmonious and well-balanced person. Contemporary education, too, has a profound relationship to the aesthetics of the situations in which people live and work. It asks the questions: Are the lifestyle of a people, the physical situation in which they live, their buildings, homes, and their human-made and natural environment well designed and maintained for beauty and harmony? Or are these elements ugly, shoddy, and discordant?

Logic

Logic, the format and process of correct reasoning, is the subdivision of philosophy that examines how we organize and express our thoughts. It relates to how we judge evidence and express our arguments. It is the pattern used to make a case for something, to provide an explanation, or to organize evidence to reach a decision. The two major patterns of logical expression are deduction and induction. Deductive reasoning begins with general principles or statements and uses minor propositions and specific cases and examples to support the starting generalization. We are all familiar with the classic statement of deduction: (1) all men are mortal; (2) Socrates is a man; (3) therefore, Socrates is mortal. We can also think of how Thomas Jefferson framed his arguments in the Declaration of Independence: (1) all men are endowed with inalienable rights of life, liberty, and happiness; (2) the American colonists possess these inalienable rights; (3) because George III, the King of England, was violating these rights, the colonists had the right to rebel against British rule and to replace it with a government that adhered to the natural rights principle. In the above examples of deductive logic, if the premises are true, then, if we reason correctly, the conclusions will also be true. Deductive reasoning tends to be that used in the more traditional philosophies, such as Idealism, Realism, and Thomism, that rest on a metaphysical base.

Inductive reasoning moves from specific instances, cases, or situations to a larger generalization that includes and encompasses them. Induction is a key element in the scientific method and the use of statistical evidence. For example, a school superintendent wants to make staffing projections to hire additional foreign language teachers. She studies enrollment patterns—the number of students enrolled in foreign language classes in the school district over a ten-year period. It is determined statistically that the highest enrollments consistently have been in Spanish language classes, followed by French, with a sharp decline in Latin. Based on past and projected student enrollments, the superintendent concludes that enrollments are likely to rise in the future in Spanish and that an additional teacher should be hired to satisfy that need. The superintendent reached this generalization with specific, quantified evidence of enrollment statistics.

The course designs used in curriculum and instruction—syllabi, manuals, books, handouts, videos, computer programs—are organized according to some pattern of logic. Some course designs state general principles and then provide cases, illustrations, and examples that explain, illustrate, and reinforce these organizing generalizations. Others introduce a number of specific examples that lead students to formulate generalizations. They are likely to involve using the scientific method, doing observations, or collecting evidence from specific sources.

The organizing principles of the traditional subject-matter curriculum tend to follow a deductive logic pattern that is sequential and cumulative. Courses, units, and lessons are organized to follow each other in a sequence that is preorganized and articulated with each other in a pattern. The traditional school pattern of organizing students into grades follows this kind of sequence. The organizing assumption of school grades is that learning is cumulative—each skill or subject learned lays a necessary foundation for the next higher-order skill or subject.

Progressive and Constructivist curricular strategies, in contrast, are inductive. Rather than having a preorganized set of sequenced courses, units, and lessons, the Progressive and Constructivist pattern assumes that the most effective kind of learning comes from what students are interested in and from their direct experiences. By examining objects in their environment, or by being involved in hands-on, process-oriented learning experiences, students will work through the specifics that will enable them to construct their own generalizations.

These different approaches to curriculum and instruction can be illustrated by two different classes that are studying the same subject, the Civil War in an American History course. In the first class, the teacher uses a deductive approach. The unit on the Civil War is presented in a chronological order, a logic based on time, in which the students study a series of earlier events relating to sectional conflicts over slavery, such as the Missouri Compromise, the Compromise of 1850, the Kansas-Nebraska Act, the Fugitive Slave Law, the Dred Scott Decision, the election of Abraham Lincoln, and the secession of the Southern States. After establishing the chronology of these events and seeing how one event had consequences for subsequent ones, the students then read a textbook in which the author identifies the causes of the Civil War. The students are expected to know the chronology and the causes, which will be examined in a test. According to the contemporary Standards Movement, this kind of knowledge provides evidence of competency.

In the second class, the teacher uses an inductive strategy in which the students examine issues of civil conflicts or civil wars within nations. The students begin with contemporary situations of civil conflict, such as tribal conflicts in Rwanda and Burundi, in Africa; religious strife between Catholics and Protestants in Northern Ireland; and ethnic conflicts in Kosovo. By examining these contemporary conflicts, they realize that the American Civil War may or may not fit a pattern. They generate questions about civil conflict that they will use to examine the American Civil War as a case study. They engage in research using primary documents, such as Lincoln's House Divided Speech, articles from southern newspapers and magazines defending slavery, articles from abolitionist magazines, Harriet Beecher Stowe's *Uncle Tom's Cabin*, and other documents from the 1850s and 1860s. After analyzing these documents, they work to formulate generalizations about the American Civil War and how it fits with, or differs from, the general pattern of contemporary civil strife. In this example, the

RELATIONSHIPS BETWEEN PHILOSOPHY AND EDUCATION

- **Metaphysics (reality):** Relates to curriculum (what we know)
- **Epistemology (knowing):** Relates to methods of instruction (how we teach)
- **Axiology—Ethics (good and bad; right and wrong):** Relates to character education and citizenship
- **Axiology—Aesthetics (beauty):** Relates to art, literature, music, dance
- **Logic (correct thinking):** Relates to how curriculum and instruction is organized

important aim of instruction is that the students have connected the present to the past and, most importantly, have learned how to use historical materials as a mode of inquiry. Note, however, that the students may or may not have arrived at a sense of chronology in which one event leads to another.

JOHN DEWEY, "THE FUTURE OF PHILOSOPHY"

In the following selection, John Dewey, a founding figure of American Pragmatism, puts forth his ideas about the role of philosophy. Dewey argues that philosophy does not deal with metaphysics—questions about ultimate being—but rather with patterns of human cultural and social relationships. As you read the selection, you might wish to consider the following focusing questions:

1. Why does Dewey argue against the proposition that philosophy should deal with metaphysical issues? What are the implications of his rejection of metaphysics for education?

2. Do you agree or disagree with Dewey's argument that philosophy should not deal with questions about unchanging and eternally true principles, but rather with changing relationships?

3. Why does Dewey argue that the business of philosophy is to examine the relationships of human culture?

4. When Dewey wrote this selection, he said that inquiry into the physical sciences had outrun developments in human society, ethics, and morality. Do you think his reasoning applies to the effects of technology on contemporary society?

5. Based on the selection, what is the role of philosophy, and philosophy of education, in contemporary society?

From John Dewey, "The Future of Philosophy," *Dewey Later Works, Volume 17*, © 1991, pages 466–470, originally published in: *The Collected Works of John Dewey* © by the Center for Dewey Studies, reprinted by permission of the publisher.

. . .

I shall begin by stating briefly the standpoint from which I see philosophy—the business of philosophy, that with which philosophy is concerned. I think that from my standpoint, the poorest idea about philosophy is that it is a theory about "being," as the Greeks called it, or about "reality," as so much of modern philosophy has assumed that philosophy was. As I may suggest later, one of the incidental positive advantages of the present retreat of philosophy is that it's becoming recently clear that philosophy hasn't made any great success in dealing with "reality." And there is hope that it may take some more human standpoint to deal with.

My standpoint is that philosophy deals with cultural problems, using culture in the broad sense which the anthropologists have made clear to us—dealing with the patterns of human relationships. It includes such subjects as language, religion, industry, politics, fine arts, in so far as there is a common pattern running through them, rather than as so many separate and independent things. The principal task of philosophy is to get below the turmoil that is particularly conspicuous in times of rapid cultural change, to get behind what appears on the surface, to get to the soil in which a given culture has its roots. The business of philosophy is the relation that man has to the world in which he lives, as far as both man and the world are affected by culture, which is very much more than is usually thought.

There wasn't any "physical world" for a very long time, or anything called "physics" as a subject matter as at present. It was only when human culture had developed to a certain point that physics became a distinctive subject matter. A lot of things had to be stripped off—animistic things. The world was previously seen through human eyes in terms of human customs, desires, and fears. It wasn't til the beginning of modern science (the sixteenth century) that a world distinctively physical came into recognized acknowledged existence. This is merely an illustration of the transforming power of culture, in this broad sense of raw material.

Because the business of philosophy is with the relations that exist between man and his world, as both are affected by culture, the problems of philosophy change as the world in which man lives changes. An example is the increased knowledge in our time of machines, technology, etc. The problems of philosophy, therefore, are simply bound to change, although there may be some underlying structures that remain throughout the changes. Therefore, the history of philosophy still has to be written. It needs to be seen and reported in terms of the distinctive features of culture. There is a sort of formalistic recognition of this fact in present histories—they are divided into sections on ancient, medieval, and modern philosophy, western and oriental philosophy. These serve as certain headings for the material. But they are not carried out in the details of philosophical systems.

I come now to my hopes and fears. The hope for philosophy is that those who engage in philosophy professionally will recognize that we are at the end of one historical epoch and at the beginning of another. The teacher and student should attempt to tell what sort of change is taking place. In all events, this recognition of changes, of ages, of epochs in the world's history isn't an invention of mine. Every history formally recognizes division into ages. We are approaching a change from one period to another; we are undergoing the same kind of change, as a change, that happened when the medieval period lost its hold on the people's beliefs and activities. We recognize this now as the beginning of a new epoch. This new epoch is largely the consequence of the new natural science, which began about the sixteenth century with Galileo and Newton, as the applications of that science revolutionized men's ways of living and their relations to each other. These have created the characteristics of modern culture and its essential problems.

The more destructive features are more prominent than the more constructive phases. For a while, no survey of the world was presented without some reference to the fission of the atom. We see now that this is significant because it is a symbol of the changes that have been going on in science.

There's no secret in the fact that physical aspects of scientific inquiry and their applications have very far outrun inquiry into human subject matter—economics, politics, and morality. This over-weighting on one side gives the clue to what should be hoped for in a further development of philosophy. The philosophers of the sixteenth and seventeenth centuries may have thought they were dealing with the theory of reality, but they were actually forwarding the new natural science. They were engaged in criticizing science as it had come down in the Middle Ages from Aristotle. They were presenting the necessity for a different kind of cosmology. In the eighteenth century, especially in France during the Enlightenment, and to some extent in England, philosophers attempted to do something of the same kind in human and social subjects, but the materials and tools were lacking. They got rid of many things, but their constructive activities never amounted to so much. I think that now we have potentially the intellectual resources that would enable philosophy to do something of the same kind for the forwarding of human and social subjects. The older physical science, after stripping away the animistic survivals, had no concern with human problems. This science was about little lumps of matter which were separated from one another, existing in external space and time, which were themselves separated from each other and from everything that happened. Physical science has nearly demolished that point of view. The material of the physical world is such that, through the increasing applications in physiology and biology, it isn't so fixedly set over against human concerns as it used to be. Science itself has got rid of matter, in

the old sense. But this does not mean that matter has become a background to be related to human concerns, which could not happen as long as the Newtonian view prevailed.

There are many obstacles in realizing the hope I speak of. One very serious obstacle is the state of the world now, which is so fearful, so frightful, in the literal sense of the word, that it's very hard to face. The tendency is to look to some unreal solution to its problems which is essentially reactionary—going back to the ideas of Greek or medieval times, or in philosophy to adopt a method of escape because we don't seem to be able to handle the actual problems, which, if we are at the beginning of a new epoch, would probably take centuries to work out effectively.

The most discouraging thing in philosophy is neo-scholastic formalism, which also happened in the Middle Ages. It is form today for its own sake, in so many cases. A form of forms, not forms of subject matter. But the subject matter is so chaotic and confused today in the world that it is difficult to handle. This is how I would explain this retreat from work in the facts of human life into purely formal issues—I hesitate to call them issues because nothing ever issues except more form! It's harmless for everyone except philosophers. This retreat accounts for the growing disinterest of the general public in the problems of philosophy.

Totalitarianism, the attempt to find a complete set of blueprints that will settle every question, is another form of reaction, and a much more dangerous form. We have seen this in fascism and now today, in my opinion, in bolshevism.

It takes considerable courage to see into the present situation. To see it through will be the work of a long period. But the hope for philosophy will be that it will take part in the initiation of movements that will be carried through by human activity.

The first step is to see as frankly as possible the kind of world that we are living in and that which is likely to come. We should at least turn our eyes toward it and face it even if we can't do much with our hands and muscles about it. But what we should not do is to spin a lot of webs to operate as screens to keep us from seeing the reality of the situation. In this respect, formalism may be a hopeful sign. It may be the beginning of a general recognition that philosophers weren't getting anywhere dealing with matter at large, as with some ultimate entity. This reaction might be the opening of a more serious attempt to face the cultural problems of today. Science has done away with so many of the dualisms of the last few centuries, mind and matter, the individual and society, etc. These are simply echoes that once had a vitality because of cultural conditions. We are growing out of these. We need to have an idea of a systematic kind of what we might grow into.

Philosophy can't settle these issues any better than seventeenth century philosophy could settle problems of physics, but today philosophers can analyze problems and present hypotheses that might gain enough currency and influence to serve so that they could be tested by the only final method of testing, which is practical activity. (Applause.)

One thing more, and that is—you who are students really have as great an opportunity as any student of any subject ever had at any time, but it will take a lot of patience, a lot of courage, and, if I may say so, considerable guts!

[Address delivered to the Graduate Department of Philosophy, Columbia University, New York, N.Y., 13 November 1947. Stenographic report in the John Dewey Papers, Box 55, folder 5, Special Collections, Morris Library, Southern Illinois University at Carbondale.]

CONCLUSION

This chapter defined and discussed philosophy and education in order to create a framework for studying philosophy of education in the rest of the book. It considered the relationships between informal education and formal education, especially schooling, curriculum, and instruction. It then examined the areas of philosophy—metaphysics, epistemology, axiology, and logic—in relationship to education. As you proceed through the other chapters in the book, you may wish to refer to the initial points made in Chapter 1. We now go on to examine some of the major systems of philosophy of education.

DISCUSSION QUESTIONS

1. How do you define education?
2. How do the areas of philosophy—metaphysics, epistemology, axiology, and logic—relate to education?
3. What is the authority for what you believe?
4. How do you know what you know?

INQUIRY AND RESEARCH PROJECTS

1. Prepare your own educational autobiography, in which you consider the persons and events that influenced your ideas about truth and values.

2. Write a paper in which you state your own philosophy of education. What do you think is real, true, good, beautiful, and logical? Keep the paper and then revise it after completing this course.
3. In a paper, state your basic values and indicate why you hold them.

INTERNET RESOURCES

For biographies of leading educational philosophers and overviews of their philosophies, consult "The History of Education and Childhood" at Nijmegen University, the Netherlands at
www.socsci.kun.nl/ped/whp/histeduc

For the philosophy of education in relation to informal education, consult
www.infed.org/thinkers

For discussions of selected philosophers of education, consult Edward G. Rozycki's "Gallery of Educational Theorists" at
www.Newfoundations.com/GALLERY. html

SUGGESTIONS FOR FURTHER READING

Heslep, Robert D. *Philosophical Thinking in Educational Practice.* Westport, CT: Praeger Publishers, 1997.
Horner, Chris, and Westacott, Emrys. *Thinking Through Philosophy: An Introduction.* New York: Cambridge University Press, 2000.
Johnson, Tony W. *Discipleship or Pilgrimage? The Study of Educational Philosophy.* Albany, NY: State University of New York Press, 1995.
Knight, George E. *Issues and Alternatives in Educational Philosophy.* Berrien Springs, MI: Andrews University Press, 1998.
Nucci, Larry. *Education in the Moral Domain.* New York: Cambridge University Press, 2001.
O'Hear, Anthony. *Philosophy at the New Millennium.* New York: Cambridge University Press, 2001.
Ozman, Howard O., and Craver, Samuel M. *Philosophical Foundations of Education.* Columbus, OH: Merrill/Prentice Hall, 1999.
Noddings, Nel. *Philosophy of Education.* Boulder, CO: Westview Press, 1995.

NOTES

1. *Webster's Third New International Dictionary of the English Language* (Chicago: Encyclopedia Britannica, 1986), p. 723.

CHAPTER TWO

IDEALISM

In this chapter we will discuss Idealism, one of the world's oldest and most enduring philosophies. The chapter begins with a definition of Idealism; proceeds to situate it in the history of philosophy; examines Idealist metaphysics, epistemology, axiology, and logic; and discusses its implications for education.

DEFINING IDEALISM

To define Idealism, we begin with two root words, *idea* and *ideal*. To have an *idea* means to have a thought, a concept, or a mental picture about something. It refers to a mental image that, while not material, may reflect reality. For example, you may have a concept in your mind of a tree, which reflects reality. However, you can also have an image of a unicorn, which is fictional.

Referring to the highest form and degree of excellence, an *ideal* is a perfect example of something—a person, belief, principle, or cause. There is, for example, the model (the ideal) of the perfect teacher who inspires students to learn and to emulate. There is the principle that human beings can create world peace. An ideal is the highest kind of principle or standard to which a person can aspire. Teachers who have high expectations and set high standards of achievement for their students are said to have high ideals.

Idealists believe that striving for perfection is a desirable goal; while human beings may not attain perfection, they can achieve much when they follow a noble standard of life. Idealists reject the inference that they are impractical utopians who live in an imaginary world. For them, the quest for excellence can be a guiding force if one has the right disposition to be the best person possible, is willing to struggle to find the truth, and wise enough to live according to it.

We now move from these commonly used meanings of Idealism to a consideration of Idealism as a philosophy of education. However, the terms *idea* and *ideal*, with which we began, will resonate throughout our discussion of Idealism as a philosophy.

Defining Idealism as a Philosophy

Idealism is one of humankind's oldest philosophies, originating in ancient India and classical Greece, further developing throughout the centuries, and reaching a high point of expression in nineteenth-century Europe and America. **Idealism**, which asserts that reality is spiritual or nonmaterial, may or may not have a religious orientation. Religious idealists believe that the Creator or God is a supernatural spiritual being, the source of all creation, and the active presence who keeps the world in existence. *Religious Idealism* is closely associated with the theologies of several of the world's major religions, such as Hinduism and Buddhism. In Hinduism, for example, ultimate reality is the unfolding or externalizing of Atman or Brahma, the supreme universal spirit. There is also a strong current of Idealism in many Christian theologies.

For philosophical Idealists, who root their beliefs in metaphysics rather than religion, reality is an extension of a highly abstract universal idea, an organizing principle or world concept, such as Plato's Form of the Good, Hegel's Absolute, or Emerson's Macrocosm.

SITUATING IDEALISM

Idealism's origins in Western thought are often traced back to the classical Greek philosopher, Plato (428–348 B.C.), who established a philosophical school, the Academy, in Athens. The study of philosophy, even today, often begins with Plato's philosophical discourses or dialogues between Socrates, his mentor, and the Sophists who were his intellectual adversaries. In Plato's dialogues, Socrates uses a method of questioning his opponents which forces them to reflect on, and attempt to defend, their positions. The questioning process, known as the Socratic Method, is illustrated in Plato's "Allegory of the Cave," which appears later in this chapter. The purpose of Socrates' questions are to get the other person to think about his beliefs and to recognize why he holds them. Are these beliefs falsehoods based on ignorance, superstition, tradition, or customs? For example, stereotyping persons of different races, ethnicities, and languages, upon examination, typically represents unfounded distortions of truth. In the case of Plato's dialogues, Socrates is trying to stimulate people to question their assumptions, to think critically, and to try to reach the truth.

Plato saw reality as emanating from the Form of the Good, an all-inclusive, perfect, highly abstract concept from which all other ideas are derived. For Plato, the goal of life is to search for the truth, good, and beauty which exists in the Form of the Good. Further, all existing things that appear to us through our senses are merely imperfect copies of eternal, unchanging, and perfect ideas or concepts. Again, this Platonic concept is illustrated in the "Allegory of the Cave," in Plato's classic work, *The Republic*. As discussed in Chapter 1, the ancient Greeks, especially the Athenians, believed that education, or *paideia*, was a highly integrated process of human formation in which a necessary and reciprocal relationship existed between the good and beautiful society and the individual person. Plato's republic, an ideal and perfect state, is governed by wise lawmakers, the philosopher–kings, experts in metaphysics who administer the fairest order of justice for all citizens. The philosopher–kings are wise and prudent rulers because their intense and prolonged study of metaphysics has brought them knowledge of the forms or universal ideas that are found in the Form of the Good.

Plato's epistemology assumed that knowledge, like the Form of the Good, was absolute and eternal; that pure ideas, rather than sensation, were the highest form of knowing; and that true knowledge came through reminiscence, the recall or remembering of ideas that are latently present in the human mind. Plato's themes still underlie much of Idealist philosophy. Some commentators on Western culture have claimed that all subsequent philosophy is a footnote to Plato.

After the classical Greek period, Idealism, often based on Plato's philosophy, resurfaced in the philosophy of Plotinus (205–270), an Egyptian philosopher, who believed that reality is an emanation from a divine source. Saint Augustine (354–430), the Bishop of Hippo and an early Christian theologian, embraced some Idealist themes. Augustine's view was that knowing is possible through the power of divine illumination, the light of God, at work in the human mind. John Duns Scotus (1265–1308), drawing inspiration from Augustine, argued that true faith was necessary for a person to reason correctly. He asserted that for the human mind to understand spiritual concepts, it needed to be illuminated by faith. With faith, it became possible for persons to understand intellectually the necessity of God's existence. In the medieval period, Idealism was eclipsed by Realism, especially Thomas Aquinas' theistic version.

During the scientific revolution of the sixteenth century, René Descartes (1596–1650), a French philosopher, began his philosophical inquiry by doubting all authorities. His reflections on truth led Descartes to a logical conclusion. Although he could doubt the existence of everything, there was one thing he could not doubt—that he was doubting. To doubt meant that he must be thinking. He, thus, arrived at the famous Cartesian principle: "I think, therefore, I am."

Situated in the era of important scientific discoveries, Descartes grappled with the issues that science, with its emphasis on sensation, posed for philosophy. Though accepting the importance of empirical observation and scientific discovery, Descartes concluded that sensation itself could not lead to incontrovertible truth; people were often deceived by their senses and knowledge derived from sensation is often flawed. The only reliable knowledge is abstract, such as that in mathematics. But such knowledge must come, Descartes reasoned, from a higher source, from God, and is implanted in the human mind as innate ideas. The conscious experience that humans have of the external world is through a series of extensions from the innate ideas in the mind such as that of shape, color, size, time, and space. Human consciousness is part of the soul, created by God. Thus, the affirmation of God became a central part of the Idealist strand in Descartes's philosophy.

Although we sense material objects by extension using our latent powers in the mind, our thoughts about them are abstract. Further, we think about things by using other thoughts as points of reference. For example, to think of something that is soft requires us to think of something that is hard. This line of thought, which consists of related concepts, goes back to and reaches a great overarching idea—that of God, the source of all ideas. Descartes's emphasis on the mind and its intellectual operations gave a renewed emphasis to the importance of the internal logic of an argument and not just to empirically verifiable evidence. Internal logic, in turn, pointed to the existence of innate ideas and to the existence of God. That part of his philosophy that deals with cognition, or thinking, puts Descartes within the tradition of Idealism.

In the late eighteenth and nineteenth centuries, Idealism enjoyed a strong revival in Europe and in America. In Germany, where Idealism became the dominant philosophy, it took on a renewed life as a strong intellectual reaction against French materialism and sensationalism, and British skepticism. Two of the leaders in the German revival of Idealism were Immanuel Kant (1724–1804) and Georg Wilhelm Friedrich Hegel (1770–1831).

Kant sought to bring the newer ideas coming from the French Enlightenment into agreement with the long-standing Idealist tradition.[1] In particular, he was reacting against David Hume's empiricism, which argued that sense data was the ultimate basis of human knowledge of the world. Rather than discounting empiricism and science as rival views, Kant sought to incorporate them into a larger framework of Idealism that emphasized human cognition and its congruency with Idealist introspection and intuition. Kant's most important books—*The Critique of Pure Reason* and *The Critique of Practical Reason*—reflected the Idealist tendency to incorporate what seemed to be discordant or even opposite elements into larger syntheses. Human knowledge, according to Kant, depends on more than sensory impressions; preexisting conceptual structures exist in the mind that organize sensory information and, by organizing it, give it meaning. Two internal cognitive organizing principles, space and time, provide this meaning. In Kant's transcendental Idealism, human knowledge is made possible by the a priori existence of intellectual powers in the mind, which make it possible to recognize the totality or completeness of something, the *noumenon*, and categorize and organize information that comes from the senses about the particular aspects, the *phenomenon*, of something encountered in experience. Ethics, he believed, is based on a priori principles that are universally and eternally applicable. These principles are made clear by a great imperative—the *categorical imperative*—that requires each person to recognize the other person, not as a means to be used and exploited, but as an end in itself, possessing the same intrinsic rights, duties, and obligations that all humans possess and share.[2] From the categorical imperative there comes a set of moral obligations that are to guide human actions; education should instill a sense of obligation, a duty, to abide by these preexisting and guiding principles.

Georg Wilhelm Friedrich Hegel, a highly influential philosopher, established the basic principles of continental European Idealism in his magnum opus, *The Philosophy of History*. Hegel interpreted history as a grand plan, the unfolding of the Absolute Idea, or Universal World Mind, in the world. This manifestation or unfolding of the Absolute took place through a dialectical process that involved the operation of a trio of ideas in which what was enfolded in an idea was unfolded or externalized. Hegel's philosophy came to be known as Absolute Idealism because of his insistence that there is only one explanation for reality—the existence of the Absolute, which, as the source and sum of all existence, is unchanging and eternally true.

According to Hegel's dialectical formula, every idea contains its opposite idea—an *antithesis*—that is enfolded within it. The clash of the idea and its antithesis results in a more comprehensive idea, a synthesis, which itself is an idea. Once again, the dialectical process is at work as the clash of ideas continues upward and onward in ever greater complexity until they reach their source, the Absolute. Karl Marx, discussed in Chapter 13, was trained as an Idealist but later renounced Hegel's metaphysics. Marx, the founder of Marxism, retained, however, the dialectical process—the inevitable clash of ideas—as the framework for his dialectical materialism, in which ideas were replaced by conflicting classes. For Hegel, the state, especially the Prussian monarchy, represented the highest physical embodiment of the Absolute—the Great World Mind—on Earth. The nation-state, a community of people of the same race and language, was endowed by a folk spirit which all its members shared. Hegelian Idealism became a support for the ideology of nationalism—that people of like ethnicity and language—should be united in a nation-state. (Nationalism is examined in Chapter 10.)

Friedrich Froebel (1782–1852), the founder of the idea of kindergarten, was heavily influenced by the reigning Idealism in his native Germany. Froebel believed there was a spark of the Divine in human beings. Each child contained a spiritual essence which was the power of her or his life force. The child's self-activity, stimulated by the inner spiritual essence, sought to be externalized. Froebel's kindergarten was designed as a special educational environment in which children could grow and develop as they followed a curriculum of gifts and occupations, each of which were interconnected in terms of related forms.[3] Froebel's important influence on education was the belief that development began within the child; education was the means by which the child's inner powers were activated and externalized. Although Maria Montessori was not an Idealist, she, too, was influenced by the view that children possess latent powers which come to the surface and need to be exercised at certain sensitive periods of human growth and development.

Although Germany was the country in which Idealism was most dominant, the philosophy had its proponents elsewhere. George Berkeley (1685–1753), an Anglo-Irish philosopher and bishop in the Church of England, was a proponent of subjective Idealism. Berkeley argued that everything that exists must be perceived by a mind. What seemed to be a material object was, according to Berkeley, ideas in the mind of the person and God.

Drawing upon Berkeley's work, a group of English philosophers, the Cambridge Platonists, sought to provide a philosophical rationale for Christianity in which Plato's Form of the Good became the Christian God. Later, the prominence of Hegel's Absolute Idealism led to a reconfiguring of Idealism in the United Kingdom by the British philosophers, T. H. Green (1836–1882) and Bernard Bosanquet (1848–1923). Opposed to empiricism, Green saw the British nation, especially in its liberal form, as the flowering of the Absolute in history. Rather than being an authoritarian super-state as some German Idealists argued, Green saw the emerging liberal state with its freedoms and representative institutions as the unfolding of the Absolute in modern times. Bosanquet, concerned with the aesthetic dimension, saw the great works in art, literature, and music as reflecting universal themes in the mind of the Absolute.

In the United States, William Torrey Harris (1835–1909), Superintendent of Saint Louis schools and a U. S. Commissioner of Education, was a strong proponent of Hegelian Idealism. Harris interpreted the Civil War as the clash between conflicting ideas. The North represented the ideas of industrialization, efficiency, and freedom while the South represented tradition, inefficiency, and slavery. The clash of these competing ideas, in Harris' interpretation, brought about a new synthesis, the United States as a great industrial world power. Josiah Royce (1855–1916), one of America's leading neo-Hegelian philosophers, emphasized the importance of the spiritual in philosophy and saw ethics as acting on moral ideals.

In the first half of the nineteenth century, Idealism also reigned in the United States, where it took the form of Transcendentalism. Ralph Waldo Emerson (1803–1882), one of America's leading philosophers, was an influential proponent of Idealism. For Emerson, the great world mind was the Macrocosm, or Over Soul, an idea that included and encompassed all other lesser ideas. Derived from the Macrocosm, lesser subordinate ideas were small replicas, or microcosms, of the great ideas from which they came. Transcendentalists looked to Nature as a great world force from which they could find the truth. Henry David Thoreau (1817–1862), a colleague of Emerson, went to Walden Pond to contemplate and find the truth revealed by nature. Transcendentalism had the important educational implications that human beings could overcome materialism by looking to nature, and could constantly improve themselves and bring about social reform. Many public school proponents, inspired by Transcendentalism, believed that state-supported education would be the means of improving and uplifting the moral and ethical character of Americans.

WHY STUDY IDEALISM?

Since few contemporary American philosophers of education identify themselves as Idealists, it may be asked: Why study Idealism? There are at least three reasons for studying Idealism: (1) because of its long history; (2) for global or ecumenical purposes; (3) because it underlies many commonly held beliefs. In the history of Western philosophy, Idealism's origins are often traced to the ancient Athenian philosopher Plato. Students of philosophy invariably either begin with or return to Plato, who asked the basic questions we still grapple with today: What are truth and justice? What is the nature of the good society? Who is the good and just person? How can we educate women and men to be truthful and just?

The study of Idealism helps to create a broad global perspective that contributes to an ecumenical understanding of cultures worldwide. Idealism provides a philosophical foundation of how reality is viewed in some of the major cultures of Asia, especially the detachment from materialism that is important in Hinduism, Buddhism, and other Oriental religions. There are also elements of Idealism in the more mystical expressions of Islam, Judaism, and Christianity. The cultivation of internal spirituality and serenity represents a present-day movement, especially among people who find a psychic emptiness with the materialism and consumerism that dominates many Western cultures and societies. It also is a force for those who look inward to find alternatives to violence in the world.

An examination of some commonly held beliefs returns us to Idealism. Educators, through the ages, have sought to develop philosophies and strategies to educate good and truthful men and women. Among these educators are those who believe that human growth is a process of spiritual unfolding of innate powers or potential that lie within the child. Among these educators were Plato; Friedrich Froebel, who developed the kindergarten; and Maria Montessori, who fashioned the prepared educative environment. There are educators who see the process of teaching as an attempt to unleash the spiritual potential that lies within all human beings. They believe that true learning requires that the false sirens of materialism and consumerism be overcome. These educators look for models of the good life and its values for children and youth to emulate. Simply stated, the call of Idealism is to seek higher ideals and the kind of life that exemplifies these ideals.

IDEALISM AS A PHILOSOPHY OF EDUCATION

Each chapter in this book will examine the major philosophies in terms of metaphysics, epistemology, axiology, and logic and then consider the educational implications of these subdivisions of philosophy. Here we consider Idealism in relation to the four major subdivisions of philosophy.

Metaphysics

As defined earlier, metaphysics refers to that which is ultimately real. How we understand reality has momentous implications for education, particularly in how we understand the meaning and purpose of life, and how institutions such as schools, and processes such as teaching and learning, are defined and how they function.[4] For Idealists, that which is ultimately real is spiritual, nonmaterial, purely conceptual, or a pure idea. There is a spiritual source, a cosmic beginning or supernatural creator from which all things originate; it is the power of that source that keeps all things in existence. Each human being has a spiritual essence or a spiritual or mental core that is her or his essence or ultimate characteristic. For Idealists, there is one great spiritual or ideational source from which all lesser beings, including human beings, are derived. Plato, for example, held that all existing things are imperfect copies of eternal, unchanging, immaterial archetypes, forms, or ideas that originate in the Form of the Good.

For Idealists, God or the Absolute Idea or Form is the most general, most abstract, and inclusive being in the universe. Human beings share in that overriding spirituality or intellectuality, but in a limited way. Human life is a striving for and search for the supreme goodness and truth that exists in God or the Absolute. Idealists believe that each human being then is essentially spiritual or intellectual. What is the most important, irreducible part of the human being is the person's spirit or mind. Religious idealists stress the spirit, while nonreligious idealists emphasize the mind. From the metaphysics of Idealism, we can begin with an educational imperative—the most important and all-embracing goal is to assist in developing the student's spirit or mind.

A dominant theme in Idealism is the chain of being according to which all existing things or ideas are positioned in an ordered chain that begins with the most complex idea of all, the Absolute or God, and proceeds downward with lessening degrees of complexity and completeness. According to the chain of being, the universe, itself, is an ordered hierarchy of being.

Epistemology

As discussed previously, epistemology examines issues of how we know. For Idealists, knowing is essentially a process of bringing to consciousness, to our spiritual and mental surface, the truth that is present within us. The Idealist theory of knowledge can be illustrated by Plato's theory of reminiscence or remembering or recalling the ideas and concepts that are already present within our minds. According to Plato, prior to birth, our spirits or minds dwelt in closeness to the Form of the Good. The brilliance of the truth, goodness, and beauty present in the Supreme Form illuminated our minds. However, the shock of being born imprisoned these pure ideas in a body of flesh and blood, with appetites, needs, and desires. The ideas present within us were repressed into our subconscious psyches. Thus, ideas, for Plato, are in the mind at birth. The quest for truth is a struggle to bring these ideas, which contain knowledge of the perfect forms, back into consciousness. It is difficult to do this, however, because the distractions and distortions of the sensory world of appearance create images that confuse us and lead us away from the path to interior eternal truths. Plato's Allegory of the Cave illustrates how those seeking truth need to overcome the false images that appear to the senses. In ancient Athens, Socrates, Plato's mentor, asked his students provocative questions about truth, beauty, and justice that helped them cut through the layers of ignorance and opinion and find the truth present within.

The modern teacher who follows Idealism's tenets, like Socrates, needs to motivate students to be truth seekers.[5] Teachers today have to combat the false images created by consumerism and disinformation that bombard people in this age of pervasive media that offers dynamic programs that appeal to the senses.

Axiology

Axiology, in philosophy, examines issues of ethical and aesthetic values. For Idealists, value formation, or character education, is highly important in a person's education. In the area of values, Idealists reaffirm their belief that human beings are essentially spiritual and intellectual. Since the origin of human spirituality and intellectuality is found in a Supreme Supernatural Being or an Absolute Principle, values, like truth, are universal, eternal, and unchanging. They are rooted in the nature of the universe's underlying spirituality and intellectuality. They are not relative to different times, places, environments, or situations.

Logic

For Idealists, logic is based on a whole-part relationship in which the whole is greater than the sum of its parts. Further, the parts must be consistent with the whole. Another way of stating Idealist logic is to refer to the relationship between the general and the specific. That which is specific is lesser and needs to conform, or agree, with that which is general. Sometimes we reach the general by examining its relationship to the specific and continue the examination until it ends in a larger unifying concept. At other times, when the general principle is established, it is possible to reason from it and state specific examples or cases that illustrate it. When we argue from a principle, our supporting arguments need to agree with that principle. Idealists, following the lead of Socrates and Plato, are quick to point out inconsistencies in thinking. In education, Idealist logic works to develop major, holistic ideas or concepts in the student's mind. Actions are to conform to these great principles. As stated in our earlier definitions of Idealism, these principles attempt to reach the highest level of generality and guide standards of excellence. Such standards do not depend on opinion polls, but are derived from universal and guiding truths.

IDEALISM'S EDUCATIONAL IMPLICATIONS

Principle of Generality and the Role of the School

Idealism asserts a universal principle of generality according to which more specific, immediate, and particular goals are derived from those that are higher, more abstract, general, and inclusive. If the primary goal of education is the student's spiritual or intellectual development, then the school's primary purpose and functions become clear. Schools are institutions, established by society, for the primary purpose of developing a student's spirituality or intellectuality. Just as God or the Absolute is eternal and universal, the purpose of education, too, is universal and unchanging. It remains the same from generation to generation. According to the principle of generality in which specific goals are to agree with more general goals, all other goals and aims are subordinate to the general goal of spiritual and intellectual development. Nothing should be permitted to interfere with, diminish, or obscure that primary goal.

Teachers and Students

If the primary goal of schooling is students' spiritual and intellectual development, then the teacher's role also becomes very clear. Teachers must assist students in developing to their potential and achieving their fullest spiritual and intellectual growth. To

IDEALISM AND THE SUBDIVISIONS OF PHILOSOPHY

- **Metaphysics:** Reality is spiritual, intellectual, and nonmaterial
- **Epistemology:** Knowing is a process of bringing interior ideas to consciousness
- **Axiology:** Values are universal, timeless, and enduring
- **Logic:** Based on whole–part and general-to-specific patterns

perform their role, teachers need to realize that they are required to be more than classroom managers. As spiritual and intellectual agents, teachers should be engaged in the great moral calling of assisting students in their spiritual and intellectual self-development. According to J. Donald Butler, the Idealist teacher is to personify reality for students, "be a specialist in the knowledge of pupils," be an ethical model that commands their respect, and be able to awaken their desire to learn.[6]

Although they may be immature physically and socially, students, too, are spiritual and intellectual persons whose purpose is to externalize, activate, and fulfill their inner potentiality. All education is self-education, stimulated by skilled teachers who, like Socrates, motivate their students to search within themselves to find the truth that is latently present. The true student, with the teacher as a guide, is on a spiritual and intellectual journey to find what is true, good, and beautiful. That journey begins with parents and teachers who cultivate the early dispositions that will incline the young to take the first right steps toward truth—and then to take larger steps forward.

Curriculum

Since metaphysics deals with questions of what is ultimately real, it has a strong influence on curriculum, or the "whatness" of education. What is it that we hold to be most real and important? How do our beliefs about reality determine what skills and subjects are taught in the school curriculum? In considering these questions from an Idealist perspective, be guided by the major principles already discussed: (1) that which is ultimately real is spiritual or ideational; (2) that which is immediate and particular is to agree with that which is more abstract and general; (3) schools are to cultivate spirituality or intellectuality.

To these three principles, we now add another working assumption about human history and culture. For Idealists, human history represents the unfolding or revealing of the ideas that are present in the mind of God, or the sum of concepts that exist in the great unifying idea of the Absolute. These ideas, like their source, are eternal, universal, and unchanging and are not dependent on, or relative to, changing times, situations, and circumstances. What is good, true, and beautiful is now and always has been good, true, and beautiful. These enduring truths and values have been embodied in great works of literature, art, and music, for example, that were fashioned in the past and have inspired people across time and generations. These classics are permanent sources of God's or the Absolute's unfolding or revelation to human beings. What the artist, writer, or composer has done is shape or fashion the enduring idea and ideal into a work of art. These works of art, literature, and music constitute the knowledge that is of the highest worth and should form the curriculum core. A book's current popularity is not the criterion for including it in the curriculum. The real test is that of time: Has it captured something that reaches, touches, and inspires people across the ages? If it has then it belongs in the curriculum core. Idealists strongly oppose those educators who argue that students should be free to choose what they want to study and not be compelled to take a required core of subjects. Failing to provide a cultural core is to break a link in the chain of being, to create a chasm between the past and the present, and to disrupt the connection between the generations—between fathers and sons and mothers and daughters.

Idealists subscribe to the doctrine of preparation. The school curriculum is designed to prepare students for adult life. It helps students develop the skills and knowledge to recognize and, indeed, to want to learn that which is important for the future. Preparation presupposes that the administrators and teachers who govern schools and organize the curriculum are mature, educated, knowledgeable adults. Students are immature but possess a desire to learn. The doctrine of preparation implies that teachers as knowledgeable adults know what is in the best interests of students to learn, whether or not they are immediately interested in learning it at the particular time.

For Idealists, preschool, early childhood education, and the kindergarten should provide children with an environment that encourages them to find areas of interest that stimulate their desire to learn. The key to this learning lies in the children's own self-activity, which, in turn, arises from the inner needs, drives, and resources of the child. The early educational experiences, building on those of the home and family, create the right predispositions to learning so that children want to participate in their education. Acting as guides and mentors, teachers arrange the educational environment so that it stimulates children to use their potentiality. Examples of this kind of arrangement are the Froebelian kindergarten and Montessori's prepared environment.

The elementary school curriculum should cultivate the basic skills of literacy, numeracy, and civility that prepare students for more advanced learning, especially for the study of the classics. In this respect, the Idealists support basic education—learning to read, write, and calculate—since these skills are the early and necessary steps on the educational path that leads to the study of the enduring philosophical, historical, and literary works of the cultural heritage. Idealists also accept the use of computer skills and electronic information-retrieval technologies as tools in acquiring information. They insist, however, that the information acquired needs to be judged and analyzed so that it supports the quest for true knowledge and does not become an end in itself. In fine arts and literature, Idealists encourage the study of the great paintings, literature and poetry, and music as means of cultivating appreciation for the high points of aesthetic achievement and as avenues to further creative expression. Civility is defined in cultural terms as a respect for another person's right to develop their spirituality and intellectuality through society and its institutions.

The principle of a hierarchy of generality is used to organize the secondary and higher education curriculum with the most general and abstract subjects being of the highest importance and deserving the most time, effort, and resources. The tool skills learned in the elementary school prepare students to read, study, discuss, and reflect on the great works of literature, philosophy, politics, and history in middle and secondary school. Mathematics, especially algebra, geometry, and calculus, with their high abstract concepts, rank high in the curriculum hierarchy. Idealists also include the physical and natural sciences, but with an emphasis on theory. If the Idealist operates from a religious orientation, then the holy and sacred books of the particular religion are a highly important part of the curriculum. For example, the Hebrew scriptures, the Christian Bible, the Hindu Gita, and the Islamic Koran are held as important texts, located at the summit of the curricular hierarchy.

Idealists identify with those who see the curriculum as a body of subjects are organized around basic principles. While Idealists teach subjects as separate disciplines, they encourage students, once they understand a subject matter and its underlying principles, to develop integrative and interdisciplinary insights into the unity of knowledge. Thorough knowledge of the disciplines makes true interdisciplinary knowledge possible. Idealists would be suspicious of educational methods that believe that it is possible for students to become interdisciplinary problem-solvers without first studying and mastering the needed subject matter expertise.

Character Education and the Inequality of Values

Although Idealists recognize that the human being in society is a complex personality with physical, social, health, and economic needs and interests, their priorities for character education are based on the principle of the hierarchy of generality discussed earlier. Human needs and interests are not of equal importance. Some are more important, or desirable, and more enduring than others. The principle of generality can be compared to a moral yardstick on which values can be ordered. Those values that relate most directly to our defining spiritual and intellectual nature are most important and enduring and rank highest on the moral scale. Our higher-order intellectual and spiritual values are those that are most abstract, general, and durable and give order to and regulate our lower, more specific values. The school curriculum and teachers need to emphasize that not every value is of equal importance, but that the decisions of life need to be based on principles that wear well over time.

Creating Perspective

Idealist-oriented character education places great emphasis on developing perspective, and on imitating models or mentors. Perspective means that the person is able to take a long-range view of ethical and aesthetic choices rather than acting on short-term immediate concerns. In a great painting, for example, the artist portrays the subject by using relationships of color, dimension, and space so that the viewer is presented with an integrated sense of wholeness. In viewing the painting, it may be necessary to stand back from it in order to see its elements as a whole, or to place it in perspective. Further, the artist needs to capture something in the painting that speaks to and moves people across time and place. In education, developing perspective does not come easily or quickly but is a deliberate, slow, gradual, and maturing process. Attaining perspective means that the person has developed a sufficient psychic distance to appreciate the wholeness and relationships of ethical and aesthetic choices. By studying the great works of art, literature, philosophy, and history, students can acquire a sense of perspective that unites them with past generations and places them within the ongoing cultural heritage.

Mentoring and Modeling

In the history of philosophy, one of the great mentoring situations occurred in ancient Athens, when Plato became Socrates' student. From Socrates, Plato learned his basic

IDEALISM'S IMPLICATIONS FOR EDUCATION

- **School:** Defined by its primary role in human intellectual and spiritual development
- **Curriculum:** Consists of skills and subjects arranged in a hierarchy of generality, with the more general and abstract having priority over the more specific
- **Instruction:** A variety of methods, with preference given to the Socratic method, modeling, and imitation
- **Teacher:** A mature person; an expert in knowledge of a subject or methods; a cultural and ethical model for students
- **Students:** Immature persons with a latent desire to know and activate their learning

strategy of probing for truth through dialogue—conversations in which the participants ask and answer each other's leading questions. Modern Idealists, too, see the teacher-learner relationship as a source of character formation. In addition to their pedagogical skills and knowledge base, Idealist teachers should be models of the culture, persons who inspire students and are worthy of their emulation. According to Butler, imitation and modeling provide students with modes of excellence and encourage them to follow these patterns. Being exposed to models of excellence should not lead to mimicry, but to awakening the desire to excel as a person.[7]

PLATO, A TRUE VISION OF REALITY

Plato's "Allegory of the Cave," found in his *Republic*, has been selected as a primary source reading because of Plato's importance as a founding figure in Western philosophy, and because of the dramatic illustration that it provides of the discerning reality in a world of images. Plato's *Republic* is a philosophical work about an ideal *polis*, or society, in which justice reigns supreme. Adjudicated and administered by philosopher–kings, justice in the Republic is the harmonious relationship of the members of the society, based on each doing what he or she is best-suited to do by their nature. In the selection from the *Republic*, we examine Plato's cave, in which he makes a famous analogy between the reality of true vision and the illusion of sensation. In the cave, men are chained so that they can see shadows on the walls, images of objects moving around outside of the cave. When a man, freed from his chains, leaves the cave and sees the real objects in the light, he at first disbelieves what he is seeing. As he slowly adjusts to the light, he recognizes that what he is seeing is real and what he saw in the cave was merely the shadow of the real object. However, when he returns to those still chained in the cave, he cannot convince them that what they believe is real is merely a shadow. As you read the selection, you may wish to consider the following focusing questions:

1. What points about metaphysics and epistemology does Plato make in the selection?

2. Suppose you were rewriting Plato's "Allegory of the Cave" in the present day. Identify and describe some of the "shadows" of contemporary life that distort a true vision of reality.

3. In your own education, can you identify any occasions or situations in which you were helped by teachers to recognize and work your way through images and shadows that distorted your view of reality?

4. After reading the selection, what questions would you ask Plato about the "Allegory of the Cave"?

Now then, I proceeded to say, go on to compare our natural condition, so far as education and ignorance are concerned, to a state of things like the following. Imagine a number of men living in an underground cavernous chamber, with an entrance open to the light, extending along the entire length of the cavern, in which they have been confined, from their childhood, with their legs and necks so shackled, that they are obliged to sit still and look straight forwards, because their chains render it impossible for them to turn their heads round: and imagine a bright fire burning some way off, above and behind them, and an elevated roadway passing between the fire and the prisoners, with a low wall built along it, like the screens which conjurors put up in front of their audience, and above which they exhibit their wonders.

I have it, he replied.

Also figure to yourself a number of persons walking behind this wall, and carrying with them statues of men, and images of other animals, wrought in wood and stone and all kinds of materials, together with various other articles, which overtop the wall; and, as you might expect, let some of the passers-by be talking, and others silent.

You are describing a strange scene, and strange prisoners.

They resemble us, I replied. For let me ask you, in the first place, whether persons so confined could have seen anything of themselves or of each other, beyond the shadows thrown by the fire upon the part of the cavern facing them?

Certainly not, if you suppose them to have been compelled all their lifetime to keep their heads unmoved.

And is not their knowledge of the things carried past them equally limited?

Unquestionably it is.

And if they were able to converse with one another, do you not think that they would be in the habit of giving names to the objects which they saw before them?

Doubtless they would.

Again: if their prison-house returned an echo from the part facing them, whenever one of the passers-by opened his lips, to what, let me ask you, could they refer the voice, if not to the shadow which was passing?

Unquestionably they would refer it to that.

Then surely such persons would hold the shadows of those manufactured articles to be the only realities.

Without a doubt they would.

Now consider what would happen if the course of nature brought them a release from their fetters, and a remedy for their foolishness, in the following manner. Let us suppose that one of them has been released, and compelled suddenly to stand up, and turn his neck round and walk with open eyes towards the light; and let us suppose that he goes through all these

From Plato, *The Republic of Plato.* Translated by John L. Davies and David J. Vaughan. London: Macmillan and Co., 1888, pp. 235–258.

actions with pain, and that the dazzling splendour renders him incapable of discerning those objects of which he used formerly to see the shadows. What answer should you expect him to make, if some one were to tell him that in those days he was watching foolish phantoms, but that now he is somewhat nearer to reality, and is turned towards things more real, and sees more correctly; above all, if he were to point out to him the several objects that are passing by, and question him, and compel him to answer what they are? Should you not expect him to be puzzled, and to regard his old visions as truer than the objects now forced upon his notice?

Yes, much truer.

And if he were further compelled to gaze at the light itself, would not his eyes, think you, be distressed, and would he not shrink and turn away to the things which he could see distinctly, and consider them to be really clearer than the things pointed out to him?

Just so.

And if some one were to drag him violently up the rough and steep ascent from the cavern, and refuse to let him go till he had drawn him out into the light of the sun, would he not, think you, be vexed and indignant at such treatment, and on reaching the light, would he not find his eyes so dazzled by the glare as to be incapable of making out so much as one of the objects that are now called true?

Yes, he would find it so at first.

Hence, I suppose, habit will be necessary to enable him to perceive objects in that upper world. At first he will be most successful in distinguishing shadows; then he will discern the reflections of men and other things in water, and afterwards the realities; and after this he will raise his eyes to encounter the light of the moon and stars, finding it less difficult to study the heavenly bodies and the heaven itself by night, than the sun and the sun's light by day.

Doubtless.

Last of all, I imagine, he will be able to observe and contemplate the nature of the sun, not as it *appears* in water or on alien ground, but as it *is* in itself in its own territory.

Of course.

His next step will be to draw the conclusion, that the sun is the author of the seasons and the years, and the guardian of all things in the visible world, and in a manner the cause of all those things which he and his companions used to see.

Obviously, this will be his next step.

What then? When he recalls to mind his first habitation, and the wisdom of the place, and his old fellow-prisoners, do you not think he will congratulate himself on the change, and pity them?

Assuredly he will.

. . .

And now consider what would happen if such a man were to descend again and seat himself on his old seat? Coming so suddenly out of the sun, would he not find his eyes blinded with the gloom of the place?

Certainly, he would.

And if he were forced to deliver his opinion again, touching the shadows aforesaid, and to enter the lists against those who had always been prisoners, while his sight continued dim, and his eyes unsteady,—and if this process of initiation lasted a considerable time,—would he not be made a laughingstock, and would it not be said of him, that he had gone up only to come back again with his eyesight destroyed, and that it was not worth while even to attempt the ascent? And if any one endeavoured to set them free and carry them to the light, would they not go so far as to put him to death, if they could only manage to get him into their power?

Yes, that they would.

Now this imaginary case, my dear Glaucon, you must apply in all its parts to our former statements, by comparing the region which the eye reveals, to the prison-house, and the light of the fire therein to the power of the sun: and if, by the upward ascent and the contemplation of the upper world, you understand the mounting of the soul into the intellectual region, you will hit the tendency of my own surmises, since you desire to be told what they are; though, indeed, God only knows whether they are correct. But, be that as it may, the view which I take of the subject is to the following effect. In the world of knowledge, the essential Form of Good is the limit of our inquiries, and can barely be perceived; but, when perceived, we cannot help concluding that it is in every case the source of all that is bright and beautiful,—in the visible world giving birth to light and its master, and in the intellectual world dispensing, immediately and with full authority, truth and reason;—and that whosoever would act wisely, either in private or in public, must set this Form of Good before his eyes.

To the best of my power, said he, I quite agree with you.

That being the case, I continued, pray agree with me on another point, and do not be surprised, that those who have climbed so high are unwilling to take a part in the affairs of men, because their souls are ever loath to desert that upper region. For how could it be otherwise, if the preceding simile is indeed a correct representation of their case?

True, it could scarcely be otherwise.

Well: do you think it a marvellous thing, that a person, who has just quitted the contemplation of divine objects for the study of human infirmities, should betray awkwardness, and appear very ridiculous, when with his sight still dazed, and before he has become sufficiently habituated to the darkness that reigns around, he finds himself compelled to contend in courts of law, or elsewhere, about the shadows of justice, or images which throw the shadows, and to enter the lists in questions involving the arbitrary suppositions entertained by those who have never yet had a glimpse of the essential features of justice?

No, it is anything but marvellous.

Right: for a sensible man will recollect that the eyes may be confused in two distinct ways and from two distinct causes,—that is to say, by sudden transitions either from light to darkness, or from darkness to light. And, believing the same idea to be applicable to the soul, whenever such a person sees a case in which the mind is perplexed and unable to distinguish objects, he will not laugh irrationally, but he will examine whether it has just quitted a brighter life, and has been blinded by the novelty of darkness, or whether it has come from the depths of ignorance into a more brilliant life, and has been dazzled by the unusual splendour; and not till then will he congratulate the one upon its life and condition, and compassionate the other; and if he chooses to laugh at it, such laughter will be less ridiculous than that which is raised at the expense of the soul that has descended from the light of a higher region.

You speak with great judgment.

Hence, if this be true, we cannot avoid adopting the belief, that the real nature of education is at variance with the account given of it by certain of its professors, who pretend, I believe, to infuse into the mind a knowledge of which it was destitute, just as sight might be instilled into blinded eyes.

True; such are their pretensions.

Whereas, our present argument shews us that there is a faculty residing in the soul of each person, and an instrument enabling each of us to learn; and that, just as we might suppose it to be impossible to turn the eye round from darkness to light without turning the whole body, so must this faculty, or this instrument, be wheeled round, in company with the entire soul, from the perishing world, until it be enabled to endure the contemplation of the real world and the brightest part thereof, which, according to us, is the Form of Good. Am I not right?

You are.

Hence, I continued, this very process of revolution must give rise to an art, teaching in what way the change will most easily and most effectually be brought about. Its object will not be to generate in the person the power of seeing. On the contrary, it assumes that he possesses it, though he is turned in a wrong direction, and does not look towards the right quarter; and its aim is to remedy this defect.

So it would appear.

Hence, while, on the one hand, the other so-called virtues of the soul seem to resemble those of the body, inasmuch as they really do not pre-exist in the soul, but are formed in it in the course of time by habit and exercise; the virtue of wisdom, on the other hand, does most certainly appertain, as it would appear, to a more divine substance, which never loses its energy, but by change of position becomes useful and serviceable, or else remains useless and injurious. For you must, ere this, have noticed how keen-sighted are the puny souls of those who have the reputation of being clever but vicious, and how sharply they see through the things to which they are directed, thus proving that their powers of vision are by no means feeble, though they have been compelled to become the servants of wickedness, so that the more sharply they see, the more numerous are the evils which they work.

Yes, indeed it is the case.

But, I proceeded, if from earliest childhood these characters had been shorn and stripped of those leaden, earth-born weights, which grow and cling to the pleasures of eating and gluttonous enjoyments of a similar nature, and keep the eye of the soul turned upon the things below;—if, I repeat, they had been released from these snares, and turned round to look at objects that are true, then these very same souls of these very same men would have had as keen an eye for such pursuits as they actually have for those in which they are now engaged.

Yes, probably it would be so.

Once more: is it not also probable, or rather is it not a necessary corollary to our previous remarks, that neither those who are uneducated and ignorant of truth, nor those who are suffered to linger over their education all their life, can ever be competent overseers of a state,—the former, because they have no single mark in life, which they are to constitute the end and aim of all their conduct both in private and in public; the latter, because they will not act without compulsion, fancying that, while yet alive, they have been translated to the islands of the blest.

That is true.

It is, therefore, our task, I continued, to constrain the noblest characters in our colony to arrive at that science which we formerly pronounced the highest, and to set eyes upon the good, and to mount that ascent we spoke of; and, when they have mounted and looked long enough, we must take care to refuse them that liberty which is at present permitted them.

Pray what is that?

The liberty of staying where they are, and refusing to descend again to those prisoners, or partake of their toils and honours, be they mean or be they exalted.

Then are we to do them a wrong, and make them live a life that is worse than the one within their reach?

You have again forgotten, my friend, that law does not ask itself how some one class in a state is to live extraordinarily well. On the contrary, it tries to bring about this result in the entire state; . . .

Then, Glaucon, have we not here the actual hymn, of which dialectical reasoning is the consummation? This hymn, falling as it does within the domain of the intellect, can only be imitated by the faculty of sight; which, as we said, strives to look steadily, first at material animals, then at the stars themselves, and last of all at the very sun itself. In the same way, whenever a person strives, by the help of dialectic, to start in pursuit of every reality by a simple process of reason, independent of all sensuous information,—never flinching, until by an act of the pure intelligence he has grasped the real nature of good,—he arrives at the very end of the intellectual world, just as the last-mentioned person arrived at the end of the visible world. . . .

CONCLUSION

In Chapter 2 we examined Idealism, one of the world's oldest and most enduring philosophies. Accentuating the spiritual and intellectual core of human nature, Idealists base their philosophy of education around enduring principles that they claim are universal and eternal. Education is about truth, goodness, and beauty which, at the highest level of generality, are the same for everyone in every place on Earth. The school is an intellectual agency, designed to lead students to realize and fulfill the higher parts of their nature. Teachers are spiritual and intellectual guides and models of ethical character who lead students on the path of self-discovery of the truth.

DISCUSSION QUESTIONS

1. Do you believe Idealism as a philosophy of education is relevant or irrelevant to contemporary education?
2. Describe and analyze how the Socratic dialogue operates as an educational strategy.
3. How can teachers be models of values? Is the Idealist conception of modeling and mentoring relevant to contemporary education?
4. Do you think contemporary American education needs ideals, models, and exemplars? Explain your answer.
5. Some educational theories point out the differences between people in terms of race, ethnicity, gender, and class. Idealism tends to minimize these differences by accentuating a universal human nature. Which side are you on? Why?
6. Describe and analyze the Idealist view of imitation, mentoring, and self-activity in education.
7. Describe how the hierarchy of generality operates in the organization of the Idealist curriculum.

INQUIRY AND RESEARCH PROJECTS

1. Have several students obtain a copy of the goals of the school district or school in which they are teaching or doing their clinical experience. As a collaborative learning project, analyze these goals and determine if they are ordered according to a principle of generality or if they are presented as having equal value? How might an Idealist react to these statements of goals?
2. Interview several experienced teachers and ask questions that elicit their ideas on the nature of the teacher and the learner. Then, determine if their ideas are similar or different from the Idealist conception of the teacher and the learner.
3. Construct, in outline form, a curriculum that is based on Idealist principles, especially those of a hierarchy of generality and the doctrine of preparation.
4. Identify, read, and review a classic work in literature. Determine why the book is a classic.
5. Go to an art gallery and study paintings that are regarded as the works of the great masters. Determine why these paintings are called masterpieces.

INTERNET RESOURCES

Paul Knierim's essay, "Re-Approaching Idealism," is available at
www.philosophyforums.com/essays/idealism.html

The Internet Encyclopedia of Philosophy discusses German Idealism at
www.utm.edu//research/iep/g/germidea.htm

For a discussion of British Idealism, consult
www.psa.ac.uk/spgrp/idealism.html

For Friedrich Schelling's Transcendentalist philosophy, consult
www.marxists.org/reference/subject/philosophy/works/ge/schelling.html

SUGGESTIONS FOR FURTHER READING

Ahrensdorf, Peter J. *The Death of Socrates and the Life of Philosophy: An Interpretation of Plato's Phaedo*. Albany, NY: State University of New York Press, 1995.

Annas, Julia. *An Introduction to Plato's Republic*. Oxford: Clarendon Press, 1991.

Bloom, Allan. *The Republic of Plato*. New York: Basic Books, 1968.

Butler, J. Donald. *Idealism in Education*. New York: Harper and Row, 1966.

Euben, J. Peter. *Platonic Noise*. Princeton, NJ: Princeton University Press, 2003.

Gaukroger, Stephen. *Descartes' System of Natural Philosophy*. New York: Cambridge University Press, 2002.

Graham, William. *Idealism: An Essay, Metaphysical and Critical*. Bristol, UK: Thoemmes, 1991.

Grier, Michelle. *Kant's Doctrine of Transcendental Illusion*. New York: Cambridge University Press, 2001.

Horne, Herman H. *The Democratic Philosophy of Education*. New York: Macmillan Co., 1932.

Irwin, Terence. *Plato's Ethics*. New York: Oxford University Press, 1995.

Kerstein, Samuel J. *Kant's Search for the Supreme Principle of Morality*. New York: Cambridge University Press, 2002.

Kuehn, Manfred. *Immanuel Kant: A Biography*. New York: Cambridge University Press, 2002.

Nehamas, Alexander. *Virtues of Authenticity: Essays on Plato and Socrates*. Princeton, NJ: Princeton University Press, 1998.

Neuhouser, Frederick. *Foundations of Hegel's Social Theory: Actualizing Freedom*. Cambridge, MA: Harvard University Press, 2000.

Pinkard, Terry. *Hegel: A Biography*. New York: Cambridge University Press, 2001.

Plato. *The Republic*. G. R. F. Ferrari, ed. New York: Cambridge University Press, 2000.

Plato. *Symposium of Plato*. Tom Griffith, trans. Berkeley, CA: University of California Press, 1989.

Rescher, Nicholas. *Human Nature in Idealist Perspective*. Princeton, NJ: Princeton University Press, 1992.

Schelling, Friedrich Wilhelm J. *Idealism and the Endgame of Three Essays*. Edited and translated by Thomas Pfau. Albany, NY: State University of New York Press, 1994.

Schott, Gary A. *Plato's Socrates as Educator*. Albany, NY: State University of New York Press, 2000.

Stauffer, Deven. *Plato's Introduction to the Question of Justice*. Albany, NY: State University of New York Press, 2001.

Webb, Thomas E. *The Veil of Isis: A Series of Essays on Idealism*. Bristol, UK: Thoemmes, 1990.

NOTES

1. Manfred Kuehn, *Immanuel Kant: A Biography* (New York: Cambridge University Press, 2002).

2. For Kant's discussion of ethics and education, see Immanuel Kant, *Education*, Annette Charton, ed. (Ann Arbor: University of Michigan Press, 1960).

3. Norman Brosterman, *Inventing Kindergarten* (New York: Henry A. Abrams, 1997), pp. 14–18, 22–29.

4. For an analysis of Idealism, see John P. Strain, "Idealism: A Clarification of an Educational Philosophy," *Educational Theory*, 25 (Summer 1975), 263–271.

5. John E. Colman, *The Master Teachers and the Art of Teaching* (New York: Pitman, 1967), pp. 28–34.

6. J. Donald Butler, *Idealism in Education* (New York: Harper and Row, 1966), pp. 98–103.

7. Ibid., pp. 108–111.

CHAPTER THREE

REALISM

This chapter focuses on Realism, whose foundations go back to Aristotle in ancient classical Greece. Realism asserts the reality of an objective order—what is out there, or external to us, is real. We begin the chapter by defining Realism, followed by an examination of its position on metaphysics, epistemology, axiology, and logic. We then draw out and discuss its implications for education.

DEFINING REALISM

In defining Realism, we begin with its root, *real.* To be real means to have an actual physical existence that is not a product of the human intellect or imagination. Realism means having a practical understanding and acceptance of the world, rather than an idealized or romanticized version of it. In philosophy, Realism means that universals, scientific principles, and ethical and aesthetic values exist independently of people's thoughts or perceptions. When people think realistically, their ideas and concepts conform to what exists in the real world of objects.

Realism is a philosophy that asserts that we live in a world of objects that truly exist and are external to us. Although objects exist outside of us, we can acquire information about them and come to know them. The basic premises of Realism are: (1) we live in a world of objects, persons, and phenomenon that are external to us; (2) we can acquire information about these objects and, indeed, come to know them and understand how they function and relate to each other; (3) generalized knowledge, or theory, about these objects is the best guide to action, conduct, and behavior. We come to know reality through our sensation of data from objects and the process of conceptualization—organizing concepts in the mind that correspond to the object in reality. Realism, with its emphasis on objective knowledge—knowing what is out there—can be contrasted with Idealism's claims that ideas about knowledge are subjective and latently present in the human mind. As will be seen in later chapters, Realism's emphasis on objective reality that exists prior to our experience contrasts with the instrumentalist view of knowledge found in Pragmatism (discussed in Chapter 5) and the phenomenological view of Existentialism (in Chapter 6).

SITUATING REALISM

Realism's origins, like those of Idealism, go back to ancient Greece. While Idealism's founder was Plato, his student Aristotle (384–322 B.C.) founded Realism.[1] Like his mentor, Aristotle was a leading ancient Greek philosopher, logician, and natural and political scientist. He established the Lyceum, a philosophical school in Athens and, for a time, was the tutor of Alexander the Great. Because he emphasized observation and classification of natural phenomena, Aristotle's version of realism is called *Natural Realism*. Aristotle defined humans as rational beings, who, when they act according to reason, exemplify the highest quality of their human nature. The life lived according to reason gives humans their greatest happiness. In ethics, Aristotle advised people to follow the *golden mean*, an ethical stance and attitude that takes a moderate position between extreme repression and uninhibited and unrestrained expression. Aristotle, for example, believed courage is a virtue that lies between cowardice and recklessness. The coward flees every moral and physical challenge while the reckless person acts rashly without a plan or strategy. The truly courageous person knows when to advance and win the battle, but also knows when to retreat strategically to live to fight another day. For Aristotle, the good life was one in which decisions were determined rationally according to knowledge and in which the person chose moderation. Together reason and moderation made it possible to lead a purposeful, balanced, and harmonious life— free from ignorance and from extremes of behavior.

From the trunk of its Aristotelian origin, Realism developed several branches. **Thomism**, named for Thomas Aquinas (1225–1274), a medieval Dominican scholastic, is a God-centered, theologically based version that is also called Theistic Realism. (Thomism is examined in Chapter 4.) **Classical Realism** is a modern version of the philosophy that returns to its Aristotelian roots.

Sense Realism emphasizes the use of the senses in gaining knowledge about the outside world, and in forming concepts about it. In education and schooling, Sense Realists emphasize the importance of using objects as the primary mode of instruction. They argue that purely verbal forms of instruction, which depend solely on words, are inadequate in forming clear ideas about reality. The term Sense Realism is used primarily in education, especially the history of education, to distinguish the methods of John Amos Comenius (1592–1670) and Johann Heinrich Pestalozzi (1746–1827) from those that are highly verbal.

Scientific Realists assert that objects exist and interact with each other in reality independently of us. By using scientific research, we can discover the structure of these objects and the patterns of how they function. **Scientific Realism** contends that scientific investigation seeks to locate, identify, describe, and explain both the "observable and unobservable" aspects of our world.[2] The epistemology used by Scientific Realists is the scientific method. While Scientific Realists rely on the scientific method as the means of arriving at the most authoritative knowledge, they see it as an instrument of discovering how the world works. Unlike the Pragmatists (discussed in Chapter 5) who also emphasize the scientific method, the Scientific Realists see it as an instrument of discovering how reality operates rather than as a means of making reality conform to our purposes. Objective reality is out there, Scientific Realists assert, regardless of our social and political preferences. Scientific theories are explanations of how physical and natural reality functions and are not simply human constructions. For Scientific Realists, patterns in phenomena are discoverable by science and are real modes of operation that govern the functioning of the physical and natural world. The patterns reveal a regularity that operates in the world. Using scientific technologies, as extensions of the senses, aids us in the discovery of the patterns of reality. This scientific knowledge is the most authoritative guide to understanding physical and natural reality.[3]

Note that in Scientific Realism, as in other varieties of Realism, the emphasis is on discovering what is out there, understanding it, and using it. This approach to science as an act of informed discovery differs from the Pragmatist emphasis on using the scientific method to construct a socially preferred or consensual definition of knowledge (discussed in Chapter 5).

WHY STUDY REALISM?

There are at least three reasons for studying Realism: (1) for its historical significance; (2) for its popularity as a commonsense, or naïve, way of knowing; (3) for its educational importance. Like Idealism, Realism is one of the major philosophies that have an enduring history in Western culture and thought. Its origins date to Aristotle in ancient Greece; it was a dominant philosophy during the medieval period when it was reformulated by Thomas Aquinas as Theistic Realism; it was used by educators such as Pestalozzi to develop object-based instruction in the nineteenth century; it was reformulated as Scientific Realism and continues to exercise an influence on contemporary thought.

Whether they officially acknowledge the philosophy or not, many people are commonsense or naïve realists in how they conceive of knowledge and thought: if it's out there and I can see it, it must be real. Scientific Realism is often called a commonsense philosophy in that its basic assertions are in line with the generally accepted way in which many people develop their view of the world as a result of direct experience. "I exist and live in a world of other persons and objects that I can see, touch, smell, or feel," is the commonsense expression of the Realist position.

VARIETIES OF REALISM DERIVED FROM ARISTOTLE'S NATURAL REALISM

- **Classical Realism:** Emphasis on human rationality in Aristotelian context
- **Theistic Realism, Thomism:** Emphasis on a God-created universe
- **Scientific Realism:** Emphasis on science and the scientific method as the most authoritative knowledge
- **Sense Realism:** Emphasis on using the human senses to acquire information about the world

Realism was significant in the development of education as schooling and instruction. In the medieval period, when universities were first being created, educators emphasized the study of the ancient texts, especially those of Aristotle, the earliest champion of Realism. In the age of science, educators such as Comenius and Pestalozzi emphasized the use of sense realism, in which the students studied objects and learned their form, number, and nomenclature. Scientific Realism has influenced educational strategies that use the laboratory as a way to discover and confirm what exists in the physical world.

REALISM AS A PHILOSOPHY OF EDUCATION

In this section, we consider Realism, as we did Idealism, in terms of the four major subdivisions of philosophy: metaphysics, epistemology, axiology, and logic and then develop some educational implications.

Metaphysics

For Realists, the basic assertion about reality is that there is a "real" world of objects that exists independently of us but that we can acquire knowledge about it. These objects have a dual composition in that they are material (composed of matter) and organized according to a design or structure (a form). Matter is the material from which objects are made. Form is the design or structure that matter takes in order to become something. Note the duality, or two-ness, that is present: reality is comprised of objects that (1) consist of matter and (2) take a form.

Human beings possess the power to sense objects—they can see, hear, feel, smell, and taste them. The sensory process brings sense impressions—information as raw data—to the mind. The human mind, like a computer, has the ability, the internal programming, to sort out these sensory impressions and to recognize the form, or structure, in which they reside and are present. When the mind forms a concept, it is based on the form of an object. Again, note that knowing results from a two-pronged function: sensation which deals with matter and abstraction, and conceptualization that deals with form. When we say the world is composed of objects, we also include the existence of other persons. The key point is that reality is objective to us—not inside us as in the case of Idealism—but external and knowable to us.

How did this world come into existence? For some Realists, the world is simply there—it exists. For Theistic Realists, or Thomists, the world was created by God, who built into creation patterns, regularity, and order. Scientific Realists look to science to provide a theory about the origin of the universe, such as Chaos Theory or the Big Bang Theory. Metaphysically, in terms of reality, the important point is that we accept the existence of the world and the objects and persons in it as external to us.

Epistemology

Realists answer the question, "How do we know?" by returning to their two-part, or dualist, conception of reality. I exist in the world. As human beings we are specially equipped to know this reality by what Aristotle identified as our defining characteristic—our rationality. Realist philosophy emphasizes the cultivation and exercise of rationality as education's primary function.

Our rationality is based on the two-fold human powers of sensation and abstraction. Human beings possess sensory organs: the eyes which have the power to see; the ears to hear; the nose to smell; the tongue and mouth to taste; and the fingers to feel. These sensory organs focus on the material characteristics (the matter) of the objects we encounter and can give us information about these objects, such as size, shape, weight, color, sound, odor. If we encounter an apple, our senses inform us that it is red, round, hard, and sweet. However, in the initial stage of our encounter, we have before us an object. Apple is the name we give it after we first use our senses and then think about it and arrive at a general concept of what constitutes or is necessary for an apple to be an apple.

Sensation of an object's matter is the first part of the knowing process. It gives us crude information about something. In computer-like fashion, our minds begin to sort this information and grasp the objects' underlying form or structure. It is the structural components, the necessary qualities, that we use to generalize the object into concepts, or large categories. To return to the example of the apple, we may discover that there are many objects that are like the apple we observed—they have the general qualities that make them an apple but do not have the qualities other objects possess. Those formal or structural qualities that are necessary for an object to be what it is are called *necessary conditions* and those that are sometimes found in the materiality of the object are *accidental* ones. For an apple, the necessary conditions are that the apple is a round, hard, edible fruit that grows on a certain kind of tree. However, some apples may be red and others yellow, some may be sweet and others sour. What we generalize to is the concept of an apple. It is the power to abstract from our sensations that gives us the power of rationality. We may enjoy or not enjoy eating apples. We may choose or not choose to buy apples. If we decide to purchase apples, we can decide how many apples we want to buy. These all can be rational decisions, if we so choose.

Axiology

Realism's ethical and moral principles are based on the belief that all human beings participate in a general human nature. All people, regardless of when and where they live, have the same general needs, hopes, fears, and desires. As Aristotle stated, the

REALIST EPISTEMOLOGY: HOW DO WE KNOW?

I possess senses that can focus on an object.
My senses give me information about the object.
My mind sorts this information into necessary and accidental characteristics.
I arrive at a concept of a general class of objects.

common defining feature of humanity is the power to be rational and to have the free-dom to make the choices that exercise this rationality. Because of this rationality, people everywhere in the world have developed and use language—the skills of oral and written expression and communication. Despite different kinship and group rela-tionships, all people have created a culture and developed a society. Despite differ-ences of expression and style, all people have created and objectified their insights into literature, music, and art forms. At the highest level of generality, there is a shared sys-tem of ethics based on a shared humanity. This general level of ethics is universal and is not circumstantial or situational. Though languages and customs vary, these varia-tions are accidents of situations. Because of our rationality, it is possible to translate from one language to another and reach common understandings. This general sense of humanness makes it possible to respect others and to speak of the rights of *all* people. The freedom to reason and to choose is an individual right, but one that requires respect for other people as reasoning beings.

In terms of aesthetics, Realists tend to believe that although there are particular cultural expressions in the arts of what is beautiful, all people have a sense of the con-cept of beauty. Through various art forms, they give this sense concrete expression. In aesthetic experience, Realists identify the object of art—the painting, musical compo-sition, or literary work—and the recipient, the person perceiving and appreciating the work of art. It is possible to make judgments about how well the artist, musician, and writer has mastered his or subject and used the appropriate medium and technique to express her or his artistic intent. Although each person—artist and recipient—brings something to the experience, the interaction between the artist and her or his work and the recipient is not completely subjective, or solely impressionistic. The more informed the recipient is about the work of art, the greater the appreciation.

Logic

For the Realist, logic involves a two-fold process of induction and deduction. In the first phase of the knowing process, the learner acquires sensory information about the outside world and then in abstraction, the second phase, sorts this information into concepts and then proceeds to categorize the concepts. These concepts can be arranged into conceptual systems, the theoretical framework of disciplined knowl-edge, or subject matters. In the first phase, the process of knowing is inductive in that it moves from specific elements of sensory information to general concepts. Sense Realists, such as Pestalozzi, devised object lessons designed to facilitate concept for-mation based on sensation. In the process of moving from sensation to abstraction, there is a logic of going from the specific to the general and from the concrete to the abstract. In addition to the sensory or inductive phase, the Realists hold that sensory data and information is the basis for generating abstractions, or concepts, about objects.

Over time, scientists and scholars, through investigation and research, have dis-covered knowledge and have organized it into conceptual systems that explain the structure of objects, their categories, and their functions. In genetics, for example, the genes of the human body can be identified and analyzed. Certain combinations of genes result in differences in the physical appearance and health of individuals. Genetic scientists study these genes and generate hypotheses. For example, certain genes cause inherited diseases and by identifying these genes, physicians can make accurate diagnoses and prescribe appropriate treatment.

Deductive logic, in Realism, takes place when reasoning is used to make specific cases or applications of a general principle. Once the authoritative knowledge has been established, it is possible to apply it to many particular instances.

REALISM'S EDUCATIONAL IMPLICATIONS

The Purpose of Education and the Function of the School

According to Realism, the purpose of education is to cultivate and develop the power of reasoning so that individuals can acquire knowledge and learn how to use it in framing and making choices. Using reason, people can become free from ignorance, superstition, and error. Informed freedom empowers people to formulate alternatives of action based on the best available knowledge in order to make intelligent and rational decisions.

Reflecting the purpose of education, the school, as a socially constructed and sustained institution, is guided by the primary purpose of informing, developing, and guiding human reason. In the context of schooling, reason is developed and exercised by the teaching and learning of subjects that are based on authoritative knowledge. Nothing should be allowed to interfere with or deter schools from fulfilling this primary role. While schools may provide health and psychological services, offer recreational activities, and sponsor athletic teams and competitions, these secondary activities should not be allowed to obscure, interfere with, or diminish the primary function.

Show and Tell: Animal, Vegetable, or Mineral

The Realist predilection for classification can be illustrated by the activity of "show and tell," often used in kindergarten and the primary grades. The pupils bring something to school—a small pet, a rock collection, a favorite toy, or a plant. They tell their classmates about the object, describe it, and indicate why they chose to bring it to school.

Illustrative of Realist epistemology, these items can be sorted or classified into categories. Using their senses, the pupils can sort them out. Some of them may be animals, such as a fish or a hamster, others may be minerals, still others might be plants. There are also human-made items, such as toys or books, which are social artifacts. As these objects are classified, the pupils are learning an important Realist principle: some things are alike and other things are different. Going back to Realist epistemology, those things that are alike share similar or related necessary qualities. Although the fish and the hamster are quite different, they breathe, eat, and move—they are living members of the animal kingdom. They do not have the qualities of plants or minerals. This rather simple illustration can lead us to higher-level and more complex Realist educational principles.

A Curriculum of Categorical Subjects

Through the process of sensation and abstraction of objects found in the environment, we arrive at concepts, a general idea that represents a class of objects that possesses the same necessary or essential qualities. For example, we can see many different kinds of trees—pines, firs, cedars, oaks, elms, lindens, and palms. They are all trees but are different types. Using the process of abstraction, we can form a concept of "treeness" based on those common characteristics or attributes all trees share. We can further sort these trees into those that are conifers (green throughout the year) and those that are deciduous (shed their leaves once a year and then sprout new leaves at the appropriate time of year, usually Spring). Trees and other plants are studied in the discipline or subject of botany. We can study botany as a body of knowledge, as an academic subject. In this study, we can learn about trees in the general sense, the theories that apply to all trees. We can also learn about trees in the specific sense, about a particular kind of tree for example. We can gain information about the geographical range of certain trees, about the climatic and soil conditions that are favorable or unfavorable to their growth, the diseases and parasites that are harmful to them, and so forth. Realists say that this kind of information, often the result of scientific research and discovery, is our best kind of knowledge and should guide our practice or behavior. While this theory based on science is valuable in its own right, intrinsically, it is also valuable in that it is a useful guide to our practice. The study of botany is a useful foundation for such practical activities as forestry and agriculture.

Not only can the study of trees in botany inform us theoretically and practically, such study can also inform us on policy issues. Environmentally, there is a scientifically based concern about the effects of reducing the earth's rain forests by harvesting their trees without a concern for maintaining the forests for the future. Some scientists believe that harvesting the trees in the rain forests contributes to the depletion of the earth's ozone layer, to the growing belt of deserts, and to increases in skin cancers. There are also issues regarding the preservation of forests in the United States and debates between those who want to harvest a larger number of trees and those who argue for more conservation. On these issues, Realists believe that informed policy decisions can be made by studying the latest and best available research. The Realist approach to decision-making is based on the belief that the defining characteristic of the human being is rationality and that it is possible and desirable to make informed rational choices.

As in the case of the example of trees and the study of botany, human knowledge, itself, can be sorted and classified into various subject matter disciplines. Among these categories or classes of knowledge, we have such subjects as chemistry, physics, zoology, biology, anthropology, sociology, languages, political science, literature, history, and so on. Although there are relationships between areas of knowledge, each subject is a separate and discrete body of knowledge. In order to approach these bodies of knowledge, we need command of the fundamental processes of literacy—reading and writing—and arithmetic. We also need to know how to locate accurate knowledge and to determine who is a legitimate authority in a field and who is not.

■ ■ ■ ■ ■

REALIST CURRICULUM

- **Elementary Education:** Fundamentals of literacy and numeracy; learning how to find information and do research; introduction of language, literature, history, arts, and science
- **Secondary Education:** Study of subjects such as history, language, mathematics, sciences, arts, literature
- **Higher Education:** The liberal arts and sciences

Instruction

Instruction, according to Realism, focuses on learning skills and subjects in a cumulative, sequential, and systematic manner. It is organized by the teacher who should have expert knowledge of the skill and subject and how to teach it. Since the curriculum is based on long-standing subjects, it is designed and structured prior to the students' encounter with it. It contains those subjects that the scholars and scientists judge to be worthy of study, the corpus of knowledge needed by an educated person.

Actual instruction can take a variety of forms. It might be a lecture, discussion of a topic, viewing of a video, library work, a search of the Internet, or independent study. The choice of format of instruction depends on what the teacher regards as the most effective way of studying and learning a particular subject. While stimulating students' interest in the subject is an important motivational device, interest alone does not determine what should be included in the curriculum. The contents of the curriculum are determined by those who are authorities, or experts, in the various disciplines. An authority is an expert who knows the content of a subject thoroughly, understands its organizing principles, and is skilled in using the methods appropriate to it.

Teachers, then, organize a particular subject, such as history or biology, prior to instruction. In preparing to teach a subject, a teacher, according to Realism, needs to know the subject thoroughly and needs to know how to teach it effectively. Again, the Realist's emphasis on duality, or the two-fold nature, of some thing or action is evident. There is content (subject-matter knowledge) and method (the process of instruction). Accordingly, teachers need to be educated in the liberal arts and sciences in order to have content knowledge, and in curriculum and instruction in order to use methods and strategies of instruction. From courses in educational psychology, teachers learn strategies that can be used to motivate students, and from courses in methods they learn how to design lessons that facilitate learning. It is important to note that there is always a subject, a body of knowledge, that is being taught and learned in all instances of instruction. Though it may be entertaining and interesting, a lesson is insufficient if there is not a body of knowledge, a subject, being taught.

■ ■ ■ ■ ■

REALIST INSTRUCTION HAS THREE NECESSARY COMPONENTS:

1. A teacher who is an expert in a subject and who knows how to teach it.
2. A skill or a subject that is the focus of instruction.
3. A student who is capable of learning the subject.

The Relationship of Theory and Practice

Realists emphasize the importance of the relationship between theory and practice. Theories, dealing with general patterns, are abstract and can transfer to a variety of particular situations. Practice is specific to particular situations. For example, theory, in educational psychology, offers explanations of how students learn or fail to learn. Practice, in particular classroom settings, deals with a teacher instructing students. Theory, at its higher level of generalization, can be applied to the particular classroom context.

More generally, education is properly directed to the study of theories, which are generalizations found in the various academic disciplines. Such theory should guide practice in the way that physics, which is more theoretical, should guide engineering, which is more applied.

Realists would rate the theoretical subjects, the liberal arts and sciences, higher in the curriculum than the practical ones, and higher than vocational training, which is limited by its specificity to particular situations. Indeed, vocational training, according to some Realists, is more effectively learned by a hands-on apprenticeship in the field than in academic settings.

The Realist placement of priority on the theoretical over the vocational has had significant implications for education and for schooling. The strongest of these implications is to create a dualism or bifurcation in education in which the theoretical ranks higher than the practical or the popular. For example, liberal studies rank higher than vocational training, fine art ranks higher than popular art, classical music ranks higher than contemporary music, and so on.

Although its metaphysical origins are different, the Realist emphasis on a hierarchy of subjects in the curriculum appears similar to that of the Idealists, discussed in Chapter 2. The dualism between theory and practice is more powerful in Europe than in the United States. In the United States more practical and vocational subjects are integrated in the curriculum, especially in the comprehensive high school. European educational systems typically have separated academic education from vocational training into distinct types of schools. It needs to be noted that Pragmatist philosophers such as John Dewey, discussed in Chapter 5, and many Progressive theorists, discussed in Chapter 18, challenged the Realist dualism that separates theory and practice.

The Realists believe that subject matter knowledge and liberal education are for all people regardless of ethnicity, race, gender, or socioeconomic class. Indeed, the same curriculum should be offered to all. Although there might be gradations and adjustments of a subject to a student's ability and readiness, all students should study the subjects that are considered necessary for the truly educated person.

Realist Ethical and Aesthetic Education

Though they prize knowledge as indispensable to rationality, Realists recognize that knowledge alone, if not reinforced by the proper dispositions and habits, may not, by itself, lead to ethical behavior. The predispositions to ethical behavior and the foundations of moral character originate in early childhood as children acquire the attitudes, inclinations, and behaviors that dispose a person to the right values. Parents, guardians, and teachers are important moral agents in developing moral habits in the young.

In aesthetic education, Realists believe that the various art forms of music, dance, painting, and literature can be studied as to their genre, structure, and style. Like the bodies of knowledge, art forms, too, can be classified and categorized. Aesthetic appreciation and creation is tied to this knowledge of genre, structure, and style. Although we can naively enjoy a song or a painting, knowledge of the work of art enhances and heightens our experience of it. While we are free to use our ingenuity and creativity in artistic, musical, and literary expression, knowledge of genre, structure, style, and technique enhance our ability and enlarge the range of artistic expression. Our life, ethically and aesthetically, is enhanced through knowledge, knowing reality, rather than by naiveté or ignorance.

HARRY S. BROUDY, "FUNCTIONS OF THE SCHOOL" AND "CRITERIA OF MORAL EDUCATION AND DEVELOPMENT"

The following primary source selection is from Harry S. Broudy, a classical Realist philosopher of education. It was selected because Broudy, drawing from Aristotle's Natural Realism, presents a clear argument that the school has a primary purpose and that moral education, following the principle of moderation, should lead to self-determination, self-realization, and self-integration. Broudy's designation of his philosophy as *classical* means that its origins go back to the ancient Greek philosopher, Aristotle. The use of the term, *realism*, means that it follows the general assumption that there is an objective order of reality that we can come to know; this knowledge is our best guide to conduct. For Broudy, the school, like other social institutions, has a primary function—the cultivation and appreciation of knowledge in the young. Unlike the Pragmatists, Progressives, and Critical Theorists (discussed later in the book), Broudy opposes a view that the school is a multifunctional institution and that the cultivation of knowledge is only one of its many functions. In "Criteria of Moral Education and Development," Broudy, like Aristotle, proposes that the purpose of education is to aim at the good life, a life that is self-determined, self-realized, and self-integrated. As you read the selection, consider the following focusing questions:

1. Do you agree or disagree with Broudy's argument that the school has a primary function? Explain your answer.

2. Based on Broudy's argument that the school has a primary function, what is the role of the teacher in such an institution?

3. Describe and evaluate the kind of person who epitomizes Broudy's criteria of moral development.

4. Do you agree or disagree with Broudy's criteria of moral development? Explain your answer.

FUNCTIONS OF THE SCHOOL

By outlining the functions of government, the family, and the church in a rational social order, the specific role of the school may become clearer.

1. The school is not a legislative agency that makes laws, nor is it an executive agency that carries them out, nor a judicial agency that passes on their legal merits.

2. The school is not a family. It does not come into being to bring children into existence. Conceivably it could undertake their total rearing from the moment of birth on, as Plato suggested it do for the children of the Guardians. But so long as we do have families in our culture, the school is not responsible for the entire rearing. Especially not for the attitudes formed by relations with parents and other children in the early years of life.

3. The school is not a church. It has no Divine authorization, authority, or special revelation.

4. The school is not Science; it is not the agency that is established primarily for the discovery and development of truth. . . .

5. The school is not an industry or business. It does not produce, transform, transport, or distribute material goods, however much it may be instrumental thereto.

6. The school is established by the group when intellectual habits need to be deliberately formed in all or some of the citizens. . . . That it reinforces some of the emotional teachings of the home and frustrates others; that it tries to promote physical and emotional good health goes without saying, but these latter cannot be the primary goals of the school without disrupting the division of labor within our social order.

When the school performs its primary job well, then anything else it manages to do is "gravy." Anything else it does *without* doing its primary job makes its title to being a school highly dubious.

It will be objected that this account of the various social agencies is too narrow; especially

From Harry S. Broudy, *Building a Philosophy of Education*, 2nd ed. Englewood Cliffs, NJ: Prentice-Hall, 1961, pp. 100–103, 243–250. Used with permission of the Krieger Publishing Company.

will it be pointed out that it seems as if *only* the church, the school, and the family do any educating. Is not then the theatre educative? Are not industry and our daily work educative? Isn't membership in a lodge or a labor union educative? Do not books, magazines, movies, television, and radio educate?

. . .These agencies provide learning opportunities, but *incidentally* to other functions that are primary for them. They educate *informally*. When the theater goes in for deliberate instruction, we call it didactic and stop going. The primary task of newspapers is not to instruct, but rather to report. Only in its editorial columns does a newspaper take an educative role. The same may be said about the educational activities of industries, labor unions, and other organizations.

One of the clearest criteria of educational genuineness is the motivation behind the activity. If it is not the perfection of the individual through the control of learning, it may be any one of many wonderful things, but it is not education. For this reason we can say that when a teacher or educator has as his or her ultimate motive any consideration other than the realization of the pupil's potentialities, he or she is no longer an educator. That educators earn their bread by teaching is important but still incidental. Nuns, priests, and parents who do not earn their living in this way nevertheless can still be teachers in the true sense of the word. When society does not pay its teachers adequately it is the fault of society, and the remedy lies not in education but in statesmanship. All of which means that teachers do at times have to be politicians, but this is never to be confused with their teaching function.

The general objection to this chapter may well be that it sets up essential functions for the various institutions as if they were somehow fixed forever. It will be held that institutions do change their functions as social conditions vary. Why, then, should not the functions of the school also change?

The answer is to be found in the interdependence of these agencies in the social order. In any organization there is the working assumption that each element will contribute its share to the whole enterprise. A failure in any part, if it persists for any length of time, disturbs the whole activity.

When any institution makes one of its incidental or secondary functions dominant, it ceases to do its principal job. To that extent the social order is maimed and begins to disintegrate. Consequently, when an institution changes its function, it makes changes necessary in all other institutions—a total rearrangement of the relations among men, and this rarely occurs without great "times of trouble," to use a phrase of Arnold Toynbee. The progress we need can be achieved by changing the *way* in which a social institution performs its function rather than by *shifting* the function. Children should perhaps be reared differently today than they were 50 years ago, but if the rearing of children is made subordinate to the economic or affectional function of the family, there will be trouble. We have changed our methods of industry, but it will be a sorry day for us all when it makes advertising instead of production its chief concern. The schools have changed their methods and can change them much more without trying to play the role of the family, the church, or the government.

CRITERIA OF MORAL EDUCATION AND DEVELOPMENT

If self-determination, self-realization, and self-integration are genuine criteria of the good life, then they are criteria for moral action.

Self-determination

Moral education aims at the development of freedom because without freedom of choice no act is moral in quality. How do we educate pupils to be free?

We might urge pupils to want to be free. Ours was a birth in freedom; freedom is celebrated in song and story as well as in history. Do we have to *urge* human beings to want to be free? Do we have to urge people to want to be free from constraint? From fear? From want? From political despotism? No one, I suggest, needs to be told to want this kind of freedom. We usually want more of it than we can possibly have.

There is, however, a freedom which not all of us want. Indeed we sometimes dread it. It is the freedom that carries the price tag of responsibility. A vigorous critic of an organization is at least momentarily disconcerted to find himself its president. Before, he could suggest the wildest schemes, the boldest measures; others would share the responsibility if they were adopted; and there would be no responsibility if they were rejected. Now matters are really up to him.

With the awareness of freedom comes the frightening realization that we have become subject to a claim that we cannot ignore. It is easier, in the short run, to have one's life shaped by others and by circumstances over which one has no control.

We are indebted to the Existentialist writers and especially to Kierkegaard for a recognition of this aspect of freedom and of the existential anxiety that is a part of human nature. We are all anxious, whether we know it or not, because we have an inkling of what human freedom means.

Moral education has to discourage flight from this kind of freedom. To make the individual pupil sensitive to the possibility that at every moment of his life there may be something that *he* can do to shape the next moment is an education for freedom. Self-determination means that one has accepted the responsibility for the making of his future and perhaps of the future of all other men.

The school, you will say, is not the place where pupils make momentous choices. How then can the school educate for freedom? It does so by way of knowledge. As we learn more about our world, our social order, and about ourselves, do we not become more and more sensitive to the claims made upon us? And with this knowledge can we ignore the question as to what our responsibility is to the community, country, family, school, and to our own selves?

Further, the use of knowledge to shape our commitments is what makes them rational rather than capricious. I cannot ever foresee all the consequences of my commitment, but if I make it on the best knowledge I can summon, my gamble with life has its supreme justification. No man can do more.

The first moral law for every man is to be as rational and as knowing in his choices as circumstances will permit. This law implies another: it is every man's duty to learn as much about the world, the society, and himself as he can.

A reliable symptom as to whether a school or a school system is working at moral education is its respect for knowledge. It matters little whether a school has one or a dozen courses marked "character education." If its attitude toward human knowing is derogatory, if it is anti-intellectualistic in its philosophy, if it gears its curriculum to the minimum needs of getting along on the job or in the group, then that school system has no genuine respect for persons as potential moral legislators in their own right. That system is not aiming at self-determination, but rather at the determination of the pupil by the group, by the economic order, by anything and everything except himself. . . .

Self-realization

We ought to choose freely, but *what* ought we to choose? So far as education is concerned, choice should be to achieve self-realization.

From where the pupil stands, self-realization lies in his own future. For the educator, the goal is the self-realization of all his pupils. Morally speaking, each pupil *ought* to realize his potentialities, and the school *ought* to cultivate the potentialities of every pupil. This seems so obvious as to be trivial, for does not human nature force us to strive for self-realization? Is there any choice, any *ought* in the matter?

The answer lies in the many levels of striving that are possible so that although striving is a universal feature of human nature, its precise character is not. Man can live after a fashion without pushing himself to the limit of his capacity. He can be ignorant of his potentialities, or he can ignore them. There is a choice here, and there can be an *ought*—if we can establish a claim upon him and get him to acknowledge the claim.

As an educator, there is an argument to which one can resort: if I, as a teacher, know the value of a sunset, a friend, a generous act, or an insight into the truth, and if I know you, as a pupil, have the capacity to realize these values, then I ought to disclose these possibilities to you and teach you how to cultivate them. If these values cannot thereafter speak for themselves, there is no more that I can say for them.

Suppose the pupil argues: Does it make any difference to anyone but myself whether I cultivate my capacities or not? Suppose I could become a first-rate poet, musician, scientist, doctor, or carpenter. Suppose I am content to remain second- or even third-rate. Can you tell me that I *ought* to become first-rate?

We can answer in the affirmative, but only if we are prepared to argue that mankind has a claim upon the full self-realization of every man. What could be the basis for such a claim?

We cannot, as a matter of justice, demand that anyone realize his powers beyond what is needed to recompense his fellow men for the values they enable him to realize. If, however, the individual can be led to experience a value of a higher order than he hitherto has achieved, and if he acknowledges it as higher, then he does have a duty to contribute the greatest values of which he is capable. Once he acknowledges that first-rate science is better than second-rate, he is obligated to become the best kind of scientist of which he is capable. He is heeding the claim of value itself. This claim is universal, that is, whatever is judged to be good or right is judged to be so for all men in the same circumstances.

That is why in the school we have to take advantage of our position as teachers to set into motion the process of self-realization. Indeed, this becomes our moral obligation. The source of this claim is the nature of man itself, for if we know anything about human nature, it is that the particular direction of human striving is not predetermined by the genes, but by the power of the human mind to envision patterns of possibility. To direct this striving to self-realization through knowledge, therefore, is what the good life demands of the school.

. . .

If, however, there is such a thing as human nature, then a value is what perfects that human nature. If health is good, it is good for all human beings; if education is good, it is good for all. If, in brief, it is my duty to realize my capacities, it is everyone's duty to do likewise. I have to respect this claim wherever it is made. Indeed I have to make that claim for all mankind.

In education, the imperative to self-realization has definite consequences. It means that we have to urge, cajole, and, so far as we are allowed, *insist* that education be not curtailed and truncated for any individual before his capacities for learning have been exploited as far as we have the resources to exploit them. It means that if a boy can learn literature, he will be required to learn it; if he can master trigonometry, he will be required to do so; if he can be artistically competent, he will be required to be competent without worrying too much whether it will get him a job, a house in the suburbs, or membership in the country club.

The vocational usefulness of his school tasks the pupil gauges with uncanny accuracy. It is the usefulness of the school studies to what Aristotle called citizenship and leisure (cultivation of one's rational powers) that the pupil cannot easily discern. Today the intellectual requirements for these are so high that unless the tools for achieving them are perfected in the secondary school, the chances of adequately cultivating one's rational resources in later life are remote.

Self-integration

Self-integration means that we have to put the claims that tug at us from all directions in some intelligible order. Value claims conflict with each other. Until we choose between alternative values, we are torn among them. To decide which values shall dominate and guide our efforts to self-realization is itself a moral decision, perhaps the most serious of all decisions. Moral education in the school, therefore, includes the learning of the means, or at least of some of them, for value integration. How do we go about this?

. . .

Knowledge might be the universal integrator, and in this book it is taken for granted that the school will devote itself to the integrating of life through knowledge. Yet it is silly to urge a boy with modest intellectual endowments to integrate his value system through erudition or to suggest to a musically gifted pupil that he take up farming as a way of simplifying and ordering life. What the school can do is to make an intelligent estimate of the pupil's integrative pattern on the basis of his potentialities. Further, much of the curriculum to be outlined is a study of what men have had to integrate and to what extent they have managed to do so. Because these struggles take place on the stages of history and art, they write our own individual problems in large and luminous letters.

These are admittedly indirect methods. Nevertheless, if the world does not make sense to a man, he is to that degree not integrated. Knowledge tries to find what sense there is in the world and to that extent is integrative for everyone. . . .

Therefore, if a general education can give a pupil a confidence in his power to acquire and use knowledge, and if it gives him a realistic sense of his own capacities, his strengths, and his weaknesses, that is, perhaps, a good beginning in integration.

CONCLUSION

This chapter examined Realism, one of the Western world's oldest philosophies. Realism has had an important impact on Western thought, especially in theology and in science. It emphasizes knowing and forming generalizations about how the real, objective, physical world works. It emphasizes that human beings are rational creatures who can know and act according to the principles that exist in the world. When our actions are based on such knowledge, we are acting realistically, or rationally. Schools exist to cultivate and exercise this rationality. Through knowledge, we can define our interests, make decisions, and choose between alternative possibilities. To be free means that we know how to acquire knowledge, organize it, and use it to chart our course in the world.

DISCUSSION QUESTIONS

1. Do you agree or disagree that Realism is a commonsense philosophy? Explain your answer.
2. How does Realism differ from Idealism?
3. According to Realism, *how* do we know?
4. What are the strengths and weaknesses of the Realist view of a subject matter curriculum?
5. Examine the curriculum, especially the required courses, at your college or university. Does it represent a Realist orientation?
6. Compare and contrast the concept of a hierarchy in curriculum in Realism and Idealism.

INQUIRY AND RESEARCH PROJECTS

1. Compare and contrast the aims of education expressed in your local school board's statement of philosophy with those of Realism, especially Broudy's position.
2. Compare and contrast the position on the function of the school taken by the author of a foundations of education text with Realism, especially the views of Broudy.
3. Design a lesson based on Realist epistemology.
4. Review the current literature on school reform; determine if it reflects a Realist orientation.

INTERNET RESOURCES

For a discussion of Neo-Realism, consult "The Philosophy of Neo-Realism" at the Radical Academy at
http://radical/academy.com/adiphilnewrealism.html

An essay on Moral Realism can be found at the Internet Encyclopedia of Philosophy at
www.utm.edu/research/iep/m/m-realis-html

For a discussion of Scientific Realism, consult Arthur Fine, "Scientific Realism and Anti-Realism," in the Routledge Encyclopedia of Philosophy at
www.gbhap-us.com/rep/q094sam.html

SUGGESTIONS FOR FURTHER READING

Alston, William P. *A Realist Conception of Truth.* Ithaca, NY: Cornell University Press, 1996.

Anagnostopoulos, Georgios. *Aristotle on the Goals and Exactness of Ethics.* Berkeley, CA: University of California Press, 1994.

Brink, David O. *Moral Realism and the Foundations of Ethics.* Cambridge: Cambridge University Press, 1989.

Broudy, Harry S. *Building a Philosophy of Education,* 2nd ed. Englewood Cliffs, NJ: Prentice-Hall, 1961.

Churchill, Paul M. *Scientific Realism and the Plasticity of Mind.* Cambridge: Cambridge University Press, 1979.

Davitt, Michael. *Realism and Truth.* Oxford, UK: Basil Blackwell, 1991.

Ganson, Dorit A. *The Explanationist Defense of Scientific Realism.* New York: Garland Publishing Co., 2002.

Garver, Eugene. *Aristotle's Rhetoric: An Act of Character.* Chicago: University of Chicago Press, 1994.

Jacobs, Jonathan A. *Being True to the World: Moral Realism and Practical Wisdom.* New York: P. Lang, 1990.

Jacobs, Jonathan A. *Practical Realism and Moral Psychology.* Washington, DC: Georgetown University Press, 1995.

Kelley, David. *The Evidence of the Senses: A Realist Theory of Perception.* Baton Rouge, LA: Louisiana State University Press, 1986.

Layder, Derek. *The Realist Image in Social Science.* New York: St. Martin's Press, 1990.

Lennox, James G. *Aristotle's Philosophy of Biology: Studies in the Origin of Life Science.* New York: Cambridge University Press, 2000.

Miller, Richard W. *Fact and Method: Explanation, Confirmation and Reality in the Natural and the Social Sciences.* Princeton, NJ: Princeton University Press, 1987.

Newman, Andrew. *The Correspondence Theory of Truth: An Essay on the Metaphysics of Prediction.* New York: Cambridge University Press, 2002.

Rescher, Nicholas. *Scientific Realism: A Critical Reappraisal.* Boston: D. Reidel, 1987.

Russman, Thomas A. *A Prospectus for the Triumph of Realism.* Macon, GA: Mercer University Press, 1987.

Smart, J. J. C. *Philosophy and Scientific Realism.* London: Routledge & Kegan Paul, 1963.

NOTES

1. For discussions of Aristotle, see D. J. Allan, *The Philosophy of Aristotle* (London: Oxford University Press, 1970); G. E. R. Lloyd, *Aristotle: The Growth and Structure of His Thought* (Cambridge: Cambridge University Press, 1968).

2. Richard Boyd, Philip Gasper, and J. D. Trout, eds. *The Philosophy of Science* (Cambridge, MA: MIT Press, 1993), p. 780.

3. Richard W. Miller, *Fact and Method: Explanation, Confirmation and Reality in the Natural and Social Sciences* (Princeton, NJ: Princeton University Press, 1987). Also, see Nicholas Rescher, *Scientific Realism: A Critical Reappraisal* (Boston: D. Reidel, 1987).

CHAPTER FOUR

THEISTIC REALISM
(THOMISM)

In this chapter, we will examine Theistic Realism, or Thomism, a philosophy that embraces a synthesis of Aristotle's Realism and Christian theology, particularly that which was articulated in Middle Ages. The terms Theistic Realism and Thomism are used interchangeably in the chapter. Thomism is derived from the name of Thomas Aquinas who articulated the philosophy of Theistic Realism. The chapter defines Theistic Realism, examines its synthesis of Aristotelianism and Christian theology, discusses its major principles, and draws out its implications for education.

DEFINING THEISTIC REALISM

Theistic Realism was developed in the Middle Ages and formed a bridge between classical Greek thought, especially that of Aristotle, and Christianity. In Chapter 3, Realism was defined as the belief that we live in a world that exists objectively and externally to us; through a dual process of sensation and abstraction, we can form concepts about that world, and this provides the basis of our knowledge. When we act according to that knowledge, we are acting rationally. (Readers can refer to Chapter 3 for the definitions of *real* as used in Realism.) We now turn to the terms *theistic* and Thomism, another name for Theistic Realism.

The root of theistic is **theism**, a belief that a supernatural and benevolent God created the world and all beings in it, and established the laws, patterns, and regularities that govern the universe. This belief is accompanied by faith in divine revelation. According to revelation, God, through inspired messages to specially designated persons, disclosed truths that were recorded in a great book, the Bible, and are accepted by the faithful as the word of the Lord.

Thomism, another name for Theistic Realism, is derived from the first name of Thomas Aquinas (1225–1274), who, in the thirteenth century, formulated the theological and philosophical body of thought and writings that were regarded as authoritative doctrines for medieval Christian scholasticism and for the Roman Catholic Church. Aquinas' working premise was that philosophy seeks truth through reason, and theology seeks it through divine revelation from God. Since what is true is eternal and the same everywhere, philosophy and theology and reason and faith are compatible and not contradictory. The Thomistic argument that reason and faith are complementary governed thinking until the sixteenth century when religion and science began to separate into different ways of thinking—religion dealing with the supernatural and science with the natural order. The debate over science and religion still resounds in education. For example, there is a continuing conflict between Creationists, who hold that God created the world and human beings, and Evolutionists, who believe that the origin of the species is a process of organisms struggling to survive in changing environments. Thomists, however, could reconcile both positions but insist that life was created by God, a Supernatural Being, who endowed humans with a materialistic body and a spiritual soul.

Theistic Realism, or Thomism, is based on a synthesis of two major sources in Western thought: Aristotle's Natural Realism and Thomas Aquinas' Christian Scholastic Theology. Theistic Realism refers to its theological orientation to Theism, the belief in the existence of God as the supernatural Creator of the universe and the beings within it, and to Realism, the philosophical belief in an external, or objective, order of reality governed by natural laws, and recurrent patterns of regularity.

Although historically associated with Catholic theology and philosophy, Thomism has attracted philosophers such as Robert Hutchins (1899–1977), Mortimer Adler (1902–2001), and others who do not adhere to Catholicism's religious doctrines and orientation. (The educational ideas of Hutchins and Adler are examined in Chapter 17, which deals with Perennialism.) Thomism's general appeal lies in its assertion that there are natural laws that are higher than the statutes enacted by political regimes or by polls of popular opinion. Not culturally relative to particular situations, times, and places, natural law—grounded in the universe itself—is universal, unchanging, and fundamental to human nature and life. Natural laws can be discovered by human reason. Human rights, then, are not given by governments or societies, but are inherent in human nature itself. The Thomist position on the existence of natural laws that govern not only the physical world but persons and societies leads to an emphasis on universal principles in human ethics and behavior. These Thomistic claims are disputed by more contemporary philosophies, such as Pragmatism (discussed in Chapter 5) and Postmodernism (in Chapter 8).

SITUATING THEISTIC REALISM IN WESTERN THOUGHT

To understand Thomism's origin, development, and significance, it is useful to consider the history of Western thought. (Western intellectual history and philosophy was developed and then situated in Europe and the Americas; it can be compared and contrasted with Eastern intellectual history and philosophy, which was developed and situated in Asia.) In Chapter 2, we examined Idealism, originally developed by Plato; in Chapter 3, we examined Realism, originally developed by Aristotle. Both philosophies originated in classical Greece and were carried into the Roman Empire after Rome conquered Greece.

Christianity, which originated in Judea in the Near East, entered the Western world by way of Greece and Rome. Among the early converts to Christianity were Greeks and Romans who were familiar with the philosophies of Plato and Aristotle, as well as with other philosophies such as Epicureanism and Stoicism. For these early Christians, however, the Bible and the teachings and doctrines of the Church Fathers were their paramount authorities and took precedence over classical philosophies, which were associated with the pagan past. Nevertheless, Plato's and Aristotle's philosophies remained important sources of thought in the Western world. In the early years of Christianity, some Christians believed the classical philosophies were dangerous rival systems of non-Theistic thought that needed to be purged from education. Other theologians, such as Saint Augustine, believed that the classical philosophies complemented Christian theology and doctrines. For example, Augustine believed that studying the liberal arts and philosophy encouraged a person to search for still higher truths. This search led to the Bible, the sacred scriptures, theology, and ultimately to a more mature and greater understanding of God.

Thomas Aquinas, a Dominican theologian at the University of Paris, sought to reconcile the apparent conflict between reason, represented by classical philosophy (especially Aristotle's Realism), and faith, represented by the Christian Bible, doctrines, and beliefs.[1] His most important philosophical and theological work, *Summa Theologiae*, written between 1269 and 1272, integrated and harmonized Aristotelian philosophy and Christian doctrine. The philosophical system based on the *Summa* is a variety of Theistic Realism that also bears his name, Thomism.

Intellectual Synthesis

Aquinas' building of an intellectual bridge between classical Aristotelian philosophy and Christian theology and his creation of a synthesis based on these systems of thought offers the opportunity to consider the difference between philosophical approaches—those that are system-building and those that use analysis and deconstruction. Aquinas' grand synthesis of Aristotle's Realism and Christian doctrine represents an integration of two major bodies of thought into one very large philosophic system. Aquinas and other system-building philosophers, such as Hegel (discussed in Chapter 2), attempted to create overarching, all-inclusive architectonic philosophies,

■ ■ ■ ■ ■

THOMISM: A PHILOSOPHICAL SYNTHESIS OF:

Christian doctrines based on the Bible, writings of the Fathers of the Church, and religious beliefs

and

Aristotle's Natural Realism

that encompass and seek to explain all existence by combining concepts found in different intellectual systems into an integrated whole. In the nineteenth century, Karl Marx's dialectical materialism, or Marxism, which is diametrically different from Thomism, represented another landmark attempt at synthesis building. (Marxism is examined in Chapter 13.) These synthetic systems are grand, all-encompassing intellectual edifices that purport to explain all of reality and existence. More contemporary philosophies such as Philosophical Analysis and Postmodernism, reject Thomism's grand approach at system building. Philosophical Analysis (examined in Chapter 7) breaks down the language used in philosophy in order to subject it to the test of empirical verification. Postmodernism, with its method of deconstructionism (examined in Chapter 8), sees such grand syntheses as Thomism and Hegelianism as representing the ideology, the rationales for power and control, of a dominant class at a particular period of history. For example, Thomism would represent the rationale used by the dominant church-related clerical hierarchy to maintain its status and power during the Middle Ages. Our approach to education and to instruction will be very different if we assume that the grand philosophical systems represent a high level of explanation, or if we take the approach that analysis represents a way of breaking through what purports to be the source of educational principles and constructs political, social, and economic insights into how power is held and exercised in modern society.

WHY STUDY THEISTIC REALISM?

There are historical and contemporary reasons for studying Theistic Realism. Thomism, which dominated Western thinking during the medieval period, especially the thirteenth century, was the standard and approved method of scholarship used in the medieval universities. As the officially sanctioned philosophy of the Roman Catholic Church, it was used as the intellectual foundation in Catholic higher education. In the twentieth century, there was a significant revival of Thomism, especially in the Integral Realism of Jacques Maritain (1882–1973). Because of its long and continuing influence, the study of Theistic Realism is useful in providing a perspective on the history of philosophy.

Thomism's influence extended beyond Catholicism. It attracted the attention of theorists who were in the tradition of Classical Humanism and Aristotelian Realism such as Mortimer Adler and Robert Hutchins in the United States. It has influenced those who want to base education on enduring principles and values as an antidote to modern society's infatuation with consumer-driven materialism and presentism's deliberate forgetfulness of the past. It has also been a strong influence on the educational theory of Perennialism, discussed in Chapter 17.

THEISTIC REALISM AS A PHILOSOPHY OF EDUCATION

Metaphysics

Thomist metaphysics included a synthesis of theological or supernatural components based on Christian doctrine and beliefs, and philosophical components derived from

Aristotle's Realism. The theological doctrines that Aquinas used in building his synthesis came from the doctrines of the medieval Christian Church. Aquinas asserted the existence of God, an omnipotent, perfect, and supernatural being, who created all existence, including human beings. Omnipotent means all-powerful; perfect means completely good; and supernatural means above and beyond nature or the physical world. God created human beings and endowed them with a spiritual soul and a physical body. During life on earth, the body connects the person to the natural and physical world. The earthly dimension of human life, the time spent on Earth, takes place at a particular time and in a particular place. After the death of the body, the soul, destined for eternal life, enables the person to enjoy the beatific vision—the complete happiness of being with God, the supernatural Creator. Through the soul, God gave human beings· an intellect, which is the basis of self-awareness and rationality, and a will, which enables them to have freedom of choice. Because of the original sin of Adam and Eve, the parents of the human race, the human being, at birth, enters the world spiritually deprived and imperfect. God sent his son, Jesus Christ, to Earth as a man in order to redeem humankind through his death, resurrection, and ascension to heaven. To aid human beings in regaining their spiritual heritage and to enjoy the vision of God, Christ established the Christian Church to teach all nations and to administer the grace-giving sacraments.[2]

Aquinas' synthesis was completed by integrating components of Aristotle's Realism into the philosophy. Among these components were the principles that:

1. Human beings live in an orderly and purposeful universe that follows patterns of regularity known as natural laws.
2. Human beings, endowed with intellect, are rational creatures.
3. Human knowledge begins with sensation and is completed with conceptualization.

While Aquinas accepted these Aristotelian principles, he believed that they were true but incomplete statements of reality. For example, Aquinas believed that Aristotle's natural process of knowing was enlightened and completed by the human being's acceptance of the truth of Christian doctrine as an act of faith, and cooperation with the enlightenment of the intellect through gifts of supernatural grace. Like Aristotle, Aquinas believed that the universe itself was rationally designed, functioned according to patterns of regularity, and that existence was purposeful and not accidental. However, for Aquinas, the power behind the purposeful universe was the mind and hand of God. While Aquinas accepted Aristotle's dictum that the greatest human happiness came from living a life based on reason, he believed that Aristotle's view was limited because he did not have the gift of Christian faith. For Aquinas, Aristotle's earthly view of happiness, while partially true, was incomplete. Human happiness was completely realized in heaven after the death of the body when the soul achieved the beatific vision of being in the presence of the Creator.

According to Aquinas, we live in a God-created world that follows natural laws and operates according to the divine plan. Further, the human being has a purpose in existence—to experience the beatific vision of God in heaven. For Thomists there are two complementary sets of goals or purposes: the ultimate ones that relate to the most important end of human existence—being in the presence of God—and those that are proximate, or nearer in time, that relate to leading a satisfying life on earth. What is important is that our proximate or immediate goals are governed by, and consistent with, the larger end or purpose, the ultimate goal for which we exist. John Dewey, a Pragmatist philosopher discussed in Chapter 5, argued that such long-term goals were not a feasible guide to human actions because they were so distant, remote, and unverifiable.

Epistemology

Thomist epistemology, or theory of knowing, relies on two sources: Divine Revelation through the Bible and Aristotelian Realism's process of sensation of natural phenomenon and abstraction of sensory data into concepts. The process of knowing is dualistic, consisting of Divine Revelation and natural sensation and abstraction. *Divine Revelation* means that God has revealed Himself to inspired individuals who have recorded these revelations in a sacred or holy book. For Christians, such as Aquinas, the sacred book was the Bible, the word of God. In the medieval Christian world view in which Thomas operated, the Bible, along with Church doctrines, formed a body of dogmatic truth, accepted on faith. The crucial elements in knowing are that the person (the knower) believes or has faith that the Bible is truly a divinely inspired book, and recognizes the Church's magisterium, or teaching authority.

Aquinas relies on Aristotle's epistemology as accurately describing how human knowing occurs through natural processes of sensation of objects in the environment and abstraction of this sensory data into concepts (see Chapter 3). Human beings, living in a real and external world of objects, use their senses to acquire information about these objects. The mind sorts this sensory data, extracts the essential qualities of objects, and arrives at concepts about the object as a class or category. By arranging these concepts in their minds, individuals can generalize from this sensory experience and construct possible alternatives of actions. This rational process enables people to exercise freedom of choice. When we make a choice based on the best available information, we are acting rationally. However, decisions are to be made according to the great purpose for which humans are created—the beatific vision of God, which gives complete happiness. Choice, Aquinas believed, followed the purpose for which human beings were created.

The truth that humans seek to guide them on their journey from Earth to Heaven is universal since it originates from the same divine source, God. For Aquinas, revelation and reason, like the supernatural and natural orders, are complementary processes. When we reason rightly, there is no conflict between faith and reason and religion and science.

Axiology

Just as they assert that truth is universal and eternal, Thomists also hold that values, too, are universal and timeless. Although some variations in human behavior exist due to necessary adaptations to different times and places, the essential values are transcendent, transcultural, and independent of differing situations. True values are valid at all times and in all places because of their origin in a loving and caring God, an eternal and universal Creator.

All people, regardless of cultural differences conditioned by time and place, are endowed with an immortal soul, and with an intellect that defines their human nature. Because of the dignity of the person, basic human rights exist that transcend geographical, political, social, cultural, and economic boundaries. The virtuous life, as prescribed by Thomists, is one in which the person follows the spiritual-religious guidelines, the prescriptions and proscriptions, for the good life as found in the Scriptures and the doctrinal teachings of the Church. Many of these prescriptions and proscriptions, as found in the Ten Commandments, relate to behaviors that lead to love of other human beings and to love of God. In conjunction with living according to the teachings of Scripture and the Church, the good life is one, as Aristotle said, that is lived according to reason. It is a life in which rationality governs the will and the appetites.

While possession of knowledge is useful in leading the good life and in forming choices of action, it needs to be directed by a rightly formed conscience—the dispositions, inclinations, and attitudes that contribute to making ethically correct decisions. For Aquinas, supernatural grace, a gift from God, inclines a person to act nobly, benevolently, and rightly. The presence of the great moral exemplar, Jesus Christ, and the saints, the holy men and women who followed him, provide the spiritual models for human imitation. In everyday life, evident moral exemplars such as parents and teachers provide the young with models of the good life that are worthy of imitation. The life of Christ and the saints, the teachings of the Church, and human rationality contribute to the forming of habits that incline a person to choose what is good and right.

Logic

Logic, for Thomists, is deductive and based on what they call *right reason*. Right reason is that by which the person's mind, illuminated by grace and guided by rationality, uses higher, or more general principles as a guide to specific behavior. The general proscriptions—not to lie, steal, and kill—relate to many specific instances in life and urge people to tell the truth and to respect others' lives and property. Following deductive logic, lower-order or case-specific principles are derived from higher, more general ones. Particular cases are to conform to the higher-level principle. If there appears to be a conflict, it should be resolved on the basis of conformity or agreement with the higher-order principle.

THEISTIC REALISM'S EDUCATIONAL IMPLICATIONS

The Purpose of Education and Schooling

Following the belief that God created a purposeful universe, education, as a universal process, and schools, as agencies designed to educate, are purposeful. They have primary purposes that are intrinsic according to their nature and function. Aquinas defined *educatio*, or education, as the life-long process of advancing individuals to spiritual and intellectual excellence in the virtuous life.[3] It is a lifelong process that involves many social agencies and persons such as the state, the church, the family, and other informal educators.[4] While other agencies play an informal educational role, the school is the formal agency, the institution, which has been given significant educational responsibilities by parents, who are the primary authorities in their children's education. Thomists believe schools exist to cultivate human rationality and to assist the church in developing the person's spirituality. While primary emphasis is given to spiritual and intellectual development (since these are the most intrinsic and important aspects of human nature), physical, social, and economic matters also need to be considered because the human being, though destined for Heaven, lives on Earth.

Dualism and the Curricular Hierarchy

Like Aristotle's Realism, which asserts the dualisms of form–matter and soul–body, Thomism, too, is a dualistic philosophy. For Thomism, the important dualisms are that of Heaven and Earth and soul and body. Certain matters relate to the soul, others to the body. Aquinas asserts that soul and body are not at war with each other but are complementary. Though they are complementary, that which is spiritual, or of the soul, is higher than and of greater importance than that which relates to the body, because the soul is destined for eternity while the body has a finite existence.

Based on the soul-body dualism, there is a hierarchy of human interests, needs, and activities with the spiritual, because of its ultimate purpose, given a higher ranking or priority than the body. In creating a curriculum, those subjects that have a theological foundation and relate to spirituality are most important and are therefore given a higher priority than those that relate to the physical world. Setting this kind of priority does not mean that subjects dealing with the physical world are unimportant; it simply means that their importance is lesser than those relating to the spirit.

As noted, the human being has a body that lives in a particular place and time. Further, the human being lives, communicates, and works in a society of other people. As communicating beings, humans have developed language, the means of oral and written expression. The human person then has an autobiography; lives at a place and has a geography; and lives at a given time and has a history. Living in societies, humans have governments. They also work to survive and have developed economies and pursue occupations. In descending order from the theological–spiritual summit of the curricular hierarchy are the subjects that relate to the human's earthly life: language, history, geography, mathematics, science, political science, sociology, and economics.

Thus far, the curricular hierarchy has the theological–spiritual subjects at its summit and the subjects dealing with earthly life positioned lower in the curriculum structure. Occupying the middle, and linking, position in the hierarchy are those subjects that relate both to spirituality and earthly life—philosophy and its subdivisions, especially metaphysics and logic, that examine reality, thinking, and valuing.

The Logic of Subject Matter Organization and Instruction

Like the Idealist and Realist curricula, the Thomist curriculum is organized into separate subject matter disciplines, which Aquinas called *scientia*, a body of accumulated, demonstrated, and organized knowledge. The organization of subject matters follows the pattern of deductive logic. Subjects are typically organized around first or major principles or premises that are either self-evident, derived from experimentation, or deduced from a higher body of knowledge. The first principles are followed by examples, cases, or situations that illustrate the principle. Then, the truth of the principle and the illustration are drawn into a conclusion.

The Thomist Teacher and Learner

As is generally the case with Realism, the Thomist teaching and learning strategy that Aquinas called *disciplina*, or deliberate instruction, refers to the process in which a teacher instructs a student in a subject such as history, mathematics, or logic.[5] Teaching requires three necessary elements: a teacher who is engaged in instruction, a skill or body of knowledge that is the object of instruction, and a student who is to learn the subject.[6] These three necessary elements may appear to be commonsensical or obvious. Yes, all instruction involves a teacher, a lesson, and a student. However, it is easy to find situations in schools where the key part—a skill or subject—is missing. In these cases, instruction degenerates into pointless discussions that are off the subject. Or instruction becomes a two-part process in which no subject is taught and the teacher uses the classroom for self-centered psychological or political purposes. There are also cases in which students' inappropriate behaviors interfere with the purpose of instruction—the learning of a skill or subject.

In the triad of teacher, subject, and student, the good teacher is a mature person who deliberately chose teaching as a vocation. A vocation, in the Thomistic context, can be defined as acceptance of a call from God to enter the life of teaching and become an educator. A vocation fulfills a desire to serve others and is motivated by love of truth, love of other people, and love of God. In the religious context in which Thomism developed, the concept of a vocation was associated with becoming a priest, monk, or

■ ■ ■ ■ ■

THOMIST CURRICULAR HIERARCHY

- **Theology:** religion, spirituality, doctrine, scripture
- **Philosophy:** metaphysics and logic
- **Liberal Arts and Sciences:** language, mathematics, science, history, geography, art
- **Necessary Skills:** reading, writing, arithmetic, prayer

nun who took vows to follow a holy way of life. Since most medieval teachers were priests or nuns, it is easy to see how the concept of vocation was extended to teachers.

In addition to heeding the call of a vocation to serve through love, the good teacher is not only inclined to educate others, but must also be knowledgeable and skilled in instruction. The good teacher is a mature person who has learned a body of truth and desires to communicate this truth to students who wish to learn and possess it. The teacher must know his or her subject thoroughly and know how to organize it for the purpose of instruction.

The knowledge of a subject and how to teach it involves the teacher in two related phases of preparation: contemplation and action. Contemplation is usually associated with the deep meditation that leads to a depth of spiritual understanding. In the case of getting ready to teach, it means doing research and thinking about a subject and how to present it. Next comes action—actually teaching the subject to students.

The Thomist conception of *scientia*, the organization of a subject into first principles, illustrative examples, and cases indicate how a teacher should plan and deliver a lesson. The teacher needs to know the level of readiness of and prior knowledge of students, and then connect the new learning to that experience by skillfully choosing the correct language, appropriate examples, illustrations, and analogies that will make the delivery of the lesson effective.

For Thomists, the student is a person of dignity and worth who possesses a soul and a mind, has a purpose for existing, a purpose in life, and a purpose for being in school. The purpose of being in school is to cooperate with the gift of supernatural grace and with the powers of intellect in recognizing the truth that is being presented. While teachers can do their best to motivate students and can work diligently to craft effective strategies for teaching, the actual process of learning can only take place within the student. All persons have a potential to learn that is part of their human nature. Students need to activate their potential for intellectually grasping and understanding truth. Having freedom of will, they may or may not choose to cooperate with instruction. Thomists believe that this cooperation comes from an interior desire to know that is further illuminated by divine grace.

■ ■ ■ ■ ■ ▬▬▬▬▬▬▬▬▬▬▬▬▬▬▬▬▬▬▬▬▬▬▬▬▬▬▬▬▬▬▬▬▬

JACQUES MARITAIN, INTEGRAL HUMANISM

In this selection, Jacques Maritain, a noted French philosopher, uses Thomistic themes as a foundation for his philosophy of Integral Humanism. Maritain was an important figure for the revitalization of Thomism in the second half of the twentieth century. He believed that a revived Thomism was needed in a world threatened by totalitarian dictators, crass materialism, and a rampant ethical relativism. This selection is included as a primary source reading because it is an example of a philosopher's attempt to create a large-scale theoretical synthesis—Integral Humanism. Maritain argues for a general education that embraces both a humanistic and religious view of knowledge and values in the modern world. In making the case for Integral Humanism in education, Maritain affirms his acceptance of the Christian ideal of the educated person, identifies education's true aims, and attacks Pragmatism as an educational misconception. As you read the selection, you might focus on the following questions:

1. How does Maritain define the Christian idea of the person? Do you agree with his definition? Is this idea appropriate for contemporary American education? Explain your answer.

2. For Maritain, what are the true aims of education? Do you agree or disagree with his argument?

3. Pragmatism has been an influential philosophy of education in the United States. Do you agree or disagree with Maritain calling it a "misconception"? (The point of difference between Maritain and Pragmatism is important in educational philosophy; you may either read ahead to the discussion of Pragmatism in Chapter 5, or delay answering this question until after you have read that chapter.)

4. According to Maritain, what is the role of the teacher? Do you agree or disagree with him?

THE CHRISTIAN IDEA OF MAN

There are many forms of the philosophical and religious idea of man. When I state that the education of man, in order to be completely well grounded, must be based upon the Christian idea of man, it is because I think that this idea of man is the true one, not because I see our civilization actually permeated with this idea. Yet, for all that, the man of our civilization *is* the Christian man, more or less secularized. Consequently we may accept this idea as a common basis and imply that it is to be agreed upon by the common consciousness in our civilized countries, except among those who adhere to utterly opposite outlooks, like materialistic metaphysics, positivism, or skepticism—I am not speaking here of Fascist and racist creeds, which do not belong at all in the civilized world.

Now such a kind of agreement is all that any doctrine in moral philosophy can be expected to have, for none can pretend actually to obtain the literal universal assent of all minds—not because of any weakness in objective proof but because of the weakness inherent in human minds.

There does exist, indeed, among the diverse great metaphysical outlooks, if they recognize the dignity of the spirit, and among the diverse forms of Christian creeds, or even of religious creeds in general, if they recognize the divine destiny of man, a community of analogy as concerns practical attitudes and the realm of action, which makes possible a genuine human coöperation. In a Judeo-Greco–Christian civilization like ours, this community of analogy, which extends from the most orthodox religious forms of thought to the mere humanistic ones, makes it possible for a Christian philosophy of education, if it is well founded and rationally developed, to play an inspiring part in the concert, even for those who do not share in the creed of its supporters. . . .

From Jacques Maritain, *Education at the Crossroads*. New Haven: Yale University Press, 1960, pp. 6–7, 10–15, 43–45.

In answer to our question, then, "What is man?" we may give the Greek, Jewish, and Christian idea of man: man as an animal endowed with reason, whose supreme dignity is in the intellect; and man as a free individual in personal relation with God, whose supreme righteousness consists in voluntarily obeying the law of God; and man as a sinful and wounded creature called to divine life and to the freedom of grace, whose supreme perfection consists of love.

. . .

Concerning the Aims of Education

We may now define in a more precise manner the aim of education. It is to guide man in the evolving dynamism through which he shapes himself as a human person—armed with knowledge, strength of judgment, and moral virtues—while at the same time conveying to him the spiritual heritage of the nation and the civilization in which he is involved, and preserving in this way the century-old achievements of generations. The utilitarian aspect of education—which enables the youth to get a job and make a living—must surely not be disregarded, for the children of man are not made for aristocratic leisure. But this practical aim is best provided by the general human capacities developed. And the ulterior specialized training which may be required must never imperil the essential aim of education.

Now in order to get a complete idea of the aim of education, it is necessary to take into closer consideration the human person and his deep natural aspirations.

THE CONQUEST OF INTERNAL FREEDOM

The chief aspirations of a person are aspirations to freedom—I do not mean that freedom which is free will and which is a gift of nature in each of us, I mean that freedom which is spontaneity, expansion, or autonomy, and which we have to gain through constant effort and struggle. And what is the more profound and essential form of such a desire? It is the desire for inner and spiritual freedom. In this sense Greek philosophy, especially Aristotle, spoke of the independence which is granted to men by intellect and wisdom as the perfection of the human being. And the Gospel was to lift up human perfection to a higher level—a truly divine one—by stating that it consists of the perfection of love and, as St. Paul put it, of the freedom of those who are moved by the divine Spirit. In any case it is by the activities that the philosophers call "immanent"—because they perfect the very subject which exerts them, and are within it the supreme activities of internal achievement and superabundance—that the full freedom of independence is won. Thus the prime goal of education is the conquest of internal and spiritual freedom to be achieved by the individual person, or, in other words, his liberation through knowledge and wisdom, good will, and love.

At this point we must observe that the freedom of which we are speaking is not a mere unfolding of potentialities without any object to be grasped, or a mere movement for the sake of movement, without aim or objective to be attained. It is sheer nonsense to offer such a movement to man as constituting his glory. A movement without aim is just running around in circles and getting nowhere. The aim, here on earth, will always be grasped in a partial and imperfect manner, and in this sense, indeed, the movement is to be pursued without end. Yet the aim will somehow be grasped, even though partially. Moreover the spiritual activities of the human being are *intentional* activities, they tend by nature toward an object, an objective aim, which will measure and rule them, not materially and by means of bondage, but spiritually and by means of liberty, for the object of knowledge or of love is internalized by the activity itself of the intelligence and the will, and becomes within them the very fire of their perfect spontaneity. Truth—which does not depend on us but on *what is*—truth is not a set of ready-made formulas to be passively recorded, so as to have the mind closed and enclosed by them. Truth is an infinite realm—as infinite as being—whose wholeness transcends infinitely our powers of perception, and each fragment of which must be grasped through vital and purified internal activity. This conquest of being, this progressive attainment of new truths, or the progressive realization of the ever-growing and ever-renewed significance of truths already attained, opens and enlarges our mind and life, and really situates them in freedom and autonomy. And speaking of will and love rather than knowledge, no one is freer, or more independent, than the one who gives himself for a cause or a real being worthy of the gift.

THE THIRD MISCONCEPTION: PRAGMATISM

Here we find ourselves confronted with the inappropriateness of the pragmatic overemphasis in education—a third error or misconception that we meet on our path. Many things are excellent in the emphasis on action and "praxis," for life consists of action. But action and praxis aim at an object, a determining end without which they lose direction and vitality. And life exists, too, for an end which makes it worthy of being lived. Contemplation and self-perfection, in which human life aspires to flower forth, escape the purview of the pragmatic mind.

It is an unfortunate mistake to define human thought as an organ of response to the actual stimuli and situations of the environment, that is to say, to define it in terms of animal knowledge and reaction, for such a definition exactly covers the way of "thinking" proper only to animals without reason. On the contrary, it is because every human idea, to have a meaning, must attain in some measure (be it even in the symbols of a mathematical interpretation of phenomena), what things *are* or consist of unto themselves; it is because human thought is an instrument or rather a vital energy of knowledge or spiritual intuition (I don't mean "knowledge about," I mean "knowledge into"); it is because thinking begins, not only with difficulties but with *insights*, and ends up in insights which are made true by rational proving or experimental verifying, not by pragmatic sanction, that human thought is able to illumine experience, to realize desires which are human because they are rooted in the prime desire for unlimited good, and to dominate, control, and refashion the world. At the beginning of human action, insofar as it is human, there is truth, grasped or believed to be grasped for the sake of truth. Without trust in truth, there is no human effectiveness. Such is, to my mind, the chief criticism to be made of the pragmatic and instrumentalist theory of knowledge.

In the field of education, this pragmatic theory of knowledge, passing from philosophy to upbringing, can hardly produce in the youth anything but a scholarly skepticism equipped with the best techniques of mental training and the best scientific methods, which will be unnaturally used against the very grain of intelligence, so as to cause minds to distrust the very idea of truth and wisdom, and to give up any hope of inner dynamic unity. Moreover, by dint of insisting that in order to teach John mathematics it is more important to know John than to know mathematics—which is true enough in one sense—the teacher will so perfectly succeed in knowing John that John will never succeed in knowing mathematics. Modern pedagogy has made invaluable progress in stressing the necessity of carefully analyzing and fixing its gaze on the human subject. The wrong begins when *the object to be taught* and *the primacy of the object* are forgotten, and when the cult of the means—not to an end, but without an end—only ends up in a psychological worship of the subject.

THE SOCIAL POTENTIALITIES OF THE PERSON

I have spoken of the aspiration of the human person to freedom, and, first of all, to inner and spiritual freedom. The second essential form of this desire is the desire for freedom externally manifested, and this freedom is linked to social life and lies at its very root. For society is "natural" to man in terms not only of animal or instinctive nature but of human nature, that is, of reason and freedom. If man is a naturally political animal, this is so in the sense that society, required by nature, is achieved through free consent, and because the human person demands the communications of social life through the openness and generosity proper to intelligence and love as well as through the needs of a human individual born naked and destitute. Thus it is that social life tends to emancipate man from the bondage of material nature. It subordinates the individual to the common good, but always in order that the common good flow back upon the individuals, and that they enjoy that freedom of expansion or independence which is insured by the economic guarantees of labor and ownership, political rights, civil virtues, and the cultivation of the mind.

As a result, it is obvious that man's education must be concerned with the social group and prepare him to play his part in it. Shaping man to lead a normal, useful and coöperative life in the community, or guiding the development of the human person in the social sphere, awakening and strengthening both his sense of freedom and his sense of obligation and responsibility, is an essential aim. But it is not the primary, it is the secondary essential aim. The ultimate end of education concerns the human person in his personal life and spiritual progress, not in his relationship to the social environment. Moreover, with regard to the secondary aim itself of which I am speaking, we must never

forget that personal freedom itself is at the core of social life, and that a human society is veritably a group of human freedoms which accept obedience and self-sacrifice and a common law for the general welfare, in order to enable each of these freedoms to reach in everyone a truly human fulfillment. The man and the group are intermingled with each other and they surpass each other in different respects. Man finds himself by subordinating himself to the group, and the group attains its goal only by serving man and by realizing that man has secrets which escape the group and a vocation which is not included in the group.

. . .

With regard to the development of the human mind, neither the richest material facilities nor the richest equipment in methods, information, and erudition are the main point. The great thing is the awakening of the inner resources and creativity. The cult of technical means considered as improving the mind and producing science by their own virtue must give way to respect for the spirit and dawning intellect of man! Education thus calls for an intellectual sympathy and intuition on the part of the teacher, concern for the questions and difficulties with which the mind of the youth may be entangled without being able to give expression to them, a readiness to be at hand with the lessons of logic and reasoning that invite to action the unexercised reason of the youth. No tricks can do that, no set of techniques, but only personal attention to the inner blossoming of the rational nature and then confronting that budding reason with a system of rational knowledge.

What matters most in the life of reason is intellectual insight or intuition. There is no training or learning for that. Yet if the teacher keeps in view above all the inner center of vitality at work in the preconscious depths of the life of the intelligence, he may center the acquisition of knowledge and solid formation of the mind on the freeing of the child's and the youth's intuitive power. By what means? By moving forward along the paths of spontaneous interest and natural curiosity, by grounding the exercise of memory in intelligence, and primarily by giving courage, by listening a great deal, and by causing the youth to trust and give expression to those spontaneous poetic or noetic impulses of his own which seem to him fragile and bizarre, because they are not assured by any social sanction—and in fact any awkward gesture or rebuff or untimely advice on the part of the teacher can crush such timid sproutings and push them back into the shell of the unconscious.

I should like, moreover, to suggest that, in order to set free creative and perceptive intellectual intuition, the path through which it is naturally awakened, the path of sense-perception and sense-experience and imagination, should be respected and followed as far as possible by the teacher. Above all the liberation of which we are speaking depends essentially on the free adhesion of the mind to the objective reality to be seen. Let us never deceive or rebuke the thirst for seeing in youth's intelligence! The freeing of the intuitive power is achieved in the soul through the object grasped, the intelligible grasping toward which this power naturally tends. The germ of insight starts within a preconscious intellectual cloud, arising from experience, imagination, and a kind of spiritual feeling, but it is from the outset a tending toward an object to be grasped. And to the extent that this tendency is set free and the intellect becomes accustomed to grasping, seeing, expressing the objects toward which it tends, to that very extent its intuitive power is liberated and strengthened. Before giving a youth the rules of good style, let us tell him first never to write anything which does not seem to him really beautiful, whatever the result may be.

In the first approach to mathematics, physics, or philosophy, let us see to it that the student actually grasps each step of the simplest mathematical demonstration, however slow this may be—that he actually understands in the laboratory how logically the statement of the physicist emerges from the experiment—that he becomes intensely involved, through the very anxiety of his mind, in the first great philosophical problems, and after that, that he really sees the solution. In asking a youth to read a book, let us get him to undertake a real spiritual adventure and meet and struggle with the internal world of a given man, instead of glancing over a collection of bits of thought and dead opinions, looked upon from without and with sheer indifference, according to the horrible custom of so many victims of what they call "being informed." Perhaps with such methods the curriculum will lose a little in scope, which will be all to the good.

Finally the very mood of the teaching is here of crucial import. If a teacher himself is concerned with discerning and seeing, with getting vision, rather than with collecting facts and opinions, and if he handles his burden of knowledge so as to see through it into the reality of things, then in the mind of the student the power of intuition will be awakened and strengthened unawares, by the very intuitivity traversing such teaching.

THE THIRD RULE

I come now to the third fundamental rule, which I shall try to express as follows: the whole work of education and teaching must tend to unify, not to spread out; it must strive to foster internal unity in man. . . .

CONCLUSION

This chapter examined Theistic Realism, or Thomism, a religiously based philosophy formulated by Thomas Aquinas in the Medieval Period. As a synthesis of Aristotle's Realism and Christian theology, it served as a large architectonic philosophy that shaped Western intellectual life, especially for the Catholic Church. Based on a dualistic definition that sees the human being as spiritual and physical, Thomism uses a hierarchy for constructing the curriculum, in which general and more abstract subjects receive priority. In Thomism, teaching is defined as a vocation of love and service to others.

DISCUSSION QUESTIONS

1. Consider Theistic Realism, or Thomism, as a synthesis of large bodies of thought. How do such large philosophical systems shape educational goals and curriculum?
2. Consider the Thomist distinction between ultimate and proximate goals and purposes. Do you agree or disagree with this distinction? Provide examples of ultimate goals and how they shape curriculum.
3. How are such terms as *educatio*, *disciplina*, and *scientia* defined? Can you find equivalent or similar terms being used, but under different names, in contemporary education?
4. Provide examples of conflicts between those who hold to principles of natural law and those who believe that enacted laws are superior.
5. Do you believe there are human rights? What is the rationale for your belief or disbelief?
6. Does Aquinas believe that moral virtue can be taught? How does his view agree or disagree with contemporary programs of character education?
7. Describe Aquinas' concept of the teacher. Do you agree or disagree with the model of the teacher?

INQUIRY AND RESEARCH PROJECTS

1. Outline a curriculum based on the Thomist principles of dualism and hierarchy.
2. Design a lesson plan that follows the Thomist strategy of teaching a subject.
3. Read and review a current book on character education. Then, determine if Aquinas would agree or disagree with it.
4. Make a list of the current educational practices that Aquinas would accept and those that he would reject.
5. In a character sketch, prepare a profile of a Thomist teacher.

INTERNET RESOURCES

For discussions of Thomism as a philosophy, and for a topical bibliography, consult Aquinas Online at
www.aquinasonline.com.htm

For the rise and progress of Thomism, consult the Jacques Maritain Center at
www.edu/Departments/Maritain/etext/thomism.htm

Thomism is discussed at
www.innerexplorations.com/philtext/the1.htm

SUGGESTIONS FOR FURTHER READING

Clarke, W. Norris. *Explorations in Metaphysics: Being-God-Person*. Notre Dame, IN: University of Notre Dame Press, 1994.

Conway, Pierre, and Spangler, Mary Michael. *Metaphysics of Aquinas: A Summary of Aquinas's Exposition of Aristotle's Metaphysics*. Lanham, MD: University Press of American, 1996.

Davies, Brian. *The Thought of Thomas Aquinas*. New York: Oxford University Press, 1992.

Donohue, John W. *St. Thomas Aquinas & Education*. New York: Random House, 1968.

Gallagher, David M., ed. *Thomas Aquinas and His Legacy*. Washington, DC: Catholic University of America Press, 1994.

Grant, Edward. *God and Reason in the Middle Ages*. New York: Cambridge University Press, 2001.

Hudson, Deal W., and Moran, Dennis W., eds. *The Future of Thomism*. Notre Dame, IN: University of Notre Dame Press, 1992.

Jenkins, John I. *Knowledge and Faith in Thomas Aquinas*. New York: Cambridge University Press, 1997.

Jordan, Mark D. *The Alleged Aristotelianism of Thomas Aquinas*. Toronto: Pontifical Institute of Medieval Studies, 1992.

McInerny, Ralph M. *St. Thomas Aquinas*. Notre Dame, IN: University of Notre Dame Press, 1981.

McInerny, Ralph M. *A First Glance at St. Thomas Aquinas: A Handbook for Peeping Thomists*. Notre Dame, IN: University of Notre Dame Press, 1990.

Moore, Andrew. *Realism and Christian Faith: God, Grammar, and Meaning*. New York: Cambridge University Press, 2003.

Torrell, Jean-Pierre. *Saint Thomas Aquinas*. Washington, DC: Catholic University of America Press, 1996.

Westberg, Daniel. *Right Practical Reason: Aristotle, Action, and Prudence in Aquinas*. New York: Clarendon Press–Oxford University Press, 1994.

NOTES

1. For a discussion of medieval scholasticism, see Edward Peters, *Europe and the Middle Ages* (Englewood Cliffs, NJ: Prentice-Hall, 1983), pp. 173–184, 220–237.

2. Neil G. McCluskey, *Catholic Viewpoint on Education* (New York: Image Books, 1962), pp. 57–79.

3. John W. Donohue, S. J., *St. Thomas Aquinas & Education* (New York: Random House, 1968), pp. 59–60.

4. Ibid., pp. 58–64, 82–89.

5. Ibid., pp. 59–60.

6. Ibid.

CHAPTER FIVE

PRAGMATISM

Pragmatism, a philosophy formulated in the United States in the early twentieth century, will be discussed in this chapter. We emphasize John Dewey's version of Pragmatism, also called Experimentalism or Instrumentalism. We will define Pragmatism, situate it historically, examine its major philosophical principles, and draw out its implications for education.

DEFINING PRAGMATISM

Pragmatism was developed by American philosophers—especially Charles S. Peirce, William James, and John Dewey—in the early twentieth century. It is not a metaphysical system; it emphasizes the practical application of ideas by testing them in human experience. Ideas are not immutable universal concepts residing in some metaphysical reality, and do not transcend human experience as Plato claimed. Rather, ideas are instruments—hypotheses, conjectures, and plans—for solving life's problems. Ideas have a social origin and relevance in that they are formulated in the context of shared experience in human association.[1] The empirical test of an idea is, does it work? Does it produce the consequences we desired when we acted?

SITUATING PRAGMATISM

Thus far in our study of philosophy of education, we have studied Idealism and Realism, which originated with Plato and Aristotle in ancient Greece, and Theistic Realism, which is identified with Thomas Aquinas during the Middle Ages. Now we deal with Pragmatism, a philosophy that originated in the United States in the early twentieth century in the work of Charles S. Peirce (1839–1914), William James (1842–1910), and John Dewey (1859–1952).

Peirce, a mathematician turned philosopher, developed a theory he called *pragmaticism*. His theory held that we can act on our best hypotheses or beliefs about something, knowing that even as we act, we can, and probably will, revise these estimates. He argued that it is possible to make sense of the indeterminate, ever-changing world in which we live. Our way of making sense of constant flux is through a theory of probability. Since certain actions bring about reactions in a way that can be expected, it is probable that such reactions will occur in the future. However, it is necessary to understand that actions and reactions, themselves, never occur in the exact same way. Our knowledge about something is probable rather than certain. However, probability provides us with a sense of intelligent direction and possible action.[2] With enough work, investigation, and thought, it is possible to formulate tentative generalizations, but never iron-clad laws, about how the world works.

James, a psychologist turned philosopher, regarded ideas as stimulated by the human need to choose between possible ways of acting in a given situation. When we choose and think, James reasoned, our conclusions can guide our actions but they are also provisional and subject to further revision. Our beliefs give us rules that we can call good and true, right or wrong, while realizing that we may, and likely will, keep revising the guidelines as we encounter different situations in the course of life.

Because of his significant influence on education, most of our discussion will focus on Dewey's variety of Pragmatism, which is called either Experimentalism or Instrumentalism.[3] According to Experimentalism, we think most accurately and completely when we use the experimental, or scientific, method to test an idea to see if it works, solves our problem, and brings about the results that we want. From the instrumentalist perspective, the human being, possessing a highly developed brain, nerve endings, and a movable thumb and forefinger, is an instrument maker, or tool maker. These instruments, part of material culture, can be used to increase human power in order to harness the environment and solve all kinds of problems.

Dewey tested his early ideas about relating the experimental method to education at the University of Chicago Laboratory School, which he directed from 1896 to 1904. The school was a laboratory for testing ideas in Dewey's philosophy of education, especially the "unity of knowledge."[4] For Dewey, the term *unity of knowledge* did not mean that all knowledge is contained and derived from one overarching great idea or form in the Platonic sense. Rather, the unity of knowledge meant that knowing is intimately related to and connected to doing. To know means to experience the consequences that come from acting on an idea, which is itself a plan of action.[5]

At the Laboratory School, students engaged in a variety of problem-solving activities in a collaborative setting. Believing that human intelligence arises from a process of social interaction, Dewey put many of the problem-solving learning episodes in a group setting. For him, the free exercise of intelligence, tested by the experimental method of science, had its best chance of working in a democratic society. A truly democratic society, he reasoned, was free of a priori absolutes that interfered with the freedom to test ideas, even if the testing challenged long-standing customs and traditions.

WHY STUDY PRAGMATISM?

Of the various philosophies examined in this book, the case for studying Pragmatism is among the most direct in that it fits so well with the American outlook and temperament, especially the tendency to action, practicality, and experimentation. American education has shown a definite belief in the idea that knowledge is valued because it can be applied in order to improve the human condition, increase productivity, and help solve problems. With its emphasis on experimental learning, Pragmatism encourages the process-oriented, problem-solving instruction that is so popular with American teachers.

PRAGMATISM AS A PHILOSOPHY OF EDUCATION

Metaphysics

In the previous chapters on Idealism, Realism, and Thomism, metaphysics was the important point of origin, containing the foundational principles upon which the whole philosophy rested. Metaphysics is the study of the reality that is beyond or above physics, the science that deals with the physical world. For Pragmatists, metaphysics is a kind of "mind game" philosophers may play. Pragmatists are not concerned with metaphysical questions that they believe cannot be answered. For them, a question must be able to be verified or proven, empirically or scientifically. People are free to play metaphysical games about the nature of ultimate reality and truth if they wish. However, Pragmatists believe that genuine philosophy needs to be concerned with real, flesh and blood issues that make a concrete difference in human life.

The traditional philosophies—Idealism, Realism, and Thomism—are based on a foundation of certitude that does not change but is eternally present, unchanging, and true. The Pragmatists discount the idea of the unchanging. For them, the universe is in constant flux and change.[6]

The Human Being Within an Environment.   Rather than looking for answers to metaphysical questions, the Pragmatists look for answers in the human situation. We know, empirically, that human beings are upright vertebrates with highly developed brains and nerves and a movable thumb and forefinger. Humans can communicate and are social. Like other organisms, they live in an environment. The identifying features of the human being as an intelligent, social, communicating, and instrument-making and -using individual living in a changing environment points to how Pragmatists look for answers to life's questions. Instead of searching for immutable answers in metaphysical realms outside of human experience, Pragmatists go directly to the interactions that people have with the environment. These interactions raise problems that need to be solved if human life is to continue and to be lived in a satisfying way. These problems become the questions that need to be answered in the human's ongoing experience. What must we do to solve a particular problem? What information, resources, and actions are needed to resolve the problem? What tools and technologies are needed to solve them? What social organization and activities will be needed to deal with the problem? Rather than trying to postulate eternal answers as the metaphysical philosophers, the Pragmatists are concerned with using a method of problem-solving that makes it possible to arrive at flexible hypotheses—answers that can be revised and reformulated to meet changing situations in human life.

> **Experience:** the human being in interaction with the environment

Epistemology

For Pragmatists such as Dewey, the essential concerns are epistemological questions: How do we know? What is the most accurate way of knowing? How do we know that our ideas and beliefs are true? Remember, in answering these questions, we cannot turn to a power or a source that is higher than human experience.

We can begin to answer these questions by looking at human life, that is, a human being living in an environment. The process of living—human survival and continuation of the species—involves interactions or transactions. In an interaction, the human does something to the environment, which in turn has an effect on him or her. The human has needs—for food, water, shelter—which can be found in an environment that contains things that satisfy these needs. However, the environment also has elements that threaten the human's survival—wild animals, serious climatic changes, and other hostile humans, for example. The essential problem is: What kind of transactions or interactions with the environment will enhance and sustain survival and make life satisfying? Dewey calls this process of interaction between the human and the environment *experience*.

The Problematic Situation.   In the course of experience—the interaction between the human being and the environment—the individual may encounter problems that block his or her ongoing activity. These problems arise when the human encounters something that is different in some way, a deviant, from previous experience. These kinds of problems can range from everyday ones to those of vast national and international importance. For example, when you began your first college courses, it was a new experience for you. You had attended high school and could draw on that prior experience, but you needed to reorganize it in the new situation. A more serious national and international problem resulted from the terrorist attacks on the World Trade Center in New York City on September 11, 2001, when two hijacked planes crashed into the Center's towers, destroying the buildings and causing great loss of life. The American people and the national government faced very serious problems that they began to solve by trying to use their past experience to deal with the new threat.

For Dewey and the Pragmatists, the successful life is one in which individuals and groups encounter, define, and solve problems. These problems are the challenges that test our abilities and develop our intelligence. They lead to our ongoing growth and development.

> **The problematic situation** occurs when the person's activity, or ongoing experience, is blocked by a new obstacle.

The Complete Act of Thought.   Thus far in our discussion of Pragmatism, we have identified the following important principles: (1) our ideas, to be validated, need to be tested empirically in actual human experience; (2) experience results from the interaction of the person with her or his environment; (3) in the course of experience, or environmental interactions, the person encounters new obstacles that block ongoing experience. With these three principles before us, we can now discuss how we go about solving these problems.

For Dewey, real thinking occurs when we use the scientific method to solve problems. He developed the following five-step rendition of the scientific method, which he called *the complete act of thought.*

1. We are in a ***problematic situation*** when our ongoing activity is blocked by encountering something new and different, a deviant from our experience.

2. In order to know exactly what is blocking the flow of experience, we need to step back and reflect on the situation and locate and ***define the problem***. In this important step, it is very important that we know what the problem is so that we can find ways to solve it and resume our ongoing experience.

3. Once we have defined the problem, we can begin to ***survey, investigate, and research it***. We can consult our past experience and see how the new problem is similar to and different from what we have experienced in our past. We can go to the library and use the Internet to research the problem and gather information about it. We can discuss the problem with friends and other people who might have experienced it.

4. After our research is completed, we can begin to think about possible ways to solve the problem by ***conjecturing possible alternatives of action***. Here, we work out in our minds what we might do and what is likely to happen when we choose that particular course of action. For example, if I do this, then this is likely to occur. We do an estimation of the results that are likely to occur and determine which of these results will solve the problem and bring about the desired consequences.

5. Up to this point we have located, defined, and researched a problem, and have structured various hypothetical ways to solve it, but we still have not acted and therefore the process is still incomplete. Now, we ***choose the alternative***, the hypothesis, that we think will solve the problem and bring about the results that we want, then ***test it by acting on it***. Hopefully, our action will solve the problem and bring about the anticipated result. We add this problem-solving episode to our total experience and can move forward until we encounter another problem. If we failed to solve the problem, we need to review the process, make the needed corrections, and try again.[7]

Problem Solving as a Method of Instruction.   If our thinking is complete when we test our ideas according to the scientific method, then the most effective method of teaching and learning is process-based problem solving. In school, as in life, all kinds of problems occur. They range from the simple sharing and taking turns of the kindergarten and primary grades, to the sophisticated experimentation done in the scientific laboratory of the medical research center. There are many situations that can be used to develop problem-solving skills. Among them are the following: establishing a balanced aquarium, designing sets for a student performance, conducting an election for a student government, dealing with issues of racial and gender discrimination, becoming involved in environmental activities, publishing a school newspaper, and so forth. There are several important features of the situations listed above: (1) they are group-centered; (2) they are interdisciplinary; (3) they can be tested in action.

As indicated, Dewey believed that we become intelligent as we develop and act on our ideas in a *group-centered* social setting. Working with others collaboratively and cooperatively enriches our experience because we can incorporate the ideas of other people into our action plan. If we have disagreements with others while developing action plans, we can work to resolve these disagreements democratically using discussion and conflict-resolution strategies. In working on situations such as those identified above, the research is *interdisciplinary* in that it involves many academic disciplines and is not confined to a single subject. For example, a social-service class project that involves an antismoking campaign directed at high school students would require research into law, health, chemistry, and the psychology of peer pressure and addiction. To determine if our solution to a problem is valid, it needs to be *tested in action*. Unlike other instructional strategies that may study an issue but not test for the validity of our ideas about it, problem solving according to the scientific method requires us to act and to judge a solution by its consequences.

Axiology

According to Dewey's world view, we live in an open-ended universe where everything is changing, relative to particular situations. The a priori principles found in the metaphysics of Idealism, Realism, and Thomism are not regarded as being empirically valid to guide human behavior. Issues of what is good, true, and beautiful have not been determined for all time by the nature of reality. Rather they are projects to be worked out in human experience. Since human experience arises in concrete and particular events and situations, the values in such experiences are also relative to the particular situation, to people living and acting at a particular time, in a particular place. The ethical and moral relativism associated with Pragmatism has provoked criticism from those who believe that action should be guided by universal ethical and moral standards. Instead of prescribing and proscribing behavior on universal standards as do Idealists, Realists, and Thomists, the Pragmatists instead argue that our values arise as we find satisfactory and satisfying ways to live that enrich our experience. What teachers can do is help students examine and clarify their values.

In the area of aesthetic values, Dewey emphasized the public nature of art. The work of art is a vehicle of shared communication and experience between the artist and those who were engaged in the aesthetic experience. Thus, the best kind of aesthetic experience could be shared by the widest possible public.

Logic

The logical criteria used by Pragmatists relies on empirical verification, validating ideas that arise in human experience to a scientific and public test. This test requires that our ideas can be stated in terms of their observable and measurable consequences. For example, a proposal to reduce air pollution by requiring that automobiles in a particular state meet specific emission controls and standards can be empirically verified. If the quality of air is improved after the controls have been in effect, then it is warranted to believe that the hypothesis was valid. Further, the proposal can be replicated in other states. This kind of test also needs to be public. Interested individuals have a right to consider the proposal and to examine the evidence.

Empirical verification, rejecting deductive reasoning from a priori first principles, is essentially inductive—coming to generalizations, or warranted assertions, based on particular instances. A warranted assertion, a generalization based on existing evidence, can be used to direct the course of experience for a time. It, however, is subject to further testing and revision in light of subsequent experience and new evidence. The Complete Act of Thought, described above in the section on epistemology, contains the basis for the logical organization of experience.

PRAGMATISM'S EDUCATIONAL IMPLICATIONS

Educational Goals and Purposes

Dewey was very wary of educational goals and purposes that came from sources, authorities, or movements that were external to the child. For example, parental desires for a student's future career, the government's goal to educate patriotic citizens, and the business sector's demand for trained workers are all examples of goals that are external to, and imposed on, the learner. Genuine educational goals come from within the person, not from some innate spiritual essence as the Idealists claimed, but rather from the person's own activity in the environment. The sole goal of education is growth, Dewey asserted. To grow means to have more activity, more problems, more resolutions to problems, and a greater network of social relationships. Growth means that the person is learning more effective, meaningful, and satisfying ways to live, in order to deal with a changing reality and direct the course of her or his own life.

The School

For Dewey, as well as other Pragmatists, the school is not a single-purpose institution with a well-defined primary purpose, as claimed by Idealists and Realists. Rather, the school is a multipurpose social institution connected to and related to the society of which it is a part. The Pragmatist approach to schooling is to get out of the four walls that enclose the schools from the rest of the culture and society and open the doors to the larger society, the community.

The school, itself, is a community of students and teachers who are mutually engaged in learning. It is a specialized environment in which experiences are simpli-

■ ■ ■ ■ ■

DEWEY'S CONCEPT OF THE ROLE OF THE SCHOOL AS A SOCIAL AGENCY

- Simplifies the complexity of the cultural and social heritage
- Purifies the heritage by emphasizing positive elements
- Integrates the heritage

fied, purified, and balanced. Since the environment is complex, experiences are simplified according to the level of learning readiness of students and arise from their own interests. Experiences are purified, in that school does not promote those that are harmful to students and diminish the possibilities for growth. Finally, experiences are balanced; that is, they are integrated and interrelated so students can see how one experience affects and leads to another.[8]

Curriculum

For Pragmatists such as Dewey, the curriculum is not antecedent to the students; it is not specified and prescribed in advance. Rather, the curriculum comes from students' experiences—their interests, needs, and problems. Dewey identified three stages in curriculum: (1) making and doing; (2) history and geography; and (3) science.[9] In the first stage, students, particularly children in the elementary grades, are involved in personal and group projects that focus on activities in which they make things. In this stage, learning is direct and active. Children might be involved in designing and planting a school garden, setting up a school store, establishing a balanced aquarium, creating posters, designing stage sets, and so on. Making and doing involves having a problem or need; establishing hypotheses or plans on how to resolve the need; carrying out the needed research; and acting on the selected hypothesis to actually test it in experience.

The second stage, history and geography, involves activities and projects that develop and add to students' conceptions of time (past-present-future) and space (or place). Time and space represent the two great categories that relate to human experience. Dewey is not so much concerned with developing a sense of dates or chronology as he is with developing the concept that events in human experience represent a flow or a continuum of activities—things that happened, are happening, and will happen. The notion of experience also means that it takes place in a setting, an environment, a place. Human places—homes, neighborhoods, towns, cities, states, and countries—are interrelationships of space.

The third stage, science, in Dewey's view of curriculum, refers to bodies of tested hypotheses, or warranted assertions, in various areas of human thought, research, and endeavor. While the natural and physical sciences are included under the larger heading "science," so are other areas such as social studies. These sciences give us fairly reliable generalizations upon which we can base our actions. However, it needs to be emphasized that these various sciences are not made up of fixed and final truths, but are tentative assertions and are subject to further research and reconceptualization.

DEWEY'S CONCEPT OF CURRICULUM

First Stage: Making and doing
Second State: History and geography
Third Stage: Sciences

Dewey's design of curriculum does not consist of separate, discrete subjects as in the case of Idealists, Realists, and Thomists. Rather, subjects are interrelated in an interdisciplinary way. We can go to the various subjects and take from them what we need to solve a problem, carry on a project, and test a hypothesis.

JOHN DEWEY, THE COMPLETE ACT OF THOUGHT

In this selection, Dewey discusses how we think when we use the scientific method. His rendition of the scientific method is called the *Complete Act of Thought*, which carries a person from the initial stage of being in a problematic situation, to acting, and thereby testing, the hypothesis selected to solve the problem. This excerpt is selected for inclusion as a primary source because of its clear exposition of Pragmatist logic and epistemology, and for its importance in designing problem-solving teaching and learning strategies. As you read the selection, you may wish to consider the following focusing questions:

1. How does Dewey's Complete Act of Thought reflect how Pragmatists define thinking, intelligence, and knowledge?

2. How is problem solving an interaction between the person and the environment?

3. What types of situations caused Dewey to examine particular problems in his experience, in this selection?

4. Identify the steps in Dewey's Complete Act of Thought.

. . . we shall make an analysis of the process of thinking into its steps or elementary constituents, basing the analysis upon descriptions of a number of extremely simple, but genuine, cases of reflective experience.

1. "The other day when I was down town on 16th Street a clock caught my eye. I saw that the hands pointed to 12:20. This suggested that I had an engagement at 124th Street, at one o'clock. I reasoned that as it had taken me an

From John Dewey, "Analysis of the Complete Act of Thought," pages 234–241, *Dewey Middle Works, Volume 6* © *1978*. Originally published in *The Collected Works of John Dewey* © by the Center for Dewey Studies, reprinted by permission of the publisher.

hour to come down on a surface car, I should probably be twenty minutes late if I returned the same way. I might save twenty minutes by a subway express. But was there a station near? If not, I might lose more than twenty minutes in looking for one. Then I thought of the elevated, and I saw there was such a line within two blocks. But where was the station? If it were several blocks above or below the street I was on, I should lose time instead of gaining it. My mind went back to the subway express as quicker than the elevated; furthermore, I remembered that it went nearer than the elevated to the part of 124th Street I wished to reach, so that time would be saved at the end of the journey. I concluded in favor of the subway, and reached my destination by one o'clock."

2. "Projecting nearly horizontally from the upper deck of the ferryboat on which I daily cross the river, is a long white pole, bearing a gilded ball at its tip. It suggested a flagpole when I first saw it; its color, shape, and gilded ball agreed with this idea, and these reasons seemed to justify me in this belief. But soon difficulties presented themselves. The pole was nearly horizontal, an unusual position for a flagpole; in the next place, there was no pulley, ring, or cord by which to attach a flag; finally, there were elsewhere two vertical staffs from which flags were occasionally flown. It seemed probable that the pole was not there for flag-flying.

"I then tried to imagine all possible purposes of such a pole, and to consider for which of these it was best suited: (a) Possibly it was an ornament. But as all the ferryboats and even the tugboats carried like poles, this hypothesis was rejected. (b) Possibly it was the terminal of a wireless telegraph. But the same considerations made this improbable. Besides, the more natural place for such a terminal would be the highest part of the boat, on top of the pilot house. (c) Its purpose might be to point out the direction in which the boat is moving.

"In support of this conclusion, I discovered that the pole was lower than the pilot house, so that the steersman could easily see it. Moreover, the tip was enough higher than the base, so that, from the pilot's position, it must appear to project far out in front of the boat. Moreover, the pilot being near the front of the boat, he would need some such guide as to its direction. Tugboats would also need poles for such a purpose. This hypothesis was so much more probable than the others that I accepted it. I formed the conclusion that the pole was set up for the purpose of showing the pilot the direction in which the boat pointed, to enable him to steer correctly."

3. "In washing tumblers in hot soapsuds and placing them mouth downward on a plate, bubbles appeared on the outside of the mouth of the tumblers and then went inside. Why? The presence of bubbles suggests air, which I note must come from inside the tumbler. I see that the soapy water on the plate prevents escape of the air save as it may be caught in bubbles. But why should air leave the tumbler? There was no substance entering to force it out. It must have expanded. It expands by increase of heat or by decrease of pressure, or by both. Could the air have become heated after the tumbler was taken from the hot suds? Clearly not the air that was already entangled in the water. If heated air was the cause, cold air must have entered in transferring the tumblers from the suds to the plate. I test to see if this supposition is true by taking several more tumblers out. Some I shake so as to make sure of entrapping cold air in them. Some I take out holding mouth downward in order to prevent cold air from entering. Bubbles appear on the outside of every one of the former and on none of the latter. I must be right in my inference. Air from the outside must have been expanded by the heat of the tumbler, which explains the appearance of the bubbles on the outside.

"But why do they then go inside? Cold contracts. The tumbler cooled and also the air inside it. Tension was removed, and hence bubbles appeared inside. To be sure of this, I test by placing a cup of ice on the tumbler while the bubbles are still forming outside. They soon reverse."

These three cases have been purposely selected so as to form a series from the more rudimentary to more complicated cases of reflection. The first illustrates the kind of thinking done by everyone during the day's business, in which neither the data, nor the ways of dealing with them, take one outside the limits of everyday experience. The last furnishes a case in which neither problem nor mode of solution would have been likely to occur except to one with some prior scientific training. The second case forms a natural transition; its materials lie well within the bounds of everyday, unspecialized experience; but the problem, instead of being directly involved in the person's business, arises indirectly out of his activity, and accordingly appeals to a somewhat theoretic and impartial interest. We shall deal, in a later chapter, with the evolution of abstract thinking out of that which is relatively practical and direct; here we are concerned only with the common elements found in all the types.

Upon examination, each instance reveals, more or less clearly, five logically distinct steps: (i) a felt difficulty; (ii) its location and definition; (iii) suggestion of possible solution; (iv) development by reasoning of the bearings of the suggestion; (v) further observation and experiment leading to its acceptance or rejection; that is, the conclusion of belief or disbelief.

1. The first and second steps frequently fuse into one. The difficulty may be felt with sufficient definiteness as to set the mind at once speculating upon its probable solution, or an undefined uneasiness and shock may come first, leading only later to definite attempt to find out what is the matter. Whether the two steps are distinct or blended, there is the factor emphasized in our original account of reflection—*viz.* the perplexity or problem. In the first of the three cases cited, the difficulty resides in the conflict between conditions at hand and a desired and intended result, between an end and the means for reaching it. The purpose of

keeping an engagement at a certain time, and the existing hour taken in connection with the location, are not congruous. The object of thinking is to introduce congruity between the two. The given conditions cannot themselves be altered; time will not go backward nor will the distance between 16th Street and 124th Street shorten itself. The problem is *the discovery of intervening terms which when inserted between the remoter end and the given means will harmonize them with each other.*

In the second case, the difficulty experienced is the incompatibility of a suggested and (temporarily) accepted belief that the pole is a flagpole, with certain other facts. Suppose we symbolize the qualities that suggest *flagpole* by the letters a, b, c; those that oppose this suggestion by the letters p, q, r. There is, of course, nothing inconsistent in the qualities themselves; but in pulling the mind to different and incongruous conclusions they conflict—hence the problem. Here the object is the discovery of some object (O), of which a, b, c, and p, q, r, may all be appropriate traits—just as, in our first case, it is to discover a course of action which will combine existing conditions and a remoter result in a single whole. The method of solution is also the same: discovery of intermediate qualities (the position of the pilot house, of the pole, the need of an index to the boat's direction) symbolized by d, g, l, o, which bind together otherwise incompatible traits.

In the third case, an observer trained to the idea of natural laws or uniformities finds something odd or exceptional in the behavior of the bubbles. The problem is to reduce the apparent anomalies to instances of well-established laws. Here the method of solution is also to seek for intermediary terms which will connect, by regular linkage, the seemingly extraordinary movements of the bubbles with the conditions known to follow from processes supposed to be operative.

2. As already noted, the first two steps, the feeling of a discrepancy, or difficulty, and the acts of observation that serve to define the

character of the difficulty may, in a given instance, telescope together. In cases of striking novelty or unusual perplexity, the difficulty, however, is likely to present itself at first as a shock, as emotional disturbance, as a more or less vague feeling of the unexpected, of something queer, strange, funny, or disconcerting. In such instances, there are necessary observations deliberately calculated to bring to light just what is the trouble, or to make clear the specific character of the problem. In large measure, the existence or non-existence of this step makes the difference between reflection proper, or safeguarded *critical* inference, and uncontrolled thinking. Where sufficient pains to locate the difficulty are not taken, suggestions for its resolution must be more or less random. Imagine a doctor called in to prescribe for a patient. The patient tells him some things that are wrong; his experienced eye, at a glance, takes in other signs of a certain disease. But if he permits the suggestion of this special disease to take possession prematurely of his mind, to become an accepted conclusion, his scientific thinking is by that much cut short. A large part of his technique, as a skilled practitioner, is to prevent the acceptance of the first suggestions that arise; even, indeed, to postpone the occurrence of any very definite suggestion till the trouble—the nature of the problem—has been thoroughly explored. In the case of a physician this proceeding is known as diagnosis, but a similar inspection is required in every novel and complicated situation to prevent rushing to a conclusion. The essence of critical thinking is suspended judgment; and the essence of this suspense is inquiry to determine the nature of the problem before proceeding to attempts at its solution. This, more than any other thing, transforms mere inference into tested inference, suggested conclusions into proof.

3. The third factor is suggestion. The situation in which the perplexity occurs calls up something not present to the senses: the present location, the thought of subway or elevated train; the stick before the eyes, the idea of a flagpole, an ornament, an apparatus for wireless telegraphy; the soap bubbles, the law of expansion of bodies through heat and of their contraction through cold. (*a*) Suggestion is the very heart of inference; it involves going from what is present to something absent. Hence, it is more or less speculative, adventurous. Since inference goes beyond what is actually present, it involves a leap, a jump, the propriety of which cannot be absolutely warranted in advance, no matter what precautions be taken. Its control is indirect, on the one hand, involving the formation of habits of mind which are at once enterprising and cautious; and on the other hand, involving the selection and arrangement of the particular facts upon perception of which suggestion issues. (*b*) The suggested conclusion so far as it is not accepted but only tentatively entertained constitutes an idea. Synonyms for this are *supposition, conjecture, guess, hypothesis*, and (in elaborate cases) *theory*. Since suspended belief, or the postponement of a final conclusion pending further evidence, depends partly upon the presence of rival conjectures as to the best course to pursue or the probable explanation to favor, *cultivation of a variety of alternative suggestions* is an important factor in good thinking.

4. The process of developing the bearings—or, as they are more technically termed, the *implications*—of any idea with respect to any problem, is termed *reasoning*. As an idea is inferred from given facts, so reasoning sets out from an idea. The *idea* of elevated road is developed into the idea of difficulty of locating station, length of time occupied on the journey, distance of station at the other end from place to be reached. In the second case, the implication of a flagpole is seen to be a vertical position; of a wireless apparatus, location on a high part of the ship and, moreover, absence from every casual tugboat; while the idea of index to direction in which the boat moves, when developed, is found to cover all the details of the case.

Reasoning has the same effect upon a suggested solution as more intimate and extensive observation has upon the original problem. Acceptance of the suggestion in its first form is prevented by looking into it more thoroughly. Conjectures that seem plausible at first sight are often found unfit or even absurd when their full consequences are traced out. Even when reasoning out the bearings of a supposition does not lead to rejection, it develops the idea into a form in which it is more apposite to the problem. Only when, for example, the conjecture that a pole was an index-pole had been thought out into its bearings could its particular applicability to the case in hand be judged. Suggestions at first seemingly remote and wild are frequently so transformed by being elaborated into what follows from them as to become apt and fruitful. The development of an idea through reasoning helps at least to supply the intervening or intermediate terms that link together into a consistent whole apparently discrepant extremes.

5. The concluding and conclusive step is some kind of *experimental corroboration*, or verification, of the conjectural idea. Reasoning shows that *if* the idea be adopted, certain consequences follow. So far the conclusion is hypothetical or conditional. If we look and find present all the conditions demanded by the theory, and if we find the characteristic traits called for by rival alternatives to be lacking, the tendency to believe, to accept, is almost irresistible. Sometimes direct observation furnishes corroboration, as in the case of the pole on the boat. In other cases, as in that of the bubbles, experiment is required; that is, *conditions are deliberately arranged in accord with the requirements of an idea or hypothesis to see if the results theoretically indicated by the idea actually occur.* If it is found that the experimental results agree with the theoretical, or rationally deduced, results, and if there is reason to believe that *only* the conditions in question would yield such results, the confirmation is so strong as to induce a conclusion—at least until contrary facts shall indicate the advisability of its revision.

Observation exists at the beginning and again at the end of the process: at the beginning, to determine more definitely and precisely the nature of the difficulty to be dealt with; at the end, to test the value of some hypothetically entertained conclusion. Between those two termini of observation, we find the more distinctively *mental* aspects of the entire thought-cycle: *(i)* inference, the suggestion of an explanation or solution; and *(ii)* reasoning, the development of the bearings and implications of the suggestion. Reasoning requires some experimental observation to confirm it, while experiment can be economically and fruitfully conducted only on the basis of an idea that has been tentatively developed by reasoning.

The disciplined, or logically trained, mind—the aim of the educative process—is the mind able to judge how far each of these steps needs to be carried in any particular situation. No cast-iron rules can be laid down. Each case has to be dealt with as it arises, on the basis of its importance and of the context in which it occurs. To take too much pains in one case is as foolish—as illogical—as to take too little in another. At one extreme, almost any conclusion that insures prompt and unified action may be better than any long delayed conclusion; while at the other, decision may have to be postponed for a long period—perhaps for a lifetime. The trained mind is the one that best grasps the degree of observation, forming of ideas, reasoning, and experimental testing required in any special case, and that profits the most, in future thinking, by mistakes made in the past. What is important is that the mind should be sensitive to problems and skilled in methods of attack and solution.

CONCLUSION

In discussing Pragmatism, this chapter focused on Dewey's Experimentalism or Instrumentalism. It examined Dewey's concept of experience as the interaction of the person with her or his environment. It pointed out that Pragmatism rejects metaphysics and replaces it with the analysis of human relationships to society and to nature. The Complete Act of Thought, approximating the scientific method, was described by Pragmatists as the best way to think and the best design for teaching and learning. Education is used in Pragmatism as the means by which the young are introduced to their cultural heritage. This introduction involves both transmission of the heritage and the possibilities for changing it.

DISCUSSION QUESTIONS

1. How does Pragmatism differ from the more traditional philosophies of Idealism, Realism, and Thomism?
2. How does Dewey define "experience"? What are the social and educational implications of this definition?
3. Identify and explain the stages in Dewey's Complete Act of Thought.
4. Pragmatists are often accused of "ethical relativism" by Idealists, Realists, and Thomists. What is "ethical relativism"? Do you think value education should be based on ethical relativism?
5. What does it mean to say that truths are warranted assertions or tentative hypotheses?

INQUIRY AND RESEARCH PROJECTS

1. Read and review a book by John Dewey.
2. Design a lesson based on the Complete Act of Thought.
3. Design a lesson based on "making and doing."
4. Design an exercise that implements Dewey's ideas about teaching history and geography.
5. Organize a debate on the proposition: Character education in schools should be based on the Pragmatist orientation to values.

INTERNET RESOURCES

For the Collections and Resources of the Dewey Center at Southern Illinois University in Carbondale, Illinois, consult
www.siu.edu/~deweyctr/

The John Dewey Project on Progressive Education at the University of Vermont can be found at
www.uvm.edu/dewey

The Pragmatism Archive, Oklahoma State University, John R. Shook, Director
www.pragmatism.org/archive/index.htm

SUGGESTIONS FOR FURTHER READING

Dewey, John. *A Common Faith*. New Haven: Yale University Press, 1934.

Dewey, John. *Democracy and Education: An Introduction to the Philosophy of Education*. New York: Macmillan, 1916.

Dewey, John. *The Early Works: 1882–1898*, ed. Jo Ann Boydston, 5 vols. Carbondale and Edwardsville, IL: Southern Illinois University Press, 1969–1972.

Dewey, John. *How We Think*. Mineola, NY: Dover Publications, 1997.

Dewey, John. *The Later Works: 1925–1953*. ed. Jo Ann Boydston, 17 vols. Carbondale and Edwardsville, IL: Southern Illinois University Press, 1981–1990.

Dewey, John. *Lectures on Ethics, 1900–1901*. Carbondale, IL: Southern Illinois University Press, 1991.

Dewey, John. *The Middle Works: 1899–1924*. ed. Jo Ann Boydston, 15 vols. Carbondale and Edwardsville, IL: Southern Illinois University Press, 1976–1983.

Dewey, John. *The Public and Its Problems*. Athens, OH: Ohio University Press, 1994.

Diggins, John P. *The Promise of Pragmatism: Modernism and the Crisis of Knowledge and Authority*. Chicago: University of Chicago Press, 1994.

Feffer, Andrew. *The Chicago Pragmatists and American Progressivism*. Ithaca, NY: Cornell University Press, 1993.

Festenstein, Matthew. *Pragmatism and Political Theory: From Dewey to Rorty*. Chicago: University of Chicago Press, 1997.

Haskins, Casey, and Seiple, David I. *Dewey Reconfigured*. Albany, NY: State University of New York Press, 1999.

Hickman, Larry A. *John Dewey's Pragmatic Technology*. Bloomington, IN: Indiana University Press, 1990.

Hoy, Terry. *The Political Philosophy of John Dewey: Towards a Constructive Renewal*. Westport, CT: Praeger, 1998.

Kestenbaum, Victor. *The Grace and Severity of the Ideal: John Dewey and the Transcendent*. Chicago: University of Chicago Press, 2002.

Martin, Jay. *The Education of John Dewey: A Biography*. New York: Columbia University Press, 2002.

Menand, Louis. *The Metaphysical Club*. New York: Farrar, Straus and Giroux, 2001.

Paringer, William A. *John Dewey and the Paradox of Liberal Reform*. Albany, NY: State University of New York Press, 1990.

Putnam, Hilary. *Pragmatism: An Open Question*. Cambridge, MA: Blackwell, 1995.

Ryan, Alan. *John Dewey and the High Tide of American Liberalism*. New York: W. W. Norton, 1995.

Tanner, Laurel N. *Dewey's Laboratory School, Lessons for Today*. New York: Teachers College Press, 1997.

Taylor, Charles. *Varieties of Religion Today: William James Revisited*. Cambridge, MA: Harvard University Press, 2002.

Welchman, Jennifer. *Dewey's Ethical Thought*. Ithaca, NY: Cornell University Press, 1995.

Westbrook, Robert B. *John Dewey and American Democracy*. Ithaca, NY: Cornell University Press, 1991.

White, Morton. *A Philosophy of Culture: The Scope of Holistic Pragmatism*. Princeton, NJ: Princeton University Press, 2000.

NOTES

1. Louis Menand, *The Metaphysical Club* (New York: Farrar, Straus and Giroux, 2001), pp. xi–xii.
2. Ibid., pp. 222–223.
3. For a recent biography, see Jay Martin, *The Education of John Dewey: A Biography* (New York: Columbia University Press, 2002).

4. John Dewey, "The Laboratory School," *University Record*, 1, 32 (November 6, 1896), pp. 417–422. For commentaries about the University of Chicago Laboratory School, see John Dewey, *The School and Society* (Chicago: University of Chicago Press, 1923); John Dewey and Evelyn Dewey, *Schools of Tomorrow* (New York: E.P. Dutton, 1915); Katherine C. Mayhew and Anna C. Edwards, *The Dewey School* (New York: Appleton-Century-Crofts, 1936); Arthur G. Wirth, *John Dewey as Educator: His Design for Work in Education (1894–1904)* (New York: John Wiley & Sons, 1966); Herbert M. Kliebard, *The Struggle for the American Curriculum, 1893–1958* (Boston and London: Rutledge & Kegan Paul, 1986).

5. Menand, pp. 322–323.

6. Dewey's rejection of metaphysics as the base of philosophy is found in John Dewey, *The Quest for Certainty: A Study of the Relation of Knowledge and Action* (New York: Minton, Balch, 1929).

7. John Dewey, "The Analysis of the Complete Act of Thought," in John Dewey, *The Middle Works, 1899–1924, Volume 6: 1910–1911*, Edited by Jo Ann Boydston (Carbondale and Edwardsville, IL: Southern Illinois University Press, 1978), pp. 234–241.

8. John Dewey, *Democracy and Education* (New York: Macmillan, 1916), pp. 22–26.

9. Ibid.

CHAPTER SIX

EXISTENTIALISM

In Chapter 6 we will examine Existentialism, a philosophy that gained attention in the twentieth century, especially after World War II. Its popularity came at a time when people were looking inward and rejecting identification with the institutions of modern mass society. This chapter examines the major features of Existentialism as a philosophy of education and the possibilities for an Existentialist education.

DEFINING EXISTENTIALISM

In defining Existentialism, we begin with its root, "to exist," and then define two words derived from it—"existent" and "existence." We then consider "existentialism" as a general expression before discussing it as a philosophy of education. To exist means that something or some person has come forth, emerged, or come into being at a particular time and place. To exist means to be actual, real, current, and not imagined, nor invented; it also means to be present in a particular situation. In terms of the philosophy of Existentialism, to exist means that a person is actually present in the world and living at a given time in a particular place.

The word "existent" refers to an actual, real being that is here at the present time. An existent person is a living individual who is really present in some place at a particular time. For the philosophy of Existentialism, it means that a person is factually and actually present in the world and is engaged in thinking, reflecting, choosing, acting and behaving in an actual situation. The person's engagement with the world is often accompanied with a sense of profound anxiety or dread that arises when the individual understands that she or he is totally responsible for the choices that are made. "Existence" means that an existent has being or is present in reality. For Existentialism as a philosophy, this means that a person is factually or actually present on the world scene, is conscious of being there, and has a sense of responsibility for making the choices that move her or him forward to self-definition.

Existentialism generally refers to a humanist orientation in philosophy or psychology that contends that human existence is so complex and profound that it cannot be defined and understood as an a priori metaphysical category; neither can it be empirically described in strictly scientific or behavioral terms. Rather than relying on metaphysics or scientific empiricism, Existentialism seeks to probe and examine the critical situations in a person's life and consider how people make decisive and self-determining choices. This means that the individual's existence precedes her or his essence. The person creates her or his own essence by the process of self-determination and self-realization that completes the project of being human. Philosophically, Existentialism refers to a person being involved in, and concerned with, the shaping of her or his own destiny, or modes of existing, with respect to the rest of the world.

To get some background for our discussion of Existentialism as a philosophy of education later in this chapter, it needs to be considered in terms of the other philosophies examined in earlier chapters. Existentialism arose as a profound reaction against these other philosophies, especially those resting on a metaphysical base.

Idealism, Realism, and Thomism—discussed in Chapters 2, 3, and 4, respectively—define human existence as being part of, and taking place in, a world or universal system. For the Idealist, existence is defined spiritually or intellectually; for the Realist, it is mental and physical; for the Thomist, it is spiritual and bodily. According to these philosophies, the person is defined by her or his essence, a metaphysically based concept of human nature. They also believe that the purpose of human existence is defined prior to the individual's own existence, and is derived from a universal system. For Idealists, the purpose of life is to know and to be reunited with the Good; for Realists, it is to live according to reason; for Thomists, it is to enjoy the Beatific Vision of God in Heaven.

While Pragmatists—discussed in Chapter 5—reject such antecedent, or a priori, definitions of human nature and purpose, they emphasize a process-oriented definition of the individual in interaction with the environment. For example, John Dewey, with his emphasis on the use of the scientific method, advised people to be scientific, sharing, and democratic.

Existentialism can be interpreted as a philosophical reaction against the metaphysical determinism of Idealism, Realism, and Thomism, in which the person is defined prior to their individual existence, and also against Pragmatism's reliance on group-determined consensus or the empiricism of scientific processes. Rejecting prior definitions and predetermined purposes and methodological exclusivity, Existentialists argue that the importance of existence—being alive in the world—lies in the person's freedom to create her or his own definition through choice. The pursuit of philosophy is not to learn about an intellectual system of thought; it is rather to engage in thinking about the most important questions of life. Who am I? How did I become what I am? What can I choose to be? What is my purpose for being here? Does my life make a difference?

SITUATING EXISTENTIALISM

Existentialism as a philosophy developed primarily in Europe. Its early origin in the nineteenth century is often traced to Soren Kierkegaard (1813–1855), a Danish theologian and philosopher, who held that truth is subjective and personal.[1] He portrayed humans as facing unrelenting and profound choice-making in an absurd world. Living in a time of religious dogmatism, Kierkegaard argued that one's religious convictions are purely a personal choice and that the human quest for God comes through searching and suffering. He was suggesting that a religious life and the will to believe, were not based on conformity to religious dogmas, but rather on a personal relation between God and the individual.[2]

In the twentieth century, Existentialism flowered in France and Germany, especially in the aftermath of World War II. The leading French Existentialist was Jean-Paul Sartre (1905–1980), whose philosophical, literary, and dramatic works portrayed people struggling to define themselves in profoundly desperate situations.[3] Arguing that existence precedes essence, Sartre asserted that human beings enter the world with no fixed or predetermined definition or purpose. The act of creating one's essence is an act of self-definition, accomplished by making significant choices about how to live life. For him, the human being is condemned to be free and to bear the responsibility of making free choices.

While Sartre was an atheist, Gabriel Marcel (1889–1973), another French Existentialist, like Kierkegaard took a religious orientation. Marcel believed that authentic spirituality came from the individual's free acceptance of faith and belief. The act of faith that created belief was itself a choice. Another leading religious Existentialist was Martin Buber (1878–1965), an Israeli philosopher, who used themes from Jewish mysticism and Existentialism to develop his philosophy. His book, *I and Thou*, held that God and the human being are engaged in a direct and profound dialogue, a spiritual conversation, which can lead the person to self-definition.

Martin Heidegger (1899–1976), a German Existentialist, founded Existentialist Phenomenology, which emphasized the need to understand *being*, especially the ways in which humans act in, and relate to, the world. For Heidegger, the search for truth comes from the individual's own intuitive self-awareness as she or he explores the subjective world of experience. This search takes place against the backdrop of the person's profound feeling of *angst*, a German word that means having a profound feeling of anxiety, anguish, or dread. Angst arises from the human being's awareness that we are totally responsible for our choices but will die and eventually disappear from the world.

Existentialism has also been influenced by *Phenomenology*, a philosophical method developed by Edmund Husserl (1859–1938), a German philosopher who argued that our consciousness and experience results from our intuition, perception, and awareness of something. Phenomenon refers to something, an object or event, that we perceive or experience directly. This contrasts with the Realist metaphysical position that asserts that our knowledge of an object must correspond to the intrinsic essence of the object. Phenomenology, then, is a method of investigating all human experiences, without regard to metaphysical issues concerning the reality of the object in the universe. The influence of Phenomenology on Existentialism is that our consciousness of our own existence lies in how we perceive and become consciously aware of our situation. Since our awareness of our situation depends on our perceptions, this awareness or consciousness is the basis for our choices and decisions—how we define ourselves. Phenomenology removes the basing of our decisions on conformity to metaphysical or universal standards from the process of self-definition. Phenomenology has also influenced Postmodernism, Liberation Pedagogy, and Critical Theory, discussed in Chapters 8, 14, and 19. It is especially evident in Paulo Freire's Liberation Pedagogy, which contends that human beings are unfinished projects.

In the United States, Existentialism enjoyed its highest popularity immediately after World War II when intellectuals reacted against the conformity of the emerging corporate society. It gained a following among those who espoused Existentialist Psychology, in which the individual was to throw off the social and economic expectations imposed by others and choose to be an inner-directed, self-defined, authentic person. Sartre explored the possibility of an Existentialist Psychoanalysis in his philosophical works. Rollo May, Viktor Frankl, Gordon Allport, and Carl Rogers applied Existentialism to various fields, including psychotherapy, learning theory, and humanist psychology. Some philosophers of education, such as Van Cleve Morris, Harold Soderquist, George Kneller, and Donald Vandenburg, explored Existentialist pedagogy as an alternative to the depersonalization, standardization, and conformity of institutions of mass education.[4]

WHY STUDY EXISTENTIALISM?

The reasons for studying Existentialism arise from the central human paradox of being a unique person, but one who lives in an indifferent world, and is conscious that the future will bring death and disappearance. Such a profound, but seemingly disturbing realization is carried by the person every day in her or his consciousness. Within the Existentialist paradox, however, lies the very profound understanding that whatever one does with their life is ultimately their own choice and responsibility.

Historically, sociologically, and psychologically, Existentialism represents not only a reaction against the traditional metaphysical systems and against the modern totalitarian political systems, but also against the sophisticated consumerism, consensus-driven conformity, and technological standardization of modern mass society. It provides an alternative way of thinking about life, choice, and the human condition.

The years of adolescence and youth, the time of junior high, high school, and college is the time when young people begin to understand that making choices is what life is about. The young person who is ready to begin the process of self-definition asks such questions as: Who am I? What do I want to be? Where do I belong? It is often a time of unconscious drift but also of serious decision making. Existentialism is a philosophy that corresponds very well to the storm and stress of the self-definition process of adolescence and youth. Using Existentialism to examine how people face the challenge of self-definition is a worthy undertaking.

EXISTENTIALISM AS A PHILOSOPHY OF EDUCATION

Metaphysics

Rejecting a priori definitions of the human person as part of a universal system, Existentialists see life as having so many possibilities that it cannot be fitted neatly into pre-existing metaphysical formulas.[5] Although Existentialists accept that we live in a physical environment, they see the physical world as simply being there, indifferent to us and our purposes. At our birth, our existence is a given, a brute fact of life, but it is then our responsibility to define our selves and to create our purpose. To exist as a person means to face the responsibility for choosing how we will live. We are faced with the disturbing question, "What difference does it make?" and the challenging statement, "I want to make a difference."

What Difference Does It Make?   For the Existentialist, an individual's existence makes no difference to the world. The world existed before the individual came on the scene and will continue to function after the individual has disappeared. An Existentialist sees the world in the following way: I had no choice about being born into this world; I simply am in it. I believe that the world around me exists—the natural phenomenon (trees, flowers, animals) and other people, with their social and cultural ways and institutions—are also here and part of my existence. I can study the sciences that explain nature and society but in the long run, in the most important way, my existence really makes no difference to the world. Like other human beings, I know that I will die sometime. My co-workers and family members may miss me for a time but my existence, for them, will eventually pass into the shadows of remembrance and eventually be forgotten and disappear. So my existence really makes no difference to anyone or anything other than myself.

I Want to Make a Difference.   Though Existentialists realize that they exist in an indifferent world and consciously face the inevitable and eventual fact of their disappearance, they also believe that they are responsible for making the choice of who they are and what they will be. To exist, to be, means to be involved in making choices that range from the mundane, to the ridiculous, to the profound. Thus, we live in the paradox—I make no difference but I can make a difference.[6] The ultimate recognition of this paradox is that responsibility falls on you alone.

The Responsibility of Making Choices and Defining Self.   Living in a paradoxical situation, an individual faces choice. A significant starting point is choosing to accept the reality of the paradox. To be this responsible for one's own definition is awesome and potentially overwhelming. There are many voices, some that claim to be experts, that tell us that we are not really responsible for defining our selves. Biologists tell us that it is the genes we inherited from our ancestors that define us. Sociologists tell us identity is based on our membership in, and identity with, a socioeconomic class. Consider how powerful the concepts of being in the middle class and having middle-class values are to many Americans. Our employers tell us we are productive functionaries in the commercial world. Marketing experts look at us as potential customers for

■ ■ ■ ■ ■

THE EXISTENTIALIST PARADOX

My existence makes no difference to the world.
I can choose to make a difference to myself.

whatever they are selling. Political leaders tell us we are defined as citizens of a particular country. The list of definitions imposed on us by others goes on and on. We can try to escape the Existential paradox, or perhaps just drift along, and accept one or all of these definitions imposed by others and become part of a social, economic, and political system. For the Existentialist, this is the easy way out of self-definition. It is really not self-definition at all, but merely an acceptance of how others have defined us or used us. However, the kind of false consciousness that comes from accepting what others tell us to believe, do, or buy does not solve the unresolvable paradox of existence, meaning, and disappearance.

In any kind of situation, the person has the ultimate choice of either accepting or rejecting it. To rebel against authority can lead to serious consequences. For some, like Gandhi and Mandela, it can lead to imprisonment. To reject conformity can make us an outsider, a stranger. To speak out against a popular idea or mood can lead to isolation or to shunning. Self-definition can be dangerous to comfortable conformity, going with the crowd, and fitting in.

Epistemology

Existentialists discern two kinds of knowing. First, there is the knowledge of the natural and physical world, which is dependent on our perception and awareness of phenomenon. Mathematics and the sciences inform us about the world in which we live. It is a world that we inhabit but did not create. For example, the laws of physics, chemistry, and biology are there whether we choose to accept them or not. The law of gravity is not one that we either choose to accept or reject. How the heart beats and the blood circulates through the human body is a fact of physiology. These are the basic facts of life; they help us make some decisions, but not the most important ones, those that deal with self-definition and the creation of our selves.

The second and more important kind of knowing is personal and subjective. It is knowledge about ourselves as persons living in a world of choice—what we shall be, who we should be friends with, what activities we should enjoy, what books we want to read, and so on. It is the knowledge that helps us make decisions in our own quest for self-definition. At the heart of this kind of knowing is our choice about what it is we want to know and how we will use that knowledge.

In considering choice-making, we might contrast the Pragmatist approach of choosing according to the scientific method (discussed in Chapter 5) and Existentialist choosing according to our own personal subjectivity. Pragmatists, like Dewey, assert that we can use the scientific method as a process in order to project and estimate the consequences of action and to generate plans that lead to achieving our ideal consequences. Further, the scientific method is public; that is, it is open to observable empirical verification. An Existentialist would say that while we may choose to use the scientific method, such a choice is not really scientific at all but is rather a personal one. If we like, we can choose other methods—prayer, astrology, or intuition, for example—as well as science.

Knowing for Existentialists is basically an epistemology of appropriation, in which the person comes to an area of knowledge and chooses what she or he wants to take from it and make her or his own.[7]

Axiology

While Idealists, Realists, and Thomists contend that values are universal and timeless and Pragmatists see them as relative to particular cultures at given times, Existentialists believe that values arise from personal and subjective choices. Of all of the subdivisions of philosophy, Existentialists give the greatest attention to axiology, which for them is the personal act of choosing and creating values. They accentuate the importance of examining and reflecting on the ethical and moral dilemmas and decisions that people face, with the full realization that valuation is personal and cannot be based on ethical measurements on a moral yardstick that exists outside of us. They place emphasis on aesthetics, especially the art, literature, drama, and films that portray human beings making the most important decisions in life. Those important decisions are the ones that require the individual to make the choices that bring about self-definition, the creation of one's own essence. The primary ethical obligation for individuals in making their own decisions and creating their own values is that they accept that they are totally responsible for who they are and what they stand for, and for the consequences of their actions.

Logic

As with the other areas of Existentialist philosophizing, logic, too, is subject to choice. We can choose to be logical or illogical—it is up to us. We can choose to be deductive, drawing our conclusions from major premises, or we can be inductive, generalizing our conclusions from specific instances. Logic is especially useful when we deal with mathematics and science—those relatively value-free areas that explain our physical and natural universe. In the self-exploratory subjects of art, music, literature, dance, film, and creative writing, for example, self-expression rather than logic is the primary consideration. Self-exploration and analysis, a kind of Existentialist philosophizing and psychotherapy, is of more importance than logic as we seek to answer the questions: Who am I? What do I want to be? What do I value? The self-examination of one's own psyche is more autobiographical and psychological than logical.

EXISTENTIALISM'S EDUCATIONAL IMPLICATIONS

The Purpose of Education

For Existentialists, the purpose of education is to cultivate in students an awareness that they are free agents, responsible for creating their own selves and purposes. This kind of awareness makes it clear that they are totally free and that their choices are not determined by environment, heredity, genetics, society, or the economy. While heredity and genetics determine physiological characteristics of pigmentation, height, eye color and so on, these characteristics do not determine personal choices.

The intensity of awareness that leads to the personal authenticity sought by Existentialists faces a major obstacle in education that is based on a socioeconomic criterion of success. A successful education, in socioeconomic terms, is one that leads to a successful life with a job that provides the income that enables a person to acquire consumer goods, a large house with a swimming pool, the latest-model car or SUV, luxury vacations, and membership in a prestigious country club. This kind of success allows people to send their children to the "right kind" of schools and colleges that will permit their children to continue the cycle of economic success. According to this criterion of success, economic goals are imposed on the young who are conditioned to accept a socioeconomic, class-referenced criterion for school success.

An important part of this cycle of success is that one learns to play roles; recognizing the cues and situations in which to act out the strategies that will lead to getting a "good job," making the right contacts, and marrying into a well-connected family. Learning to play the roles that lead to success is an important part of contemporary schooling. Existentialists find learning to play the roles of success in school phony, leading to a nonauthentic, other-defined life. When engaged in role playing, the individual is acting according to a script defined by others, rather than being true to her or his own authentic choices. This leads to covering up the true self with roles and images.

School Organization

Just as Existentialism opposes the definition of the person based on metaphysics, it also rejects the consensus-creating conformity of the modern corporate- and consumer-driven society. It opposes any organization of the school that restricts the genuine interaction of students with each other as individuals or that categorizes them. It opposes the standardization of education, the rigidity of scheduling, and the tyranny of testing that restricts the interpersonal relationship between teacher and student, and among students. The important quality to these relationships is that they are between individuals who value each other as free selves, and as equals. If one individual sees the other as belonging to some kind of racial, ethnic, class, or functional category, they are no longer equal. This can result in "otherness," in which a student's primary identification is that of being "gifted," "handicapped," a "jock," or a "nerd," rather than being seen as a person. The various cliques that abound in high schools, for example, while providing students with a kind of group-based security and membership, also reward conformity and punish uniqueness. Membership in a clique or gang that excludes others and stereotypes that short-cut possibilities of valuing differences define other students by categorical definitions.

Curriculum and Instruction

In terms of curriculum, Existentialists construct two divisions: givens and self-formations. A given is knowledge that is taken for granted and is used to perform skills and to provide certain kinds of information. The tool skills, such as reading, writing, computing, and researching, are taught in the elementary school and are largely givens. Seen as ways of decoding and communicating, they are useful skills that can be employed to access bodies of knowledge. Much of the schooling in the primary grades consists of acquiring, practicing, and mastering these basic skills. For Existentialists, this kind of skill learning takes place in childhood, a time prior to the Existential moment of awareness of the responsibility of choice.

Although the elementary school years occur prior to the Existential moment (when a person is conscious that she or he is responsible for her or his choice), they are a time in which the predisposition to respect of self and other students should be created. Teachers should try to create a learning environment in which pupils are free to express themselves via creative writing, art, and drama, and are encouraged to respect and value the creations and expressions of their peers.

After skill acquisition, the next step in curriculum is studying those subjects that inform us about the physical, natural, social, and political world in which we live. The natural and physical sciences—biology, chemistry, physics, and mathematics—are truly "givens." The knowledge transmitted in these subjects should be accurate and well-organized and the instruction should be done by competent teachers. Instruction in these "givens" takes place throughout the upper grades. It continues on into higher education. However, these subjects are largely value-free. They inform us; they provide useful information; they can be applied. However, they do not carry strong possibilities for value formation and self-definition.

For Existentialists, the most important areas of curriculum are the value-laden subjects—history, literature, art, drama, film, dance, music, creative writing—that hold strong possibilities for personal reflection and expression. History is approached not as a chronology or as the politics of the past, but rather as the engagement of individuals at moments of crisis, ultimately leading to self-realization. History can be a narrative about John Brown's choice to be zealous in the cause of abolition; the story of Martin Luther King's decision to go forward in the civil rights movement despite the threat of death; Mahatma Gandhi's and Nelson Mandela's decision to accept imprisonment as a consequence of leading the struggle for independence in India and South Africa. It is about the decision of fire fighters and police officers to face death while rescuing others at the World Trade Center in New York City on September 11, 2001. This kind of history involves getting inside individuals, both famous and ordinary, and reflecting on the choices that they made at a decisive moment in their lives. In so doing, the students take, or appropriate, from history what they want in order to examine their own autobiographies.

Value-Laden Subjects and Self-Reflection

Literature, too, provides excellent opportunities for value reflection and self-examination. For example, *The Diary of Anne Frank* is found on reading lists for middle and high schools throughout the country. It is an autobiographical account of a Jewish girl's adolescence spent hiding in sealed attic rooms during the Nazi occupation of the Netherlands. Her diary, kept from the beginning of her family's concealment until their capture by the Nazis, is the story of continuing and daily choices—a coming of age through self-definition—in a truly absurd and terrifying world ruled by extreme prejudice and hatred. Not only does the diary depict her choices but it also describes the choices made by the Dutch employees of Anne's father who secretly brought them the food that sustained them, and the choice made by the unknown person who turned the family in to the Nazis. It also tells the story of the terrible consequences when one group, in this case the Nazis, subjects another to the most brutal kind of "othering," reducing Europe's Jews to "others" to be hunted, persecuted, isolated, and exterminated. Anne died in a concentration camp.

Art, drama, music, dance, and creative writing provide opportunities for students to express themselves while exploring their own values. For example, acting in a play can allow a student to appropriate a script and play the role in such a way as to bring to the surface of consciousness their innermost feelings.

Teaching

Teaching in the two areas of curriculum—the givens and the value-laden subjects—takes two forms. In the givens, the mathematical and scientific areas which tend to be value-free, teaching is directed toward understanding and using the subject matter. These areas tend to have an interior logic that forms the basis for organizing lessons. Even when dealing with value-free subjects, teaching should be done as much as possible in an I-Thou relationship that does not depersonalize the student or turn the teacher into an educational functionary. An I-Thou relationship is one that begins and remains as an interaction between individuals who value each other as persons for their own identity as a free existent. It means valuing the person for what he or she is and stands for. An I-Thou relationship is a delicate one that is jeopardized or even destroyed when one individual in the relationship decides to treat the other person as something other than a free and authentic self. If one person in the relationship seeks to use the other person for selfish motives, then it is distorted. Even in these value-free subject areas, opportunities present themselves for value explorations that deal with the humane use of science and technology in a world that is becoming increasingly corporate, mechanized, and violent.

The value-laden arts and humanities, which provide the richest occasions for value exploration, create excellent opportunities for Existentialist teaching. Here, teachers can pose the leading questions about the meaning of life and death that stimulate students to probe their own psyches. They can also encourage students to pose their own leading questions to lead to self-examination. In contrast to the Socratic method discussed in the chapter on Idealism, there is, for the Existentialist, no right or wrong answer that can come from this self-reflection. In fact, the answer might not emerge until a moment of important choice in the student's future.

Learners

Existentialists present the view that learning is an engagement by students in their own self-construction as individuals. The learner, like all individuals, is an unfinished project and, if she or he chooses to do so, can consciously engage in the action of creating her or his own essence—the self-definition that gives personal meaning to life.

As indicated throughout this chapter, it is difficult to talk about individuals as students because that places them in a category. It is better to speak of them as young people who are engaged in creating themselves. The goal is to raise learners' consciousness that they are responsible for making the choices that lead to their own self-realization.

Assessment

An issue currently attracting attention and stimulating heated debate is assessment of students' academic achievement and progress. The trend, reinforced by state and federal government-mandated policies, is to rely on standardized, usually objective tests, normed to national populations. This kind of assessment is regarded as objective because it is impersonal and is designed to rank students. When parents ask, "How is my son or daughter doing?" the answer comes simply by finding the individual's placement in a ranking of students in the local district, state, or nation. This kind of standardized testing flies in the face of what Existentialists regard as true assessment.

Existentialists prefer to use *authentic assessment*, in which students maintain portfolios or journals that allow them to set their own goals and determine their own achievement of these goals. Their own papers, drawings, essays, and other items help them track their own educational journey.

■ ■ ■ ■ ■

VAN CLEVE MORRIS, "THE CURRICULUM OF A FREE EXISTENT" AND "AN EXISTENTIALIST PEDAGOGY"

In this selection, Morris discusses how Existentialism as an educational philosophy differs from more traditional approaches, especially Realism. This reading has been selected because Morris presents a very clear statement of how Existentialism can be used as a guide to curriculum and instruction and to teaching and learning. He examines education's possibilities for creating self-awareness and self-definition and then discusses the curriculum areas that have potential for creating an intensity of awareness. As you read the selection, you may wish to consider the following focusing questions:

1. According to Morris, how do we write our own script regarding knowledge and curriculum?

2. How would an Existentialist teacher respond to the student who says, "So what?"

3. How does an Existentialist define the concept of the "self"? Revisit the reading from Broudy in Chapter 3. Compare and contrast the Existentialist view of self, as presented by Morris, with that presented by Broudy, a Classical Realist.

4. What are the similarities and differences in how an Idealist (discussed in Chapter 2) and an Existentialist would use the Socratic method or dialogue?

5. What are the possibilities for an Existentialist teaching of the arts, humanities, and history?

THE CURRICULUM OF A FREE EXISTENT

... But let us attend to the student's *attitude* toward these boxes of knowledge, his leaning toward, his stretching out to these granite blocks of truth. This is where Existential education begins.

The existentialist attitude toward knowledge radically affects the teaching of those subjects which are dependent upon systems of thought or frames of reference: it states that school subjects are only tools for the realization of subjectivity.

This view of the curriculum is a specialized version of the Existentialist's entire epistemology. It is an epistemology diametrically opposed to the so-called "Spectator Theory" of knowledge made popular by the Realists. It is the view of knowledge not from the standpoint of the spectator but from the standpoint of the *actor*, onstage and actively implicated in the "role" of man.

Look at knowledge, if you will, in the most traditional way of the Spectator Theorist, viz., as encyclopedic in character. Knowledge may be thought of as an organized universe of cognitive propositions such as might be found in the Britannica. Every library is a kind of "walk-in" encyclopedia, a storage vault of information. But note, he who walks in is the center of the action; he must decide which propositions, among the world's billions of propositions, are meaningful and significant and therefore worth believing. He is the actor, the active agent. He chooses his knowledge.

An allegorical aside may clarify this last. It is as if man had been cast in a role for which no part had been written. We have awakened to our existence to discover a script in our hands.

But the script is blank. We "write" our own script in speaking hitherto unwritten lines; we act it out, ad libs and all. Indeed, the whole play, all of life, is ad lib.

Part of the dialogue we invent and act out, i.e., part of our stream of ad libs, is epistemological; that is, some of the lines we speak are propositions of a cognitive sort. We utter possible truths about the world. But they are all uttered from the standpoint of the *actor* who sees them as true only in light of the role he is trying to develop by pronouncing them. If, therefore, some of the dialogue is scientific, it is because those who speak these lines are "playing the role" of man—"creating the part," as they say in the theater—as if they intended man's meaning in the world to be "the vehicle of scientific cognition."

But there are other lines, other ad libs, other soliloquies, other asides that can be spoken. Those who speak them have a different idea of how the "part" of man should be played. There is no preterhuman playwright who has certified one set of lines or one "interpretation" of the role as more authentic than any other. Each of us creates his own interpretation of the part.

Working from this allegory, we may say that the library of any university or the curriculum of any school, insofar as it represents the extant knowledge of the world, represents the "scripts" that have thus far been written, the lines spoken by others in their interpretation of the "role" of man. They are there for the taking, but each learner must do the taking. They are possible lines to be spoken if the learner wishes to employ them in realizing his own subjectivity. The curriculum is not there to be mastered (as the traditionalist would say), nor is it there to be experienced (as the Experimentalist might say). It is there to be *chosen*. The subject matters and experiences in a curriculum shall be merely *available*; to be learned, they must first be opted for, sought out, and appropriated by the student.

One might well ask at this point whether, in all that is presently "available" in contemporary conventional curricula, any subjects or learning experiences would particularly lend themselves to Existentialist development. Are there components of today's curricula which might be adaptable to the above analysis, which seem to provide even in their present form the possibility of teaching in the first-person mode wherein genuine, individualized appropriation can be encouraged? Certainly whatever experiences in the school are most likely to arouse the individual's own private way of looking at life will be elevated to first position in anything that might some day be called an Existentialist school. Are there such experiences in present-day school programs?

I think there are two possibilities for an affirmative answer to this question. By far the more obvious but, in the long run, perhaps of lesser significance is that region of the curriculum we customarily label the *arts*. Experiences in music, the dance, drama, creative writing, painting, and the plastic arts seem to me the chief contenders for this kind of education. In these "subjects," if you want to call them that, the idea has already gained headway that what the child produces in his classroom or homework assignments is very largely *his*. (If this is not altogether true of music, I think it is still true of the other areas mentioned.) We can credit the Progressive educator for this development; he is the one who, in these areas, liberated the child from the heavy hand both of traditional canons of form and of contemporary, "other-directed" conventions of style. The learner's dance or short story, his snatch of dialogue or role playing, his clay figure or water color is somehow *not* expected to match what has gone before. It is expected to be his own authentic

expression of what he sees in his own world. Not only that, but the motivation to produce these "works" is not primarily to exhibit them to others but rather to work out, from the center of one's private experience, certain meanings that the world may have for oneself.

If Existentialism ever gains a foothold in educational thinking in this country, it will probably begin its work in these "self-creating" subject matters. Thanks to the Progressive, we have already established a precedent to work from, a precedent for the kind of teaching in which the learner sees himself in the role of creative innovator in the learning process.

The less obvious but eventually more significant area of learning is, unfortunately, one that has no name. We shall call it "normative." Included in this category are not only subject matters per se but experiences of all sorts which awaken the decision-making awarenesses of the learner.

Among the subject matters of a normative sort, I believe that history and literature would probably provide the most fuel for an Existentialist teacher. As indicated in the previous example of history, the implicit question of *meaning* and *significance* always lies just beneath the surface of historical subject matter. The question "So what?" can be made explicit on an instant's notice in every history classroom during the study of virtually any historical period or any particular event. If the old cliché that the purpose of studying history is to illuminate the present has any meaning, it must be that the "illumination" is of a normative sort; that is, such study presents to us various hypotheses as to how life in the present might be lived, how we might solve our problems. The whole point of examining the past is to identify really live options on the management of present events in the name of a desired future. If we are to "learn from history," what else could the cliché possibly mean?

Every historiographer grants that the past does not give us direct instructions on how to manage the present. It merely helps us, as he might put it, to *understand* the present. But of what worth would mere understanding be if it did not at least suggest what was possible in the way of social action? Such aloof, insulated "understanding" would be a splendid luxury, but it could hardly persuade anybody to labor at the study of history. It would be a case of "present-ism" in its most vicious form, having no critical dimension concerning what was right and what was wrong about contemporary civilization. History can be understood only forward, not backward. "It is the future which decides whether the past is living or dead." For the past to live, it must in one way or another awaken possibilities for things to come, the region out ahead where human projects are worked out.

The study of literature is equally relevant for the awakening of strategic choice making on the part of the learner. And by "strategic" I mean choice making of a magnitude which bears on the shape and direction of an entire human life. Shakespeare's *Hamlet*, a perennial figure, comes immediately to mind. It is a work in which the agonies of personal definition make a persistent whisper to the student: "What would *you* have done?" Wherever ethical questions are raised for which convenient precedents in present-day experience are not available—there one will find the kinds of literature capable of arousing the existential awareness of the learner.

A literature of even greater power, in my judgment, is twentieth-century drama. We have grown weary of Hollywood happy endings; modern playwrights have helped us rediscover the "tragic sense of life." Tragedy is not merely the blatantly *un*happy ending, or the melodramatic, but that struggle to make sense of human existence and to find personal meaning in an apparently indifferent world. In this kind of struggle genuine affective involvement can be generated. In the student's personal involvement with the works of such authors, let us say,

as Samuel Beckett, Tennessee Williams, Arthur Miller, Jean Paul Sartre, or Albert Camus may be found the makings of an "awakening" experience for him.

. . .

AN EXISTENTIALIST PEDAGOGY

It must be clear by now that Existentialism is not a philosophy in the conventional sense. It is not a body of thought about the nature of world and man. Its message is far simpler and at the same time more profound, viz., Existentialism wishes merely to establish the starting place for the philosophical enterprise itself, the place from which all thought about the meaning of life must set out. This place is the human *self*.

Existential education assumes the responsibility of awakening each individual to the full intensity of his own selfhood.

An instructional method which pretends pursuit of such a goal must obviously possess some working knowledge of the "self." Just what is it? Certainly, the "self" is not an object in the world with a static essence or whatness. Nor is the "self" merely a verbal construct to stand for an occurrence or event in an empirical sociology. The word "self" must be understood as a phenomenon—literally, from the Greek, "that which reveals itself"—best represented . . . by the word *"awareness."* The technical Existentialist "definition" (if there is a definition) of "self," therefore, might be "the phenomenon of the awareness of subjectivity"—that is, the awareness of being an unanalyzable, undefinable point of origin for all subsequent awareness. It is this prime awareness of self which becomes possible, but not automatic, on the occasion of the Existential Moment. And it is this awareness which the Existentialist teacher would seek to intensify.

As the earlier chapters have shown, there are three constituent awarenesses which make up the psychological content of "self":

1. I am a *choosing* agent, unable to avoid choosing my way through life.
2. I am a *free* agent, absolutely free to set the goals of my own life.
3. I am a *responsible* agent, personally accountable for my free choices as they are revealed in how I live my life.

The teacher's imperative is to arrange the learning situation in such a way as to bring home the truth of these three propositions to every individual.

THE SOCRATIC PARADIGM

It is something of a pleasant surprise to find in the educational theory of antiquity a paradigm to work from, namely, the classic figure of Socrates as teacher. Unfortunately, however, the paradigm is ambiguous.

For one thing, Socrates' injunction "Know thyself" bears a superficial and misleading resemblance to the Existentialist injunction for each person to become aware of his own subjectivity. Socrates, and the Greeks generally, viewed the self as some sort of essential content in the human structure; if an individual could be summoned to "Know thyself," supposedly the self was an entity that could be known. There is nothing in Existentialism to coincide with this understanding. Indeed, the self as a transcending phenomenon fashioned out of free choices is supremely *un*known and *un*knowable. One can become aware of the self as a phenomenon, but not know it.

Another ambiguity lies in the fact that Socrates' famous interrogative method took two forms. On some occasions Socrates posed questions whose answers he already knew; on other occasions, he posed questions whose answers he did *not* know but was earnestly seeking. The former instances are represented in those episodes in Plato's dialogues where we most often meet him in the teacher's role. The classic illustration is to be found in *The Meno*, wherein Socrates proceeds, through an artful line of questioning, to get an ignorant slave boy to formulate the Pythagorean theorem. In this pedagogic exercise, Socrates knew in advance the conclusion toward which his teaching was directed. Every question therefore enjoyed an a priori focus and intent. What appeared on the surface to be a kind of "psychic remembering" on the part of the pupil led Socrates' student Plato to formulate his notion of learning as reminiscence or recollection of a previously known set of ideas. In reality, however, most of the "remembering" was already built into the structure of the questions by virtue of the planned sequence of queries. . . .

The latter instances of questioning represented Socrates' other methodological mode: to seek for truth which he did *not* already possess. He ambled about Athens asking questions, some of them extremely embarrassing to the alleged wise men of the day and to the people in power. (As we all know, his incessant questions made him appear to his infuriated fellow citizens as a nuisance and troublemaker and they finally sentenced him to the cup of hemlock.) The bulk of Plato's dialogues show him in these kinds of interchanges. In *The Republic* and *The Theaetetus*, for example, Socrates is genuinely seeking after that which he does *not* understand and does *not* know; he is the epitome of the *seeker after truth*. The irony, however, is that we do not picture Socrates in these episodes as a teacher. He seems to us more like the inquirer or what we would now call the researcher. He is probing for new truth, and we do not customarily associate this activity with the direct act of teaching. But here is precisely where Socrates foreshadows the Existentialist's educational theory. We must renew and reactivate this association of the teacher with the inquirer. We must revive the Socratic paradigm, not in the mode of *The Meno* but in the mode of *The Republic*. And I do not mean that the Existentialist teacher is always searching for new truth in the manner of the "serious" research scholar. Rather, he is searching for personal truth. Personal truth is always *new* to the individual searching for it himself; and, for that matter, it is always new to the teacher also.

Thus, if we adopt the Socratic paradigm, the teacher will concentrate on asking those questions to which he does *not* know the answer. In the most literal and profound of ways, he will learn along with his students.

The understanding of teaching as the asking of questions to which no one knows the answer will no doubt seem outrageously bizarre. It certainly runs counter to all conventional conceptions of teaching and learning. Moreover, it places the teacher under heavy obligations of imagination and insight. It is not easy to ask such questions; anyone who has attempted the "Socratic method" knows that it is one of the most difficult of teaching procedures. But difficulty must be measured against yield, namely, the possible awakening of the student to his awareness of choice, freedom, and responsibility in his own selfhood.

SOME EXAMPLES

The Arts

We saw in the previous chapter that the arts represent one portion of conventional curricula that would possibly be susceptible to Existentialist treatment. We have at last outgrown the "copying" phase and the "representational" phase of art instruction. We have graduated to a newer methodological position which places the teacher in the role of "evoker" and "awakener" of the child's artistic expression. Noticeably absent from art classrooms is the insistence upon following the canons of some alleged artistic standard. In its place is the insistence by the teacher that the student stand on his own and by himself in portraying the world in water color, in oil, in soap or clay, as *he* sees it and *not* as his teacher or his classmates or the so-called "masters" see it. The teacher is, I

think, enacting the Socratic paradigm of arousing the pupil to artistic expression which the teacher cannot anticipate. The teacher does not know in advance what he is after; all he knows is that it is important for the pupil to *feel* his own experience through the medium of his paintbrush or carving knife or cutting tool. *What* the student creates is less important than that he *does* create something which he can see as his own private artistic statement about his experience.

For students who may be ill at ease in the manual arts, the teacher may employ experiences in the literary arts of short-story writing and poetic expression. Spontaneity is the principal caution; nothing is quite so preposterous as to "assign" a student the task of writing an original poem "to be handed in tomorrow." But, wherever poetic or prose inclinations reveal themselves, the teacher should immediately seize on such opportunities and quicken the student's desire to express himself in his own way. In this connection, I am reminded of the final examination Robert Frost once gave to one of his classes. At the close of the course, the students gathered dutifully with their blue books, ball-points poised for three hours of question answering. Mr. Frost entered the room at the appointed hour and wrote the entire examination on the blackboard in two words: "Write something." Then he left.

For students not facile with pencil and paper, the teacher can turn to the dramatic arts. Drama, it seems to me, is perhaps the most powerful of all the arts in evoking existential awareness. In dramatic interpretation the pupil can literally assume the role of existential actor, making clear to himself—in the act of making something clear to his audience—what he considers the most important of his own subjective feelings. How one interprets a role inevitably reflects how one views his own life and its meaning in the world.

By way of an indirect example of such teaching, I have sometimes speculated on the appropriateness of an assignment like the following: The student in the eleventh-grade English class is asked to imagine himself a kind of benign Frankenstein (the college student might imagine himself a Watsonian Behaviorist psychological lab technician with a newborn baby assigned exclusively to him). The assignment is to write a description of the ideal human being that might be created, the individual with the finest set of attitudes, personality traits, life aspirations, and personal values. When the paper was turned in, the teacher would read it over and jot at the bottom of it a sequel assignment: "Now prepare a second paper in which you compare and contrast the individual you have created with yourself at this moment." This paper, in turn, would be submitted, the teacher would go over it, and the student would then be instructed to prepare and turn in a final, culminating assignment, namely, an explanation why there was a discrepancy between the ideal and the actual individual since there is no excuse for not appropriating the attitudes, aspirations, values, etc., of the ideal individual as conceived. The point of the assignment would be to arouse disquiet in the student by showing him that he bears responsibility for falling short of his ideal goal.

Literature and the Humanities

. . . the Existentialist educator would seek to intensify the *normative* aspect of all subject matter. This is where personal judgment, in the manner of the Socratic pupil, can be exercised. The humanities obviously offer some of the most pregnant possibilities for such emphasis.

The conventional teaching of literature and the humanities assumes that literary documents, like natural phenomena in the sciences, lie outside the student's immediate life. They are to be studied and learned in the same way that one might study biology or mathematics, viz., to be comprehended as so much more verbal material concerning the world that lies beyond and independent of the learner. To look at the humanities in this way, the Existentialist educator might say, is to mutilate them and to destroy their most prominent contribution to human learning, namely, the awakening of sensibilities, the intensification of feelings in the individual.

To read the tales of Chaucer's pilgrims, to hear the lines of T. S. Eliot's "The Hollow Men," to study the essays of Ralph Waldo Emerson is *not* to be studying English. It is, rather, to be placing one's capacities for feeling at the disposal of an author who seeks to arouse feeling to a new, more intense level of awareness. To study literature is to lay bare the nerve endings of one's emotions and to invite stimulation from the author's work, much as the playgoer, upon entering the theater, deliberately opens his perceptive apparatus to receive symbolic experiences from the stage which will arouse new and hitherto unfelt emotions in his subjective consciousness. Consider any major theme of humanistic writing—death, love, suffering, guilt, freedom—and let the student in the classroom be put in touch with increasingly strong doses of what the important figures in our literary past have had to say about them. Of these, certainly the most powerful is the theme of death. Are we ready to induct high school youngsters into a subjective consideration of this most profound of human encounters? Are we prepared as teachers to have them really get inside this most existential of all human problems? The Existentialist teacher would insist on it. And he would introduce it to the youngster with materials ranging from Jack London's "To Build a Fire" to Caryl Chessman's *Cell 2455, Death Row*. Let the student get inside the heart of the man freezing to death, of the man before the firing squad or sitting in the electric chair or the gas chamber. Let him ponder the problem of capital punishment. Let him ponder the meaning of his own life by deliberately pondering the truth that on some future day it will be abruptly canceled from the universe with no trace remaining, as abruptly as any firing squad might cancel it.

History

The normative element subsides as we leave the arts and humanities and enter other subject matters which only partially lend themselves to Existentialist forms of teaching. History is a case in point because it can be taught in many different ways: as the chronological sequence of cause and effect through time, as the emergence and evolution of civilizations through the ages, as a series of heroic figures who have both shaped and been shaped by their times, or as an analysis of the ways in which human societies have solved their problems. These I think summarize the conventional "uses of the past," in Mueller's phrase. The Existentialist teacher of history would, however, find them all lacking. For one does not find the normative element in the study of history by viewing the past as something to be *used*. The past is not used; it is created. That is to say, what makes the past normative, expressive of the good-bad dimension of life, is not to be found in the past itself but in how we today view the past. It is our apprehension of what there is in history to value or reject which introduces the normative element into it. In this sense we *create* the value content of our heritage by viewing that heritage, and studying it, and teaching it to others in a particular light.

I realize that this conception of history, while enjoying some credence in historiographic circles, has only tenuous acceptance in American common sense. But it is essential to an Existentialist philosophy of historical education and is therefore worth some comment.

Kierkegaard used to say that you cannot learn from history until you have a life, an existence, of your own against which to judge history. History is no better a guide to behavior than contemporary society. For man cannot acquire moral and ethical principles from other men or other social institutions except by choosing them from the baseless platform of his own awareness of what is going on in contemporary life. He finds meaning in history only in terms of present circumstance.

There is no more appropriate way to exemplify this condition than to bear witness to American history itself. What does the United States Constitution say? What it says is plain enough; the Archives Building in Washington, D.C., still has the original. But what does it *mean*? This question cannot be answered except by living men. And the Supreme Court of this nation does not hesitate to interpret it for us, the living. The complaint is correct that in *interpreting* the Constitution this Court is actually *legislating*. And thanks for that! For if the Constitution were placed out of reach of living men, if they were barred from saying what it means in contemporary affairs, it would lose all significance as an historical document. Precisely because it is endowed with meaning by *the living* it remains a living document. Its meanings are authored in the here and now.

So it is with all of history. Past events may be said to exist in a brute, documentary, "archive" sense. But what they *mean* is always for us to say. The study of history is always an affair of the living present. Indeed, it is an affair of the future, of man's efforts to transcend his present situation in choosing his way forward to new and hitherto unexperienced spheres of awareness. Are we to say it is otherwise—that contemporary man is bludgeoned into certain views about his own past merely because that past *is* past and out of reach? What more insane and preposterous position could be taken? If we mean to be the masters of our fate, then certainly we must be the captains of our past. For a man to be "compelled" by history, he must freely *choose* to be compelled. He does not have to follow precedent. In the last analysis, he is the author of his own precedents. Only with this understanding can we regard the future as free and really at our disposal.

What we have said concerning a collective view of history can now be personalized in Kierkegaard's terms. Our own private sense of history, in the same fashion, originates in our private consciousness concerning the meaning of the past for ourselves. It is the epistemological notion of *appropriation*... brought literally to bear on a commonplace subject matter of every school. Historical subject matter is to be appropriated, i.e., "made one's own," in the act of being learned. It must be opted for, adopted, and assimilated into a private life before it can be considered knowledge in any scholastic sense.

To make history one's own and to make one's own history is to become involved in the interpretation of the past. It is to become personally implicated in the thrust and charge of events. It is to become emotionally a participant in the human enterprise. If we fought a Civil War, let each student feel the full voltage of that catastrophe; let him feel the exultation and heartbreak which that greatest of all national blunders burned into the American consciousness. Let him *feel* that war, as well as merely comprehend it as a 100-years-later bystanding spectator.

CONCLUSION

In this chapter we examined Existentialism as a philosophy that emphasizes the consideration of the crucial nature of the self as a freely existing person, responsible for defining her- or himself by making crucial decisions about life's purpose and meaning. We emphasized that the purpose of education cannot be fixed by statements of antecedent goals and expectations separate from the students' own struggle to create their essence. Through an epistemology of appropriation, the student determines the meaning of what he or she studies. The arts, literature, the humanities, and history represent curricular areas that are most congenial for studying and reflecting on the meaning of life and how the choices we make shapes who and what we are.

DISCUSSION QUESTIONS

1. How does Existentialism differ from the more traditional Idealist, Realist, and Thomist philosophies?
2. What does it mean to recognize, reflect on, and accept personal responsibility for choice and self-definition?
3. What does it mean to have an "intensity of awareness"?
4. Do you think Existentialism has much appeal for contemporary teachers and students? Explain your answer.
5. Consider the "strip mall," found in cities throughout the country, from the perspective of Existentialism. What kind of choices does it present?
6. Distinguish between an important and a trivial choice. How are the two kinds of choices often confused?

INQUIRY AND RESEARCH PROJECTS

1. Identify and review a book, motion picture, or television series that portrays individuals in situations where they must make important life-defining decisions.

2. In your clinical experiences, have you found any examples of Existentialist teaching? If so, describe them; if not, why do you think that they are absent?
3. In your clinical experiences, have you found any situations in which teachers or students turn other students into "others" or objects? Examine the context or background in which this occurs.
4. Prepare a character sketch of an Existentialist teacher.
5. Design a lesson plan based on Existentialist pedagogy.

INTERNET RESOURCES

For a discussion of Existentialism, consult
www.tamer.com/csw/exist/existentialism.html

The major themes of Existentialism are discussed at
www.conect.net/ron/exist.html

SUGGESTIONS FOR FURTHER READING

Barrett, William. *Irrational Man: A Study in Existentialist Philosophy.* New York: Anchor Books, 1990.
Billington, Ray. *East of Existentialism: The Tao of the West.* London and Boston: Unwin Hyman, 1990.
Chamberlain, Jane, and Ree, Jonathan. *The Kierkegaard Reader.* Oxford, UK: Blackwell Publishers, 2001.
Cohen-Solal, Annie. *Sartre A Life,* trans. Anna Cancogni. New York: Pantheon Books, 1987.
Dobson, Andrew. *Jean-Paul Sartre: A Theory of History.* New York: Cambridge University Press, 1993.
Greene, Maxine. *Teacher as Stranger: Educational Philosophy for the Modern Age.* Belmont, CA: Wadsworth Publishing Co., 1979.
Hall, Amy Laura. *Kierkegaard and the Treachery of Love.* New York: Cambridge University Press, 2002.
Hannay, Alastair. *Kierkegaard.* New York: Cambridge University Press, 2001.
Hendley, Steve. *Reason and Relativism: A Sartrean Investigation.* Albany: State University of New York Press, 1991.
Kaufman, Walter. *Existentialism from Dostoevsky to Sartre.* New York: New American Library, 1975.
Kneller, George. *Existentialism and Education.* New York: John Wiley & Sons, 1958.
McCulloch, Gregory. *Using Sartre: An Analytical Introduction to Early Sartrean Themes.* London and New York: Routledge, 1994.
Morris, Van Cleve. *Existentialism in Education: What It Means.* New York: Harper & Row, 1966.
Pattison, George. *Kierkegaard: Religion and the Nineteenth-Century Crisis of Culture.* New York: Cambridge University Press, 2002.
Peters, Helene. *The Existential Woman.* New York: Peter Lang, 1991.
Sartre, Jean-Paul. *Being and Nothingness: A Phenomenological Essay on Ontology.* New York: Washington Square Press, 1992.
Sartre, Jean-Paul. *Existentialism and Human Emotions.* New York: Philosophical Library, 1957.

NOTES

1. For Kierkegaard's profound challenge to traditional philosophy, see Alastair Hannay, *Kierkegaard* (New York: Cambridge University Press, 2002).

2. For Kierkegaard and the Christian religion, see Amy L. Hall, *Kierkegaard and the Treachery of Love* (New York: Cambridge University Press, 2002) and George Pattison, *Kierkegaard, Religion and the Nineteenth Century Crisis of Culture* (New York: Cambridge University Press, 2002).

3. Annie Cohen-Solal, *Sartre A Life*, trans. Anna Cancogni (New York: Pantheon Books, 1987).

4. Van Cleve Morris, *Existentialism in Education: What It Means* (New York: Harper & Row, 1966) and Harold O. Soderquist, *The Person and Education* (Columbus, OH: Charles E. Merrill, 1964).

5. George F. Kneller, *Existentialism and Education* (New York: John Wiley & Sons, 1966), p. 19.

6. The concept of the existential paradox and many of the ideas about an Existentialist pedagogy in this chapter are derived from Van Cleve Morris, *Existentialism in Education* (New York: Harper & Row, 1966), pp. 31–53, 69–78, 110–116.

7. Ibid., pp. 120–122.

CHAPTER SEVEN

PHILOSOPHICAL ANALYSIS

Generally, Philosophical Analysis, or Language Analysis, a philosophy developed in the twentieth century, restates philosophical and other issues, clarifying the language used to express them. It holds that problems, especially those relating to education, are most logically resolved by asking questions about the use of words in specific contexts.

DEFINING PHILOSOPHICAL ANALYSIS

Since we have already defined *philosophy*, we now look at the words, *language* and *analysis*. *Language* is the verbal and written communication system used by the people in a particular group, locality, district, or country. It includes the speech, diction, syntax, and grammar, and also refers to the terminology used in an academic area of specialization, such as education, psychology, law, medicine, and so forth.

Analysis means to separate or divide something into its constituent parts or elements to find out what it contains, and then to examine the individual parts closely, and study the structure as a whole. It may also include examining the details of each of the parts and how the parts relate to each other.

Building on these definitions, **Linguistic Analysis** is then the philosophical method used to establish meaning in language. Initially this method was applied to philosophical statements, and was later applied to specialized and ordinary discourse. Linguistic Analysts test for the meaning conveyed by language by breaking down or reducing larger and more complex and compound statements into their smaller, simpler parts. In order to establish meaning, they often define or redefine the words used in the original statement until they arrive at a clear understanding of what is being expressed. The process of analysis, breaking down and explaining the parts of the statement, continues until the statement's meaning is established. In the case of some statements, meaning cannot be established.

The Words We Use

Philosophical Analysis is a philosophy that seeks to examine and clarify our use of language by establishing the meaning of what we say and write. Analytical Philosophers

107

believe that the major contribution to be made by philosophers is the analysis of the concepts conveyed by language. Because of the specific focus on language, Philosophical Analysis is also called Linguistic Analysis.

In our ordinary conversations, we often say or hear the phrases, "I know what you're saying," "I hear you," "What do you mean?" In typical teenage jargon, one often hears the comparative words, "it's like." When we listen to war coverage on radio or television, we are likely to hear such phrases as "friendly fire," "collateral damage," and "coalition of the willing." In our professional discussions and readings as teachers, we hear such nice-sounding phrases as "quality education," "educating the whole child," "authentic assessment," an "effective school," and "critical thinking."

What do these phrases really mean? What do they mean for the speaker *and* for the listener? Let's consider some of these much used phrases:

"I know what you're saying" and "I hear you" mean that you think you are on the same communication wavelength as the speaker and understand what is being said. They mean that you understand, and likely agree with, the speaker. "What do you mean?" conveys that, even though you are using the same language, you don't understand what the speaker is trying to communicate.

The popular teenage phrase, "it's like," can mean many things. It can merely be a vocal pause, like an "ah" or an "um." Or it can be an analogy, when two objects, situations, or persons are being compared and found similar, at least for the speaker. Occasionally, the hearer will disagree and say that it's "not like" that at all.

The terms "friendly fire" and "collateral damage" convey meanings that are profoundly more serious than the terminology suggests. The meaning of "friendly" when used to report a battle is deadly, not friendly. Friendly fire means that casualties have resulted from being fired upon by one's own forces. "Collateral damage" means that a missile or bomb has gone off its trajectory and has struck an unintended target. It may be a school or a hospital rather than a military installation that has been hit. A "coalition of the willing" describes other countries that agree with our political policies, particularly in respect to war.

In all of these examples, we need to use other language, and more explanation and analysis to determine what is really being said and reveal the speaker's meaning. Our search for the meaning of terms used in education such as "quality education," "educating the whole child," "authentic assessment," "effective school," "critical thinking," and "no child left behind" will continue later in the chapter.

SITUATING PHILOSOPHICAL ANALYSIS

Philosophical Analysis, or Language Analysis, arose in the early twentieth century as a reaction against speculative metaphysical philosophies such as Idealism, Realism, and Thomism (discussed in Chapters 2, 3, and 4). Its drive to clarify language and thinking by reducing the emotive and subjective elements also put it in sharp contrast to Existentialism, discussed in Chapter 6.

G. E. Moore (1873–1958), Bertrand Russell (1872–1970), and Gilbert Ryle (1900–1976), three British philosophers, led the charge against Idealism and other speculative metaphysically based philosophies. Representing a bridge from Realism to

Analysis, Moore emphasized the common-sense view that objects really exist, but disavowed a metaphysically based framework for his philosophy. Instead, he turned his attention to the language that we use to express our conception of reality. Russell, an influential philosopher and logician, worked to move philosophy away from metaphysics and to base it, especially epistemology, on scientific logic. He sought to analyze what he believed was the logical structure of language. Ryle sought to develop a philosophical method, Analytical Philosophy, that clarified and analyzed the meanings conveyed by language.

On the European continent, interest in language analysis as a mode of philosophical thinking was sparked by the Vienna Circle, a group of philosophers who met in 1920s and 1930s Vienna. Claiming that philosophy should model itself after science, the Circle was hostile to the older, more traditional philosophies, such as Idealism and Realism, that were grounded on metaphysics. A leader in the Circle was Moritz Schlick (1882–1936), who developed *Logical Empiricism*, an effort to apply the scientific method to philosophical issues. Schlick's work, an intense critical analysis of the language used by philosophers, sought to detect their faulty definitions and misuse of terms. Ludwig Wittgenstein (1889–1951) was an important member of the Circle who left his native Austria to teach at Cambridge University in the United Kingdom.[1] Wittgenstein's *Tractatus Logico-philosophicus* (1922) was a significant book that stimulated the field of language analysis called *Logical Positivism*. Wittgenstein used the language in which scientific propositions are stated to analyze ordinary discourse. He concluded that meaningful statements are either logically true, as in the case of mathematics, or can be verified empirically—tested scientifically—in experience.[2]

Positivism had been developed earlier by Auguste Comte (1798–1857), a French social reformer who argued that the truth of knowledge claims must be validated by testing them according to the scientific method. The Logical Positivists asserted that only statements that could be verified empirically were candidates for meaning; those that could not be so verified, while they might have meaning for their speaker, were meaningless to others. Logical analysis was a means of reducing statements to the point where they could be tested empirically. The test of empirical verification meant that metaphysical and religious statements were incapable of being proved either true or false since they rested on what their adherents called the irreducible.

Some philosophers of education in the United States, Canada, and Australia eagerly accepted Philosophical Analysis, which virtually dominated the field in the 1960s and 1970s. They found the Analytical approach to be especially useful in clarifying the often jargon-laden and ambiguous language used in the field of Education that borrowed heavily from the social sciences of anthropology, sociology, and psychology. They also sought to unload the often popular homiletic preachments about "educating the whole child" and "learning by doing" that abounded in Education texts.

How Analysis Works

Analysis is done based on the concept that some of our language statements are immediately meaningful because of their inner logic, or have the possibility of being made meaningful if they can be stated in empirical terms that can be verified and tested. However, other parts of our language are emotional, poetic, or subjective, and are meaningful only to the person who voices them. Emotive language may express a belief or a value preference—a like or dislike—that is personal and interior to the individual, but may not be understood by others.

Analysis operates according to the premise that if our language is not immediately and overtly clear and meaningful, we can make it so by reducing it into smaller parts that are more direct, simple, and empirical. To test the meaning of language empirically means that we can state it in terms that are publicly observable and convey the same meaning to everyone, in much the same way that a chemical formula, such as "H_2O = Water" means the same thing to everyone.

WHY STUDY PHILOSOPHICAL ANALYSIS?

Philosophical Analysis represents a major shift in how philosophers do their work. It was a significant historical shift in thinking and writing about philosophy, and moved the emphasis from metaphysical debate to the analysis of philosophical and ordinary language.

Philosophical Analysis is a useful tool in helping to decode, unload, and decipher the language used both in our ordinary discourse as individuals, citizens, and consumers of information, and our professional discourse as educators. We are constantly bombarded by information from radio, television, newspapers, the Internet, colleagues, politicians, and experts (some of whom are our professors). Today, much of the information we receive, especially advertising, is delivered in "sound bites," "infomercials," "factoids," and "courtesy calls," via the telephone, World Wide Web, and television. What is the real meaning of these snippets of information? Do they really contain valid knowledge? In our ordinary life, we need to be able to unload, unpack, and critically assess the claims made by commentators, preachers, politicians, self-help gurus, drug companies, and advertisers.

In our professional life as teachers, we constantly encounter old bromides such as "educate the whole child" and "I teach children, not subjects," and new catch phrases such as "effective schools," "zero tolerance," "relevant education," "engaged learning," that promise to solve the nation's educational problems quickly and efficiently. Many of these educational promises are conveyed in language that is promising but also vague and ambiguous. While noble and high-sounding, they are often a kind of preachment or a political statement of somebody's good intentions or ideological preferences. Philosophical Analysis offers a way to determine if these educational statements are really meaningful and can be used to guide us as professional educators.

PHILOSOPHICAL ANALYSIS AS A PHILOSOPHY OF EDUCATION

Metaphysics

Analytical philosophers are not concerned with metaphysics, which they regard as purely speculative and lacking the prospect of being verified empirically. The Idealist statement, "reality is spiritual or mental" and the Existentialist statement, "existence precedes essence," for example, cannot be tested empirically. Analysts would regard them as statements expressing faith commitments, or personal emotive statements about how we would prefer reality to be. With Analysis, then, we turn away from metaphysics and deal with the meaning of our concepts, as expressed in ordinary or scientific and professional language.

Epistemology

As indicated, with Philosophical Analysis, the purpose of philosophizing is to establish and clarify language. It is not to make claims, as done by the speculative philosophies, about the nature of reality. Neither are Philosophical Analysts concerned about theories of knowledge that are speculative. They are concerned about the meaning of our language, which can be differentiated into three kinds of statements: analytical, synthetic, and emotive.

Analytical Statements.   An analytical statement is true by its own internal logical definition, by virtue of the terms it contains. In an Analytic sentence, the predicate is contained in the subject. Thus, the sentence, "All men are male human beings" is analytical because the subject "men" contains the meaning of the predicate, "male human beings." We can simply reverse the sentence to "All male human beings are men," which is also analytical. Many of our mathematical propositions are analytical. Consider the important arithmetical proposition, $1 + 1 = 2$, which is foundational to knowledge of mathematics. Note that the meaning of the predicate is contained in the subject, and vice versa. In these statements, the concepts are logically meaningful. However, they do not tell us anything we did not already know when we stated the subject. We already know that 2 is the same as 1+1 and are merely affirming our knowledge commitment when we so state it.

At this point, you might say, "So what? Why waste my time with something that is so obvious that I have known it since I learned to talk?" Let's explore the topic of Analytic statements to identify some instances of how frequently we use false analytical statements in a vague and confused way in our language. For example, consider the Idealist statement, "Human history is the story of the unfolding of the Absolute Idea." Although this statement appears to be analytical, is it really such? It is not logically analytical. What does the "unfolding of the Absolute Idea" really mean? The predicate cannot be verified and if reversed with the subject it is not really the same. What we are really stating here is our emotional preference—I wish human history were the unfolding of an absolute spiritual reality—or our faith commitment that human history is the unfolding of the Absolute Idea.

Another example is the statement, "Knowledge is power." Although we can further define the terms "knowledge" and "power," they are not the same. They represent a belief commitment, rather than a logically meaningful statement.

Let's take another example of a sentence that masquerades as analytic. "Portfolio use is authentic assessment in the classroom." Is "portfolio use" the same as "authentic assessment"? The answer is no. The subject, "portfolio use," is not the same as "authentic assessment." In fact, the adjective, "authentic" is an emotional word, a political word, that states our commitment to use portfolios.

Synthetic Statements.   A synthetic statement, a sentence in which the predicate is not included in the subject and that can be empirically verified by an observable public test, is also a candidate for meaningful discourse. Synthetic statements such as "Martin Maybury weighs 180 pounds" may be verified immediately by weighing Martin on an accurate scale. Or the statement, "The Mississippi River is 2,470 miles long" again can be immediately verified by measuring the length of the river from its source in its headwaters in Minnesota to its terminus in the Gulf of Mexico.

There are other kinds of synthetic statements, however, that are not immediately verifiable but need to be reduced to terms that will render them so. Consider the statement, "Post-secondary education is a 'gendered experience' that is not only manifestly different for women but may also be structured toward masculine rather than feminine intellectual orientations and learning styles." We can immediately begin to unpack the terminology and reduce it to simpler terms such as "College and university education is different for women and may be more favorably organized for the ways in which men, rather than women, learn." However, we still don't know if the statement is true until it is tested empirically. We would need to define the terms "post-secondary education," "gendered experience," "manifestly different," "for women," "structured for masculine" "feminine intellectual orientations," and "learning styles." Once these terms are made verifiable, we can test them or can gather data and information from other researchers to test them.[3]

Or consider President George W. Bush's challenge that "no child be left behind," used to promote his administration's educational legislation. The phrase appears to be simple, clear, and dramatic. The "no child" subject is empirically self-evident, but what does "be left behind" mean? It is a candidate for meaning, if it can be verified. It needs to be reduced into measurable terms. We get an idea of what "left behind" means as we study the Education Law of 2001 which requires states to administer the National Assessment of Educational Progress test every two years to students in the fourth through eighth grades, to serve as an indicator of student achievement in a particular state and its school districts. Test results would then be used as criteria to allocate federal funding for districts in need of academic improvement. We can see that "left behind" really means "as determined by standardized test results."

Emotive Statements.   While communication can consist of analytical and synthetic statements, our language is also full of emotive statements by which we convey our feelings of hope, joy, sorrow, pain, love, hate, likes, and dislikes. These feelings can be expressed by statements such as "I love Mary," "Christmas is a time for joy," "All we have to fear is fear itself." While these are important feelings in the range of human experience and expression, the meaning is exclusively ours and cannot be shared in the same way with others. Other people may also claim to experience these feelings, but we have no way of knowing if they are like our sentiments. Philosophical Analysts do not deny the importance of these statements to the persons who make them, nor do they minimize the role of art, religion, drama, music, and poetry in our lives as means of human expression, recreation, and enjoyment. However, they advise us to know what kind of language we are using and to be able to distinguish meaningful and verifiable statements from those that are not. They warn us that when emotive statements masquerade as empirically verifiable statements they can be misleading and sometimes even dangerous.

Axiology

The Analytic philosophers seek to use language analysis to clearly separate the language that deals with fact from that which deals with values. They are especially concerned with clarifying sentimental or jargon-filled terms that confuse facts with values. Facts are those expressed in two meaningful kinds of statements: analytical and synthetic. Values are conveyed by emotive statements that express preferences. While the Analytic philosophers appreciate the importance of values and our value beliefs and actions, they do not consider it their function as philosophers, to advise others on life's ethical and moral issues. G. E. Moore, for example, refuted metaphysical philosophy's attempts to base values on what was claimed to be universal and eternal relations between humans and the universe. Values, he claimed, were emotional and signified the person's approval or disapproval of some action.

Logic

Analysts tend to believe that it is possible to find a logical structure to language and that this logic can be used as a tool to clarify ambiguous statements and to make them meaningful. Some analysts order this logical structure into symbols, or try to express it mathematically. Analytical statements, which are logically true, are tautological in that the terms are true and reversible. The validity of synthetic statements can be tested by using empirical methods that are inductive. Emotive statements expressing personal preferences, however, are not subject to logical testing. When so viewed, the task of philosophy is to formulate the logical rules underlying language usage.

PHILOSOPHICAL ANALYSIS'S EDUCATIONAL IMPLICATIONS

Philosophical Analysis does not attempt to formulate the purposes of education or to prescribe the function of the school. It does seek to devise new modes of curriculum and instruction. Using analysis, it seeks to clarify the language used in education.

There are several reasons why the language used by educators is often ambiguous and vague. In their origins, educational institutions were often sponsored and supported by religious groups and denominations. A typical form of teaching in churches is the sermon or homily, which exhorts people to follow the doctrines and teachings of the church. Much homiletic language takes the form of analogies, parables, and exhortations that relate to values, and to ethical and moral prescriptions and proscriptions. Often, emotive statements are presented as if they were factual analytical or synthetic statements. Though public schools in the United States no longer are used for religious formation, the language of exhortation remains a part of education.

Public education in the United States is political. It is a responsibility and function of the school districts established within each state. It relates to how American children are socialized politically to become citizens. Almost every local district's statement of philosophy will cite "good citizenship" as a goal. What makes a "good citizen," however, is often ambiguous. Does it mean performing patriotic rituals or does it mean to think critically about civic decisions? Many statements about the purpose of education, including some emanating from professional educators, are based on particular ideological agendas whose goals may be hidden. Some reflect a conservative agenda for perpetuating the social, economic, and political status quo; others may reflect a radical agenda for dramatically changing the social, political, and economic order.

Education as an interdisciplinary field borrows heavily from the social sciences, especially psychology and sociology. In their development from social studies to social sciences, these fields created scientific terminology that often contains considerable professional jargon. These highly specialized terms need to be unpacked in order for them to become meaningful.

To illustrate the analysis of educational assertions, we might consider the following kinds of statements about: (1) philosophical and ideological policy related to setting goals and objectives; (2) the purpose of schools; (3) curriculum and instruction; and (4) teacher talk in the classroom.

Philosophical and Ideological Policy Statements

In the nineteenth century, official government policy was directed to assimilate Native Americans into the dominant culture. Consider the following statement as an expression of this policy about the education of Native Americans: "The kind of education they are in need of is one that will habituate them to the customs and advantages of a civilized life, . . . and at the same time cause them to look with feelings of repugnance on their native state."[4] This policy statement at first glance appears to be synthetic, but upon analysis it is an emotive one. It is an ideological exhortation to undertake a policy designed to impose the dominant white culture, which the speaker has determined is "civilized," upon the Native Americans, to encourage them to abandon their own culture.

An editorial, "Casting out bad teachers" in the *Chicago Tribune*, argued that school principals should take a leadership initiative in removing incompetent teachers and not allow them to hide behind tenure laws. The editorialist contended that it is easy to know who the good and bad teachers are. Indeed, students are able to separate competent from "lousy" teachers. The editorial stated: "The system of how we protect mediocrity in teaching has gotten so calcified and thick it's no longer possible to see through it."[5] Here the editorialist is using a metaphor to say that the system's density blocks a clear vision into its inner workings. Though using metaphorical language, the editorialist is calling for a change in the regulations governing tenure and teacher remediation.

The Purpose of Schools

Analysts do not seek to prescribe the purpose and role of schools. Rather, they seek to apply the tools of analysis to what others have to say about the purpose of schools.

In discussing the schools' role in teaching acceptance and respect for cultural diversity, Baruth and Manning state: "Schools, however, must do more than pay lip service—the curriculum must reflect diversity, and learning materials must show culturally diverse people in positive and meaningful roles."[6] (Our purpose in using this statement is not to argue for or against multiculturalism in the curriculum, but rather to analyze this statement that proposes a role for schools.) Although the statement appears to be synthetic and subject to empirical verification, a closer examination shows that the authors value diversity and want the school curriculum to reflect their commitment to multiculturalism. Several terms require further analysis, such as "more than lip service." The term is a colloquialism that means more than it says. It means that political pronouncements that endorse multiculturalism but do not implement it are inadequate and insufficient in infusing multiculturalism into the curriculum. The use of "must" is strongly imperative and is a value-laden term encouraging quick action. The phrase "positive and meaningful roles" also needs further reduction to examine what constitutes a positive and meaningful role.

Curriculum and Instruction

John Goodlad's *A Place Called School: Prospects for the Future* was a well-received study that proposed initiatives for reforming schools on a school-by-school basis. Regarding classroom instruction, Goodlad advised, "By finding more efficient ways to handle routines and by learning to manage the classroom with a minimum of time lost to social activity and controlling students' behavior, teachers can increase the amount of time spent on learning and, presumably, enhance achievement."[7] Here, we have an example of a synthetic statement that argues that more time spent on direct instruction is likely to result in higher student achievement. Even with such a seemingly obvious statement, we can use analysis to clarify its meaning. Key questions to be asked are: What are "more efficient ways"? "What are "routines"? How can we measure and minimize time lost "to social activity and controlling students' behavior"? Most importantly, how can we verify and determine that an increase in time spent on instruction will lead to higher student achievement?

Teacher Talk

Consider the following quotation from a teacher named Toni: "Those are the days that I get pleasantly surprised because all of sudden there's a flow. You and the children are moving together toward the common vision. We're just all on the same mind set, all flowing together. There's just a sense of collaboration. And that's the neatest feeling every time."[8]

What kind of ideas are conveyed by these sentences? Although they appear to be synthetic, they are highly emotive. What is the meaning of "flow," "common vision," and "same mind set"? Can these terms be empirically verified so that they convey meaning to others? Or, are they merely a preferential statement of what Toni likes?

■ ■ ■ ■ ■

GEORGE F. KNELLER, "THE TASK OF CLARIFICATION"

In this selection, Kneller discusses why so much of the language used in education is ambiguous and suggests what we might do to clarify it.

1. Why does Kneller believe that it is necessary to analyze the language of educational discourse?

2. Why are the meanings of words generally used in education often ambiguous?

3. Kneller provides a discussion of the analysis of the term, "adjustment." Clarify the meaning of the currently significant term, "standards." What are standards and what do they mean?

THE TASK OF CLARIFICATION

The aim of analysis is to clarify our thinking about education by examining the logical features of the expressions and the arguments in which this thinking is expressed. According to the analytic philosopher, these features often pass unnoticed because they are not exhibited in the grammatical form of what is said. This lack of awareness sows weakness and confusion in educational thought. Some educators pursue the apparent logic of their words and, in so doing, lose the intended logic of their ideas. Others keep the logic of their ideas but drive it into words that misrepresent it. Some communicate meanings they never intended; others fail to communicate those they did intend. Faulty communication exacerbates educational disputes, diverting attention from genuine issues to differences that spring from the misuse or misunderstanding of words. Being unaware of the informal logic of the expressions they use, educators are divided by the very language with which they seek to communicate.

It follows that, if we are to understand the problems, policies, and concepts of education, we must first examine carefully the language of educational discourse. The informal analyst does not propose that we purify this language, let alone replace it. His sole stipulation is that we learn to use language properly, which means respecting the informal logic of words and expressions. To bring this logic to light, we must investigate the different possible uses of words and expressions, in education and elsewhere, since the meaning of a word or phrase, and hence the inferences we can draw with its help, varies according to context. When we know the true possibilities of language, we shall begin to communicate effectively. Effective communication may not guarantee mutual agreement, but it does guarantee mutual understanding.

Some of education's fundamental ideas—which themselves are foci of educational discussion and presuppositions of many other educational ideas—are dominant concepts of great generality in a number of realms of discourse, such as philosophy, psychology, and general life. They include 'knowing,' 'thinking,' 'understanding,' and 'explaining.' When examining them, the educator must cast the net of analysis wide enough to take in their many different uses and neutralize their great ambiguity. In the process he can rely on the analyses already made of these concepts by professional analytic philosophers. Philosophers of education are indebted, for example, to Gilbert Ryle's studies of mental-conduct concepts in *The Concept of Mind*. Other concepts are germane to education itself, such as 'subject matter,' 'mastery,' 'readiness,' 'mental discipline,' 'maturity,' and 'character training.' These may be narrower in scope than the former, but as a rule they have not been analyzed by professional philosophers. Moreover, they are not only topics of theoretical debate but also the fiercely defended justifications of many practical school policies; this fact alone adds to the difficulty of analyzing them.

There is a dual reason for the ambiguity of educational discourse, namely that the study of education draws heavily on ideas in general currency as well as on the ideas emerging from a range of related disciplines. As a result, not a few educational expressions carry a number of meanings corresponding to the different spheres in which these expressions are used, and, in consequence, are highly equivocal. Take, for example, the concept of 'adjustment,' which is used, among other places, in general life, in psychology, and in education. Two uses may be distinguished here: (1) the common use, as in "X is adjusting to Y"; and (2) its use, in certain psychological theories of adjustment. In ordinary life we use 'adjust' to mean, among other things, "bring into proper relations." Thus, when we say, "John is adjusting to the school," we mean that he has solved the necessary problems in order to bring himself into proper relations with the school. When we disagree about what

proper relations are, we are really disagreeing about what is "proper" and hence about values.

Psychologists tend to use the concept of adjustment differently. C. J. B. Macmillan considers the term as it is used by Laurence E. Shaffer and Edward J. Shoben, Jr. in their introductory textbook, *The Psychology of Adjustment* (Houghton Mifflin, 1956). The authors state that "life is a series of. . . sequences in which needs are aroused and then satisfied," that "adjustment means the reduction or satisfaction of drives," and that "behaviors are adjustive because they reduce tensions."

As used in ordinary language, the concept of adjustment differentiates actions by which a person enters into proper relations with his environment from actions by which he retreats or somehow changes it. The psychological concept makes no such distinction; it states that adjustment is "tension reduction." In this sense all behavior amounts to adjustment since all behavior is said to be a response to a stimulus or drive. According to this usage, says Macmillan, to adjust is simply to behave. Such a definition is valueless, he says, because it excludes the possibility of nonadjustment. When used by educators who do not distinguish this definition from the customary sense of adjustment, it creates confusion both in educational theory and classroom practice.

None of these difficulties indicates that the concept of adjustment is educationally vacuous but rather, a problem exists that can be clarified (though not necessarily solved) by means of philosophic analysis. The analysis, says Macmillan, will have three phases: (1) a rigorous investigation of the various possible meanings of the concept of adjustment; (2) a definition of one or more precise meanings applicable to the term as it is used in education; (3) an examination of the implications of these meanings for various educational theories now using this concept.

CONCLUSION

In this chapter we examined Philosophical or Linguistic Analysis as it applies to the philosophy of education. We dealt with the meaning of language by considering analytic, synthetic, and emotive statements. We focused on the language used in education to indicate areas of confusion and obscurity. Philosophical Analysis is a useful tool that can be used to analyze ordinary language as well as language used in specialized areas such as professional education.

DISCUSSION QUESTIONS

1. What are the uses of Linguistic Analysis in educational situations?
2. Define and provide examples of analytical, synthetic, and emotive statements.
3. Why is so much of the language related to educational goals subject to differing interpretations?
4. Analyze the meaning of the following: "authentic assessment," "excellence in education," "let no child be left behind," "educating the whole child," and "education that makes a difference."
5. In your clinical experience, do you find instances in which well-meaning people create misunderstandings with the language they use to communicate with each other?

INQUIRY AND RESEARCH PROJECTS

1. Examine a chapter of a book used in teacher education. Select several key statements and analyze them. Try to establish their meaning.
2. As a class exercise, have members of the class write their own definitions of teaching. Provide copies of these definitions to the class and determine what they mean.
3. Kneller asserts that some words generally used in education have different uses. Conduct the following exercise in your class in philosophy of education. Have the members of the class write out their definitions of words such as "knowing, learning, thinking, understanding, and explaining." Then determine if the definitions agree or disagree. Try to develop some common definitions of these terms that are meaningful to the group.
4. Record several commercials from radio or television programs. Determine if the statements used are analytical, synthetic, or emotive.

INTERNET RESOURCES

For discussions of the Philosophy of Language, access
http://dmoz.org/Society/Philosophy/Philosophy_of_Language/Pragmatics/ Discourse_Analysis

The analysis of Ordinary Language is examined at
www.philosophypages.com/hy/6u.htm

For the examination of the language of educational issues, contact
http://eric-web.tc.columbia.edu/monographs/til7-issues.html

SUGGESTIONS FOR FURTHER READING

Austin, David, ed. *Philosophical Analysis: A Defense by Example*. Boston: Kluwer Academic Publishers, 1988.

Buzaglo, Meir. *The Logic of Concept Expansion*. New York: Cambridge University Press, 2002.

Charlton, William. *The Analytic Ambition: An Introduction to Philosophy*. Cambridge, MA: Blackwell, 1991.

Cohen, L. Jonathan. *The Dialogue of Reason: An Analysis of Analytical Philosophy*. New York: Oxford University Press, 1986.

Davis, Wayne A. *Meaning, Expression, and Thought*. New York: Cambridge University Press, 2002.

Dummett, Michael A. E. *Origins of Analytical Philosophy*. New York: Cambridge University Press, 1994.

Ebbs, Gary. *Rule Following and Realism*. Cambridge, MA: Harvard University Press, 1997.

Edmonds, David, and Eidinow, John. *Wittgenstein's Poker: The Story of a Ten-Minute Argument Between Two Great Philosophers*. New York: Harper-Collins Publishers, 2001.

Grayling, A. C. *Wittgenstein: A Very Short Introduction*. Oxford, UK: Oxford University Press, 1996.

Hutchinson, Brian. *G. E. Moore's Ethical Theory: Resistance and Reconciliation*. New York: Cambridge University Press, 2001.

Kaminsky, James S. *A New History of Educational Philosophy*. Westport, CT: Greenwood Press, 1993.

Klagge, James C., ed. *Wittgenstein: Biography and Philosophy*. New York: Cambridge University Press, 2001.

Ostrow, Matthew B. *Wittgenstein's Tractatus: A Dialectical Interpretation*. New York: Cambridge University Press, 2001.

Parikh, Prashant. *The Use of Language*. Chicago: University of Chicago Press, 2001.

Perloff, Marjorie. *Wittgenstein's Ladder: Poetic Language and the Strangeness of the Ordinary*. Chicago: University of Chicago Press, 1996.

Soames, Scott. *Philosophical Analysis in the Twentieth Century: The Age of Meaning*. Princeton, NJ: Princeton University Press, 2003.

Soames, Scott. *Philosophical Analysis in the Twentieth Century: The Dawn of Analysis*. Princeton, NJ: Princeton University Press, 2003.

Sorenson, Roy A. *Pseudo-Problems: How Analytical Philosophy Gets Done*. New York: Routledge, 1993.

Wittgenstein, Ludwig. *Culture and Value*. Chicago: University of Chicago Press, 1980.

NOTES

1. For a biography of Wittgenstein, see James C. Klagge, ed., *Wittgenstein: Biography and Philosophy* (New York: Cambridge University Press, 2001). For a very lively and entertaining book on disagreements between two leading philosophers, Wittgenstein and Karl Popper, see David Edmonds and John Eidinow, *Wittgenstein's Poker: The Story of a Ten-Minute Argument Between Two Great Philosophers* (New York: Harper-Collins Publishers, 2001).

2. A clear discussion of Wittgenstein's philosophy is provided in A. C. Grayling, *Wittgenstein: A Very Short Introduction* (Oxford, UK: Oxford University Press, 1996).

3. The quotations are from an article, "Prime Numbers" in *The Chronicle of Higher Education*, (December 21, 2001), p. A7 which discussed a report, "How Much Do Students Learn in College," whose primary author was Lamont A. Flowers.

4. George Wilson, "How Shall the American Savage Be Civilized?" *Atlantic Monthly* (November 1882), p. 604, as quoted in David W. Adams, *Education for Extinction: American Indians and the Boarding School Experience, 1875–1928* (Lawrence, KS: University Press of Kansas, 1995), p. 21.

5. "Casting out bad teachers," *Chicago Tribune*, Section 1 (December 23, 2001), p. 18.

6. Leroy G. Baruth and M. Lee Manning, *Multicultural Education of Children and Adolescents* (Needham Heights, MA: Allyn and Bacon, 1992), p. xiii.

7. John I. Goodlad, *A Place Called School: Prospects for the Future* (New York: McGraw-Hill Book Co., 1984), p. 101.

8. Mari E. Koerner, "Teachers' Images: Reflections of Themselves," in William H. Schubert and William C. Ayers, ed., *Teacher Lore: Learning From Our Own Experience* (New York: Longman, 1992), p. 49.

CHAPTER EIGHT

POSTMODERNISM

In Chapter 8 we will discuss Postmodernism, an influential contemporary philosophy that challenges the more traditional philosophies, especially those based on metaphysics. We will define Postmodernism, situate it as a philosophical movement, identify and examine its major premises, and draws out its implications for education.

DEFINING POSTMODERNISM

To define postmodernism, we need to examine the words, *post* and *modernism*. The word *post* has several meanings, each of which can be applied to this philosophy. As a prefix, post means coming after, later, or following in time. So the obvious meaning in this context is after or following the modern period of history. Post used as a noun refers to a timber that is used to support a structure; posts also can refer to the timbers or poles that mark a boundary. As we shall see later in the chapter, Postmodernists are inclined to reject the existing theoretical posts that are used to support philosophical structures; they also want to pull down the fences or boundaries that they believe separate fields of thought or subjects from each other.

To understand the Postmodernist use of *modern*, we need to go beyond its common usage as up to date, current, or contemporary and think about it in terms of periodization of history. In itself, periodization—determining when an historical epoch or period began and ended—is always difficult since historical change does not occur with abrupt starts and stops but often occurs gradually and unevenly. Further, historical periods are often identified in hindsight many years after they have occurred. Postmodernists, however, label the contemporary period in history as the postmodern era.

In Western history, the modern period's onset is usually cited as beginning with the coming of the Renaissance around 1500 A.D. and then continuing onward. Among some theorists, especially in literature and philosophy, the modern period's defining characteristics originated during the Eighteenth-Century Enlightenment, the "Age of Reason," and then continued with scientific discovery, exploration, industrialism, imperialism, the World Wars, the nuclear era, and the Cold War. In the Postmodernist critique, however, the Enlightenment established the following contours of modernity:

- Human reason can discover how the universe, nature, and society function.
- The scientific method, relying on empirical discovery and verification, is held to be the surest guide, the most rational means, of finding the truth.
- Science can discover natural laws that yield rational explanations of reality and provide prescriptive guidelines for improving human life and society.

For those following the Postmodernist perspective, the Enlightenment ideology, though proclaiming "liberty, equality, and fraternity," in fact, became the dominant rationale for a new capitalist ruling class, an exploitative class system, and a racist imperialism. The scientific innovations spawned by the Enlightenment led to the nineteenth-century industrial revolution in which science, applied to engineering, was used to invent new techniques of exploiting natural resources and mass-producing goods. Postmodernists believe we are now in the post-industrial era, in which the factory assembly modes of production have been replaced by a new era—the information age of high technology and services. For them, the modern era ended in the latter half of the twentieth century.

Postmodernism can be illustrated by contrasting it with the opposing ideology of modernization. C. E. Black's comparative study of modernization provides an example of the modernist thinking that Postmodernists resolutely oppose. Predicting that the future would be determined by ongoing modernization, Black defined modernization "as the process by which historically evolved institutions are adapted to the rapidly changing functions that reflect the unprecedented increase in man's knowledge, permitting control over his environment, that accompanied the scientific revolution."[1] According to Black, modernization, which originated in Western Europe and the United States in the nineteenth and twentieth centuries, was being exported and implemented in societies throughout the world, causing a global transformation affecting all human relationships. Black predicted that the process of modernization would transform traditional, less technologically developed societies into modern ones. For Postmodernists, Black's definition and prediction of the global extension of modernizing tendencies represents what is wrong in modernization theory. It implies that one kind of experience, the modern, is destined to override and submerge all other varieties of human organization, especially those categorized as primitive, backward, or traditional. Further, it divides people into two groups: those who are modern and those who are not (and are, thus, marginalized). Modernization, including its contemporary form of globalization by multinational corporations, unleashes still more exploitation and marginalization in the world, and leads to modern societies disempowering those judged to be less modern.[2]

For Postmodernists, the Enlightenment version of reason was not a universal dictum as its proponents claimed, but was merely one rationale, constructed by the rising middle class, to justify its rebellion against and overthrow of the privilege and power of landed aristocrats and absolute monarchies. In turn, the middle classes used the canons, the texts, that expounded on the legitimacy of reason to rationalize their own ascendancy to power and subordination of other groups such as the industrial working class, Marx's proletariat. (Marxism is discussed in Chapter 13.) Black's concept of modernization masquerading as a universalizing global process, provided a theoretical rationale

■ ■ ■ ■ ■ ▬▬▬▬▬▬▬▬▬▬▬▬▬▬▬▬▬▬▬▬▬▬▬▬▬▬▬▬▬▬▬▬▬▬▬

POSTMODERNISM REJECTS:

1. Metaphysical philosophies' claims that there are universal and eternal truths and values.
2. Enlightenment ideology's claims that there is one method and approach to rationality.
3. Modernization's claims that it is the irresistible social and economic force of the future.

for the superiority of modernizers over those judged less modern. Modernization could be used to justify a new form of economic and cultural imperialism, taking the benefits of modernity to the less fortunate, traditional, and backward people of the world.

Canons as Rationales

In Postmodernist terms, we discussed the Enlightenment endorsement of reason as a class-constructed, time-bound rationale, rather than a universal and timeless principle. Modernization theory, too, can be seen as a rationale, constructed by the beneficiaries of industrialization and globalization, rather than as an irresistible historical force. Postmodernists refer to historically constructed rationales, such as reason and modernization, as canons. The claims to authority expressed in a canon have an interesting origin and the story of their development explains how canons are used to rationalize the possession of power by some and not others.

    In ancient Greece, a *canon* (kanon) was a measuring rod, a kind of yardstick. Measurements, based on the kanon, were held to be accurate in establishing the dimensions of something, especially landed property. By the Fourth Century, canon had taken on a broader and elevated meaning as a rule or a law. During the Middle Ages, canonical designated an authentic, religious, or scriptural text, officially approved by the Church. For example, the governing legal code of the Roman Catholic Church is referred to as canon law. Over time, a more general use of canon developed and can be used to refer to the great texts—the definitive and classic works—that have authority in a culture, a political and social order, an academic discipline, or a profession. For example, the books taught in the "great books" curriculum espoused by the Perennialists, are regarded as having a greater authority than other lesser books. (See Chapter 17 for a discussion of Perennialism.) In the former Soviet Union, Marxist–Leninism was the ideological canon of undisputed political authority. (For Marxism, see Chapter 13.) For Islamic fundamentalists, the Koran is the supreme religious text or canon; for Christians, it is the Bible.

    Questioning the authority of canons, Postmodernists challenge their validity and see them in limited terms as constructions made by a given group or class at a particular time in history, and not endowed with an enduring, universal authority. As mere historical pieces, canons can be analyzed, or deconstructed. In deconstructing a canon or text, Postmodernists ask a series of questions: What events and situations gave rise to the canon? Who gives a canon a privileged status in a culture or society? Who benefits from the existence and acceptance of a canon? Why do canons in a particular culture and society exclude underrepresented and marginalized people?

Postmodernists want to know and examine the criteria used to establish some, but not other, works as canons. They argue that the criteria for analyzing and appraising a canon is internal to the work. There is no legitimate external—spiritual, natural, or universal—criteria for giving a work a privileged authoritative status in a culture and society. Postmodernists conclude that canons are established and raised to authority by those who hold social, economic, political, and educational power, and are used to legitimize and sustain that power.

While the discussion of canons may seem overly theoretical, it is important in establishing policy and practices in society, politics, and education. If we think of the curriculum as a contested area, we can see how the construction and deconstruction of canons operates. There have been many arguments for and against a cultural core in education, especially in secondary and higher education. Many core requirements reflect the traditional canons of Western culture. Postmodernists challenge these canons as representing male-dominated, European-centered Western culture, which takes on an added capitalist dimension in the United States. They contend that these canons have no extrinsic value over any other work. It is time, they argue, that the works of underrepresented groups—African, Asian, Hispanic, and Native Americans; feminists; those in the "Third World;" and gays and lesbians—be included in the curriculum, even at the core, if a core still remains.

Othering, Subordinating, or Marginalizing

As we proceed with our discussion of Modernism and Postmodernism, we introduce the concepts of "othering," subordinating, or marginalizing. "Otherness" or othering, in this context, means setting up a dichotomy between the modern and the less than modern. Those who are modern like us are "with it," up to date, or current; others, such as those in less technologically developed countries or in urban slums are traditional or primitive. Terms such as "other," "primitive," "less technologically developed," and "non-Western," often found in the literatures (canons) of economics, political science, and education, upon analysis reveal a stereotypic view of society in which the alternatives to these terms are regarded as higher and better and those included in these categories as subordinate and at the margins of institutions and society. Often these concepts are conveyed in what purports to be scientifically objective literature but in reality is racist, classist, and sexist language constructed by the dominant group, especially by its spokespersons.[3]

SITUATING POSTMODERNISM

Rather than being a single system of philosophy like Idealism or Realism, Postmodernism is more an orientation or perspective. As an orientation, it includes individuals whose parent fields are sociology, anthropology, literature, art, architecture, and education, as well as philosophy. Sharing the Postmodernist perspective are some who work in such areas as feminist theory and multiculturalism. What unites these different voices is a shared antithesis to modernism and what it represents. As an antithesis, Postmodernism is iconoclastic in its break with the past and its dissection or deconstruction of claims to universality and objective certainty.

The early antecedents of Postmodernism are identified with the philosophers Nietzsche and Heidegger. Contemporary Postmodernism is associated with such theorists as Jacques Derrida and Michel Foucault.

Antecedents of Postmodernism

Friedrich Nietzsche (1844–1900), an iconoclastic German philosopher, attacked metaphysically based philosophies.[4] He dismissed the long-standing philosophical assumption that metaphysics was disinterested speculation into a universal structure of reality. Rather, Nietzsche reduced metaphysics to a human invention, a construction, that was a substitute for discarded ancient religious myths and the supernaturalism that provided a sense of certitude about an unchanging world beyond earthly experience. Metaphysicians—Idealists, Realists, and Thomists—invented, or constructed an unchanging other-world that is always good, true, and beautiful. (These philosophies are discussed in Chapters 2, 3, and 4.) Their cosmic invention provided a kind of philosophical tranquilizer for anxious people who could not accept the reality of a world that was incomplete, changing, and always in the ferment of becoming. Certain outstanding individuals, Nietzsche claimed—"the supermen"—accepted that they were living in an incomplete world and were responsible for making their own rules.[5] For Nietzsche, philosophy could not and did not explain an ultimate reality. Rather, philosophical statements were metaphors, perspectives, and rationales constructed by certain articulate individuals at a particular time in history. These philosophical statements should be analyzed for their genealogy—for the historical, psychological, economic, sociological, and educational situations in which they were made.[6]

Martin Heidegger (1899–1976), a German philosopher, was a leader in developing Existentialist Phenomenology. (Existentialist Phenomenology is examined in Chapter 6.) While Nietzsche conjured up a superman who created his own rules for life, Heidegger developed an Existentialist theory of the authentic person, who was self-defined and lived with the ever-present feelings of dread, disappearance, and the awareness of death as a consciously known inevitability. According to Existentialist Phenomenology, what is true for us is not found in some universal category such as Plato's Form of the Good. Rather, we make our own truths based on our intuitions, perceptions, and reflections that arise in our experience. Free from metaphysical antecedents, we are not placed in an existing reality but construct our own reality as it comes from our intuitions and experiences.

Derrida

Jacques Derrida (1930–), an Algerian-born French philosopher, is often identified as a major contributor to the contemporary Postmodernist perspective, especially to the version known as Poststructuralism. One of Derrida's important contributions to Postmodernism is his development of the method of deconstruction. Examining Western philosophy's origins in ancient Greece, Derrida finds that philosophers such as Plato and Aristotle and their later disciples embarked on a search for the general rational purposes they believed were inherent in, and ordered and governed, the universe. (Plato and Aristotle are discussed in Chapters 2 and 3.) Their belief in the existence of this rational principle, or *logos* in Greek, was based on their interpretation of how reality functioned.

Later philosophers continued to search for universal principles of rationality inherent in the universe itself. It was believed that the human being, by Aristotle's definition, possessed a reasoning mind that made it possible to find the *logi*, the rational principles, and act according to them.

To deconstruct *logos*, it is necessary to analyze its origins in the ancient Greek philosophical tradition and its continual replay in the history of Western philosophy. What is assumed to be the principle of rationality in the universe, according to Derrida, is not an objective reality but rather how philosophers represent it in their writings or texts. A text, as used by Derrida and the Postmodernists, may be, but is not necessarily, a work in print. While the philosophical works are inscripted, other texts may be an oral dialogue, a movie or a play, or some form of cultural representation. In educational terms, a text can be a curriculum guide, a video, or a book, including a textbook.

Despite continued attacks on metaphysics by the Pragmatists and by the Postmodernists, Derrida finds that metaphysical interpretations, the assumption that rational principles or *logi*, remain deeply embedded in Western culture. Indeed, meaning in Western cultures is *logo*-centric, centered in and often controlled by these inherited metaphysical principles.

Deconstruction is a method of getting inside the texts to explore different shades of meaning in addition to those designated as an officially sanctioned canon. Getting inside the text means to: (1) identify the *logo*-centric principles that it embodies; (2) trace the origin and development of the meanings conveyed, with special sensitivity to justification by appealing to the *logi*; (3) determine how the knowledge claims, meanings, and interpretations in the text affect our ideas, beliefs, and interpretations. The aim of deconstruction is not simply to engage in language analysis but to understand how texts, rather than reflecting metaphysical principles, are historically and culturally specific constructions that involve political power relationships. Recall that in Chapter 7 on Linguistic Analysis, the concern is to establish the meaning of a statement. For Postmodernists, the issue is not only establishing meaning, but examining when, how, and why the statement was made. Unlike the Analysts' insistence on using logical or empirical verification to establish the meaning of language, the Postmodernists are concerned with its nuances and emphases. They are concerned with particularizing the various meanings that different groups give to language.

Derrida believed that philosophers need to break free from the metaphysical search for an underlying universal rationality and cease attempting to construct colossal world views. Rather, they should embark on a rigorous analysis, a deconstruction, of the language used to legitimize the theoretical foundations for social, cultural, political, economic, and educational institutions. These supposed foundations are conveyed in discourses—oral and written narratives—that purport to explain reality and to justify allegiance to existing institutions and situations. What we must deal with is not reality, then, but how the authors, the originators, and users of the discourses view and interpret reality. Since interpretations reflect a particular person's experience, we need to examine how individuals and groups use language, arising from their experience, to construct meaning and to legitimize and justify their control of institutions.

For Postmodernists, the philosophical task is to deconstruct ideas about institutions and culture in order to uncover the rationale builder's underlying assumptions, presuppositions, and meanings. These rationales, often referred to as the foundations of culture, are expressed in the language of a text and assume the authority or special status of a canon. All discourse, philosophical, historical, and scientific, is presented in texts. A text, itself, is not reality but what an author may think is true and valuable. Deconstruction involves identifying and explaining the author's meaning, or version of reality, as well as what the reader brings to the text in terms of experience. This deconstruction of an author's intentions involves "unpacking" the author's assumptions and meanings as they are expressed by word choices, examples, metaphors, and puns.[7] In other words, philosophy involves an analysis of language as it is used in relationships; it is a socially charged study in grammar.[8]

For Derrida, the efforts to deconstruct language involve identifying and analyzing the differences in how people understand and use language. To deconstruct requires us to find the differences in meanings and relationships in the various voices engaged in discourse. The language used to express statements of any kind is constructed by shades of meaning, emphasis, accentuation, and nuance; the only means of interpreting these statements is to use still other words that enable us to compare and contrast the statement being deconstructed with other statements. Establishing meaning requires interpretation—using other words that tell us what it is and is not.[9] At the same time that the act of interpreting is taking place, there is a need to defer final results in establishing a central meaning due to the complexity, fluidity, and drift of language—how it is used at different times in different places.[10]

Foucault

Michel Foucault (1926–1984), a French social philosopher and historian, exerted a major shaping influence on Postmodernism as well as general scholarship about history, society, culture, politics, economics, and education. He argues that notions of "truth" originate in historical contexts and create relationships of power in cultures, institutions, and social systems. To examine Foucault's complex and often opaque philosophy, we begin with three of his major working premises: (1) the relationship of "truth" and power; (2) "regimes of truth," and (3) the use of discourse.

Like Derrida, Foucault rejects the possibility of universal truth, discoverable by metaphysical speculation. Truth does not come from the insightful glimpse into the universe about which metaphysicians speculate. Justice does not come from the all-knowing judgments of Plato's philosopher–kings; nor, is it found in the impartial decisions made by John Stuart Mill's disinterested citizens. (Plato's philosopher–king is discussed in Chapter 2 and Mill's disinterested citizen in Chapter 11.)

Joining other Postmodern philosophers, Foucault rejects the Enlightenment's enthronement of reason, which claims that rational individuals, using the scientific method, can discover truth as an objective body of knowledge. He also discounts the Enlightenment premise that this kind of objective knowledge is open to all and that it can fairly and equitably benefit all people.[11]

The various social and behavioral sciences that originated in the Enlightenment and were developed in the modern period—sociology, economics, anthropology, psychology—profess to be objective, empirical, and scientific ways of describing and examining human behavior. From this professedly objective or neutral description, social scientists have developed prescriptions or guidelines that tell how "normal," socially sound, good citizens—men, women, children—should behave. The social sciences categorize people into types and roles based on a standard of the normal; these lead to norms or rules of behavior. Just as there are approved norms, there are also patterns of deviant behavior. Depending on their degree of deviancy, individuals in these categories can be remediated or reeducated, and if need be institutionalized in asylums and prisons. The process of empirically based standard setting, characteristic of the modern era, is a way in which one group categorizes, manipulates, and exercises power over others. The Enlightenment orientation, especially as it claims to be scientifically objective, merely represents the discourse used by a regime of truth.

Foucault examines how claims of possessing the "truth" creates relationships of power in specific contexts. Using the term "truth" as a title to ownership of knowledge that certain individuals and groups claim to possess, he does not argue that some universal truth exists that is superior to the version a particular group claims to know. Neither does he assert that some individuals and groups have more truth, or a clearer vision of truth, than others. Rather, all persons and groups have some version of truth that gives them power in their relationships with others. At certain historic periods and places, however, the truth–power formula favors, or empowers, some groups over others. These truth–power relationships produce "regimes of truth," the ideologies, institutions, and practices by which people control, regulate, govern, and even define, each other. Foucault's exegesis examines social, political, economic, and educational policies and practices—the exercises of power—based on assumptions that those who hold and use power have a right to do so because they know or possess some truth, unknown to others. Discourses, developing "in the contexts of specific historically constituted power relations," use the claim to possess truth to shape attitudes and behaviors of people living in that context. The language used in these discourses is chosen in order to legitimate the exercise of power enjoyed by those who control a regime of truth.[12]

We can illustrate the relationship of truth and power by looking briefly at the kind of discourse used in the standards movement in education. The discourse states as truth that: (1) all children have a right to an education that is excellent and no child should be left behind; (2) an excellent education is one in which students achieve academically; (3) academic achievement can be measured fairly and objectively through the use of standardized tests; (4) these tests will identify the students who are achieving and those who are being left behind; (5) the tests will identify the schools that have a high record of academic success as well as those whose students fail; (5) schools with high failure rates can be remediated; (6) if the remediation is unsuccessful, students in these schools can transfer to schools with higher test results.

Using Foucault's mode of analysis, we can determine the truth–power relationship that operates in the discourse about standardized tests as measures of academic achievement. The analysis begins with political claims, based on a democratic ideology that children have a right to an excellent education. The general claim quickly shifts, however, to an assertion that standardized tests provide objective evidence about the quality of that excellence as determined by successful mastery of certain academic skills and subjects. Now the knowledge claim begins to relate to power relationships: Who is mandating the testing? Who is making up the test? Who is interpreting the test results? How will be results be used? What are the roles of politicians, parents, teachers, and students in the process of setting standards and using tests to verify if they have been met?

Foucault examines the truth–power relationship in specific contexts, establishing what he calls a "genealogy" of how the techniques of power originate and are used as statements of legitimacy and control. Foucault is not arguing for a utopia in which power relationships are absent. Rather, he is saying that both past and contemporary societies exhibit truth–power relationships that develop definitions of right and wrong, normalcy and deviancy, and that to recognize this reality better prepares us to deal with it. He advises that the relationship between truth and power is always present in social contexts, including educational ones. In particular, Foucault warns us to be wary of those who claim to know universal truth, claim to be altruistic in its application, and justify their actions based on universal moral and ethical principles. Instead of one truth that is universally manifested, there are many claims to truth found in all societies and in all situations. These multiple discourses represent multiple regimes of truth. Discourses can justify one group's claim to truth but also can be used by another group to resist it.[13] The relationship of truth to power is slippery and shifting, with some group's claims ascendant and the other's suppressed or inarticulated. The interplay of discourses, each representing a truth claimed by a particular group, can be examined. Applying analysis to discourse allows us to locate the relationship of knowledge and power in a given society at a given time. Perhaps those who are currently marginalized can use their insights to resist and liberate themselves from social control by dominant groups. Analysis of the truth–power relationship might be used to identify examples that are negative and pernicious and others that carry possibilities of liberation. It may also help us avoid the dogmatism of those who claim to know it all.

WHY STUDY POSTMODERNISM?

Postmodernism is one of the leading contemporary philosophical orientations. It is especially influential in academic fields such as literary criticism and educational foundations. In education, it is related to Liberation Pedagogy, discussed in Chapter 14, and Critical Theory, discussed in Chapter 19. Beyond these fields, Postmodernism has penetrated into the general vocabulary. Postmodernist influences can be found in such related movements as Poststructuralism and Postindustrialism. The study of Postmodernism acquaints us with an influential philosophical persuasion and helps in locating and interpreting one of the currently influential positions in education.

POSTMODERNISM AS A PHILOSOPHY OF EDUCATION

In the next section, we examine how Postmodernism can be considered in relationship to the major areas in philosophy: metaphysics, epistemology, axiology, and logic.

Metaphysics

Postmodernists regard many philosophical texts of the past, such as Plato's *Republic*, Aristotle's *Nichomaechean Ethics*, and Aquinas' *Summa Theologiae* to be metanarratives, the expositions of spokespersons for favored groups, rather than universal metaphysical explanations of reality and values. (For discussions of these works, see Chapters 2, 3, and 4.) They reject the grand philosophical systems purported to explain reality as an architecture of the universe, and the metaphysical assumption that an ultimate ground of being, a transcendent cosmic reality, exists beyond and above the physical world. For Postmodernists, traditional philosophical systems, resting on metaphysical foundations, are not explanations of ultimate reality. They are rather the discourses—the written texts—produced by the intellectuals of a given period of history that rationalized and explained the knowledge that gave power to some, but denied it to others. Metaphysics, they contend, imposed constraints from which, with its demise, we are well liberated.[14]

Postmodernism was not the first philosophy to reject metaphysics. Earlier in the twentieth century, the Pragmatists—William James, Charles Peirce, and John Dewey—had abandoned metaphysics as empirically unverifiable "non-sense." Dethroning metaphysics, the Pragmatists gave their trust to the scientific method as a true use of intelligence that could either empirically verify or disprove claims to truth. Rather than objective and universal "truth," the Pragmatists argued that our "truths" were really probabilities or warranted assertions. The scientific method, a product of the modern world, was proclaimed to be a public, dispassionate, and verifiable way of solving problems. (For a discussion of Pragmatism, see Chapter 5.) Postmodernists, unlike Pragmatists, reject claims that the scientific method is really objective and ideologically unbiased. It is "scientific" and "objective" only for those who share the commitment to use its terminology. Scientific knowledge is merely what is acceptable to a particular group or circle who share a commitment to that idea.[15]

Especially pernicious, contend Postmodernists, is the claim that scientific objectivity can be extended to areas other than natural and physical science. Some experts in fields such as psychology, sociology, political science, and education claim that they can approach their areas of inquiry with scientific objectivity and arrive at disinterested knowledge claims. Postmodernists believe that such claims are feigned or false. All knowledge claims and the texts that convey them represent power relationships. Claims to objectivity are used to deflect critical analysis.

Epistemology

Postmodernism argues against traditional philosophies' epistemological claims that we can know objects as they correspond to reality. Rather than looking outside of human experience and history for truth, they advise us to look within the human past and present to see how claims to truth have originated, been constructed and expressed, and have had social, political, and educational consequences. What people claim as a truth takes on meaning only when it is expressed in conceptual and symbolic form through language. Concepts do not correspond to objects existing in some supernatural or metaphysical reality; they are human constructions based on experience. Knowledge claims are constructions used to explain and control human life and institutions. Claims to knowledge, the constructions that explain and control, are expressed symbolically in sounds, signs, gestures, words and language.[16] These language-expressed and language-bound claims of truth can be approached, dissected, decoded, or deconstructed by "unpacking" what is asserted to be true. Working through language reveals that what purports to be knowledge is a human-made construction. Language expression and use is a means of controlling knowledge and of giving control to those who purport to understand and interpret it. Historically, certain texts or metanarratives—religious works, great books, the classics—have been given a prominence and status as speaking of universal truths to a worldwide, transgenerational audience.

Challenging the universal claims of these metanarratives, Postmodernists contend that they, too, are the constructions of once-powerful historical elites, now used to legitimize and empower new elites by investing them with the signs and symbols of the old order. Further, they believe that there are many ways to describe human experience, each of which has its own validity, rather than just those that claim to speak in universal terms. With their emphasis on a multiplicity of dialogues and voices, Postmodernists encourage multiculturalism in education.

Deconstructing or decoding a text is a relentless effort to discern meaning and relationships. Indeed, every knowledge claim or statement can be deconstructed by looking at the various contexts in which it is used, and how it is used. What did the text mean at the time of its origination or construction? What groups established and used the meaning of the text at its origination? What has the text come to mean over the course of history? What does the text mean at the present time for different groups?

In terms of formal education, these questions focus on how curriculum is constructed. What texts represent official knowledge in the curriculum? How are these texts interpreted in order to establish and maintain the power relationships between different groups? Which texts (i.e., which experiences) are included and which are excluded? Postmodernists see the curriculum as a locus of struggle, a cultural war, between groups struggling to establish knowledge claims and to assert power.

Axiology

The Postmodernist rejection of metaphysical systems and the analytical tools they use to examine the language of dominant and suppressed groups reveal much about their views of ethics and aesthetics. Postmodernists reject the Idealist, Realist, and Thomist metaphysical claims that there are universal and eternal values that prescribe and proscribe ethical and moral actions. Such claims proclaim that they possess absolute knowledge about what is universally and eternally good or bad or right and wrong need to be deconstructed. For Postmodernists, such claims to authority represent the strategy dominant groups use to control subordinate ones. By tracing the genealogy of moral injunctions, it is possible to identify who made the claim that something was either right or wrong and why the claim was made. By historical analysis, it is possible to discern the social consequences of the claim, especially on certain groups. In the modern world, contemporary dominant groups cling to or resurrect these past statements of moral authority to justify their efforts to control the behavior of subordinate groups. Often, dominant groups are not content to state their commitment to particular values but seek to impose them on others by law and criminal codes and silence those who dissent and punish those who violate the rules. Dominant groups seek to instill what they define as the rules of ethical standards into the general society through the agencies of informal education and through schooling. Often these rules are justifications for the exploitation of less economically and socially favored groups. Instilling a sense of guilt in the victims of oppression is a powerful means of social control.

Postmodernists do not say that there is no standards for judging moral and ethical behavior. Rather, they say that there is no single set of moral standards. There is a multiplicity of moral discourses. They advise that values, like knowledge claims, need to be seen as growing out of the experiences of groups who live in differing situations. Ethical values—the sense of right and wrong—reflect the conditions under which persons live and how they cope with their situations. When values are seen as coming from group experience, those that are exploitative can be identified, resisted, and changed. Values, for Postmodernists, should be expressions of what a group cherishes and enjoys and should be expressed in open discourse.

Postmodernists are most concerned with analyzing the ethical discourses that groups use to explain their relationships to the wider society, especially as they are expressed in ideology and politics. It is important to understand how a group's unique experiences have shaped their ethical and moral values. Instead of a single, uniform, and monolithic moral code, there are many ethical discourses that contest for the right to be voiced. The major ethical struggle takes the form of an initiative to expand human rights against those who seek to restrict them to certain preferred groups. The quest for genuine ethics requires a struggle to empower those who are denied justice and equality.

In aesthetics, Postmodernists resist those who define beauty and artistic appreciation and expression in universal terms. For example, they question the designation that some works of art or music are classics; such works, for them, are historical constructions. The sense of the beautiful depends on a particular group's experience. Dominant classes and groups tend to control the museums and art galleries where paintings and sculptures are exhibited and the orchestra halls where musical concerts are presented. Often popular expressions of art and music are judged to lack the standards prescribed by experts in these fields. The museum or art exhibit is often a situation of confrontation between those who control an artistic field and those who wish to exhibit art that had not conformed to the established canons. In contrast, Postmodernists argue that there are many ways to express art and music and that these various expressions should have an opportunity to be seen and heard.

The Postmodernist argument for ethical and aesthetic pluralism has important implications for education, especially for the curriculum. Rather than using universal claims to determine what is valuable and ethical and looking to the experts who cater to dominant groups to tell us what is beautiful, teachers should look to the experiences of the students whom they are educating.

Logic

In terms of logic, Postmodernists advise that we take a careful and critical look at what is stated to be logical or illogical. They do not quarrel with the basic deductive or inductive systems of logic but rather advise that we need to consider the position, authority, and power of those who commend some actions as logical but condemn others as illogical or irrational. They are especially wary of those who use deductive logic to generalize rules of behavior from alleged first principles and apply them to specific categories of people. This kind of manipulation of logic can be used to justify and maintain the status quo that favors some individuals and groups over others. The claim that some proposals are illogical can be used to silence dissenters who do not accept what is asserted to be an irrefutable first principle. For example, the general premise that "a woman, by her nature, is to be a wife and mother" leads to a conclusion that it is illogical for a right-thinking woman to choose to be something other than a wife and mother. Upon analysis, this premise is an example of what is really patriarchal preferences and male dominance over women. It is a remnant from earlier periods of history when women's roles were rigidly prescribed. What is stated as a logical premise based on the nature of women is really a convention, a period piece, that marginalized women. Postmodernists would argue that while a woman may choose to be a wife and a mother, she is free to choose some other career. It is crucial to look behind the logic claims to determine who is making them and why they are making them.

POSTMODERNISM'S EDUCATIONAL IMPLICATIONS

In the following section, we examine Postmodernism's implications for education, schooling, curriculum, and instruction.

Postfoundationalism

In discussing Postmodernism, we pointed out that it is a point of view, a persuasion, or an orientation, rather than a school of systematic philosophy. In much the same way, Postfoundationalism, based on Postmodernism, presents an orientation or a way of interpreting the goals of education and analyzing educational institutions. Postfoundationalism is highly suspicious of foundation building—the way in which we establish grounds for our basic educational beliefs and practices. For example, in teacher education programs, it is commonplace to refer to the foundations of education—to the history, philosophy, and sociology of education, and to educational psychology—as those disciplines that contain the principles upon which sound practices rest. The leading mode of educational analysis is statistical, using statistics about methodological effectiveness or student achievement to arrive at findings that are then generalized to explain the particular educational phenomenon and guide practice. Foundationalism and reliance on statistical interpretation, for Postfoundationalists, represent the modernist tendency to identify a particular kind of rationality as superior to all others. Again, reliance on academically based foundations and statistical inquiry represents how one group, usually the educational elite, puts forth claims to truth that give them power and deny it to others.[17]

Instead of using foundations derived from parent academic disciplines, Post-foundationalism would use the foundational disciplines—history, philosophy, and sociology of education—in a different way. Instead of transporting and transposing generalizations from these disciplines, the methods of history, philosophy, and sociology would be applied at the local, grassroots school levels. Research in history would examine the past of students who attend the school and live in its local community. Philosophy would encourage students to reflect on and interpret their own experiences. Sociology would examine local networks and associations and analyze their impact on those who live in the community.

Critics of Postfoundationalism's rejection of the foundations of education as derivations and applications from the scholarly disciplines of history, philosophy, and sociology of education accuse them of failing to create adequate generalizations that have the potentiality of transferring from one locale to another. At some point, the critics contend, studies of local situations need to generate broader comparisons and contrasts. Local schools and communities will have similar conditions, situations, and problems. These similarities can be brought together in larger explanatory generalizations to form a theory that encompasses and transcends the locality. In other words, local investigations when carried forward to encompass larger territories will lead to metageneralizations.

Postmodernism is highly suspicious of metanarratives in education, especially the so-called great works of Aristotle, Plato, Aquinas, Rousseau, Pestalozzi, and others who purport to speak in a universal voice for educational goals and purposes. It challenges these metanarratives as reflecting Eurocentric and patriarchal constructions of educational theory.

Schools

As educational institutions, public schools in the United States are part of a social, political, and economic system, which in turn, has justified the use of the texts of official knowledge. These canons of public education proclaim the public school to be the agency that educates the children of all the people, provides equality of opportunity, encourages social and economic mobility, and is necessary for continuing and perpetuating a democratic society. Postmodernists, however, contend that public schools, like other institutions, are used to reproduce a social order that is patriarchal in that they favor men over women; Eurocentric in that what is said to be knowledge is a construction of white people of European ancestry; and capitalist in that private property and the corporate attitude are enshrined in the free market ideology. Given these official foundations, the dominance of a white, European male is approved, reinforced, and reproduced in institutionalized education. Other groups—people of color, women, and gays and lesbians, for example, are excluded from the official narratives. They are placed at the margins of the schools and society.[18]

Curriculum and Instruction

Postmodernism questions how knowledge has been organized and presented in Western cultures, especially in Aristotelian natural categories and Enlightenment designations based on science and social science. According to the Aristotelian categorization of knowledge, subject matters, corresponding to metaphysical reality, can be organized hierarchically in the curriculum. (For a discussion of the Aristotelian categories of knowledge, refer to Chapter 3.) For Postmodernists, Aristotelian categorization, though premodern, is not an objective representation of nature but instead represents how classical and scholastic elites constructed knowledge. For several thousand years, this Aristotelian categorization contributed to the control of formal education by dominant political aristocracies and religious elites. Domination, based on Aristotelian metaphysics, is still found in Realism, Thomism, and Perennialism. (For these perspectives, see Chapters 3, 4, and 17.)

Postmodernists reject the construction of knowledge that developed with the birth of the modern age in the Eighteenth-Century Enlightenment. In their search to discover the natural laws that governed the universe and society, the eighteenth-century *philosophes* turned to empiricism, as in the case of John Locke, rather than to metaphysics as did the earlier Aristotelian Realists and Thomists. However, modern science and social science, too, represent a construction of knowledge by new elites—scientists, economists, and political scientists. These new elites of the Enlightenment and post-Enlightenment periods proclaimed the scientific method to be an unbiased, fair, and neutral mode of acquiring knowledge. Modern versions of science in the social studies, psychology, and education claim scientific objectivity. Postmodernists argue that scientific claims to objectivity are either delusional or contrived. Claims to knowledge, they allege, are never neutral, but represent the establishment of a relationship of power between those who claim to know the truth and those upon whom the truth is imposed. For Postmodernists, the modernist construction of knowledge, along with the language used to convey it, represents the strategy of modernist elites to take and keep power.

Both the premodern Aristotelian metaphysical categories and the modern sciences and social sciences remain encased and encoded into subject matter disciplines. The controlling elites have constructed canons or texts that contain definitions, cases, and illustrations that demarcate a subject's boundaries or borders. As with any boundary, these canons give a sense of ownership to the experts who control them, and to the interests they serve. In academic institutions, the experts in each subject matter have constructed theoretical fortifications that act as impenetrable boundaries that protect their power and their turf.[19]

Based on an ideology stemming from the Enlightenment, the controlling elites, once colonialist, have fashioned a neocolonialist version of the curriculum that is Eurocentric, patriarchal, and classist. By subjecting the canons of the vested subjects to rigorous critical analysis, they can be seen as the historically constructed rationales that justify the racist, sexist, and classist biases of the dominant groups. Once they are seen as rationales rather than as a description of universal truths, these canons can be deconstructed so that the purposes of those who originally created and used them can be examined. Further, the canons and the texts that convey them can be unmasked as the representation of a particular class or group seeking power rather than as having a broad and universal legitimacy. With such official knowledge dethroned, it becomes possible to replace the canons with the representations of marginalized groups whose voices have been excluded.

Postmodernists refer to instruction as a "representation," a cultural expression or discussion. A "representation" refers to the "processes" that individuals and groups "use to interpret and give meaning" to their experience, through language, stories, images, music, and other cultural constructions.[20] Teaching, especially the transmission of the official curriculum, involves making representations to students through language to provide students with descriptions of reality. However, the official curriculum—the approved representations—is only one version of reality, usually that of a society's dominant and controlling group. Postmodernists urge teachers to become conscious of how powerful they are in representing reality to students and to critically assess the representations they make in their teaching. The official curriculum either neglects or gives an officially sanctioned "spin" to how the experience of marginalized groups, especially African, Hispanic, and Native Americans; women; and gays and lesbians is represented. Rather than transmit officially approved knowledge, the process of representation needs to be used critically and reflectively to present a wider range of human experience.[21]

A Postmodern curriculum should not be organized into discrete subject matter disciplines, separated by impermeable boundaries and guarded by experts. Arising in its local context, it should offer a fluid and flexible means of examining issues of personal and group identity, and social, political, and economic problems. It should encourage dialogues that question existing assumptions, particularly those contained in the officially approved curriculum. Recognizing that all societies and their institutions are made up of forces contending for power and control, the curriculum should make students aware that they live in an ideologically charged environment that requires them to become social critics and critical actors. The curriculum, like the school, should be transformed into an agency that empowers individuals, especially those who have been marginalized by the existing power structure.

CRITICS OF POSTMODERNISM

Although Postmodernism occupies an influential position in contemporary philosophy of education, it has many critics. Idealists, Realists, and Thomists find its rejection of metaphysics to be another in a series of attacks that seek to replace universal truth and values with cultural and situational relativism. Postmodernism, they contend, is a poorly articulated, highly repetitive, and wearisome attack against academic and ethical standards in education. Its attack on metaphysics causes claims to knowledge and value to be reduced to the most immediate of situations and it weakens efforts to generalize human experience to a higher plane. Further, they argue that Postmodernism masks a nostalgia for the remnants of Marxism. Discredited by the collapse of

Marxist-Leninism, residues of Marxist ideology have found a refuge among some Postmodernists.

In addition to the proponents of metaphysically based philosophies, those who see philosophy as dealing with the commonalties in human nature and experience see Postmodernism as an ideology that seeks to politicize education and schooling by emphasizing differences in race, class, and gender. They contend that it represents a failure to recognize the commonalties, or universals, in human nature and behavior. These critics argue that it is crucial to affirm the common patterns in human life and society, across boundaries of time and place, in order to generalize about human freedom and human rights. Otherwise, all that remains are situations that are so specific we can make no judgment of them. Although Postmodernists have raised issues of oppression, domination, and disempowerment, they operate from a particularistic situational framework that rejects generalizations that explain human nature and behavior in the larger world.

JACQUES DERRIDA, POSTMODERN PHILOSOPHY

In *Who's Afraid of Philosophy?*, Derrida expresses his views on certain Postmodernist themes such as institutional memory, legitimization, and deconstruction. Despite the difficulties in interpreting Derrida and other Postmodernist philosophers, their work has had an important impact on contemporary education, especially the foundations of education and curriculum theory. The selection from Derrida is included so that readers can become acquainted with a significant voice in contemporary philosophy. As you read the selection, you may wish to consider the following focusing questions:

1. According to Derrida, how do institutions and schools include and exclude memories. Consider memory to be a view of the past. What does it mean to have a selective memory? How does inclusion and exclusion affect the identity of certain groups? Which groups tend to be included and which are excluded from the curriculum?

2. What does it mean to be legitimate? How are the subjects found in the curriculum legitimate? Do you think that establishing legitimacy is biased or objective?

3. How does Derrida define deconstruction? Have you encountered the use of deconstruction of texts in your education?

But something else can always happen *against its will*, affecting the structure of its very space. It can, first of all, *forget* its own elect: we know that it sometimes loses their names in ever more inaccessible depths. This selectivity no doubt signifies, first of all, the finitude of an institutional memory. The paradox lies elsewhere, however, even if it is *also* the effect of an essential finitude: what we call an institution must sometimes remember what it *excludes* and selectively attempts to doom to being forgotten. The surface of its archive is then marked by what it keeps outside, expels, or does not tolerate. It takes the inverted shape of that which is rejected. It lets itself be delineated by the very thing that threatens it or that it feels to be a threat. In order to *identify itself*, to be what it is, to delimit itself and recognize itself in its own name, it must espouse the very outlines of its adversary, if I can put it thus. It must wear its adversary's features, even bear its name as a negative mark. And the excluded thing, whose traits are deeply engraved in the hollows of the archive, imprinted right on the institutional support or surface, can end up in turn becoming the subjectile that bears the memory of the institutional body. This is true for the founding violence of states and nations and the peoples it never fails to suppress or destroy. And this never takes place once and for all, but must necessarily continue or repeat itself according to diverse processes and rhythms. But this is also true, on an apparently more modest scale, of academic institutions, philosophy in particular.

. . .

Taking many forms and admitting of many degrees (exclusion, misunderstanding, marginalization, inhibition, insufficient development), this nonlegitimation in itself calls for refined analyses, ones that are at once preliminary and interminable. To be able to claim also to be philosophical, such an analysis must not be merely operative. In principle it must include in its space the treatment of its own conceptual instruments, beginning with the concept of legitimation, which is so useful and which, with its often careless reference to right, law, legality (positive or not), dominates the social sciences, notably when they concern culture, education, and research. To borrow a convenient distinction from Fink (even if its pertinence is bound to be essentially limited), we would have to make a *thematic* concept of the *operative* concept of legitimation, de-instrumentalize it as much as possible (it is never possible purely and absolutely) in order to interrogate philosophically its genealogy, scope, and conditions of validity. We will see the limits of thematization reimprinted in those of objectification.

To submit an operative concept to philosophical thematization is not only, in this case, to submit scientific efficacy to epistemological or philosophical reflection. It is not to fold knowledge back into speculation. In the best of cases, precisely the one that must be sought out, this amounts to reviving, enlarging, or radicalizing scientific conceptuality, methods, and practices themselves. The concepts of legitimation or objectification, for example, are fruitful and effective, notably in the work of Pierre Bourdieu, because they can also, in a given situation, correspond to a sociologically determined figure of the social sciences in their relation to all kinds of instances, in particular to the history of discourse and philosophical institutions, whether it be a question of the legality (or legitimacy) of the law or the objectivity of the object.

. . .

Deconstruction, which produces itself first of all as the deconstruction of these oppositions, therefore immediately concerns, just as much and just as radically, the institutional structures founded on such oppositions. *Deconstruction is an institutional practice for which the concept of the institution remains a problem.* But since, for the reason I am in the process of pointing out, it is not a "critique" either, it destroys no more than it discredits critique or institutions; its transformative gesture is other, its responsibility is other and consists in following as consistently as possible what I have above and elsewhere called a graphics of iterability. That is why the same responsibility rules at once philosophy (the struggles for the recognition of the right to philosophy, the extension of philosophical teaching and research) *and* the most vigilant practice of deconstruction. To consider this a contradiction, as certain people do, is to understand as little about deconstruction as about philosophy. It amounts to considering them terms foreign or opposed to one another. As for the responsibility to which I am referring here, it is no longer purely philosophical, in fact, nor can it be determined by philosophical concepts of responsibility (the freedom of the subject, consciousness, the I, the individual, intention, voluntary decision, etc.), which are still *conditions* and thus *limitations* of responsibility, sometimes limitations in

the very determination of the unconditional, the imperative, and the categorical. If, therefore, the responsibility we are calling for (or rather, which is recalling itself to us here) exceeds the philosophical as such, we will call it, for obvious reasons, neither "higher" nor "more profound" than philosophical (or indeed moral, political, ethical, or juridical) responsibility, nor simply foreign to it. It is even *engaged* in philosophical responsibility, which does not mean thoroughly inscribed in philosophy, for it is also engaged by injunctions that command at once more imperatively and more gently, more discreetly and more uncompromisingly: among other things, that one "think" the philosophical determinations of responsibility, the imperative, or the unconditional, which is also to say, their socio-institutional determinations.)

CONCLUSION

In this chapter we examined Postmodernism, a leading contemporary philosophical persuasion. We emphasized the Postmodernist rejection of metaphysics and the Enlightenment concept of reason. We pointed out that knowledge claims are not statements of objective truth but are social constructions of dominant groups or their spokespersons. Postmodernism opposes giving credence to metanarratives and avows that they are historically situated social constructions developed by dominant groups to legitimize their positions and privileges. Schools have functioned as agencies of indoctrination in the social constructions of dominant groups. While dominant groups control the representations made in schools, other groups are marginalized. Instead of being agents of dominant groups, teachers need to examine the representations they make and encourage a plurality of voices, especially those of traditionally silenced individuals. Rather than being docile transmitters of officially approved regimes of truth, teachers should function as agents of critical change.

DISCUSSION QUESTIONS

1. Compare and contrast the concepts of "modern" and "postmodern." Are you a modern or a postmodern person?
2. Examine the statement "Some societies are advanced and others are primitive" from a modernist and postmodernist perspective.
3. Why is Postmodernism such a significant influence on literary and educational thinking?

4. Do you believe that truth and values are universally or locally defined? Why?

5. How would you go about deconstructing a text in education?

INQUIRY AND RESEARCH PROJECTS

1. Using deconstruction, examine a syllabus in a course in teacher education at your college or university.

2. Examine a textbook in world history at either the secondary or higher level. Is the general interpretation modernist or postmodernist?

3. Arrange a debate on the topic: Curriculum should be based on how people in the local community view the world.

4. As a class project, analyze several of the passages in the selection from Derrida with the assistance of your instructor. You might wish to refer to Chapter 7 on Philosophical Analysis before you begin.

INTERNET RESOURCES

For excerpts and bibliographies on Derrida, consult Derrida:Online at
www.hydra.umn.edu/derrida.htm

For discussions of Foucault, consult Michel Foucault: Resources at
www.qut.edu.au/edu/cpol/foucault/.htm

SUGGESTIONS FOR FURTHER READING

Aronowitz, Stanley, and Giroux, Henry A. *Postmodern Education: Politics, Culture, and Social Criticism.* Minneapolis: University of Minnesota Press, 1991.

Ball, S., ed. *Foucault and Education.* London: Routledge, 1991.

Best, Steven, and Kellner, Douglas. *Postmodern Theory.* New York: Guilford, 1991.

Cahoone, Lawrence E. *From Modernism to Postmodernism: An Anthology.* Oxford, UK: Blackwell Publishers, 1996.

Derrida, Jacques. *Of Grammatology.* Baltimore: Johns Hopkins University Press, 1976.

Doll, William E., Jr. *A Post-Modern Perspective on Curriculum.* New York: Teachers College Press, Columbia University, 1993.

Faulconer, James, and Wrathall, Mark, eds. *Appropriating Heidegger.* New York: Cambridge University Press, 2000.

Foucault, Michel. *The Archeology of Knowledge and the Discourse of Language.* New York: Pantheon Books, 1972.

Foucault, Michel. *Power/Knowledge.* Translated by Colin Gordon, Leo Marschall, John Mepham, and Kate Sopher. New York: Pantheon, 1980.

Giroux, Henry A. *Postmodernism, Feminism, and Cultural Politics: Redrawing Boundaries.* Albany: State University Press of New York, 1991.

Hoeveller, David J., Jr. *The Postmodern Turn: American Thought and Culture in the 1970s.* New York: Twayne Publishers, 1996.

Jencks, Charles. *The Post-Modern Reader.* London: Academy Editions, 1992.

Kincheloe, Joe L. *Toward a Critical Politics of Teacher Thinking: Mapping the Postmodern.* Westport, CT: Bergin & Garvey, 1993.

Lyotard, Jean-Francois. *The Postmodern Condition: A Report on Knowledge.* Translated by Geoff Bennington and Brian Massumi. Minneapolis: Minnesota University Press, 1984.

Lyotard, Jean-Francois. *Toward the Postmodern.* Edited by Robert Harvey and Mark Roberts. Atlantic Highlands, NJ: Humanities, 1993.

Rabinow, Paul, ed. *The Foucault Reader.* New York: Pantheon, 1984.

Rose, Margaret. *The Post-Modern and the Post-Industrial: A Critical Analysis.* Cambridge: Cambridge University Press, 1991.

Rosenau, Pauline M. *Post-Modernism and the Social Sciences: Insights, Inroads, and Intrusions.* Princeton: Princeton University Press, 1992.

Schacht, Richard, ed. *Nietzsche's Postmoralism: Essays on Nietzsche's Prelude to Philosophy's Future.* New York: Cambridge University Press, 2000.

Slattery, Patrick. *Curriculum Development in the Postmodern Era.* New York: Garland Publishing, 1995.

NOTES

1. C. E. Black, *The Dynamics of Modernization: A Study in Comparative History* (New York: Harper and Row, 1966), p. 7.

2. For critiques of globalization, see Joseph E. Stiglitz, *Globalization and Its Discontents* (New York: W.W. Norton Co., 2002) and Amy Chua, *World on Fire: How Exporting Free Market Democracy Breeds Ethnic Hatred and Global Instability* (New York: Doubleday, 2003).

3. Edward K. Berggren, "Deconstruction and Nothingness: Some Cross-Cultural Lessons on Teaching Comparative World Civilization," in Rebecca A. Martusewicz and William M. Reynolds, *Inside/Out: Contemporary Critical Perspectives in Education* (New York: St. Martin's Press, 1994), pp. 24–25.

4. Friedrich Nietzsche, *The Will to Power,* trans. Walter Kaufmann (New York: Vintage, 1967).

5. For Nietzsche as a predecessor of Postmodernism, see Richard Schacht, ed., *Nietzsche's Postmoralism: Essays on Nietzsche's Prelude to Philosophy's Future* (New York: Cambridge University Press, 2000).

6. David E. Cooper, *World Philosophies: An Historical Introduction* (Oxford, UK, and Cambridge, MA: Blackwell, 1996), p. 467.

7. George R. Knight, *Issues and Alternatives in Educational Philosophy* (Berrien Springs, MI: Andrews University Press, 1998), p. 86.

8. Jacques Derrida, *Of Grammatology* (Baltimore: Johns Hopkins University Press, 1976).

9. Cooper, p. 473.

10. Howard A. Ozmon and Samuel M. Craver, *Philosophical Foundations of Education* (Columbus, OH: Merrill/Prentice Hall, 1999) p. 356.

11. Knight, pp. 86–87.

12. Jennifer M. Gore, "Enticing Challenges: An Introduction to Foucault and Educational Discourses," in Rebecca A. Martusewicz and William M. Reynolds, *Inside/Out: Contemporary Critical Perspectives in Education* (New York: St. Martin's Press, 1994), p. 110.

13. Gore, p. 114.

14. Cooper, p. 476.

15. Ibid.

16. Rebecca A. Martusewicz and William M. Reynolds, *Inside/Out: Contemporary Critical Perspectives in Education* (New York: St. Martin's Press, 1994), pp. 11–13.

17. Cooper, p. 466.

18. Angeline Martel and Linda Peterat, "Margins of Exclusion, Margins of Transformation: The Place of Women in Education," in Rebecca A. Martusewicz and William M. Reynolds, *Inside/Out: Contemporary Critical Perspectives in Education* (New York: St. Martin's Press, 1994), p. 152.

19. Martusewicz and Reynolds, pp. 3–4.

20. Elizabeth Ellsworth, "Representation, Self-Representation, and the Meanings of Difference: Questions for Educators," in Rebecca A. Martusewicz and William M. Reynolds, *Inside/Out: Contemporary Critical Perspectives in Education* (New York: St. Martin's Press, 1994), p. 100.

21. Ibid., pp. 100–101.

CHAPTER NINE

IDEOLOGY AND EDUCATION

In the preceding chapters, we examined philosophy of education—the relationship to and implications of philosophy on educational goals, schooling, curriculum, teaching, and learning. This chapter defines ideology, considers its similarities and differences to philosophy, identifies its components, and investigates implications for education.

DEFINING IDEOLOGY

Ideology is the belief (idea) and value system of a group, especially in relation to politics, society, economics, and education. A *group* can be citizens of a country; members of a racial, ethnic, or language group; members of a political party; or, in some cases, a professional society. For example, consider what it means to be an American in terms of national group identity. After the terrorist attacks on the World Trade Center in New York City and the Pentagon in Washington, D.C. on September 11, 2001, television advertisements showed people of different races and ethnic groups saying, "I am an American." The ads conveyed the message that Americans, though of different races and ethnicities, share something in common—their sense of being, their identity, as an American.

While Americans were being rallied and united, their adversaries, personified by Osama Bin Laden, used a videotape telecast over an Arabic-language station, to appeal to their version of Islam to encourage followers to commit more terrorist attacks as part of a jihad, or holy war. These two very different ideological messages, carried in a dramatic and vivid way by television, have had their counterparts in the past. Famous rallying speeches in American history such as Lincoln's "House Divided," Wilson's "Making the World Safe for Democracy," Roosevelt's "Day That Will Live in Infamy," and Martin Luther King's "I Have a Dream" appealed to American core beliefs and values to generate and mobilize a people.

Although our examples of ideological messages are dramatic ones, ideology also functions less dramatically as well. It is the ideas and beliefs that give groups a sense of belonging, or identity, holds them together, and provides their agendas for action.

Distinguishing Ideology from Philosophy

At first glance, ideologies and philosophies might seem to be much the same. They both deal with ideas; they both explain why the world is as it is; they both are prescriptive and proscriptive in that they purport to tell us how we should or should not live; they both carry strong implications for education and schooling. Indeed, some ideologists refer to their thought systems as world views or philosophies.

Despite these similarities, there are significant differences between philosophy and ideology. The more traditional philosophies, such as Idealism, Realism, and Thomism, were based on a metaphysical foundation—the universal and eternal truth and values that transcend place and time and are applicable to all people, everywhere, regardless of group identity. Ideologies, in contrast, are usually based on specific conditions of place, time, and group membership. Pragmatism, especially Dewey's Experimentalism, argued that experience, although shaped by context, was a historically ongoing and worldwide process, as was the application of the scientific method, the method of intelligence. (For a discussion of Pragmatism, see Chapter 5.) In contrast, ideologists, arising in specific settings, look to nation, race, ethnic and language group, political party, and class to create group solidarity.

SITUATING IDEOLOGY

Ideology as a form of group identity has probably existed since humans banded together in kinship groups, clans, and tribes. Over the course of history, group identity and solidarity became more complex. Membership as a subject of an empire in China, Japan, and Egypt generated a large racially based political bond in ancient times. In classical Greece, culture, language, religion, and citizenship came to a focus in the *polis* or city state. Homer's epic poems, the *Iliad* and *Odyssey*, used myth and history to create the sense of what it meant to be Greek, in contrast to the non–Greek-speaking barbarians. Greek children and adolescents were introduced to the dramatic events in their history through the Homeric epics and, through ideology, began to identify with their cultural heritage and tradition. For the ancient Jews, who regarded themselves as

■ ■ ■ ■ ■

DIFFERENCES BETWEEN IDEOLOGY AND PHILOSOPHY

1. Traditional philosophies are metaphysical—above and removed from particular contexts of time and place; ideologies are contextual, arising in particular times and places.
2. Philosophies claim universal or worldwide applicability, regardless of time and place; ideologies are based in given historical, political, and economic situations.
3. Philosophies claim that they are relevant to all people, everywhere, at any time; ideologies emphasize specific membership based on identity with a nation, tribe, ethnic group, political party, or socioeconomic class.

God's "Chosen People," the Torah and Talmud were the great texts that created a sense of religious and ethnic group identification. For the Christians of the Middle Ages, the Church created the sense of being identified with a universal Christendom. However, in each of these examples, group identification and meaning came from an actual geopolitical entity such as an empire, or from being a member of a body of religious believers.

It was not until the late eighteenth and nineteenth centuries that ideologies developed in their more modern contexts. In late eighteenth-century France, some Enlightenment theorists, the Ideologues, were engaged in seeking to understand how human beings formed their ideas. They concluded that ideas arose from the human beings' interaction or involvement with their contexts—when and where they lived. Ideas, thus, were seen as developing in specific contexts rather than as metaphysical universals.

As a result of the significant social changes caused by the American and French Revolutions, the Napoleonic Wars, the rise of nationalism, and the beginning of industrialism, new and powerful forms of political, social, cultural, and economic identification arose and eclipsed older forms of identity. Liberalism became the ideology of the rising middle classes and served as a revolutionary ideology that proclaimed individual rights against the vested aristocracy. (For a discussion of Liberalism, see Chapter 11.) Conservatism developed as an antiliberal reaction that urged the restoration of commitments to traditional institutions such as the family, church, and king. (Conservatism is discussed in Chapter 12.) Various forms of Socialism, ranging from utopian to Marxist, sought to raise the consciousness of the working classes and rally them against capitalist exploitation. (See Chapter 13 for a discussion of Marxism.)

Karl Marx, who developed a theory of scientific socialism, known as dialectical materialism, used the term *ideology*, to denigrate rival systems of thought as misleading, false consciousness. Marx condemned the nationalism of official state ideologies and the semiofficial liberal and conservative ideologies as the delusional false consciousness created by ruling classes to mislead and confuse the working classes. False consciousness was a way of blocking the development of true consciousness about the realities of socioeconomic domination and exploitation.

The various ideologies carry with them very powerful educational implications. Through means of informal education, such as speeches, pamphlets, and books, the leaders and spokespersons of the various ideologies sought to justify their positions and persuade the uncommitted to join with them in either creating a new social order or in restoring the glories of a past age. In terms of formal education, the various ideologies each had their own version of the purpose of education, the roles of schools and teachers, the construction of the curriculum, and how children should be socialized, politically and economically, into the world.

WHY STUDY IDEOLOGY?

Ideology is so pervasive in our lives, in our group identification and membership, and in shaping our behavior, that it is virtually impossible to avoid it. Ideologies range from the very general and inclusive (being an American), to the still general but more restricted (being an African American or Mexican American), to the still more limited (being a member of a teacher's organization such as the American Federation of Teachers). They even operate in the cliques or subgroups found in high schools such as the "brains," the "jocks," the "goths," and so on. By studying what an ideology is and how it functions, we get a clearer idea of identity, membership, belonging, and acting as a member of a group.

COMPONENTS OF AN IDEOLOGY

An ideology—a group's shared beliefs and values—is expressed as: (1) a view and interpretation of its past, its history; (2) an appraisal of its current condition or situation in terms of its past; (3) some idea of how the group, if they do certain things, can maintain or improve their situation; (4) a policy for deliberate maintenance or change that can be implemented by action. We shall now illustrate these ideological components in two ways: how they relate to the general group identity of Americans, and how they relate to what has been called the "public school ideology."

Viewing the Past

A group's collective memory of its past is important in shaping members' sense of identity or "we-feeling." We can look at histories of various nation-based groups, such as the American people, the English, the French, the Russians, and so forth. There are histories of racial and ethnic groups as well: African Americans, Irish Americans, or Polish Americans. There are histories of special-interest groups, such as the American Federation of Teachers, the American Medical Association, and the American Legion. Some of these histories are academic interpretations of past events and their meaning, in which the historian aims for an accurate portrayal of what happened in the past; others are popular histories that highlight a group's achievements and contributions. An ideology uses these histories to appropriate certain parts of it to shape group identity, membership, purpose, and meaning. For example, who were the leaders or main characters in the group's past, what did they do, and how might we emulate them?

Perhaps even more important in explaining and giving meaning to a group's heritage is myth. A *myth* is a legendary story, often concerned with actual persons and events but with embellished or imagined significant events included to make the story more dramatic and compelling. For example, every schoolchild knows the story of

AN IDEOLOGY INCLUDES:

1. An interpretation of a group's past that may be both historical and mythical.
2. An account of a group's present condition.
3. A strategy and an agenda for improving or maintaining the group's situation.
4. Some idea of social change—improvement or maintenance—related to the group's welfare.

George Washington and the cherry tree and of Abraham Lincoln's determination to read. Myths frequently use allegories or parables to give added power to their messages. A myth relates to something that is so powerful and meaningful that its validity is not questioned in the usual way, and as such is not subject to critical or scientific inquiry.

We are all familiar with the myth of Santa Claus, the spirit of Christmas, and imaginary gift-giver. Santa is personified as a stout and jolly man, a lively and happy old fellow, with a white beard, who, dressed in a red suit, arrives on a sleigh pulled by eight tiny reindeer to bring toys to good little girls and boys. Santa symbolizes the holiday season, but is also a symbol of the commercialism that drives the U.S. economy during the December holiday season. The answer to the question, "Is there a Santa Claus?" is yes. Even though he does not exist as a real person, the spirit of Santa does exist. He symbolizes giving, loving, kindness, and sharing. As we grow older, Santa loses some of his power but his image is ingrained in our minds and reinforced each year during the holiday season. Further, the image of Santa Claus invokes and brings to consciousness many memories of past Christmases.

Being an American.   What does it mean to be an American? How was our American identity formed? How should we behave as good Americans? These three questions blend fact (what is an American?) and value (how should a good American behave?). What it means to be an American is learned informally by living in the United States, and formally by being schooled in this country. Throughout the year, there are holidays and commemorative events that celebrate certain events in the American past: Memorial Day to remember the fallen military service people of past wars; the Fourth of July to commemorate the signing of the Declaration of Independence; President's Day to honor America's Presidents collectively but to pay special homage to George Washington, who is seen as the Father of the country, and Abraham Lincoln, who saved the Union; Thanksgiving, to remember the shared meal of the Pilgrim settlers and Native Americans; Martin Luther King's birthday to remember the life of the African-American civil rights leader. Perhaps in future years, the events of September 11, 2001 will be remembered with a day of national mourning. Each of these events conveys a powerful and publicly shared message. They are celebrated by the whole country and children in schools have special observances. This allows them to internalize the meaning of these events as they draw pictures, hear stories, and sometimes act out an event, such as Thanksgiving. These combinations of history and myth stand out, making an enduring imprint on an individual's memory and the group's collective remembrance. Although academic history tells us that brutal battles occurred between Native Americans and white settlers, the partially mythical image of the peaceable feast of Thanksgiving remains and although Lincoln compromised at various times on the slavery issue, his image at the Lincoln Memorial in Washington is seen as that of the Great Emancipator.

Through the uneven combination of history and myth, an idea has evolved about what it means to be an American. This concept of group identity embraces the following: With the exception of the Native Americans, all other Americans came from other countries or regions; the colonists, rebelling against British rule, declared their independence and created a new republican government of representative institutions; with great heroism and fortitude the Americans settled a rich but wild country, moving constantly westward until the republic reached from the Atlantic to the Pacific Oceans; the Civil War preserved the Union and ended slavery; Americans defended freedom in various wars of the twentieth and twenty-first centuries. The American past represents a shining example of an exceptional people living in a bountiful land. Although we study American history as a required course in elementary and high school, and often in college, the combination of history and myth outlined above is a powerful means of creating national group identity. Historians may attempt to provide a critical and sometimes unflattering interpretation of our past. They tell us about genocide against the Native Americans; slavery imposed on African Americans; robber barons who recklessly exploited their workers and the environment for profit; and continuing racial and class exploitation; but the mythical–historical images remain and give us identity and meaning. During times of crisis, this sense of meaning, grounded in ideology, gives us national purpose—Remember the Alamo, Remember the Maine, Remember Pearl Harbor, United We Stand.

Assessing or Appraising the Present

In assessing or appraising the present, an American's identity can be complicated by membership in other more specific subgroups, often with their own ideologies. For example, Republicans and Democrats, while holding to the general American ideology, will have a somewhat different assessment of the present situation and what needs to be done to improve the economy, health care, foreign policy, and so forth. This is also likely to be true for members of different religious, racial, and ethnic groups. Some African Americans are likely to appraise the current social and economic situation differently than white, upper-class Americans. Members of the National Association of School Boards are likely to have a different assessment of the conditions and compensation of teachers than members of the American Federation of Teachers. If we return to our discussion of "I am an American" and "United We Stand," the larger sense of "American-ness" is a more general, inclusive, and overarching membership than that of the more specific subideologies.

The general appraisal of the American condition in the twenty-first century is that the landscape has changed. Many more people live in large metropolitan areas (big cities and their suburbs) than on farms and small towns in rural areas. The small town's main street and small family-owned businesses have been replaced by large corporate enterprises—symbolized by the strip mall and its fast food restaurants. The large industries of the past—iron and steel—have yielded to high tech and service ones. Internet, CNN, C-Span, and electronic data retrieval have made getting the latest news and information a rapid process that takes only a few seconds or minutes, rather than hours or days. The nuclear family, portrayed in the "Dick and Jane" readers, now coexists with alternative family styles. In the schools, the monocultural curriculum of the past has given way to cultural diversity and multiculturalism. Indeed, the cultural and physical landscape of the United States has changed. As we appraise the American condition in the first years of the twenty-first century, we might well ask how the attitudes, behaviors, ethics, and morals of the American people reflect this change.

After the terrorist attacks on the World Trade Center and the Pentagon on September 11, 2001, the response to the tragedy that claimed 3,000 lives began to reveal the attitudes and values that make up part of the American condition. There were the heroes and heroines, the ordinary people and the fire fighters and police officers, who came to the aid of victims, often at a cost of their own lives. There was the President, who like Presidents in the past, rallied a stricken nation. There were countless American flags waving from porches and cars. Throughout the land, there were groups sometimes spontaneously singing "God Bless America." It seemed that the Baby Boomers and their teenage children were responding, as had earlier generations, to times (such as after the attack on Pearl Harbor) when their country was in peril. What was revealed was the persistence of strong ideological continuities in the American psyche, even in a United States that was rapidly changing.

A Policy and Plan of Action

After the events of September 11, 2001, a strong sense of anxiety gripped the nation. Terrorist attacks, in the past, were events that took place in other countries—in Northern Ireland or Israel—not in the United States. What had happened? Why did it happen to us? Why did some people hate Americans so much that they wanted to destroy us, our way of life, and our country? Commentators and experts, the "talking heads" of modern television news programs, tried to provide answers, but their loud and conflicting opinions did not answer these powerful core questions about the attacks. What happened was that ideological symbols of "American-ness" provided the necessary answers with symbol and metaphor. There were the new heroes, the fire and police personnel of New York City and Washington, D.C., who took their place alongside the veterans of earlier wars, and there were the old symbols—the flag and "God Bless America"—that expressed a renewed patriotism.

The official policy emerged as a determined "War on Terrorism," at home and abroad. The U.S. government sent armed forces to Afghanistan to root out and destroy Osama Bin Laden and the al Qaeda terrorists. Security was tightened at airports by increased passenger and luggage inspections. Suspicious foreigners in the United States were detained by federal law enforcement officers. A new federal agency, the Office of Homeland Security, was established. These steps can be seen as ideology being implemented in response to a new challenge. Now that we have used a contemporary illustration to show how an ideology functions, we turn more specifically to education by looking at the public school ideology.

THE PUBLIC SCHOOL IDEOLOGY

In the United States, there is a very general and commonly held set of beliefs about the origins and continuing merits of public schooling and its contributions to American life. It is sometimes referred to as the *public school philosophy* but is really an ideology, as we have defined it, rather than a philosophy in the true sense. The public school ideology enjoys strong support from what might be called the public school lobby—school board members, school administrators, teachers, and parents identified with organizations such as the Parents and Teachers Organization, the National Education Association, the American Federation of Teachers, and the National Association of School Boards. We now examine the components of the public school ideology in the same way that we examined the general American ideology above. Our purpose in doing so is to move the analysis of ideology closer to education and schooling.

An Interpretation of the Origins of Public Schools

According to the public school ideology, public schools in the United States originated as a crusade against ignorance. In the 1830s and 1840s, enlightened men and women united in the common-school crusade to establish tax-supported, publicly controlled schools that would educate all the children of all the people. Dedicated leaders of the movement were the eloquent and tireless Horace Mann (1796–1859) of Massachusetts and the steady and diligent Henry Barnard (1811–1900) of Connecticut. A history of education text calls these leaders, "educational statesmen" who "dedicated their ability and capacity for leadership to blazing new trails that led to a more extended and better education for American children."[1] According to histories that celebrate the achievements of the common-school leaders, these statesmen combated ignorance, petty politics, special interests, and religious sectarianism, and eventually succeeded in laying the foundations for today's public schools. As a result, public schools are established, supported, and controlled by states rather than churches; they are democratically controlled by elected school boards; they successfully assimilate millions of immigrant children, bringing them the promise of American life; they provide educational opportunity for all children, enabling them to rise as high as their talents will permit; they are staffed by dedicated administrators and teachers who work for the best interests of children; and they provide the education that is necessary for good citizenship, economic productivity, social participation, and a satisfying life.

The story of the origin of public schools given above contains both history and myth. Revisionist historians advise us that many of the leaders of the common-school movement were not altruistic but were, themselves, often serving special interests. For example, Mann and Barnard, the "educational statesmen" lauded in celebrationist historiography, were "promoters of bureaucracy," who the revisionists believe were bent on destroying "democratic localism" as an educational alternative to the larger idea of state-controlled and -regulated schooling.[2] Revisionist historians also tell us that public schools were instruments of social control used by dominant groups to reproduce the socioeconomic conditions that put them in a favored position. Further, they challenge the rhetoric that public schools served all the children of all the people. The revisionists remind us that before the ratification of the Thirteenth Amendment, the children of enslaved Africans did not attend public school. They remind us that opportunities were limited for children of immigrants and other minority groups, and often for girls. They also point out that there are great inequalities in the educational resources available from district to district—public schools are still not equal. Despite the revisionist efforts to correct the historical record, the public school ideology is strong, and resonates throughout the country. The revisionist audience is a small one, mainly students in a few classes in the history of American education.

Appraising the Current Condition of Public Schools

As students of education, you are well aware of the complexity and controversy that abounds in attempts to appraise the current condition of American public education. These appraisals include international comparisons, campaign oratory from politicians, philosophical critiques, and ideological statements of opinion that range from the radical right to the radical left. Visit the education section of any large bookstore and you will find a large number of books about what is wrong with American public education. Likewise, in many education courses, especially in the social, philosophical, and historical foundations, you will probably hear more criticisms than affirmations about public education. The appraisal that follows is to illustrate how the public school ideology views the current condition of American public education, rather than to deny the existence or minimize the importance of the many critical views.

Those who are loyal to the public school ideology will typically answer critics with the following defense: Public schools have a historical record of success in that they provided opportunity for all students regardless of race, creed, ethnicity, and socioeconomic class. If rates of school retention and completion are lower for certain minorities, it is not the fault of the schools but of larger social and economic conditions beyond the control of the schools. While it may be statistically true that students in other countries, such as Japan or Germany, score higher in mathematics and science than their American counterparts, this finding needs much more interpretation and should not be taken at face value. American public schools are comprehensive institutions that are open to all children, regardless of socioeconomic class, academic aptitude, or career destination. Schools in many other countries rigidly segregate students so that it is only the academically talented who complete secondary school and go on to higher education. Thus, international comparisons are invalid and unfair. Administrators and teachers in public schools work in situations where much is expected of them from politicians, parents, and the public. Unlike their counterparts in other countries, they are called upon to perform many nonacademic functions. Despite these demands, they are competent and perform their responsibilities well. The real problem in American public education is not administrative inefficiency and bureaucracy, nor is it teacher incompetence. The real problem is a society that does not give a high enough priority to education and as a result under-funds its schools. As a result, buildings are often dilapidated, curriculum is archaic, and teachers are underpaid. All this can be remedied if the country sets the right priorities and gives more support to the public schools.

Maintaining and Improving Public Education

As mentioned earlier in the chapter, some ideologies, such as reactionary and conservative ones, want to maintain the status quo. To a large extent, the public school ideology wants to maintain the public school system. Other ideologies, especially those that are not currently in power, want to change things so that they can take power.[3] Typically, ideologies of the radical political left and their educational counterparts such as Liberation Pedagogy and Critical Theory (examined in Chapters 14 and 19) want to bring about a sweeping transformation of the social and educational system. Other ideologies, such as those based on Liberalism, accept the changes that are necessary to preserve the system. (For coverage of Liberalism, see Chapter 11.) Public school ideologists are willing to accept limited and moderate reforms intended to renew and preserve the system. (More will be said about how different ideologies approach change in subsequent chapters.)

The major goal of advocates of the public school ideology is to maintain the public schools against threats to their continued prominence and existence as the primary educational institutions in the United States. While many of these advocates have a vested interest in so doing, the great majority of them believe that public schools are necessary for the preservation of the American system of democratic government and are the best hope for social stability and progress, and for economic productivity.

Advocates of the public school ideology are alert in organizing their ranks to criticize, weaken, and eventually defeat those who propose alternatives to public education. They often return to the argument used by the common-school founders that nonpublic schools, especially those that are church-related and socioeconomically based, are socially divisive and weaken the social integration of American society. Foremost in their argument is that public support that provides tax-generated revenues to nonpublic schools will weaken the already under-funded public schools. The argument defending separation of church and state is used against those who wish to give aid to religious and church-related schools. Vouchers that could be used by the parents to pay tuition to nonpublic schools, they contend, would enable some to leave public schools. This would leave the poorest and least-prepared students in the public schools, especially in inner cities, and create greater socioeconomic and racial segregation. For advocates of the public school ideology, a less serious threat is presented by those, often on the left, who argue for a radical and sweeping change in public education. They believe that the system itself and the limited staying power of the small radical groups will blunt any serious changes.

The advocates of the public school ideology tend to be very open to, and often highly enthusiastic about, minor incremental and additive changes that they call reforms, which may renew or improve certain parts of the system but leave it basically as it is. Among these kinds of changes are: adding more days to the school calendar, having year-round schools, including preschool in the system, adding more computer-assisted instruction, requiring teachers to take more in-service courses, alternating between limited school decentralization (site-based management) and recentralization, adding more phonics to the reading program, adding a service requirement for high school graduation, adding conflict resolution units to the curriculum, and so forth.

The real goals of the advocates of the public school ideology are to protect the system and work for increased public support and funding. More funding will allow administrators and teachers to really do their job—educating the children of all the people.

■ ■ ■ ■ ■

PAULO FREIRE, EDUCATION AS A FORM OF INTERVENTION IN THE WORLD

In this selection, Paulo Freire, the leading founder of Liberation Pedagogy, writes that all education is conditioned and shaped by ideology. The selection is included because of Freire's prominence in contemporary education, especially for Critical Theorists and radical educators. Freire accuses educators who claim to be ideologically unbiased or disinterested of being either unconscious of the reality in which they live, or surreptitiously agents who transmit a hidden ideology. As you read the selection, you may wish to consider the following focusing questions:

1. What is the basis of Freire's argument that ideology always influences education? Do you believe that you are ideologically committed or ideologically neutral?

2. How do the dominant groups and classes use schooling to reinforce their ideology? Can you give examples of such reinforcement in educational situations you have experienced or observed?

3. In the selection, Freire cites the statement, "unemployment today is an end-of-the-century inevitability" as representing a rationale of the dominant ideology. Can you identify similar statements that express educational views representing the dominant ideology? For example, consider some of the explanations given for academic underachievement in inner-city schools.

EDUCATION AS A FORM OF INTERVENTION IN THE WORLD

Another kind of knowledge whose existence I cannot doubt for a moment in my critical educative practice is that education, as a specifically human experience, is a form of intervention in the world. In addition to contents either well or badly taught, this type of intervention also implies both the reproduction of the dominant ideology and its unmasking. The dialectical nature of the educational process does not allow it to be only one or the other of these things.

Education never was, is not, and never can be neutral or indifferent in regard to the reproduction of the dominant ideology or the interrogation of it. It is a fundamental error to state that education is simply an instrument for the reproduction of the dominant ideology, as it is an error to consider it no more than an instrument for unmasking that ideology, as if such a task were something that could be accomplished simplistically, fundamentally, without obstacles and difficult struggles. These attitudes are serious errors, and they indicate a defective vision of both history and consciousness. On the one hand, we have a mechanistic comprehension of history

From Paulo Freire, *Pedagogy of Freedom: Ethics, Democracy, and Civic Courage*. Translated by Patrick Clarke. Lanham, MD: Rowman & Littlefield, 1998, pp. 90–95. Used with permission of Rowman & Littlefield Publishers.

that reduces consciousness to a simple reflex of matter, and on the other, we have a subjective idealism that tries to make the role of consciousness fit into the facts of history. As women and men, we are not simply determined by facts and events. At the same time, we are subject to genetic, cultural, social, class, sexual, and historical conditionings that mark us profoundly and that constitute for us a center of reference.

From the perspective of the dominant classes, there is no doubt of course that educational practice ought to cover up the truth and immobilize the classes. Conversely, these same interests are capable of being "progressive" when it suits them. Progressive by half, so to speak. They are able to bring into being technical advances that are understood and often carried out in a "neutral" way. It would be extremely naive on our part to believe that the ranchers' lobby would agree that our schools, both rural and urban, should discuss the questions of agrarian reform as an economic, political, and ethical problem of the greatest importance for the development of the country. This task falls to progressive-minded educators, both inside and outside the schools. It's a task also for nongovernmental organizations and democratic-minded unions. On the one hand, we might expect modern-minded business with urban roots to be sympathetic to the cause of agrarian reform, because its interests in the expansion of the market seem "progressive" in the face of rural conservatism. On the other hand, the "progressiveness" of modern business, welcome as it is in contrast to the retrograde truculence of the ranchers, does not have to think twice about where its loyalty lies when confronted with a clash between human interests and the interests of the market.

I continue to ponder Marx's observation about the necessary radicality that enables me to be permanently aware of everything that has to do with the defense of human interests, which are superior to those of particular groups or classes of people.

Recognizing that precisely because we are constantly in the process of becoming and, therefore, are capable of observing, comparing, evaluating, choosing, deciding, intervening, breaking with, and making options, we are ethical beings, capable of transgressing our ethical grounding. However, though transgression of this grounding exists as a possibility, we can never claim transgression as a right. And, of course, we cannot sit idly by and fold our arms in the face of such a possibility. Hence my categorical refusal of fatalistic quietude, which, instead of condemning ethical transgression, tries to absorb it as if it belonged to "right" thinking. I cannot be complicit with a perverse system, exempting it from responsibility for its malice, by attributing to "blind forces" the damage caused to human beings.

Of course (and I restate my belief), modern business leaders accept, stimulate, and support technical training courses for their workers. What they obviously refuse is an education that both includes technical and scientific preparation and speaks of the workers' presence in the world. A human and ethical presence, debased every time it is transformed into pure shadow.

I cannot be a teacher if I do not perceive with ever greater clarity that my practice demands of me a definition about where I stand. A break with what is not right ethically. I must choose between one thing and another thing. I cannot be a teacher and be in favor of everyone and everything. I cannot be in favor merely of people, humanity, vague phrases far from the concrete nature of educative practice. Mass hunger and unemployment, side by side with opulence, are not the result of destiny, as certain reactionary circles would have us believe, claiming that people suffer because they can do nothing about the situation. The question here is not "destiny." It is immorality. Here I want to repeat—forcefully—that nothing can justify the degradation of human beings. Nothing. The advance of science or technology cannot legitimate "class" and call it "order" so that a minority who holds power may use and squander the fruits of the earth while the vast majority are hard pressed even to survive and often justify their own misery as the will of God. I refuse to add my voice to that of the "peacemakers" who call upon the wretched of the earth to be resigned to their fate. My voice is in tune with a different language, another kind of music. It speaks of resistance, indignation, the just anger of those who are deceived and betrayed. It speaks, too, of their right to rebel against the ethical transgressions of which they are the long-suffering victims.

The fatalistic philosophy of neoliberal politics of which I have been speaking is a case in point of how human interests are abandoned whenever they threaten the values of the market.

I cannot imagine, for example, a modern manager allowing one of his workers the right to discuss, during a literacy class or during an in-service training course in the factory, the pros and cons of the dominant ideology. For example, to discuss the question "unemployment today is an end-of-the-century inevitability." And, in that context, to ask: Why is agrarian reform not also an inevitability? And why not make putting an end to hunger and misery inevitable as well?

It's extremely reactionary to say that what only interests workers is achieving the highest grade of technical efficiency and that they do not want to get involved in ideological debates that, in any case, lead nowhere. It is in the context of the work situation that the worker needs to engage in the process of becoming a citizen, something that does not happen as a consequence of "technical efficiency." It is the result of a political struggle to re-creation of a kind of society that is both humane and just.

Thus, since I cannot be a teacher without considering myself prepared to teach well and correctly the contents of my discipline, I cannot reduce my teaching practice to the mere transmission of these contents. It is my ethical posture in the course of teaching these contents that will make the difference. It is a posture made up of my commitment to thoroughness, my investment in excellence, and my competent preparation that reveals humility rather than arrogance. It is a posture of unconditional respect for the students, for the knowledge they have that comes directly from life and that, together with the students, I will work to go beyond. My coherence in the classroom is as important as my teaching of contents. A coherence of what I say, write, and do.

I am a teacher who stands up for what is right against what is indecent, who is in favor of freedom against authoritarianism, who is a supporter of authority against freedom with no limits, and who is a defender of democracy against the dictatorship of right or left. I am a teacher who favors the permanent struggle against every form of bigotry and against the economic domination of individuals and social classes. I am a teacher who rejects the present system of capitalism, responsible for the aberration of misery in the midst of plenty. I am a teacher full of the spirit of hope, in spite of all signs to the contrary. I am a teacher who refuses the disillusionment that consumes and immobilizes. I am a teacher proud of the beauty of my teaching practice, a fragile beauty that may disappear if I do not care for the struggle and knowledge that I ought to teach. If I do not struggle for the material conditions without which my body will suffer from neglect, thus running the risk of becoming frustrated and ineffective, then I will no longer be the witness that I ought to be, no longer the tenacious fighter who may tire but who never gives up. This is a beauty that needs to be marveled at but that can easily slip away from me through arrogance or disdain toward my students.

It's important that students perceive the teacher's struggle to be coherent. And it is necessary that this struggle be the subject of discussion in the classroom from time to time. There are situations in which the teacher's attitude or practice may appear contradictory to the students. This apparent contradiction usually occurs when the teacher simply exercises authority in coordinating the activities of the class in a way that seems to the students an excess of power. At times it may be the teacher who is uncertain whether she or he over-stepped the limits of authority or not.

CONCLUSION

In this chapter, ideology was defined as the beliefs and values about its past conveyed to a group by an oral or written story based on selective group memory. The telling of the story gives the group's members a sense of identity and meaning, and also suggests how the group can either maintain or improve its political, social, and economic condition. Based on a mixture of history and myth, an ideology provides explanations of why things are as they are, or why and how they should be changed for the group's benefit. Along with beliefs, ideologies are prescriptive; they recommend ways to move the group in a desired direction. While they arise in particular contexts, some ideologies develop a world view that seeks a larger justification. Resting on beliefs and values embedded in the past, ideologies are action-oriented and directed toward shaping social, political, economic, and educational institutions and processes in a way that will benefit the group. When controlled by a dominant group, schools are used to mold students' beliefs and values into their model of the preferred citizen and personality type. Dominated or suppressed groups tend to challenge the dominant group with a rival and counter ideology that they hope will someday supplant the dominant group's position. Often a group—such as a political party or the public school lobby—may appeal to ideological justifications as a form of legitimacy based on a higher and seemingly more general authority.

DISCUSSION QUESTIONS

1. What is an ideology and how does it work in society and education?
2. What are the components of an ideology?
3. Do you agree or disagree with the author's discussion of "American-ness"? Explain why you agree or disagree.
4. Do you agree or disagree with the author's discussion of the "public school ideology"? Explain why you agree or disagree.

INQUIRY AND RESEARCH PROJECTS

1. Identify a particular group and determine its view of its past, assessment of its present condition, and plans for the future.
2. Reflect on your own educational past. Can you detect evidence of ideological imposition? In particular, what school activities and experiences were used to shape an ideological commitment?

3. In your field studies or teaching at a particular school, can you detect how children are taught the myths and symbols of a particular ideology?

INTERNET RESOURCES

For a wide range of articles on ideology, refer to the Keele Guide to Political Thought and Ideology at
www.keele.ac.uk/depts/por/ptbase.htm

For definitions and sources on ideology, consult
www.xrefer.com/entry/552374

SUGGESTIONS FOR FURTHER READING

Apple, Michael W. *Ideology and Curriculum*. New York and London: Routledge & Kegan Paul, 1979.
Apple, Michael W. *Official Knowledge: Democratic Education in a Conservative Age*. New York and London: Routledge & Kegan Paul, 2000.
Bailey, Leon. *Critical Theory and the Sociology of Knowledge: A Comparative Study in the Theory of Ideology*. New York: Peter Lang, 1994.
Balaban, Oded. *Politics and Ideology: A Philosophical Approach*. London: Avebury, 1995.
Ball, Terence, and Dagger, Richard. *Political Ideologies and the Democratic Ideal*. New York: Harper-Collins College Publishers, 1995.
Boudon, Raymond. *The Analysis of Ideology*. Translated by Malcolm Slater. Chicago: University of Chicago Press, 1989.
Eagleton, Terry. *Ideology: An Introduction*. London: Verso, 1991.
Guillaumin, Colette. *Racism, Sexism, Power, and Ideology*. London and New York: Routledge, 1995.
Hoover, Kenneth R. *Ideology and Political Life*. Belmont, CA: Wadsworth, 1994.
Karabel, Jerome, and Halsey, A. H., eds. *Power and Ideology in Education*. New York: Oxford University Press, 1977.
Katz, Michael B. *Class, Bureaucracy, and Schools: The Illusion of Educational Change in America*. New York: Praeger Publishers, 1971.
Mondale, Sarah, and Patton, Sarah B., eds. *School: The Story of American Public Education*. Boston: Beacon Press, 2001.
Paris, David C. *Ideology and Educational Reform: Themes and Theories in Public Education*. Boulder, CO: Westview Press, 1995.
Spring, Joel. *Conflict of Interests: The Politics of American Education*. New York: Longman, 1988.
Staff of *Education Week*. *Lessons of a Century: A Nation's Schools Come of Age*. Bethesda, MD: Educational Projects in Education, 2000.
Stevens, Edward, and Wood, George H. *Justice, Ideology and Education: An Introduction to the Social Foundations of Education*. New York: McGraw-Hill Higher Education, 1994.
Ward, Irene. *Literacy, Ideology, and Dialogue: Toward a Dialogic Pedagogy*. Albany, NY: State University of New York Press, 1994.

NOTES

1. Newton Edwards and Herman G. Richey, *The School in the American Social Order* (Boston: Houghton Mifflin Co., 1963), p. 310.

2. Michael B. Katz, *Class, Bureaucracy, and Schools: The Illusion of Educational Change in America* (New York: Praeger Publishers, 1971), p. 28.

3. For a discussion of the competing ideologies and interests in American education, see Joel Spring, *Conflict of Interests: The Politics of American Education* (New York: Longman, 1988).

CHAPTER TEN

NATIONALISM, AMERICAN EXCEPTIONALISM, AND ETHNONATIONALISM

In this chapter, we examine Nationalism, one of the most prominent and influential of the ideologies examined in the book. We begin by discussing Nationalism, then turn to American Exceptionalism, an important American expression of nationalism, and continue on to an examination of ethnonationalism, a powerful contemporary global trend. Although these three ideologies are related, we shall also examine some of their differences.

DEFINING NATIONALISM

If we look at a political map of the world, we note that there are nearly 200 countries or independent and sovereign nation-states. A *nation-state* can be defined as a polity, a country, that is independent and sovereign in that it has its own government, makes its own laws, and controls the territory within its borders. Importantly, it has the power of determining who is and who is not a citizen of the nation-state. Among nation-states are large ones, such as the United States, Canada, the Russian Federation, the People's Republic of China, and India. Next in area of land mass come France, Spain, Germany, Nigeria, Mexico, and many other countries. There are the significant island nations of the United Kingdom and Japan. There are many small nation-states, such as Latvia, Estonia, Jamaica, Belize, Monaco, Belgium, and Luxembourg. We have named only a few of the nation-states, or countries, that can be found on the political map of the world. All of these nation-states have the following in common: (1) they are sovereign in that they have their own governments; (2) they are independent in that they are not officially controlled in the political sense by another country; (3) they have their own political, legal, military, and educational institutions. It is important to reiterate that they have their own school systems that, as part of their educational mission, seek to socialize children as national citizens. We will turn to how schools develop citizens through programs of national socialization later in the chapter.

As noted above, nation-states are countries that occupy a particular geographical territory, have their own political institutions, and embody some sense of the ideology called Nationalism. We now turn to a definition of Nationalism. The key to understanding Nationalism as an ideology is to focus on the idea of the *nation*. A nation is composed of a large group of people, often called its popular body politic or citizens, who live within the boundaries of a particular geographical area. To state the obvious but also the necessary, Americans live in the United States, Mexicans live in Mexico, Japanese live in Japan, and so on. Citizens of nation-states are consciously aware that they belong to a particular national group and are participants in its cultural, political, religious, and educational institutions. The idea of the nation leads to **Nationalism**, the ideology that embodies and expresses the sense of national identity, the "we-feeling" of common cultural identity and loyalty to the country shared by the people of the country or the nation; it further expresses the group's national spirit or patriotism and its national interests. We can illustrate this "we-feeling" with a question: What does it mean to be American, Japanese, French, or Mexican, for example? Further, how do people acquire this sense of "we-feeling"? The idea of citizenship in the nation is nationality; that is, being designated as a citizen by being born in the country or naturalized in it as an immigrant. National citizenship makes the "we-feeling" official and identifies a person as citizen of a particular nation-state. Official citizenship is documented by a birth certificate, an identity card, a voter's card, or a passport.

SITUATING THE NATION-STATE AND NATIONALISM

To understand how nation-states and Nationalism arose, we need take a brief historical sojourn into the late eighteenth and early nineteenth centuries. The American Revolution in 1776 and the French Revolution in 1789 were important catalysts for stimulating Nationalism. An important ideological premise of the American rebels against British colonial rule was their emerging sense that they were no longer resettled Englishmen but were a distinct people, possessing inalienable rights of "life, liberty, and pursuit of happiness," and who had the right of self-government. The sense of American Nationalism, joined with republicanism, was used to convince the former colonists that they belonged to a new American nation, an identity that was larger and more encompassing than being a New Yorker, a Virginian, or a Carolinian.

The French Revolution, with its slogan of "liberty, equality, and fraternity," brought the popular masses into direct contact with their national government. It sparked the idea that the French people, rather than the Bourbon monarchy, ruled France. The French Revolution and the efforts of Napoleon to remake Europe into a system of French puppet states sparked a strong tide of counter-Nationalism among the British, the Russians, the Spanish, Germans, and other national groups. After Napoleon's final defeat at Waterloo in 1815, the idea of the country as a nation-state, rather than a dynastic monarchy, grew increasingly powerful throughout Europe. Throughout the nineteenth century, the spirit of Nationalism intensified. It led the great European powers to colonize Africa; it also fed the rivalries and alliances that led to World War I and II.

The idea of the nation-state was exported to South America, Asia, and Africa by European imperialists. When the former European colonies gained their own independence, they followed the model of the nation-state organization and became independent, sovereign countries.

Nationalism and Nation-States' Structures

Nation-states create a structure of institutions designed to preserve and promote the nation's survival, maintenance, and interests. They have governments, presidents, prime ministers, parliaments, and congresses; they have treasuries, banks and taxation agencies, police and military forces—armies, navies, air forces—to protect their citizens and maintain their borders; they have diplomatic services to handle their relations with other nation-states; they have educational systems that reinforce the sense of national identity and educate young people as citizens according to models of political socialization.

Nation-States and Schools

In the nineteenth century, many nation-states began to establish national school systems. Their initial efforts were halting steps toward national school systems. In the United Kingdom, Parliament began to give financial grants to school societies in the 1830s; France established national primary schools; and the common, or public, school movement began in the United States. Part of the goal in building national school systems was to create key agencies to foster the sense of national identity, or political socialization, and to instill patriotism and citizenship.

In some countries, the national schools either cooperated with or replaced existing religious schools. By the end of the nineteenth century, national school systems were found throughout the world. (Although the United States does not have a national school system, its state systems, collectively, serve to create American identity and citizenship.) In the twentieth century, as new nation-states appeared after winning independence from colonial powers, they, too, established some version of a national school system.

In the United States, public schools provide academic learning to students, but also seek to educate good citizens. The philosophies of school districts throughout the country include promoting citizenship—educating good citizens—as one of their stated goals. Throughout the nineteenth and early twentieth centuries, the public schools' version of educating good citizens emphasized a program of Americanization, designed to assimilate immigrant children into a preferred version of what it meant to be a good American. For example, Ellwood P. Cubberley, a prominent educator, advised public school teachers on how to assimilate immigrant children. Cubberley stated, "Everywhere these people tend to settle in groups or settlements, and to set up here their national manners, customs, and observances. Our task is to break up these groups of people as a part of our American race, and to implant into their children, so far as it can be done, the Anglo-Saxon conception of righteousness, law and order, and popular government, and to awaken in them a reverence for our democratic institutions and for those things in our national life which we as a people hold to be of abiding worth."[1]

Cubberley voiced the concept of being American that dominated public school thinking. The ideal of American nationality was already completed and not subject to alteration. It was modeled on the white, English, Protestant interpretation of the American past. For Cubberley, the immigrants were not to contribute to an expansive and more culturally diverse definition of being an American but were to imitate what was already a completed product.

The public schools used English as the language of instruction to the virtual exclusion of other languages, and taught a select version of American history and literature. The schools stressed standards of behavior that were identified with being a good American: obedience to the laws and established authorities; respect for private property; a willingness to compete, but also to respect the rights of others; diligence; and punctuality.

Today, after a long struggle, multiculturalism has replaced Americanization in the public school ideology. Respecting cultural diversity is now heralded as one of the important behaviors of a good American. James Banks, a leading multicultural educator, in contrast to Cubberley's monocultural stance, argues for a broad transformation of American education that incorporates and infuses the perspectives of many groups into the concept of the good American. According to Banks, "The key curriculum issues involved in multicultural curriculum reform is not the addition of a long list of ethnic groups, heroes, and contributions, but the infusion of various perspectives, frames of references and content from various groups that will extend students' understandings of the nature, development and complexity of U.S. society."[2]

However, the question of how broad or how narrow, how inclusive or exclusive the definition of the good American should be and what the role of schools should be in educating the good American remains highly controversial. In writing about the cultural wars over the definition of an American, James Hunter states: ". . . the contemporary cultural war is ultimately a struggle over national identity—*over the meaning of America*, who we have been in the past, who we are now, and perhaps most important, who we, as a nation, will aspire to become in the new millennium."[3]

Forming Nationalism's "We-Feeling"

In this subsection, we examine how Nationalism works to create a sense of "we-feeling," a sense of fraternal brotherhood and sisterhood based on living in a particular national political space and of being a citizen of that nation. The bonds of national togetherness are found in a common language, common folk and patriotic origins, a common religion, and common expressions of culture.

A Common Language.   A common language is important in forming national group identity. A common language brings people together with shared understandings—ideas, beliefs, and values—and separates them from those who, not speaking the same language, lack this sense of mutuality. Indeed, the ancient Greeks referred to non-Greek speakers as barbarians. Again, we must state the obvious but very important: the English speak English, Germans speak German, Japanese speak Japanese,

Russians speak Russian, and so on. Americans speak English as the unofficial "official" language. Speaking the common language identifies the speaker as belonging to the language group and sharing it with other similar speakers.

While a common language is a means of everyday discourse and communication, it is much more than that in terms of culture. It conveys the nuances of how an idea, belief, or value is expressed. A language expresses the meanings of time, space, honesty, loyalty, beauty, friendship, politeness, and family in the national contexts in which they are used. The language expresses how things are and how they should be. By simply being born into a national culture, children, as part of their development, acquire that country's language. Instruction in schools further refines the child's skill in using the language. (Language politics and education in multiracial, multiethnic, and multilingual nation-states are discussed later in the chapter.)

School systems throughout the world devote much curriculum space and instructional time to teaching language. In the primary or elementary schools, reading instruction is one of the central activities. A child's academic success depends heavily on how well she or he masters the language. As the child learns the language, ideas, beliefs, and values become more contextualized, made more particular, to the national setting. Language instruction begins in the first grade where it may take the form of stories about civic helpers such as fire, police, and postal personnel, or biographical stories about presidents, athletes, scientists, and others who can serve as models. In learning to read the stories, children acquire not only decoding skills but also information and values related to their country. Language instruction continues through middle and high school where an effort is made to improve comprehension, emphasize proper usage, and have the student become increasingly fluent and sophisticated in using the language.

Common Folk and Patriotic Origins.   A sense of "we-feeling" is cultivated by the remembrance of common folk or patriotic origins that are celebrated in anthems, songs, stories, holidays, and other events. In the United States, such common celebratory occasions of remembrance are Memorial Day, Thanksgiving, and Independence Day. They are marked by parades, the posting of the American flag, and the singing of the national anthem. In France, Bastille Day, July 14th, the posting of the tricolor flag and the singing of the Marseilles invokes the historic memories. Each nation has these celebratory events, its heroes, its days of commemoration.

In schools, these events, celebrated with songs, stories, and reenactments, take on a heightened significance for the students, especially for elementary pupils. They are becoming part of the nation as they participate in its patriotic rituals. Much like the rituals of religion, those of patriotism elicit an automatic response. The American flag, the "red, white, and blue" stirs love of country, the pledge to the flag expresses loyalty to the nation, "to the republic for which it stands. . . one nation indivisible."

A Common Religion.   Another ingredient in generating "we-feeling" in many countries is a common religion, often an "official church." In Greece, Russia, Serbia,

Bulgaria, and Romania, the Orthodox Church provides not only religious but also cultural cohesion. In Italy, Poland, Ireland, and Spain, Roman Catholicism provides a religious and cultural bonding. In Israel, Judaism is the religious and cultural link. In Egypt, Pakistan, Malaysia, Afghanistan, and Iran, it is Islam that is deeply embedded in the culture. In Thailand, Buddhism is embedded in the culture. In many countries, churches and religious institutions are powerful informal educational forces and the teaching of religion, especially that of the dominant church, can be found in the state-operated schools.

The United States is an exception in that it does not have a common religion. Church and state are separated by law. The country is religiously pluralistic—there are Protestants, Roman Catholics, Orthodox, Jews, Moslems, and members of other religious denominations.

Common Expressions of Culture.   Nationalism is expressed in the architecture, art forms, literary works, music, poetry, and drama that reflect a national life style. Certain cultural works gain a prominence that expresses the national mood. In the United States, the books of James Fenimore Cooper, Ralph Waldo Emerson, Henry David Thoreau, Herman Melville, Mark Twain, Ernest Hemingway, and F. Scott Fitzgerald express the American literary style and idiom. The architecture of Louis Sullivan and Frank Lloyd Wright express the concepts of American design. Certain buildings, such as the White House, the Washington Monument, the Lincoln Memorial, the Empire State Building, and the Sears Tower, evoke the consciousness of being an American. The terrorist attack on and the destruction of the Twin Towers of the World Trade Center on September 11, 2001 was an attempt to destroy features of the American landscape that convey a sense of the powerful American economy and position in the world.

For Germans, the literary masterpieces of Johann Wolfgang von Goethe and Friedrich Schiller and the music of Ludwig van Beethoven and Richard Wagner evoke the sense of being a German. Wagner's music in particular, although containing some of the world's greatest compositions, also was stridently nationalistic.

In France, nationalist themes were conveyed by Alexander Dumas and Victor Hugo, especially the latter's literary masterpiece, *Les Miserables*. The epic murals in the Louvre and the Chamber of Deputies portray glorious events in France's history. The Eiffel Tower and Arc de Triomphe immediately bring France to mind. In Italy, the stirring operas of Giuseppe Verdi convey a sense of Italian nationalism. Frederic Chopin's stirring Polonaise aroused Polish patriots to rally for their country's freedom.

The names and themes mentioned above provide only a few examples of how nationalism and national culture are expressed in works of art. These works of art, literature, music, and architecture become reference points on the psychic maps of those who share a common national culture. Importantly, they constitute a significant part of the school curriculum and are consciously used to bring the young into contact with and engage them in their national heritage. They are found in courses in literature, music, art, and drama, the subject areas that are laden with values. They are the means of appreciating, participating in, and expressing the national culture.

AMERICAN EXCEPTIONALISM

We now turn to American Exceptionalism, a specific type of nationalism that has exercised a profound impact on American history, culture, and education. We begin by taking a closer look at the words *to except* and *exceptional*, which are at the root of exceptionalism. *To except* means to exclude or to leave out; it emphasizes the exclusion of those who are different. For American Exceptionalism, those who are not Americans are excluded or left out. The word *exceptional* designates an instance or a case of something or someone that does not conform to the general rule. The word *exceptional*, as we will use it here, is celebratory in that it connotes something or someone that is uncommon, excellent, superior, unique, or extraordinary. In terms of **American Exceptionalism**, it means that Americans and their country, the United States, are unique and differ from other countries. The American nation, its people, and their culture are different from the people of other countries; they are extraordinary.

Situating American Exceptionalism

A young French visitor to the United States, Alexis de Tocqueville, spent 1831 and 1832 traveling around the country. He was a penetrating observer of American institutions, culture, and manners. Returning to France, he wrote his classic book, *Democracy in America*, published in 1835. His sage comparisons about the differences between the American and European temperaments were prophetic and have stood the test of time. Noting "the peculiar and accidental situation in which Providence placed the Americans," Tocqueville wrote, "Everything about the Americans, from their social condition to their laws, is extraordinary; but the most extraordinary thing of all is the land that supports them."[4] He observed that underlying the democratic fabric of American society was a widely shared concept of equality. Americans, he observed, see that "democratic institutions flourish" in their country but fail elsewhere. Americans "have an immensely high opinion of themselves and are not far from believing that they form a species apart from the rest of the human race."[5] Politically, Americans were committed to the ideal of majority rule but also believed in the respect for the minority and the possibility that a minority might become a majority. Further, Americans looked for practical solutions to problems rather than to grand theories. Religion, Tocqueville predicted, would become more flexible and adaptable in the United States but would nevertheless inform a generalized national ethic. He noted that Americans were joiners, forming numerous clubs, societies, and interest groups.

As the United States moved westward to occupy the vast territory lying between the Atlantic and Pacific Oceans during the nineteenth century, American Exceptionalism was expressed in terms of the nation's "manifest destiny." According to the doctrine of American Exceptionalism, God had favored Americans above other peoples. Protected by the moat-like barriers and isolation afforded by the two great oceans, they were given a continent of vast resources to settle and exploit. In their protected habitat, Americans created the best of all possible systems—a republican form of government, democratic institutions, and a free-enterprise economy. The United States was to be the beacon light of progress that shone on and illuminated less fortunate lands and peoples. The United States was a model of how people could and should live, a moral and political exemplar for the rest of the world.

American Exceptionalism as an ideology operates, as do all ideologies, on a selective collective memory. The account of the United States as an exceptional nation celebrates and glorifies cultural, political, and educational achievements, and does not emphasize events that are rather deliberately repressed rather than brought to consciousness in the collective memory, such as the genocide against Native Americans; slavery and racial segregation of African Americans; class conflicts and exploitation of workers and others; and destruction of the natural environment.

American Exceptionalism and Education

When the common-school leaders created public schools, they conceived of them as sociocultural, as well as educational, agencies for forging a sense of American cultural nationalism and identity. The public schools themselves were the exceptional institutions created by an exceptional people.[6] Even before public schools were established in the first half of the nineteenth century, the revolutionary and early national educator, Noah Webster, set about the task of creating a language that while still English, would be distinctly American. He wrote spelling and reading books that helped to standardize the American language. His most masterful achievement was writing the dictionary that still bears his name. Like Franklin, Jefferson, and other founding fathers, Webster defined who Americans were by contrasting them with Europeans. Americans represented the new world while Europeans clung to old ways and customs. Americans practiced the equality of the frontier while Europeans were divided by birth into rigidly ascribed and separated classes. Americans were industrious, innovative, and experimental while Europeans sought the security of conforming to the past and keeping things as they once were.[7]

The public schools, originally called common schools, differed from those of Europe. Unlike European schools, American public schools were accessible to all the children of all the people. While European schools were organized and attended on the basis of socioeconomic class, American public schools were comprehensive institutions that enrolled children of all classes. While Europe's schools were designed to perpetuate the status quo and maintain class distinctions, American public schools were designed as agencies of upward social and economic mobility. Thus, like the nation itself, American public schools were celebrated as exceptional institutions that could be found nowhere else in the world.

Note that the account of public schooling given above is based on American Exceptionalism. In this account, the school system is celebrated and acclaimed. This kind of interpretation does not include some of the failings of American public education. It does not deal with slavery, racial segregation, forced assimilation of immigrants, and gross inequalities from district to district and state to state in the funding of public education.

ETHNONATIONALISM

So far we have discussed Nationalism as a general ideology that glorifies and expresses identification and membership in a nation-state and American Exceptionalism as a unique American expression of Nationalism. We now turn to Ethnonationalism, an important contemporary force that is having a profound impact on the post–Cold War world. The prefix *ethno* is borrowed from the Greek word *ethnos* that means race, culture, or people. The term *ethnic*, also derived from the Greek root, pertains to the members of a race or nationality who speak the same language and share a distinctive culture. Ethnonationalism is an ideology that combines the sense of ethnic identity with a movement for independence or autonomy from a larger political unit.[8]

Distinctions Between Nationalism and Ethnonationalism

At first, Nationalism and Ethnonationalism may seem to be very similar. In the few nations where there is a single ethnic group, such as Japan and Iceland, Nationalism and Ethnonationalism do indeed converge. In many other nations, however, they may diverge.

Nationalism, focused on nation-states, has worked to shape loyalties that focus on the nation. For example, racial and ethnic groups such as African Americans, Hispanic Americans, German Americans, and Japanese Americans are expected to embrace the larger national identity of being an American. **Ethnonationalism** focuses primary identification and loyalty to one's particular racial and ethnic group. While Nationalism focuses on the nation as a larger and more encompassing entity, Ethnonationalism may erode larger commitments and replace them with a more particular racial or ethnic identification.

Ethnonationalism as an Ideology

Ethnonationalism rests on the belief that an individual is a member of a unique group that is descended from common ancestors and has a blood relationship with others of the group.[9] The belief in a common ancestry does not depend on DNA verification or other scientific tests. It is based on myth and history, in some instances a creation story that is emotionally powerful. The various enthnonational groups have strong traditions and narratives, often epics, about the group's origins, history, triumphs, and adversities. The transmission of the group's language and heritage from the older generation to the younger takes place through informal methods—stories, myths, celebrations, coming-of-age rituals—as well as formal education in schools.

Educational Implications.   As indicated, education is a process that creates group identity and the sense of "we-feeling." Informal education—living in the particular ethnocultural milieu of family, kinship group, ethnic community, church, and community—socializes children into that particular ethnic group. In instances where the particular ethnic group is dominant, schools, too, continue the process of ethnic socialization. However, in instances where the particular ethnic group is subordinate, its children may attend schools where the language of instruction and the curriculum reflect the dominant group's culture rather than its own. Historically, the process of Americanization in the United States represented the use of schooling to impose the dominant group's culture on subordinate groups. The process, if successful, leads to the erosion of the subordinate culture and brings its members into the dominant culture. Some of the controversies over bilingual, bicultural education reflect ethnonational issues in the United States.

In some countries, ethnonational issues are interwoven with language issues. Is there to be an official language or are there to be several languages used in government and education? When ethnonational issues surface in education, they involve: (1) using the ethnic group's language rather than the dominant group's official language; (2) including the ethnic group's traditions, literature, and history in the curriculum; (3) constructing a school milieu that celebrates and reinforces ethnic group membership and identity.

Defenders of the nation-state as the central focus of identity argue that using several languages rather than the dominant national one is divisive and will weaken the nation. Those who seek ethnonational recognition, autonomy, or independence challenge the nation-state argument by contending that every group has the right to ensure its ongoing existence.

The Tide of Contemporary Ethnonationalism

A very strong trend in recent history has been the revival of Ethnonationalism as a result of the disintegration of some multiethnic nation-states. After the disintegration of the Union of Soviet Socialist Republics in 1990, it was replaced by a number of independent nation-states, such as Russia, Ukraine, Belarus, Uzbekistan, Kazakstan, and Armenia. Czechoslovakia peacefully divided into two independent nation-states: the Czech Republic and Slovakia. The disintegration of Yugoslavia was marked by ethnic cleansing and violence as Croatia, Slovenia, Macedonia, and Bosnia overcame Serbian opposition to become independent nation-states. The wars in Bosnia and Kosovo were marked by serious human rights violations such as ethnic violence and genocide which, in turn, led to NATO intervention that included involvement of U.S. military forces.

In Africa, Ethnonationalism takes the form of tribalism. In countries such as Nigeria, Burundi, Rwanda, the Sudan and others, the primary identification is to the tribe rather than to the nation-state. In Nigeria, for example, the political and educational situation has been complicated by the attempts of Yorubas, Hausas, and Ibos to gain hegemony over each other.

In the Western world, Ethnonationalism has asserted itself in political and educational conflicts in Canada where the French-speaking Quebecois energetically seek to maintain their language and culture against Anglicization; in Belgium, where the Flemish resist Walloons; and in Spain, where the Basques seek greater autonomy.

The Ethnonationalism Dilemma.   Nationalism, resting in the nation-state or country, and Ethnonationalism, resting in the ethnic group, pose a contemporary world dilemma. Nations such as the United Kingdom, France, China, and the United States have the right to maintain their integrity and security. Ethnic groups have the right to maintain their ethnic cultures, languages, and traditions. In some instances, the tensions between these two rights have erupted in violent confrontation and conflict. Some subordinated ethnic groups such as the Kurds, who live in Iraq, Iran, and Turkey, the Chechens in Russia, and the Albanians in Kosovo have resorted to armed conflict to win their independence. Some of the Basques in Spain and the Chechens in Russia have used terrorist tactics to win greater autonomy or independence.

LOOKING TO THE FUTURE

As we have discussed, the world is organized into nation-states—independent, sovereign countries—each of which uses Nationalism to create and maintain a sense of national identity. National school systems socialize that nation's children to create good citizens. How this socialization takes place is important for the future of the nation-state. It can involve identity with one's own country, but also respect for the people of other countries. Or, it can take the form of chauvinism, which exalts one's country over all others. Extreme Nationalism has led to world wars and conflicts. Ethnonationalist conflicts have generated violence against civilians, often with a large number of victims being women and children. Those who propose nonviolent ways to solve these issues often turn to education, emphasizing programs of conflict resolution and muliculturalism.

Ethnic identification can be a source of group pride and self-esteem. It can be a positive celebration of one's ethnic heritage that also respects the racial and ethnic heritages of other people. If, however, ethnic identification becomes a strident assertion of one group's superiority over others it can lead to suspicion, stereotyping, and violence against members of other groups. Strident Ethnonationalism can degenerate into ethnocentrism, the belief in the inherent superiority of one's group, seeing members of other groups as inferior.

In the United States, the United Kingdom, and in other countries, there has been an effort to develop and implement multicultural programs into the schools.[10] Multicultural programs encourage a respect for cultural pluralism and diversity in which each racial and ethnic group is seen as having the right to express its distinctive culture and in which this expression is viewed as an enriching contribution to the larger national culture.

A serious issue in multicultural educational programs is finding the right balance between identification with the larger national culture and the particular racial or ethnic subculture. With rising Ethnonationalism, with increasing violence of group against group, and with the use of terror to achieve goals of ethnic autonomy or independence, it becomes imperative to find the principle of balance.

NOAH WEBSTER, AN EDUCATION FOR AMERICANS

Noah Webster, author of the dictionary that bears his name, was an advocate of American cultural Nationalism. He believed that Americans, as an independent people, should shape their own language and their own education. This selection is included as a primary source because Webster was an influential educational voice for cultural Nationalism. A truly American education was important, Webster believed, in creating a distinctive identity for citizens of the new republic. As you read the selection, you may wish to reflect on the following focusing questions:

1. Why does Webster oppose sending young Americans abroad for a foreign education?

2. How do you think Webster would react to the foreign-study programs offered by many colleges and universities?

3. How are Webster's arguments an example of American Exceptionalism?

. . . Before I quit this subject, I beg leave to make some remarks on a practice which appears to be attended with important consequences; I mean that of sending boys to Europe for an education, or sending to Europe for teachers. That this was right before the revolution will not be disputed; at least so far as national attachments were concerned; but the propriety of it ceased with our political relation to Great Britain.

In the first place, our honor as an independent nation is concerned in the establishment of literary institutions, adequate to all our own purposes; without sending our youth abroad, or depending on other nations for books and instructors. It is very little to the reputation of America to have it said abroad, that after the heroic achievements of the late war, this independent people are obliged to send to Europe for men and books to teach their children A B C.

But in another point of view, a foreign education is directly opposite to our political interests and ought to be discountenanced, if not prohibited.

Every person of common observation will grant, that most men prefer the manners and the government of that country where they are educated. Let ten American youths be sent, each to a different European kingdom, and live there from the age of twelve to twenty, & each will give the preference to the country where he has resided.

The period from twelve to twenty is the most important in life. The impressions made before that period are commonly effaced; those that are made during that period *always* remain for many years, and *generally* thro' life.

Ninety-nine persons of a hundred, who pass that period in England or France, will prefer the people, their manners, their laws, and their government to those of their native country.

From Noah Webster, *The American Magazine*, May, 1788, pp. 307–373.

Such attachments are injurious, both to the happiness of the men, and to the political interests of their own country. As to private happiness, it is universally known how much pain a man suffers by a change of habits in living. The customs of Europe are and ought to be different from ours; but when a man has been bred in one country, his attachments to its manners make them in a great measure, necessary to his happiness; on changing his residence, he must therefore break his former habits, which is always a painful sacrifice; or the discordance between the manners of his own country and his habits, must give him incessant uneasiness; or he must introduce, into a circle of his friends, the manners in which he was educated. All these consequences may follow at the same time, and the last, which is inevitable, is a public injury. The refinement of manners in every country should keep pace exactly with the increase of its wealth—and perhaps the greatest evil America now feels is, an improvement of taste and manners which its wealth cannot support.

A foreign education is the very source of this evil—it gives young gentlemen of fortune a relish for manners and amusements which are not suited to this country; which, however, when introduced by this class of people, will always become fashionable.

But a corruption of manners is not the sole objection to a foreign education; an attachment to a *foreign* government, or rather a want of attachment to our *own*, is the natural effect of a residence abroad, during the period of youth. It is recorded of one of the Greek cities, that in a treaty with their conquerors, it was required that they should give a certain number of *male children* as hostages for the fulfilment of their engagements. The Greeks absolutely refused, on the principle that these children would imbibe the ideas and embrace the manners of foreigners, or lose their love for their own country: But they offered the same number of *old* men, without hesitation. This anecdote is full of good sense. A man should always form his

habits and attachments in the country where he is to reside for life. When these habits are formed, young men may travel without danger of losing their patriotism. A boy who lives in England from twelve to twenty, will be an *Englishman* in his manners and his feelings; but let him remain at home till he is twenty, and form his attachments, he may then be several years abroad, and still be an *American*. There may be exceptions to this observation; but living examples may be mentioned, to prove the truth of the general principle here advanced, respecting the influence of habit.

It may be said that foreign universities furnish much better opportunities of improvement in the sciences than the American. This may be true, and yet will not justify the practice of sending young lads from their own country. There are some branches of science which may be studied to much greater advantage in Europe than in America, particularly chymistry. When these are to be acquired, young gentlemen ought to spare no pains to attend the best professors. It may, therefore, be useful, in some cases, for students to cross the atlantic to *complete* a course of studies; but it is not necessary for them to go early in life, nor to continue a long time. Such instances need not be frequent even now; and the necessity for them will diminish in proportion to the future advancement of literature in America.

It is, however, much questioned whether, in the ordinary course a study, a young man can enjoy greater advantages in Europe than in America. Experience inclines me to raise a doubt, whether the danger to which a youth must be exposed among the sons of dissipation abroad, will not turn the scale in favor of our American colleges. Certain it is, that four fifths of the great literary characters in America never crossed the Atlantic.

But if our universities and schools are not so good as the English or Scotch, it is the business of our rulers to improve them—not to endow them merely; for endowments alone will never make a flourishing seminary—but to furnish them with professors of the first abilities and most assiduous application, and with a complete apparatus for establishing theories by experiments. Nature has been profuse to the Americans, in genius, and in the advantages of climate and soil. If this country, therefore, should long be indebted to Europe for opportunities of acquiring any branch of science in perfection, it must be by means of a criminal neglect of its inhabitants.

The difference in the nature of the American and European governments, is another objection to a foreign education. Men form modes of reasoning or habits of thinking on political subjects, in the country where they are bred—these modes of reasoning may be founded on fact in all countries—but the same principles will not apply in all governments, because of the infinite variety of national opinions and habits. Before a man can be a good Legislator, he must be intimately acquainted with the temper of the people to be governed. No man can be thus acquainted with a people, without residing amongst them and mingling with all companies. For want of this acquaintance, a Turgot and a Price may reason most absurdly upon the constitutions of the American states; and when any person has been long accustomed to believe in the propriety or impropriety of certain maxims or regulations of government, it is very difficult to change his opinions, or to persuade him to adapt this reasoning to new and different circumstances. . .

It is therefore of infinite importance that those who direct the councils of a nation, should be educated in that nation. Not that they should restrict their personal acquaintance to their own country, but their first ideas, attachments and habits should be acquired in the country which they are to govern and defend. When a knowledge of their own country is obtained, and an attachment to its laws and interests deeply fixed in their hearts, then young gentlemen may travel with infinite advantage and perfect safety. I wish not therefore to discourage travelling, but, if possible, to render it more useful to individuals and to the community. My meaning is, that *men* should travel, and not *boys*.

But it is time for the Americans to change their usual route, and travel thro a country which they never think of, or think beneath their notice.—I mean the United States.

While these States were a part of the British Empire, our interest, our feelings, were those of English men—our dependence led us to respect and imitate their manners—and to look up to them for our opinions. We little thought of any national interest in America—and while our commerce and government were in the hands of our parent country, and we had no common interest, we little thought of improving our acquaintance with each other or of removing prejudices, and reconciling the discordant feelings of the inhabitants of the different Provinces. But independence and union render it necessary that the citizens of different States should know each others characters and circumstances—that all jealousies should be removed—that mutual respect and confidence should succeed—and a harmony of views and interests be cultivated by a friendly intercourse. . . .

Americans, unshackle your minds, and act like independent beings. You have been children long enough, subject to the control, and subservient to the interest of a haughty parent. You have now an interest of your own to augment and defend—you have an empire to raise and support by your exertions—and a national character to establish and extend by your wisdom and virtues. To effect these great objects, it is necessary to frame a liberal plan of policy, and to build it on a broad system of education. Before this system can be formed and embraced, the Americans must *believe* and *act* from the belief, that it is dishonorable to waste life in mimicking the follies of other nations, and basking in the sunshine of foreign glory.

CONCLUSION

This chapter examined the ideology of Nationalism and the related ideologies of American Exceptionalism and Ethnonationalism. Nationalism has had far-reaching effects on society and schooling. It is so penetrating that it extends itself into the other ideologies treated in this chapter and the ones discussed in later chapters. American Exceptionalism is the American belief that the United States is a unique country with a special mission in the world. Ethnonationalism is examined as a force that can cause unrest and readjustments throughout the world as suppressed groups seek autonomy or independence from larger nation-states.

DISCUSSION QUESTIONS

1. What kind of cultural identity should public schools promote?
2. What are the roots of American Exceptionalism? Why do many people think the United States has a special mission in the world?
3. Examine the relationship or issues between multiculturalism and American identity.
4. How do times of crisis, such as the "War on Terrorism," promote Nationalism in society, politics, and education?
5. What are the strengths and dangers presented by Nationalism, American Exceptionalism, and Ethnonationalism?

INQUIRY AND RESEARCH PROJECTS

1. Reflect on your own educational experiences. How have these experiences been a source of nationalist identification?
2. Examine several books that advocate multiculturalism in American education. How do these books treat Nationalism and Ethnonationalism?
3. Examine several projects that deal with Holocaust education. How do these projects deal with Nationalism and Ethnonationalism?
4. Do an analysis of the newspapers and television news programs. Identify the instances in which Nationalist or Ethnonationalist conflicts are the subject.
5. Review several American History textbooks used in elementary or secondary schools. How do these books deal with Nationalism and American identity?

INTERNET RESOURCES

An excellent guide to sources on Nationalism is the Nationalism Project at **www.nationalismproject.org**

Nationalism is discussed at the Modern History Source Book at **www.fordham.edu/ha/sall/mod/1784herder-mankind.htm**

SUGGESTIONS FOR FURTHER READING

Alter, Peter. *Nationalism.* New York: Edward Arnold, 1994.

Banks, James A., and Banks, Cherry A. McGee. *Multicultural Education: Issues and Perspectives.* Boston: Allyn and Bacon, 1989.

Barkan, Elazaer, and Shelton, Marie-Denise. *Borders, Exiles, Diasporas.* Stanford, CA: Stanford University Press, 1998.

Brass, Paul R. *Ethnicity and Nationalism: Theory and Comparison.* Newbury Park, CA: Sage, 1991.

Breton, Albert; Galeotti, Gianluigi; Salmon, Pierre; Wintrahe, Ronald, eds. *Nationalism and Rationality.* Cambridge, UK, and New York: Cambridge University Press, 1996.

Callahan, David. *Unwinnable Wars: American Power and Ethnic Conflict.* New York: Hill and Wang, 1997.

Chua, Amy. *World on Fire: How Exporting Free Market Democracy Breeds Ethnic Hatred and Global Instability.* New York: Doubleday, 2003.

Connor, Walker. *Ethnonationalism: The Quest for Understanding.* Princeton, NJ: Princeton University Press, 1994.

Diamond, Larry, and Plattner, Marc F. *Nationalism, Ethnic Conflict, and Democracy.* Baltimore: Johns Hopkins University Press, 1994.

Farnen, Russell F., ed. *Nationalism, Ethnicity, and Identity: Cross National and Comparative Perspectives.* New Brunswick, NJ: Transaction Publishers, 1994.

Gellner, Ernest. *Encounters with Nationalism.* Oxford, UK, and Cambridge, MA: Blackwell Publishers, 1994.

Ignatieff, Michael. *Blood and Belonging: Journeys into the New Nationalism.* New York: Farrar, Straus, and Giroux, 1994.

Kecmanovic, Dusan. *The Mass Psychology of Ethnonationalism.* London: Routledge, 1997.

Kellas, James G. *The Politics of Nationalism and Ethnicity.* New York: St. Martin's Press, 1991.

Nieto, Sonia. *Affirming Diversity: The Sociopolitical Context of Multicultural Education.* New York: Longman, 1992.

Smith, Anthony D., ed. *Ethnicity and Nationalism.* New York: E. J. Brill, 1992.

NOTES

1. Ellwood P. Cubberley, *Changing Conceptions of Education* (Boston: Houghton-Mifflin 1909), pp. 15–16.

2. James A. Banks and Cherry A. Banks, *Multicultural Education: Issues and Perspectives,* 2nd ed. (Boston: Allyn and Bacon, 1993), p. 203.

3. James Davison Hunter, *Culture Wars: The Struggle to Define America* (New York: Basic Books, 1995), p. 59.

4. Alexis de Tocqueville, *Democracy in America,* J. P. Lawrence, ed. (New York: Perennial Classics/Harper-Collins Publishers, 2000), p. 280.

5. Ibid., p. 374.

6. For American Exceptionalism, see Seymour M. Lipset, *American Exceptionalism: A Double-Edged Sword* (New York: W.W. Norton & Co., 1996).

7. Frances Fitzgerald, *America Revised: History Schoolbooks in the Twentieth Century* (New York: Random House, 1979), p. 74.

8. Walker Connor, *Ethnonationalism: The Quest for Understanding* (Princeton, NJ: Princeton University Press, 1994), p. xi.

9. Ibid., pp. 74–75.

10. Banks and Banks, pp. 3–4. Also see, Sonia Nieto, *Affirming Diversity: The Sociopolitical Contest of Multicultural Education* (New York: Longman, 1992).

CHAPTER ELEVEN

LIBERALISM

In this chapter, we examine Liberalism, one of the most significant ideologies in Western and American culture and society. We will define Liberalism, examine it as an ideology, and discuss its implications for education.

DEFINING LIBERALISM

To define Liberalism, we go to its root, the term *liberal*. A liberal is a person who believes progress is possible and desirable, and that the human condition can be improved by reforming society, the economy, politics, and education. Opposing repressive political regimes, liberals support representative forms of government that protect and secure personal and civil rights. They believe individuals should enjoy the greatest possible freedom and that this freedom should be guaranteed by constitutional protections, due process of law, and the protection of civil liberties. In education, liberals are not bound by tradition but believe in the free flow of ideas and the testing of ideas in human experience. **Liberalism** is an ideology that expresses these beliefs about human freedom, seeks to protect those freedoms with procedures of representative institutions, and promises that it is possible to improve the human condition by reform and education.

WHY STUDY LIBERALISM?

Since the late eighteenth century, Liberalism, in its various expressions, has been one of the major ideologies in American and Western society, politics, and education. It has had a particularly pronounced impact on the history of the United Kingdom and the United States. The Liberal ideology has been used as the rationale for a larger social, health, and educational role and services by government. Liberalism has also argued that schools, in addition to their academic functions, should have a larger social role. For example, schools should be used to promote racial integration, to solve problems such as drug and alcohol abuse, to inform students about safe sex, to encourage conflict resolution, and to promote multiculturalism. Today, Liberalism vies with Conservatism as one of the two major competing ideologies in the United States.

SITUATING LIBERALISM

The definition of Liberalism given above may sound very appealing. You might ask: Who would quarrel with it? Who would not want freedom of thought, civil rights, and due process of law? The answer is that Liberalism today is under serious attack and many Americans, especially religious fundamentalists, see Liberalism as a dangerous ideology that has weakened traditional values. Conservatives oppose Liberalism as an ideology that, by encouraging cultural relativism and pluralism, has weakened cherished traditions and values. (For a discussion of Conservatism, refer to Chapter 12.) Neo-Marxists and Critical Theorists attack Liberalism as promoting a false consciousness, an ideological smoke screen, that is a cover for special political and economic interests and educational bureaucrats. (See Chapter 13 for a discussion of Marxism and Chapter 19 for Critical Theory.) We can try to determine why Liberalism is so controversial by considering its origins, history, and development.

The Age of Reason

Liberalism's origins begin with the Eighteenth-Century Enlightenment, the "Age of Reason," a powerful intellectual movement that eventually reshaped the European and American world view. The key ideas of the Enlightenment were voiced by the *philosophes*, a circle of intellectual critics that included such notables as Denis Diderot, Etienne Condillac, and Jean-Jacques Rousseau. The philosophes believed that human beings could achieve unlimited and ongoing progress if allowed to apply their reason to the problems of society.[1] For them, the application of reason meant using the method of scientific inquiry, not only to examine natural and physical phenomena, but to examine human life and society. Such inquiry, they believed, would enable them to discover the natural laws that not only regulated natural phenomena but could be applied to social, political, economic, and educational institutions. If these natural laws were discovered and permitted to function freely without repression from church and state, human life and society could be reformed, improved, and perfected. However, powerfully entrenched special interests and institutions were in place that blocked the needed inquiry and the projected reforms. Among the institutions that blocked reform were the monarchy, in which a king ruled with unquestioned authority by the grace of God; the aristocracy who occupied places of ascribed influence and privilege not by merit, but simply by their birth into privileged noble families; a Church that emphasized the unquestioning acceptance of its dogma; a society and economy based on rigid social-class divisions and the proposition that the "poor would always be with us"; and schools and teachers who told students that "they lived in the best of all possible worlds."

The philosophes' questioning of the institutions of the old order generated a practice of challenging authority that worked to undermine the establishment. These ideas contributed to the republican ideology of the American Revolution of 1776 and the French Revolution of 1789.

The Enlightenment theorists made the following contributions to Liberalism: (1) the belief that scientific inquiry could be applied to society and social institutions; (2) the human condition could be improved by social, political, economic, and educational reforms; (3) progress was a real possibility for the human future. In Chapter 8, Postmodernism was examined. Recall that the Postmodernist philosophers attack the Enlightenment construction of reason as a contributing factor to the conditions of oppression they attribute to modernism.

The Enlightenment theorists developed some important ideas about education that would become part of Liberalism's educational agenda. They challenged the traditional assumption that education should be entrusted to the church. Religious dogmatism, they argued, was antithetical to rational scientific inquiry. They questioned the usefulness of the classical curriculum of Greek and Latin inherited from the Middle Ages and the Renaissance and urged the addition of scientific and practical subjects into education. They argued that education should be used to cultivate informed and critical thinkers who used their reason, rather than training dogmatic and superstitious conformists.

John Locke and the Contract Theory

John Locke (1632–1704), an English philosopher and political theorist, is especially important for establishing the foundations of Anglo-American Liberalism. His *Essay Concerning Human Understanding* (1690) is a classic statement of empiricist philosophy.[2] In it, Locke attacked the Platonic theory of innate ideas and argued, instead, that the human mind, at birth, is a blank slate and that our ideas come to us from sensation of the external world. He also wrote *Some Thoughts Concerning Education* (1693), in which he asserted that the aims of education are to cultivate virtue and wisdom and to prepare individuals to manage their personal, economic, and political affairs prudently and morally.

It was Locke's *Two Treatises of Government* (1690), however, that had the greatest influence on Liberalism's ideological development.[3] Challenging the divine right of kings theory of government, Locke made what was then a bold assertion of individual rights. Each individual, he said, is born with the inalienable natural rights of life, liberty, and property. People come together and establish a government to protect these

■ ■ ■ ■ ■

THE ENLIGHTENMENT'S CONTRIBUTION TO LIBERALISM

1. Use of the scientific method to discover the natural law governing society
2. The need for reform of existing institutions
3. The possibility of human progress

rights against those who would try to violate them. Government arises from the consent of the people who are governed. Government, thus, results from a contract, a mutual agreement among those who are governed.

To ensure that government does not become too powerful, Locke built several safeguards into his system. First, there is the principle of representative government and the election of its members by majority rule, determined by simply counting the votes. Candidates who receive the most votes are elected to office—as legislators or members of the executive branch. Of course, with a majority, there is a minority, whose rights are to be respected. Majorities and minorities are temporary; in the next election, the current majority may become a minority and vice versa.

Further, the government is divided into three branches: a legislature that passes the laws, a judiciary that interprets and adjudicates them, and an executive that enforces them. With this threefold division of powers, no one branch is to become more powerful than the others.

Locke's system also included the safeguard of fixed terms for those elected to office. Elected officials come from the people, serve for a fixed term, and then return to the people who elected them to office. Importantly, Locke warned that if a government violates the conditions of the contract with the people, the people have the right to rebel against and alter or overthrow it.

Locke's warning against repressive government strongly appealed to the colonists in North America who rebelled against the English rule of King George III. Thomas Jefferson, who wrote the Declaration of Independence, borrowed Locke's ideas to justify the American Revolution against a tyrannical king. In so doing, Jefferson asserted that Americans, as individuals, possessed the inalienable rights of life, liberty, and pursuit of happiness. When the Constitution of the United States was established, it contained the important Lockean provisions of representative government, checks and balances, and majority rule.

Classical Liberalism's Doctrines

In nineteenth-century Europe and America, a body of political, social, and economic doctrines called Classical Liberalism developed. The following section examines these doctrines, which represent an important phase in liberalism's history. It is also important to note that some of these economic ideas were readily accepted in the United States and, ironically, became part of American Conservatism. (Conservatism is examined Chapter 12.)

■ ■ ■ ■ ■

LOCKE'S CONTRIBUTIONS TO LIBERALISM

1. The individual person comes first in society.
2. Every individual has the inalienable rights of life, liberty, and property.
3. Government is a contract between the people and the government.
4. Government should be a representative system of checks and balances.
5. The political system is governed by majority rule.

Liberalism in its origins and in its classical phase was a reaction against authoritarian governments, especially those of absolute monarchies and landed aristocracies. As an ideology, Liberalism gained its greatest support from the middle classes—the lawyers, bankers, businessmen, and industrialists—who were shut out of positions of power in the old order based on one's birth. (In the early nineteenth century, the European class structure basically consisted of three classes—the upper aristocratic class, the lower peasantry and small farmers, and the business and professional classes located between them, and thus known as the middle class.) In place of a rigid hierarchical society, Liberals argued for social mobility, in which individuals could climb as high as their merits, especially measured by industriousness and productivity, would take them.

In asserting themselves against the vested interests of the time, Liberals sought safeguards and protections against authoritarian governments in the form of what can be called negative freedoms—freedom from government control and imposition. Namely, they wanted laws that prevented governments from interfering with freedom of speech, press, assembly, and religion. For their own protection, they wanted the due process of common or public law, and freedom from arbitrary arrest and confinement.

Economically, the middle-class liberals, whose position rested on earned rather than inherited wealth, were the rising upwardly mobile class. Believing that their productivity and industriousness would be best rewarded in a political situation free of restraints, they endorsed a free market, laissez-faire, capitalist economy. They justified such an order by appealing to what they called the natural laws of supply and demand. Based on Adam Smith's *The Wealth of Nations*, supply and demand meant simply that when goods were scarce there would be a demand for them in the market. Entrepreneurs would rush to produce the scarce item and make a profit in so doing. However, after a time, the demand would be satisfied, overproduction would occur and the price would fall. Competitive enterprising individuals would then invest in and produce the next item of scarcity and so on. In the process, there would be periods of economic prosperity, followed by periods of recession. People who invested unwisely would lose their money and some workers would be unemployed. However, in this model the government was to stay out of the economy. It should not get involved in providing relief to the unemployed, nor should it interfere with how businesses operate. If allowed to function naturally, the free market would, by its own operation, create greater efficiency of production and labor and eventually generate a higher level of economic prosperity, which would benefit everyone.

Classical Liberalism had implications for religion and education. Liberals opposed the idea that there should be an established church that was officially recognized and supported by the state. Many of these Liberals were dissenters from official churches, such as the Church of England in the United Kingdom. Like Jefferson in the United States, they opted for separation of church and state. Further, many Liberals believed that Church-related or -controlled schools would be too dogmatic to give the kind of critical education that industrious, competitive persons needed in a modern economy based on merit rather than birth. They also opposed using funds raised by public taxation to establish or support any religion.

In the early nineteenth century, most secondary schools and especially the colleges and universities emphasized the traditional classical curriculum—Latin and

■ ■ ■ ■ ■

CLASSICAL LIBERAL PROPOSITIONS

1. Assertion of individualism, especially in the economy
2. Freedom from government controls and restraints on individuals
3. Operation of the natural law of supply and demand
4. Productivity and economic progress through competition in the free market
5. Need for practical, applied, scientific education, free from Church control

Greek languages and literature—that was considered the hallmark of an educated person. Absent from the traditional classical curriculum were subjects such as mathematics and science as well as the applied studies of engineering, accounting, and so forth that were needed for an innovative, competitive, industrial economy. Liberals wanted educational reforms. They wanted greater access to schools, especially secondary and higher institutions, and a more scientific curriculum that could be lead to economic productivity.

Liberalism in Transition: Utilitarianism

In the early nineteenth century in the United Kingdom, *Utilitarianism*, a new philosophy developed by Jeremy Bentham, attracted those who wanted to reform social, political, legal, and educational institutions. Utilitarianism, as its root indicates, argued that philosophy should have utility; that is, it should be useful rather than just an intellectual exercise. Bentham drew into his circle such leading reformers as James Mill and his son, John Stuart Mill.

Bentham's Utilitarianism, a reconceptualization of Lockean Liberalism, questioned some laissez-faire Classical Liberal doctrines. Utilitarians argued that at certain times, the state, or government, needed to enact reforms, modernize institutions, and deliberately seek to improve the human condition through legislation and education. Bentham believed that all human decisions, including those needed in order to reform society, could be made by the principle of utility—that which brings the greatest good for the greatest number of people. Utility could be determined by using a calculus, a way of adding up the amount and degree of pleasure or pain that would occur when a decision was acted upon. Bentham believed that institutions such as the parliament, the law courts, the prisons, and the schools had become so weighted down by tradition that they functioned poorly and needed to be reformed and modernized according to the principle of utility.

Among the Utilitarians was the social and political critic John Stuart Mill, who revised Bentham's ideas into a ringing statement of human liberties.[4] Mill believed that society and its institutions, including schools, should be open to all ideas, even unpopular or unconventional ones. In an open-minded society, ideas could be discussed, debated, clarified, and revised. In an open forum the best ideas would win out and no areas would be closed to consideration, even if they were part of cherished tradition grounded in religion or custom. The individual's freedom, Mill asserted, was limited only to the point where it interfered with another person's freedom. Espousing political and educational reform, Mill became a proponent of women's rights and suffrage.

The Utilitarianism of Bentham and John Stuart Mill moved Liberalism in a new direction. Not only was it an ideology that sought to safeguard individual and civil liberties but now it was to be an instrument of social, political, economic, and educational reform. The new social reformist strain in Liberalism split the Liberal ranks. Some Liberals remained loyal to the Classical Liberal doctrines of noninterference by government and laissez-faire in the economy. In the United States, these Classical Liberal doctrines became a key part of the Conservative ideology, examined in Chapter 12. Other Liberals saw the government as a necessary agency of social reform. The new social reformist Liberals were gradualists, not revolutionaries. They believed that reform should take place incrementally and bring about a gradual improvement that restored existing institutions to an efficient and good working order, rather than overturning them.

Based on our survey of Utilitarianism, we can speculate on how a Utilitarian would reform schools. They would accept schools as necessary and beneficial institutions. However, over time, schools, like other institutions, can become overly formal and too traditional. The curriculum and methods of teaching might become irrelevant to socioeconomic change. They might not reflect scientific discoveries and technological innovations. When this happens, the schools need to be reformed and reinvigorated. Curriculum and instruction could be reconceptualized to incorporate new areas of knowledge. New subjects and skills might need to be added and obsolete ones removed. Such a process of educational reform would save schools as an institution and make them more relevant and efficient. This kind of incremental and gradual innovation would work for the good of the greatest number of students and teachers.

American Modern Liberalism

In the United States, Liberalism experienced a significant transformation in the early twentieth century when it was infused by ideas from the Progressive movement. The Progressive movement arose in the first two decades of the twentieth century and is associated with efforts to reform American politics, society, economics, and education. Progressive reformers depended on investigative journalists such as Upton Sinclair for his exposé of the meat-packing industry in *The Jungle* and Ida Tarbell for her exposé of the Standard Oil Company to inform the public about political corruption, business

■ ■ ■ ■ ■

THE UTILITARIAN CONTRIBUTIONS TO LIBERALISM

1. At times, society needs rationally directed and scientifically based reform.
2. Reforms should produce the greatest good for the greatest number of people.
3. Human decisions and actions can be calculated according to the amount, and degree, of pleasure or pain they produce.
4. Reforms should be *within* the system and should be peaceful and gradual.
5. With these guidelines for reform, human rights and responsibilities can be preserved and extended to the greatest number of people.

monopolies, unsanitary food, and dangerous drugs. Progressive politicians, such as Presidents Theodore Roosevelt and Woodrow Wilson and Senator Robert LaFollette, emphasized legislation that would reform government, curb business monopolies, and conserve natural resources. Like the Utilitarians, Progressives wanted to use peaceful and gradual means to solve problems in society by enacting laws that regulated the economy while preserving the free-enterprise system. (See Chapter 18 for a discussion of Progressivism.)

In the 1930s, President Franklin Roosevelt's New Deal sought to use the federal government to bring the country out of the Great Depression of the 1930s. Roosevelt designed programs to provide relief to the millions of unemployed people and their families, to stimulate economic recovery, and to reform the system through regulations. Roosevelt's New Deal, like the earlier Progressive Movement, used incremental reforms to preserve and revitalize the system rather than radically transforming or overthrowing it. The important point of both the New Deal and the earlier Progressive Movement was the reliance on government, especially the federal government, to act as a major agency of reform. This change in modern Liberalism was almost diametrically opposed to the Classical Liberalism view that government should stay out of society and the economy.

Along with the new Liberals involved in politics, several leading educators, too, called for the development of a new Liberalism that urged the government to provide the needed social services in what had become an industrial, corporate society. Foremost among these educators was the prominent Pragmatist philosopher John Dewey, who urged that Liberalism become an active ideology that would create a cooperative society to promote the economic well-being, social welfare, and education of all of the people.[5] George S. Counts, a Reconstructionist educator, called upon teachers to join with other Progressive groups in working for a more planned, collaborative, and sharing society.[6] Harold Rugg called upon the schools to prepare people to use new technology for social betterment.

As a result of the New Deal and similar movements, Liberalism was transformed into Modern or Social Welfare Liberalism. While Liberals still prized individual freedom and civil rights and liberties, they now extended their ideological perspective to allow government to play a greater role as an agency of reform and regulation. The government, especially the federal government, was to improve the general welfare by providing pensions, health care, social security, and aid to hitherto disadvantaged groups; ending racial segregation and promoting integration, affirmative action programs, and protection for persons with disabilities; and giving aid to people at the poverty level.

Liberals now believed that education was about more than learning basic skills and subjects. Public schools were redefined as agencies to promote gradual social change. They were to provide compensatory education to help economically disadvantaged children; devise means of ending racial segregation and promoting racial integration; mainstream children with disabilities into regular classrooms; provide early childhood education; develop programs of sex education, drug and alcohol abuse programs, and AIDS education; and create a climate of multiculturalism. In other words, the new Liberal agenda made schools into much more than academic institutions—they were to become multipurpose institutions involved in remedying social ills and solving social problems.

■ ■ ■ ■ ■

MODERN LIBERALISM'S PRINCIPLES

1. The American political and economic systems benefit and are maintained by internal reform and regulation.
2. In the modern technological and corporate society and economy, the federal government is the national agency responsible for reform and regulation.
3. In a modern society, the government has a role to play in providing social, unemployment, health care, educational, and other human services.
4. Education, schools, and teachers have social roles and responsibilities, as well as academic ones.

The new Liberal approach also changed the role and function of teachers. Teachers were no longer simply to teach skills and subjects; their roles became broader and included social work and counseling functions.

MODERN LIBERALISM'S CORE BELIEFS

In this section we will identify and comment on Liberalism's core beliefs—the principles lying at the heart of the ideology. Chapter 12 will include a discussion of American Conservatives' appropriation of the Classical Liberal economic doctrines. Here, Liberalism's core principles are positioned within the modern or social-welfare orientation that characterizes Liberalism in contemporary America.

An Optimism About People

When you meet other people for the first time, how do you react? Are you eager to meet them, or are you cautious, wary, or suspicious? As a teacher, how do you feel when you meet your students for the first time? Do you expect some to be well-behaved, cooperative learners and others to be ill-disciplined troublemakers who will disturb your teaching and their classmates' learning? Underlying these questions is what you believe about human beings and their behavior.

Liberals tend to have an optimistic view of human nature. They see people as either good by nature, as did Rousseau, or at least morally neutral at birth with the possibility of becoming ethical persons. They reject the pessimistic view of human nature that sees people as inherently evil, weak, wicked, and lazy. For Liberals, the "trust principle" is an important one. They trust or believe that if a person lives in the "right" kind of social environment and has the opportunity for the "right" kind of education, she or he will do the "right thing." Notice, the emphasis on "right" kind in the sentences above. When a person does the "wrong thing," Liberals would say there is something wrong with their social environment or their education, and not inherently with them. If we know what the "right" kind of society and education is, we can change or reform both environments. We can then turn them into environments that will provide positive experiences and motivate individuals to do what is right. Note that Liberals tend to put the primary responsibility on society and education for changing behavior, rather than on the individual.

Closely related to the Liberal optimism about human nature is the corollary belief in human freedom. If people are basically good at heart, or if at least they are not inherently evil, then they can enjoy the greatest possible freedom. To be sure, for Liberals, freedom does not mean doing whatever you please, without regard to the consequences for yourself and for others. With freedom comes responsibility, especially to use the right kind of procedures. Since people are good or have the possibility of being good, then they should be free to think, to express themselves, and to act. Schools and teachers should be places of freedom of thought and of expression.

Liberalism's trust in human benevolence runs up against the traditional Christian belief that human beings are born in sin, retain a tendency to evil, but can be redeemed by faith. Fundamentalist Christians, for example, would consider the Liberal school atmosphere to be overly permissive and a misuse of freedom that permits students to be disruptive. Conservatives would see the Liberal attitude about social reform, "fixing things" through social and educational engineering, to be so naïve that it compounds social ills. Conservatives believe that there is evil in the world and some people will chose to be criminals and thus should be punished.

Social Intelligence

Based on their assumptions about the goodness of human nature, or at least its benign neutrality, Liberals believe that individuals can and should use their minds in ways that are socially intelligent. Social intelligence means that individuals, acting together, can cooperatively solve their problems. The stalwart modern Liberal, John Dewey, argued that the scientific method could be used to solve problems that ranged from the personal to the social and political. In a democracy, people, free to use their reason, can define problems, interpret information, consider the evidence, make the correct decisions, and act on them. To develop social intelligence we need to have an open society, a marketplace of ideas, free of absolutes, customs, and traditions that interfere with the questioning attitude necessary for critical thinking.

Educationally, the Liberal call for social intelligence and critical thinking has many important implications. Schools should be places of academic freedom, where teachers are free to teach and students are free to learn, without having their freedom curtailed by censorship or arbitrary controls. The curriculum should be open to new ideas and to methods of inquiry in which students are free to ask questions and challenge the status quo. Libraries should not be censored but should include controversial books. Teachers should encourage the development of social intelligence in students by using methods that emphasize open discussions, permission to share and to question ideas, and freedom to make decisions based on the evidence.

There are several objections to the Liberal concept of social intelligence. Existentialists, valuing human subjectivity, warn that the Liberal concept of social intelligence may be so focused on the group that personal freedom is submerged to the group's will. (See Chapter 6 for a discussion of Existentialism.) Some Conservatives argue that the so-called "open society," so prized by Liberals, is a misnomer for a permissive society in which truth and values depend on how a particular group defines a given situation. Within this kind of group-based determination of ethics, there are no universal standards of behavior and everything ends up being clouded by relativism.

Secularism

Although they may or may not be religious in their personal lives, Liberals believe that religious identification and church membership are individual matters, not public ones. Individuals should be free to practice their religion but should not impose their beliefs on others through state-ordered observance, support, or controls. There should be no religious test in order to obtain citizenship or hold public office.

The Liberal tendency to secularism comes from their long struggle against the establishment of religion as part of the state and educational systems. Liberals in Europe opposed the establishment of an official state church, such as the Church of England in England or the Roman Catholic Church in France. Thomas Jefferson, who reinterpreted Lockean Liberalism to justify the American Revolution, argued against the establishment of a state church or religion in the United States. For Liberals who follow Jefferson's line of reasoning, there should be separation of church and state, and church and public schools. Believing that religious dogmas can block freedom of inquiry, Liberals contend that public schools need to be free from religious controls. They oppose religious instruction, religious observances and prayer, the posting of the Ten Commandments, and the teaching of Creationism in public schools.

The separation of church and state, so strongly supported by Liberals, has generated some strong opposition in the United States. The chief opposition comes from Christian Fundamentalists, often associated with the neo-Conservative ideology. Fundamentalists contend that the United States is a Christian nation and the ideas of the founders of the republic were based on Christian ideals. They argue that Liberals, while denying the right of others to religious instruction, have imposed their own creed, Secular Humanism, on public schools. They see Secular Humanism as a relativistic philosophy that places all truth and values in human beings and society rather than in God. Secular Humanism, they contend, asserts that right and wrong are relative, and depend on what the group says they are in different situations.[7]

The Right to Private Property

Since its origins with John Locke, Liberalism has maintained the core principle that individuals possess the inalienable right to acquire and own property. In modern terms, the Liberal assertion of property rights means that individuals have the right to employ and fire other people, and to earn income, invest it and make a profit (to earn a return or financial dividend on their investment). This self-motivated economic interest stimulates people to learn and to earn.

When Modern Liberalism took on its social service and social welfare character, a revision or modification of the concept of the right to property occurred. Modern Liberals now argue that the government needs to assist individuals in the lowest socioeconomic levels, especially those at the poverty level, with resources—food, health care, low-cost housing, and job training—needed to help them improve their situation. Government also needs to encourage affirmative-action programs that give preference in college and university admissions, and in employment, to members of underrepresented minority groups. To support this assistance, those in higher income groups should be taxed at a higher rate—a progressive tax—to generate the needed revenues for social, health, and educational services. For Modern Liberals, property, while still an individual right, should not be permitted to override the right of a person to the necessities of living a decent life—to having access to health care, housing, and education.

It is on the property issue that Classical Liberalism, now part of American Conservatism, and Modern Liberalism take divergent ideological paths. Contemporary Conservatives argue that excessive taxation, caused by the programs of the Liberal social welfare state, is taking away the right to own property. Liberalism, they say, has been transformed into a form of state socialism.

Individuals and Associations

Liberalism, a middle-of-the-road ideology, tends to perform a delicate balancing act. It asserts both the primacy of the individual, and the importance of human association in politics, society, the economy, and education. Locke proclaimed that the inherent and inalienable rights to life, liberty, and property are possessed by individuals and are not bestowed by government, nor determined by membership in society. Further, as John Stuart Mill argued, individuals have the right to pursue their rights and interests as long as they do not injure or restrict the rights of others. Thus, Liberalism endorses the free and competitive interplay of individuals in society.

Modern Liberalism reaffirms these individual rights, often framed as human rights and civil liberties, but simultaneously emphasizes the importance of human association in government, society, and education. For Liberalism to work, there needs to be a shared social consensus to use the processes of peaceful, nonviolent reform and change. Consensus means that there is a meeting of the individual minds, a social agreement, to hold to certain principles and to follow agreed-upon processes to solve problems. The maintenance and use of representative institutions in a democratic society requires a consensus that promotes their validity, viability, and workability.

In our everyday life, the Liberal idea of working together to promote the general welfare while holding individual rights can be summed up by the word, "committee." Most of us have served on a committee. A committee is composed of individuals who have a common cause, problem, or project. Individuals are expected to speak their mind but also to arrive at some kind of group agreement or consensus so that the problem can be solved or the project accomplished by collaborative efforts.

In schools, we can see the Liberal dichotomy at work in how both the individual and the group are emphasized simultaneously. Children are encouraged to be creative or even competitive, to do their own work, to respect the work of others, and to respect private property. At the same time, they are also encouraged to be good group members, to take turns and share, to use collaborative learning to solve group problems, and to be team players. The Liberal dichotomy in schools merely mirrors the larger dichotomy in American society. Individual competition and initiative is prized but so is being a team player and an effective member in a corporate economy.

Emphasis on Process—Playing by the Rules

Liberals are process oriented in their devotion to the scientific method, to due process before the law, and to using parliamentary procedures in enacting legislation. The Liberal emphasis is on *process*—using appropriate methods or procedures to make things work fairly, effectively, and efficiently—especially in government, society, and education. Liberals tend to use the following process in dealing with issues: (1) identify a problem to be solved, such as regulating traffic, improving airport security, or providing prescription drugs for seniors; (2) define and research the problem by calling expert witnesses to testify, collecting statistics, and conducting public hearings; (3) based on the research, propose and enact legislation to solve the problem and regulate the society so that the problem does not reappear.

Educationally, the Liberal emphasis on process operates in two dimensions: (1) respecting the process as a method of learning and problem solving and (2) knowing how to use the process. For the process to work, those who use it need to be committed to, and value, it. In other words, children need to acquire the belief that using the process is fair. It begins with taking turns in using playground equipment and not permitting the biggest, strongest, and most assertive child to monopolize it. The process is developed by internalizing a sense of playing by the rules in sports, debates, and contests. Based on the commitment that we should play by the rules, skills in using the method are developed: understanding how the method works; practicing its use; and applying it in actual situations.

Liberals tend to endorse process-oriented education in which students learn by doing. In Dewey's "Complete Act of Thought," the scientific method is applied to problems using the following procedure: (1) recognize that one has a problem; (2) define the problem; (3) research the problem; (4) develop possible ways to solve the problem; (5) choose one of these possibilities and act on it to test it.

Many school activities are centered around a group, in what Dewey called associative learning, which today is called "Collaborative Learning." Students work together and engage in a mutual effort and share information to jointly solve a problem. In so doing, they not only solve a particular problem, but also learn how to function as responsible team players in a democratic society.

Other ideologies do not object to following rules or playing fairly. However, Conservatives would find the Liberal emphasis on process and procedure to be excessive. They would allege that Liberals tend to be so preoccupied with the process that they ignore substance and content. Further, they warn that using the process does not determine if something or some action is good or bad, right and wrong.

While not opposed to the concept of using a process, neo-Marxists and Critical Theorists would say that the Liberal process means playing with a "marked deck" in that it is rigged to favor the dominant group. They say that the Liberal process is merely a routine played to ensure that those who control politics and the economy maintain their dominance. (See Chapter 13 for a discussion of Marxism and Chapter 19 for Critical Theory.)

Being in the Middle Can Be Uncomfortable

Contemporary Liberalism is an ideology that takes a moderate middle-of-the-road position, between Conservatives on the right and Socialists, neo–Marxists, Critical Theorists, and others on the left. In times of crisis, Liberalism often comes under pressure from those who call for hurried, sweeping, transformative, revolutionary change. Taking a cautious, moderate, and incremental approach to solving social, political, economic, and educational problems, Liberals are suspicious of advocates of sweeping grand designs that promise to bring about some kind of utopia. Liberals such as John Dewey, for example, were highly suspicious of both Fascists, on the right, and Marxists, on the left, who promised to create a perfect world order by purging those identified as undesirables because of their race, religion, or class. Liberals look with dismay upon those who hold extreme positions but are able to change sides so quickly.

Being in the middle can be both comfortable and uncomfortable. You might reflect on what it means to be "caught in the middle" when your friends are having an argument. Being in the middle is comfortable when there is a consensus, that is, when the majority of people share the same commitment to use the same process. It is uncomfortable when, especially in times of crisis, the extremes gain more strength and want to bring about a change that does not follow the established rules. For example, should civil rights be maintained and due process followed when there is a threat of terrorist attacks? Liberals will opt for freedom of speech, assembly, and expression, even to the uncomfortable point of allowing those who want to destroy these freedoms to speak and organize against them.

In educational theory, especially the foundations of history and philosophy of education, Liberals often find themselves very much in the middle. They are pushed from the right by religious fundamentalists who want to insert particular religious doctrines into the schools and by neo-Conservatives who want to define the schools as strictly academic institutions and to limit social programs. They are pushed from the left by neo-Marxists and Critical Theorists who want to use the schools as agencies for a radical transformation of society. When faced by these diametrically opposed forces, often "true believers" in the rightness of their particular ideology, the liberal arguments for peaceful discussion, following parliamentary procedures, and taking a vote in which the majority rules, often seem to be pale remedies for pressing social problems. Though not dramatic, Liberals believe that commitment to following the process, even if it means being in the middle, is the best way to maintain democratic institutions.

Progress

Liberals believe it is possible to improve the human condition and situation. They do not believe that the poor will always be poor. Instead, they look for ways to ameliorate the conditions of poverty and ignorance through social and educational programs. If we apply social intelligence to solving problems, they believe the future can be progressively better than the past. This sense of making things better affirms the belief in progress. Liberals believe that society can be dynamically changed for the better and human intelligence can create a better society, system of government, and educational system. The liberal outlook is directed toward reforming the present as a means of making the future better. The Progressive movement in education was based on the belief that education could be improved upon, be more liberating, and socially relevant.

LIBERALISM'S EDUCATIONAL IMPLICATIONS

Throughout the chapter, we provided a running commentary to point out some of the general implications of Liberalism for education, especially educational theory. At this point, we will discuss some implications for educational practice.

The Purpose of Education and Schools

Liberals have an open-ended outlook on the purpose of education. They see education as the process by which human intelligence is exercised, enabling individuals and societies to adjust to change and to develop innovative ways of directing change in order to secure maximum social and economic benefits. The key is to encourage individuals to look forward to change rather than fearing it. Further, individuals and societies should not drift along, but should deliberately develop plans and strategies to achieve the desired consequences.

For Liberals, there is no one single or primary purpose of schools, as there is for Idealists, Realists, and Conservatives. Liberals see a need for schools to be adaptive and anticipate social and economic change. Accordingly, the purpose and function of schools is to be fluid, flexible, and responsive to social change and problems. The school should be a multifunctional agency that performs, along with its academic function, other functions such as providing for vocational preparation, health care, counseling, recreation, and other social needs.

Policy

A contemporary development in educational foundations is the idea of policy studies, in which areas of study such as history, philosophy, sociology of education, and comparative education are used to inform strategic planning for educational institutions. Liberals tend to see policy as a flexible planning attitude that establishes goals for the immediate future and allocates resources to accomplish these goals. The kind of planning goals favored by Liberals are rarely radical or transformative, but are designed to solve problems when they appear. The basic intent is to maintain the system of education by making it sufficiently flexible to incorporate new technologies and solve new problems. For example, the age of electronic information presents a challenge and an opportunity for schools. Liberals would develop plans and allocate resources to include technology in the classroom by giving it a place alongside the more conventional areas. In setting educational priorities, it might be necessary to drop some subjects to fit technology into the schedule and to provide adequate resources for its inclusion in the curriculum.

Curriculum and Instruction

Based on their flexible, multifunctional approach to schooling, curriculum and instruction would be constructed and designed to fit changing social needs and problems. The curriculum cannot be established to last for all time but is subject to revision and reconceptualization depending on social changes, needs, and problems. The basic elementary skills—reading, writing, communicating, and calculating—would stay in place. However, Liberals would continue to experiment with innovative methods of teaching them. Subjects such as history, science, language and literature, and mathematics, would be found in the intermediate and secondary curriculum but these subjects would be constantly revised to incorporate new developments and insights.

Depending on current issues and problems, new subjects will need to be added to the curriculum. For example, the AIDS epidemic requires safe-sex education; the rising incidences of school violence require programs of conflict resolution; the increasing cultural diversity of the United States requires multicultural programs; the problem of drug abuse requires substance education; the increasing obesity of Americans requires health education programs. The curriculum in not set in stone but should be the educational response to changing needs and problems.

The school milieu, the educational environment, should be organized to encourage the values and attitudes Liberals prize. Student government provides an opportunity for students to learn and practice the processes of democratic decision making. Student newspapers and radio and television stations provide an opportunity for students to engage in the free flow of information and communication. Various clubs and organizations encourage students to develop their own interests and learn to work with others.

Teachers and Students

The Liberal teacher should be a flexible instructor who is ready to diverge from the prepared lesson plan when the occasion presents itself. If there is a breaking news story, a significant current event or controversy, the teacher should be ready to discuss it with students and hopefully, but not necessarily, relate it to the subject being studied. For example, the reaction to the War on Terrorism can be examined as the events occur and put into the perspective of similar situations of the past. For example, incidents of ethnic profiling of persons of Arabic descent in the aftermath of September 11, 2001 can be related to the internment of Japanese Americans during World War II.

Students, in the Liberal educational context, are individuals, each with their own needs, interests, aspirations, fears, and hopes. Students are encouraged to be both individuals and members of the group. Group membership, too, is subject to flexibility and change. Rather than racially or ethnically based group identification, student groups, in the Liberal view, should be organized around interests. As interests change, so does group membership.

■ ■ ■ ■ ■ ▬▬▬▬▬▬▬▬▬▬▬▬▬▬▬▬▬▬▬▬▬▬▬▬▬▬▬▬▬▬

JOHN STUART MILL, ON LIBERTY

In this selection, John Stuart Mill develops the Liberal argument for individual freedom versus arbitrary restraint of government, church, and other authorities, and also versus the growing pressures and conformity of mass society. This selection from Mill's *On Liberty* is included because it is a classic, eloquent, and forceful enunciation of the basic Liberal principles of freedom of thought and individual expression that underlie the liberty of individuals in society and also provide us the freedom to teach and to learn. As you read the selection, you may wish to consider the following focusing questions:

1. What does Mill define as the limits of human liberty? Do you think contemporary American society and education limits personal freedom and expression? Do you believe that there should be certain areas in which freedom of expression should be limited?

2. Consider Mill's argument about freedom from restraints and freedom to define oneself. What are the restraints from which we should be free? What are the possibilities that we should enjoy in order to define ourselves?

3. Why does Mill insist on the right to express unpopular opinions? Examine contemporary American society. Are unpopular opinions freely expressed or are they silenced?

4. How would Mill respond to the statement: Education is the transmission of the cultural heritage?

5. How well does Mill's argument resonate in a time of heightened national security and anxieties posed by the threat of terrorism?

The object of this Essay is to assert one very simple principle, as entitled to govern absolutely the dealings of society with the individual in the way of compulsion and control, whether the means used by physical force in the form of legal penalties, or the moral coercion of public opinion. That principle is, that the sole end for which mankind are warranted, individu-

From John Stuart Mill, *On Liberty*. New York: Henry Holt and Co., 1885, pp. 7–12, 20–26, 29–32, 43–45, 90–100.

ally or collectively, in interfering with the liberty of action of any of their number, is self-protection. That the only purpose for which power can be rightfully exercised over any member of a civilized community, against his will, is to prevent harm to others. His own good, either physical or moral, is not a sufficient warrant. He cannot rightfully be compelled to do or forebear because it will be better for him to do so, because it will make him happier, because, in the opinions of others, to do so would be wise, or even right. These are good reasons for remonstrating with him, or reasoning with him, or persuading him, or entreating him, but not for compelling him, or visiting him with any evil in case he do otherwise. To justify that, the conduct from which it is desired to deter him, must be calculated to produce evil to some one else. The only part of the conduct of any one, for which he is amenable to society, is that which concerns others. In the part which merely concerns himself, his independence is, of right, absolute. Over himself, over his own body and mind, the individual is sovereign.

It is, perhaps, hardly necessary to say that this doctrine is meant to apply only to human beings in the maturity of their faculties. We are not speaking of children, or of young persons below the age which the law may fix as that of manhood or womanhood. Those who are still in a state to require being taken care of by others, must be protected against their own actions as well as against external injury. . . .

It is proper to state that I forego any advantage which could be derived to my argument from the idea of abstract right, as a thing independent of utility. I regard utility as the ultimate appeal on all ethical questions: but it must be utility in the largest sense, grounded on the permanent interests of a man as a progressive being. Those interests, I contend, authorize the subjection of individual spontaneity to external control, only in respect to those actions of each, which concern the interest of other people. If any one does an act hurtful to others,

there is a *prima facie* case for punishing him, by law, or, where legal penalties are not safely applicable, by general disapprobation. . . .

But there is a sphere of action in which society, as distinguished from the individual, has, if any, only an indirect interest; comprehending all that portion of a person's life and conduct which affects only himself, or if it also affects others, only with their free, voluntary, and undeceived consent and participation. When I say only himself, I mean directly and in the first instance; for whatever affects himself, may affect others through himself; and the objection which may be grounded on this contingency, will receive consideration in the sequel. This, then, is the appropriate region of human liberty. It comprises, first, the inward domain of consciousness; demanding liberty of conscience, in the most comprehensive sense; liberty of thought and feeling; absolute freedom of opinion and sentiment on all subjects, practical or speculative, scientific, moral or theological. The liberty of expressing and publishing opinions may seem to fall under a different principle, since it belongs to that part of the conduct of an individual which concerns other people; but, being almost of as much importance as the liberty of thought itself, and resting in great part on the same reasons, is practically inseparable from it. Secondly, the principle requires liberty of tastes and pursuits; of framing the plan of our life to suit our own character; of doing as we like, subject to such consequences as may follow: without impediment from our fellow-creatures, so long as what we do does not harm them, even though they should think our conduct foolish, perverse, or wrong. Thirdly, from this liberty of each individual, follows the liberty, within the same limits, of combination among individuals; freedom to unite, for any purpose not involving harm to others: the persons combining being supposed to be of full age, and not forced or deceived.

No society in which these liberties are not, on the whole, respected, is free, whatever may be its form of government; and none is completely free in which they do not exist absolutely and unqualified. The only freedom which deserves the name, is that of pursuing our own good in our own way, so long as we do not attempt to deprive others of theirs, or impede their efforts to obtain it. Each is the proper guardian of his own health, whether bodily, or mental and spiritual. Mankind are greater gainers by suffering each other to live as seems good to themselves, than by compelling each to live as seems good to the rest.

. . .

. . . Let us suppose, therefore, that the government is entirely at one with the people, and never thinks of exerting any power of coercion unless in agreement with what it conceives to be their voice. But I deny the right of the people to exercise such coercion, either by themselves, or by their government. The power itself is illegitimate. The best government has no more title to it than the worst. It is as noxious, or more noxious, when exerted in accordance with public opinion, than when in opposition to it. If all mankind minus one, were of one opinion, and only one person were of the contrary opinion, mankind would be no more justified in silencing that one person, than he, if he had the power, would be justified in silencing mankind. Were an opinion a personal possession of no value except to the owner; if to be obstructed in the enjoyment of it were simply a private injury, it would make some difference whether the injury was inflicted only on a few persons or on many. But the peculiar evil of silencing the expression of an opinion is, that it is robbing the human race, posterity as well as the existing generation; those who dissent from the opinion, still more than those who hold it. If the opinion is right, they are deprived of the opportunity of exchanging error for truth: if wrong, they lose, what is almost as great a benefit, the clearer perception and livelier impression of truth, produced by its collision with error.

. . .

Before quitting the subject of freedom of opinion, it is fit to take some notice of those who say, that the free expression of all opinions should be permitted, on condition that the manner be temperate, and do not pass the bounds of fair discussion. Much might be said on the impossibility of fixing where these supposed bounds are to be placed; for if the test be offence to those whose opinions are attacked, I think experience testifies that this offence is given whenever the attack is telling and powerful, and that every opponent who pushes them hard, and whom they find it difficult to answer, appears to them, if he shows any strong feeling on the subject, an intemperate opponent. But this, though an important consideration in a practical point of view, merges in a more fundamental objection. Undoubtedly the manner of asserting an opinion, even though it be a true one, may be very objectionable, and may justly incur severe censure. But the principal offences of the kind are such as it is mostly impossible, unless by accidental self-betrayal, to bring home to conviction. The gravest of them is, to argue sophistically, to suppress facts or arguments, to misstate the elements of the case, or misrepresent the opposite opinion. But all this, even to the most aggravated degree, is so continually done in perfect good faith, by persons who are not considered, and in many other respects may not deserve to be considered, ignorant or incompetent, that it is rarely possible, on adequate grounds, conscientiously to stamp the misrepresentation as morally culpable; and still less could law presume to interfere with this kind of controversial misconduct. With regard to what is commonly meant by intemperate discussion, namely, invective, sarcasm, personality, and the like, the denunciation of these weapons would deserve more sympathy if it were ever proposed to interdict them equally to both sides; but it is only desired to restrain the employment of them against the prevailing opinion: against the unprevailing they may not only be used without general disapproval, but will be likely to obtain for him who uses them the praise of honest zeal and righteous indignation. Yet whatever mischief arises from their use, is greatest when they are employed against the comparatively defenceless; and whatever unfair advantage can be derived by an opinion from this mode of asserting it, accrues almost exclusively to received opinions. The worst offence of this kind which can be committed by a polemic, is to stigmatize those who hold the contrary opinion as bad and immoral men. To calumny of this sort, those who hold any unpopular opinion are peculiarly exposed, because they are in general few and uninfluential, and nobody but themselves feels much interested in seeing justice done them; but this weapon is, from the nature of the case, denied to those who attack a prevailing opinion: they can neither use it with safety to themselves, nor, if they could, would it do anything but recoil on their own cause. In general, opinions contrary to those commonly received can only obtain a hearing by studied moderation of language, and the most cautious avoidance of unnecessary offence, from which they hardly ever deviate even in a slight degree without losing ground: while unmeasured vituperation employed on the side of the prevailing opinion, really does deter people from professing contrary opinions, and from listening to those who profess them. For the interest, therefore, of truth and justice, it is far more important to restrain this employment of vituperative language than the other; and, for example, if it were necessary to choose, there would be much more need to discourage offensive attacks on infidelity than on religion. It is, however, obvious that law and authority have no business with restraining either, while opinion ought, in every instance, to determine its verdict by the circumstances of the individual case; condemning every one, on whichever side of the argument he places himself, in whose mode of advocacy either want of candor, or malignity, bigotry, or intolerance of feeling

manifest themselves; but not inferring these vices from the side which a person takes, though it be the contrary side of the question to our own: and giving merited honor to every one, whatever opinion he may hold, who has calmness to see and honesty to state what his opponents and their opinions really are, exaggerating nothing to their discredit, keeping nothing back which tells, or can be supposed to tell, in their favor. This is the real morality of public discussion: and if often violated, I am happy to think that there are many controversialists who to a great extent observe it, and a still greater number who conscientiously strive towards it.

. . .

. . . No one's idea of excellence in conduct is that people should do absolutely nothing but copy one another. No one would assert that people ought not to put into their mode of life, and into the conduct of their concerns, any impress whatever of their own judgment, or of their own individual character. On the other hand, it would be absurd to pretend that people ought to live as if nothing whatever had been known in the world before they came into it; as if experience had as yet done nothing towards showing that one mode of existence, or of conduct, is preferable to another. Nobody denies that people should be so taught and trained in youth, as to know and benefit by the ascertained results of human experience. But it is the privilege and proper condition of a human being, arrived at the maturity of his faculties, to use and interpret experience in his own way. It is for him to find out what part of recorded experience is properly applicable to his own circumstances and character. The traditions and customs of other people are, to a certain extent, evidence of what their experience has taught *them*; presumptive evidence, and as such, have a claim to his deference: but, in the first place, their experience may be too narrow; or they may not have interpreted it rightly. Secondly, their interpretation of experience may be correct, but unsuitable to him. Customs are made for customary circumstances, and customary characters; and his circumstances or his character may be uncustomary. Thirdly, though the customs be both good as customs, and suitable to him yet to conform to custom, merely *as* custom, does not educate or develop in him any of the qualities which are the distinctive endowment of a human being. The human faculties of perception, judgment, discriminative feeling, mental activity, and even moral preference, are exercised only in making a choice. He who does anything because it is the custom, makes no choice. He gains no practice either in discerning or in desiring what is best. The mental and

moral, like the muscular powers, are improved only by being used. The faculties are called into no exercise by doing a thing merely because others do it, no more than by believing a thing only because others believe it. If the grounds of an opinion are not conclusive to the person's own reason, his reason cannot be strengthened, but is likely to be weakened, by his adopting it: and if the inducements to an act are not such as are consentaneous to his own feelings and character (where affection, or the rights of others, are not concerned) it is so much done towards rendering his feelings and character inert and torpid, instead of active and energetic.

CONCLUSION

In this chapter we examined Liberalism as an ideology. We traced the history of Liberalism from its origins in the Enlightenment, through John Locke and the British Utilitarians, to classical and modern Liberalism. The core values of Liberalism—a belief in progress, an openness to change, a willingness to experiment, and a tendency to innovate—were identified. Liberalism was identified as encouraging a secular, progressive system of schools. Relying on democratic parliamentary processes, its approach to change and reform is gradual and incremental rather than transformative.

DISCUSSION QUESTIONS

1. How do contemporary Americans tend to define Liberalism?
2. Compare and contrast classical and modern Liberalism.
3. Why do Liberals tend to emphasize process and procedures?
4. What are the strengths and weaknesses of Liberalism?
5. Why are Liberals often in the middle on policy issues?

INQUIRY AND RESEARCH PROJECTS

1. Listen to some of the "talk shows" on radio or television. Is the Liberal position represented? If so, what are the major elements of the Liberal perspective presented on these programs?
2. With the approval of your instructor, develop a questionnaire that elicits student reaction to the major principles of Liberalism. Allow students to respond anonymously and then compile the findings to determine the degree to which they agree or disagree with Liberalism.

3. In recent years, there has been a resurgence of neo-Conservatism in politics and in education. Why do you think Liberalism has been on the defensive?
4. As a class project, compile a clippings file of articles from newspapers and magazines that deal with topics such as school uniforms, mandatory standardized testing, creationism vs. evolutionism, the use of the phrase "under God" in the Pledge of Allegiance, and other current issues. Determine how Liberals would react to each issue.
5. Trace the development of Liberalism as an ideology in Western culture.

INTERNET RESOURCES

For an essay on Liberalism and its history, consult
http://library.thinkquest.org/3376/Genkts.htm

For a lecture on Rawls' political liberalism, consult
http://info/bris.ac.uk/~plcdib/lect 10.html

Gerald F. Gaus analyzes Liberalism as a political theory and a philosophy at
http://plato.stanford.edu/entries/liberalism.html

For a definition and discussion of exponents of Liberalism, consult
www.xrefer.com/entry/552617.html

For a glossary of terms related to Liberalism, consult
www.cs.nd.ac.uk/people/chis.holt/home.informal/lounge'politics'liberalism.html

SUGGESTIONS FOR FURTHER READING

Donner, Wendy. *The Liberal Self: John Stuart Mill's Moral and Political Philosophy*. Ithaca, NY: Cornell University Press, 1991.

Eberle, Christopher J. *Religious Conviction in Liberal Politics*. New York: Cambridge University Press, 2002.

Freeden, Michael. *The New Liberalism: An Ideology of Social Reform*. Oxford: Clarendon Press, 1978.

Gans, Chaim. *Liberalism and Cultural Nationalism*. New York: Cambridge University Press, 2003.

Gaus, Gerald F. *Justificatory Liberalism: An Essay on Epistemology and Political Theory*. New York: Oxford University Press, 1996.

Gaus, Gerald F. *The Modern Liberal Theory of Man*. New York: St. Martin's Press, 1983.

Hunter, James D. *Culture Wars: The Struggle to Define America*. New York: Basic Books, 1991.

Ivison, Duncan. *Postcolonial Liberalism*. New York: Cambridge University Press, 2002.

Kymlicka, Will. *Liberalism, Community and Culture*. Oxford: Clarendon Press, 1989.

Locke, John. *An Essay Concerning Human Understanding*. Ed. Peter H. Nidditch. Oxford: Clarendon Press, 1975.

Locke, John. *The Second Treatise of Government in Two Treatises of Government*, Ed. Peter Laslett. Cambridge: Cambridge University Press, 1960.

Losonsky, Michael. *Enlightenment and Action from Descartes to Kant*. New York: Cambridge University Press, 2001.

Mill, John Stuart. *On Liberty and Other Essays*. John Gray, ed. New York: Oxford University Press, 1991.

Mill, John Stuart. *Principles of Political Economy*. New York: Augustus M. Kelley, 1976.

Rawls, John. *Justice as Fairness: A Restatement.* Cambridge, MA: Harvard University Press, 2001.

Rawls, John. *Political Liberalism.* New York: Columbia University Press, 1993.

Rawls, John. *A Theory of Justice.* Cambridge, MA: Harvard University Press, 1999.

Riley, Jonathan. *Liberal Utilitarianism.* Cambridge: Cambridge University Press, 1988.

Ryan, Alan. *John Stuart Mill.* New York: Pantheon Books, 1970.

Spector, Horacio. *Autonomy and Rights: The Moral Foundations of Liberalism.* Oxford: Clarendon Press, 1992.

Steiner, Hillel. *An Essay on Rights.* Oxford: Basil Backwell, 1994.

Thomas, William. *Mill.* New York: Oxford University Press, 1985.

Urbinati, Nadia. *Mill on Democracy: From the Athenian Polis to Representative Government.* Chicago: University of Chicago Press, 2002.

NOTES

1. For a classic discussion of the Enlightenment, see Carl L. Becker, *The Heavenly City of the Eighteenth Century Philosophers* (New Haven, CT: Yale University Press, 1960).

2. John Locke, *An Essay Concerning Human Understanding*, Raymond Wilburn, ed. (New York: Dutton, 1947).

3. John Locke, *Two Treatises of Government*, Peter Laslett, ed. (New York: New American Library, 1965).

4. John Stuart Mill, *On Liberty*, Alburey Castell, ed. (Wheeling, IL: Harlan Davidson, 1947). Also, see Alan Ryan, *John Stuart Mill* (New York: Pantheon Books, 1970) and William Thomas, *Mill* (New York: Oxford University Press, 1985).

5. John Dewey, *Liberalism and Social Action* (New York: Capricorn, 1963). Also, see Allan Ryan, *John Dewey and the High Tide of American Liberalism* (New York: W. W. Norton, 1995).

6. Lawrence J. Dennis and William E. Eaton, *George S. Counts: Educator for a New Age* (Carbondale and Edwardsville, IL: Southern Illinois University Press, 1980).

7. James Davison Hunter, *Culture Wars: The Struggle to Define America* (New York: Basic Books, 1991), pp. 24–28.

CHAPTER TWELVE

CONSERVATISM

In chapter 12 we will examine Conservatism as an ideology that seeks to preserve what it considers to be the vital aspects of culture. In the late twentieth and early twenty-first century, Conservatism has had a marked resurgence in politics, society, the economy, and education. We will define Conservatism, trace its origins and development, identify its basic principles, and draw out its implications for education.

DEFINING CONSERVATISM

Conservatism is an ideology that emphasizes the preservation of institutions in what is believed to be their primary and traditional form and function. The word's root, *conserve*, means to keep, maintain, preserve, or prevent loss or decay. The meaning of *Conservative* can be further explained by taking a closer look at the terms *primary*, *traditional*, and *to keep*, which are essential elements in this ideology. The adjective *primary* means the most important, essential, basic, and original (the first in its origin).

The adjective *traditional*, based on the word *tradition*, means to hand down, to transmit, or pass on existing beliefs and values from one generation to the next. Here, *to hand down* can be visualized by thinking of parents giving a family legacy, as an inheritance, to their children who, in turn, will pass it on to their offspring. *To keep* means to have and to hold; to receive something and to hold it as one's own possession.

We can use the words *primary*, *traditional*, and *to keep* to further develop our definition of Conservatism. Conservatives believe that institutions have a primary role and function in society. For example, marriage is the primary institution for a man (a husband) and a women (a wife) to live together in wedlock. Conservatives believe that the primary function of marriage is sacred and that other relationships such as a man and woman living together out of wedlock or a same-sex marriage distorts and violates the high purpose of this institution. The family's primary purpose is to provide the home environment in which a married man and woman raise their children. For Conservatives, alternative family styles distort the family's primary role and function as an institution.

Schools' primary purpose is to provide an academic education to students. When they take on nonacademic custodial, therapeutic, and social functions as recommended by Liberals, schools dilute, weaken, and distort their primary role in society.

Now, we can add the adjective *traditional* to *primary*. Traditional implies the transmitting of beliefs about knowledge and values from one generation, the adults, to the next, the children. An important part of cultural transmission is to provide the young with the correct idea of how institutions are to be maintained and how they are to function. Conservatives want to keep institutions functioning according to their primary and traditional purpose.

Ideologically, Conservatism has two goals in regard to institutions: (1) to maintain and preserve those institutions that are functioning according to their intended original or primary purpose; (2) to restore those institutions which have been altered or changed and are no longer functioning according to their original, primary, and traditional purpose. If schools have taken on nonacademic custodial, social, and therapeutic functions, these functions should be removed so they can return to and perform their original, traditional, and historic academic functions. Teachers are to teach academic skills and subjects and not dilute or distort their traditional roles by trying to be baby-sitters, therapists, counselors, or social workers. Time that is spent on nonacademic functions takes time and energy away from the primary academic purpose for which schools were established.

WHY STUDY CONSERVATISM?

Since Ronald Reagan was elected President in 1980, Conservatism has been one of the major ideologies in the United States. It was espoused by Presidents Reagan, George H. Bush, and George W. Bush, who called himself a "compassionate conservative." Millions of Americans identify themselves as Conservatives, and Liberalism, once dominant, has been in retreat in recent years. Conservatives have strong views on society, the economy, religion, the family, education, and schooling. Many Conservative ideas have been articulated as policies and enacted as laws. Among them are reductions in welfare assistance and the use of mandated standardized testing to assess students' academic achievement. For these reasons it is important to study Conservatism.

SITUATING CONSERVATISM

Although there have been individuals of a conservative temperament throughout history, Conservatism's origins as an ideology can be traced to the British statesman and political theorist Edmund Burke (1729–1797). His *Reflections on the Revolution in France* (1790), which condemned the excesses and violence of the French Revolution, became a classic Conservative ideological statement. The French revolutionaries, Burke wrote, had attempted to either distort or destroy traditional institutions. Their trial and execution of King Louis and Queen Marie Antoinette, the decimation of the French aristocracy, and their attack on the Catholic Church had undermined the primary institutions that had once given cultural and political stability to France as a nation and society. With the cultural safeguards provided by these traditional institutions ripped asunder, the Revolution had produced mob rule and a dictatorial "reign of terror" with mass arrests, trials, purges, and executions. Robespierre and other zealots of the French Revolution believed that the ends justified the means as they attempted to create a utopia, a perfect society on earth. They believed the mass executions were justified as the necessary steps in eliminating those who stood in the way of creating a perfect republic. Burke warned that such counsels of perfection and revolutionary excess were doomed to fail. Human beings, who themselves are imperfect, cannot possibly create a perfect society.

Warning against the sweeping changes wrought by revolutionary violence, Burke argued that "A spirit of innovation is generally the result of a selfish temper, and confined views. People will not look forward to posterity, who never look backward to their ancestors." He proclaimed that tradition, the accumulated and time-tested wisdom of the human race, was a cultural inheritance, a legacy, to be kept by one generation and passed on to the next. Social, political, religious, and educational institutions—family, state, church, and school—were not convenient societal agencies to be experimented with, as Liberals claimed. They were institutions, founded upon a primary set of purposes that were unique to each of them. Together, they held the culture and society together, maintained them, and passed them along as an inheritance from the past generation, to the people of the present, who, in turn, would transmit them to future generations. Right and wrong, ethics and morality, were not matters to be determined by taking a vote, conducting a poll, or reaching consensus; they were the historical and traditional results of humankind's long march from barbarism to civilization. Standards of civility and propriety, enshrined in customary manners and behavior, represented the ways in which humans had worked out their behavior and relationships to each other so that harm and violence were kept to a minimum. Based on his interpretation of the events of the French Revolution, Burke warned that to ignore tradition or to recklessly try to change society was to invite social calamity. In extolling the British system as one rooted in Conservative principles, Burke concluded:

> Our political system is placed on a just correspondence and symmetry with the order of the world, and with the mode of existence decreed to a permanent body composed of transitory part; wherein, by the disposition of stupendous wisdom, moulding together the great mysterious incorporation of the human race, the whole, at one time, is never old, or middleaged, or young, but in a condition of unchangeable constancy, moves on through the varied tenor of perpetual decay, fall, renovation, and progression.[1]

■ ■ ■ ■ ■

BURKE'S CONTRIBUTIONS TO CONSERVATISM

1. Tradition is the accumulated wisdom of the human race.
2. Existing social institutions have traditional, primary purposes.
3. Civilized and civil culture is an inheritance to be transmitted from generation to generation.

GENERAL CONSERVATIVE PRINCIPLES

Over the course of the nineteenth century, Conservatism developed, in Europe, as a counterforce to Liberalism, Marxism, Socialism, and other ideologies. In the United States, too, Conservatism had its cultural and political advocates. However, in the United States, a rather unique variety of Conservatism developed. At this point, we examine the general principles of Conservatism. We discuss the American version of the Conservative principles later in the chapter.

A Weak Human Nature

Unlike the Liberal's benign or neutral view of human nature, Conservatives see the human being as an imperfect and flawed creature. For some Conservatives, human nature is downright sinful; for others, it is damaged. Because of this inherent imperfection, individuals have a tendency to egotism, selfishness, and violence. The source of human weakness lies with our instincts and impulses. While our instincts are designed to keep us alive and drive us to obtain food, water, and sexual activity, they need to be checked or curbed so that they do not drive us into excessive and self-wounding and addictive behaviors. With the right kind of upbringing in a good family, the right kind of education in an effective school, and the culturally ingrained practice of civility, we can curb and reign in our tendency to self-gratification and impulsive behavior. Social institutions—state, church, family, school—establish the correct guidelines for human behavior. By following these guidelines we can avoid violence, anarchy, and exploitation.

Conservatives fear social unrest and the alienation of individuals from their society and culture. The community promotes cultural and social control that integrate individuals through such institutions as family, church, and school. The family is the most intimate of human institutions and its essential relationships allow traditional values to be transmitted in a familiar, personal, and nurturing way from parents to their children. The church, intertwined in the culture and reinforcing the family, promotes and interprets moral and ethical values in a religiously charged context. For example, the Judeo–Christian commandment, "Honor thy father and mother," gives divine sanction to family authority. Schools continue, reinforce, and extend the value formation begun in the family and the church. These primary institutions transmit the traditional core of knowledge and values, protecting individuals from alienation and social instability.

Like Plato in *The Republic*, Conservatives favor an organic society, one in which the various parts, the social classes, function in mutual cooperation to promote the general health and well-being of society, much like the organs function together for the health of the body. They oppose atomistic society, in which each individual pursues her or his special interests without concern for the general welfare. They also warn against the tastes generated by the mass media that tend to pull public values down to the lowest common denominator.

Respecting the Past

Conservatism is historically rooted in a version of the past that constructs a sense of tradition. It is the power of past experience, organized as customs and traditions, that shapes social institutions and human relationships. Tradition is the legacy, the repository, of humankind's collective and tested wisdom that maintains social stability and continuity from one generation to the next. Tradition represents the cultural heritage. Traditions—expressed in religion, law, literature, art, and music—are the basis of human culture. It is through culture that people build a sense of identity and meaning that gives them a sense of roots, a genealogy of belonging. For Conservatives, a particular event in the past is not a unique transitory historical moment but becomes part of our collective memory. What operates in a well-ordered society is a continuum that unites the past, the present, and the future. Education, both informal and through the school curriculum, should create a sense of belonging and identification that gives each person a place in the culture. History, literature, drama, and music can be used to create a sense of cultural identity that connects the young to a great and vital past. Language, literature, and history should celebrate the achievements of the past, the major events of the group's collective life, and the heroes and heroines who best exemplify the group's values and aspirations.

Historically Evolved Institutions and Change

Conservatives believe that human institutions are the products of historical evolution and perform necessary primary functions in society. Human institutions, each serving a primary purpose in society, have been shaped by a continuum of historical experience; they are the products of the test of time. This continuum, this historical continuity, should not be broken by revolutionary actions or the untested innovations and social experiments of Liberalism and Socialism. Social experimentation will only cause moral confusion, weaken the safeguards provided by civility, and bring about social disequilibrium and cultural disarray.

The Conservative world view emphasizes a decided preference, indeed, a longing, to maintain historically evolved institutions in a way that is true to their original primary purposes. Relying on tradition as a source of authority, Conservatives take a cautious and moderate disposition to change. They tend to endorse the saying, "The more things change, the more they stay the same." Conservatives do recognize the importance of scientific and technological change. However, they believe that these kinds of changes in the material realm—that of science and technology—be subordinated to and put into historical perspective and traditional cultural controls. While changes will inevitably occur, they need to be accommodated and incorporated into the traditional cultural heritage, rather than changing the heritage itself.

Excellence, Equality, and Hierarchy

European, more than American, Conservatism, emphasizes that the society that is functioning well is guided by leaders who form an aristocracy of culture and civility, an elite of well-educated, public-spirited individuals. This ideal is similar to that expressed in Plato's *Republic* that society should be governed by publicly spirited intellectuals, the philosopher–kings. This better educated, more prudent, more talented group is to lead and guide their less-educated, less-talented followers. What is implied here is that not all people are equal in intelligence and ability. Some are better in these areas than others. The role of schools, given this proposition, is to identify those who are gifted and provide them with the kind of education that cultivates their leadership potential.

When the social and political order is functioning properly, it is organized according to the principle of the hierarchy. The members of society fall into a graded or ranked order, with the most able taking leadership positions at the hierarchical summit and the less talented taking their places in the subordinate classes or grades.

CONTEMPORARY AMERICAN CONSERVATISM

With the election of Ronald Reagan as President in 1980, Conservatism in the United States enjoyed a strong revival in politics, culture, economics, and education. In some ways, American Conservatism reflects the general conservative principles identified above. In other ways, however, it is more of a hybrid ideology that encompasses several ideological strands, including the market-driven economy and values associated with Classical Liberalism. (Classical Liberalism was discussed in Chapter 11.)

A Conservative Version of the Cultural Heritage

American Conservatives, like Conservatives in general, look to the past and to tradition as a source of authority. As is true of other ideologies, they have created their own sense of the past and their own interpretation of history. They view the American past as the history of a unique and exceptional people. (Refer to Chapter 10 for a discussion of American Exceptionalism.) Americans are a good people, ordained by Divine Providence to settle in a new world, to tame the wilderness, and to establish a republic, governed by law and civility. As in the days of the ancient Hebrews when Mosaic Law was regarded as a covenant between the Jews and God, American government, too, is a covenant in which the people adopted a Constitution as their instrument of self-government. For them the Constitution rests on the tradition of essential Christian principles and precedents from Anglo-American common law. Unlike Jefferson's call for separation of church and state, Conservatives see the United States as "the city on a hill," the New Jerusalem, originating from the religious principles that the Puritan fathers brought to New England.

In the frontier settlements of the western territories that became the United States, the pioneers were community builders. As soon as they had constructed their crude cabins, the next structures to be created were the town meeting place, the church, and the school. These institutions were the transplanted agencies of civility.

Along with the concept of community building, another interpretation about the winning of the West entered American Conservatism. The West was settled by rugged individuals, who through their own courage and initiative conquered a hostile environment. They and their families stood on their own two feet and did so without government handouts. The rifle and the gun were the necessary instruments they used to protect themselves against hostile Native Americans and outlaws. For some American Conservatives an important aspect of this version of the past is *rugged individualism*, which differs greatly from the European version of Conservatism that rests on governance by a well-intentioned, well-educated elite. Also arising from this version of the settlement of the West is the American Conservative worldview that individuals have the right to keep and bear arms, an important safeguard provided by the Constitution.

Conservatives recognize that the United States is a country of immigrants, of people who came to America to find the personal freedom and economic opportunity denied to them in their home countries. By the time most immigrants arrived, they found an American culture already in existence. The characteristics of this culture were: (1) the use of the English language; (2) the general Protestant ethic; (3) respect for the Constitution and the law; (4) a willingness to work hard and to be self-supporting. Immigrants succeeded when they (and their children) acquired and participated in the existing, dominant culture. Conservatives argue that America's most recent immigrants—from Asia, the Middle East, and South America—should imitate the way in which the older stock of European immigrants became Americans.

Of course, many historians question the accuracy of this version of the past. However, for an ideology, that is not the point. The version of the past, myth entwined with history, becomes a guiding point in shaping the ideology. While we are speaking specifically of the Conservative ideology here, the same mixture of myth and history would be used to shape ideology for Liberals, Marxists, and others.

The Conservative version of the successful integration of immigrants into American life, politics, and society has immense educational implications. First of all, there is the notion that a model of American culture exists that was defined in the early decades of the republic. New generations, be they native born or immigrants, are to absorb and assimilate into this model. The model is not open-ended and changing—it is rooted in a specifically defined version of the American cultural heritage and tradition. Education, then, is to further the process of assimilation into the model. Schools are to transmit an American cultural core to students so that they adopt, and adapt to, the model. This means that the English language should be the language of instruction, rather than allowing bilingualism. Schools should impart a solid cultural core based on American history and literature, rather than teaching multiculturalism. The values inculcated by the school focus on respect for legitimate authority, hard work, diligence, and civic responsibility.

Philosophers, such as Postmodernists (discussed in Chapter 8) and Critical Theorists (discussed in Chapter 19), argue that the version of the settling of the West and the assimilation of immigrants is not an accurate rendition of history. It is a construction of the dominant group and is a selective view of the past that rationalizes their hegemony over subordinated groups such as Native-, African-, Hispanic- and other Americans. The American Conservative rendition of the past is conveyed by various canons—legends about the winning of the West in motion pictures and television programs, popular novels, and some academic histories.

In terms of international relations, Conservatives tend to think of the United States as a country inhabited by morally good people who do the right thing in foreign affairs. The United States represents a model that other countries would do well to imitate. Some Conservatives in the past tended to be isolationists, believing that the United States should have as little as possible to do with other countries and avoid entanglement with them. This view has been eroded by the larger world role that the

United States now plays as a result of the wars of the twentieth and twenty-first centuries. However, the tendency to believe that the United States has the right to make unilateral decisions that affect world affairs remains. Current Conservative foreign policy tends to divide the world into good or evil countries with good or evil leaders. Foreign policy is presented in religious-sounding, either-or moral terms—"you are either with us, or against us."

Market Economics

In general, American Conservatives have adopted the economic theories that originated as Classical Liberalism. They have revived Adam Smith's ideas of the law of supply and demand, the importance of competition, the market economy, and the free enterprise system. The ideas that were once directed to individual business entrepreneurs and industrialists are now applied to the larger and more interconnected corporate economy. Recall that Chapter 11 indicated how Modern Liberals have profoundly revised these ideas and prefer that the government play a larger role in providing social services.

In opposition to the Modern Liberal social welfare state, American Conservatives advocate an open-market, free-trade, supply-and-demand economy; competitiveness; and the deregulation and privatization of social and (some) educational services. A free and competitive marketplace, they maintain, will encourage the most industrious and able individuals to achieve and produce without having to fear the weight of carrying the less productive on their economic shoulders. Conservatives believe that government intervention in regulating the economy leads to higher taxes and inefficient bureaucracy. It is important to restore the economy to its free-flowing condition by deregulating it; that is, by removing the controls of government regulatory agencies.

American Conservatives have little of the European Conservative's sense of paternalism, in which the upper classes look after the welfare of the poorer classes. For American Conservatives, the paternalism of the modern welfare state keeps those who receive aid in a state of dependency. Conservatives charge that the social welfare assistance programs enacted by Liberals actually create and maintain an underclass of people who are dependent on welfare checks. Let all compete, and make sure that misguided Liberals do not impose social welfare schemes that limit individual initiative.

Conservatives believe that modern welfare-state Liberals enacted bureaucratic regulations that weakened American economic productivity. Further, the public schools, hampered by performing too many nonacademic functions, have downgraded the importance of basic academic skills and subjects that contribute to productivity. They have replaced the tried and true, traditional values of hard work, diligence, respect for authority, and patriotism with the progressive permissiveness of values clarification. Rather than preparing the well-trained workforce and managers needed in an entrepreneurial society, public schools, too often controlled by misguided Liberal educationists, have miseducated children.

In addition to reforming schools by restoring what they believe are the primary academic roles, Conservatives contend that there should be greater educational freedom of choice. They argue that the public school system has become a virtual educational monopoly supported by public taxation. They call for a program of government-subsidized vouchers that would enable parents to send their children to the private school of their choice. In such a competitive educational arena, it would be possible to distinguish the most effective and efficient schools from those that are mediocre. Effective schools would attract academically inclined and motivated students. Thus, the voucher system, a form of educational privatization, would make schooling an arena of challenging competition.

Religious Fundamentalism

Christian fundamentalists, sometimes called the "religious right," are often strongly affiliated with the Conservative ideology. Like many of their counterparts in Europe, Conservatives in the United States believe religious principles provide the moral foundations of a properly functioning society. A good society is one that recognizes its religious foundations and emphasizes them throughout its institutions. While some Christian Conservatives would challenge the doctrine of separation of church and state, many would argue that the courts have interpreted the doctrine too rigidly. They believe the United States, as a nation, rests on a generalized Christian ethic, summed up nicely by "in God we trust." They do not want an official state church, but do want a conscious affirmation by government and educational authorities that America's institutions rest on a religious core of values.

Christian Conservatives fear that some trends in modern society have undermined fundamental values.[2] They assert a need to restore "family values" and maintain the family as an institution in which a married man and woman rear their children. In the good family, the husband and wife have a faithful and continuous relationship. Women's roles are as homemakers, childrearers, and caregivers; men are the primary breadwinners. Christian Conservatives reject alternative family arrangements and are especially opposed to same-sex arrangements.

Religious Conservatives, Christian Fundamentalists, and Roman Catholics are also opposed to the Supreme Court's decision in *Roe versus Wade*, which legalized abortion. Conservatives say that abortion denies the unborn child's right to life.

Christian Conservatives' educational agenda is to restore religious values to schools. Many of them favor prayer and the posting of the Ten Commandments in the schools. They oppose the teaching of Darwin's theory of evolution as a scientific truth about the origin of humankind and want Creationism taught. Sex-education programs need to be carefully monitored so that they stress abstinence from sexual relations before marriage.

In terms of entertainment, motion pictures, and television, Christian Conservatives oppose programs that violate what they regard as the fundamental norms of decency. These are programs that portray sexual relations among unmarried people, promiscuity, and similar behaviors.

CONSERVATISM'S EDUCATIONAL IMPLICATIONS

The Purpose of Education and Schools

Conservatives believe that education is society's way of transmitting the cultural heritage. Each of the essential human institutions—family, church, state, and school—have well-defined primary responsibilities in transmitting the cultural heritage from generation to generation. The primary purpose of schools is to educate children and adolescents in academic skills and knowledge. (For discussions of other philosophies that emphasize academics as the primary function of schools, see Idealism in Chapter 2, Realism in Chapter 3, and Theistic Realism in Chapter 4.) Schools, Conservatives argue, perform their primary function best when they also introduce and transmit the cultural heritage—its skills, knowledge, and values—to the young. They promote cultural continuity through language, history, literature, and the arts. Educators should safeguard and protect the traditional curriculum from those who want to experiment, add nonacademic frills, and impose nonacademic functions on schools and teachers. They warn against being deluded by panacea-like promises that the introduction of a new subject or method will make teaching and learning easier or more effective. From time to time, certain changes, such as the introduction of computers and electronic information technologies can be integrated, as long as they are linked to and reinforce the cultural heritage.

The Conservative Cultural Core Curriculum

Conservatives believe that the curriculum should transmit a cultural core rooted in Western Civilization and American culture. As noted earlier, ideologies each have a version of what constitutes the cultural heritage. The heritage of Western Civilization, as Conservatives define it, is based on the great ideas and events of European history. Conservatives admire the ideas of such thinkers as Plato, Aristotle, Aquinas, Luther, Calvin, Locke, Burke, and others.

Postmodernists, Deconstructionists, and Critical Theorists contend that what the Conservatives claim as the heritage of Western Civilization is really the ideology devised by a dominant group at a particular time in history. Feminists argue that what Conservatives proclaim as a heritage actually represents the patriarchal rhetoric of white males. Multiculturalists argue what the traditional core emphasizes as Western Civilization is really white Eurocentrism. Lynne Cheney accuses those who attack a core, grounded in the Western culture, of deliberately downgrading "ideas and practices associated with the United States and its Western heritage, including ... the Enlightenment legacy of scientific thought."[3] Defending Conservatism, Dinesh D'Souza argues that truly liberally educated students need to be "conversant with some of the classic formulations of other cultures, and with the grand political and social currents" that are increasingly interacting with Western culture. This kind of education "is best pursued when students ... search for universal standards of judgment which transcend particularities of race, gender, and culture," thus providing them with the "intellectual and moral criteria" to evaluate their own—and other—cultures.[4]

In addition to Western Civilization, Conservatives want the curriculum to emphasize what they identify as the core knowledge and values of American culture. This means that students should be taught American history and literature and should be expected to know the important persons and events that shaped the country. These subjects should not be taught in a way that downgrades American patriotism or minimizes the great achievements Americans made in creating their nation. It should emphasize knowledge of the Constitution, and respect for law and duly constituted authorities. Conservatives would oppose the version of multiculturalism that minimizes American core values and sees the United States as a nation of unassimilated racial and ethnic groups.

Values of Order and Civility

Conservatives argue that schools have been moving in the wrong direction in terms of values and behavior. Misguided by Dewey's Pragmatism, Liberalism, and Progressivism, the moral climate of schools has been eroded by hedonism, permissiveness, irresponsibility, and inappropriate dress and behavior. In the past, teachers and schools were respected. This respect was earned by emphasizing the moral values—patriotism, diligence, hard work, respect for private property, and the practice of manners and civility—that made the United States a great nation. Conservatives say it is time to reassert the core values in schools and tolerate zero misbehavior and violence. Schools should be places in which students learn to respect their country, their teachers, and each other.

The Conservative Policy Agenda

American Conservatives have a definite educational agenda. They want to restore the school to what they believe is its primary function—instruction in academic skills in a climate that emphasizes traditional moral values. They believe restoration is needed because decades of miseducation by Dewey's Pragmatists, Liberals, Progressives, Cultural Relativists, and Secular Humanists have undermined the academic and moral foundations of the public school. (For discussions of Pragmatism, see Chapter 5, for Liberalism Chapter 11, and for Progressivism Chapter 18.) Today, Postmodernists, Liberation Pedagogues, Critical Theorists, extreme multiculturalists, and others are using teacher-education programs to undermine American patriotism and values. (See Chapter 8 for Postmodernism, Chapter 14 for Liberation Pedagogy, and Chapter 19 for Critical Theory.) Pragmatism's ethical relativism insidiously weakens traditional moral values and patriotism. Postmodernism's argument that the important value-carrying works of Western civilization are merely historic constructions designed to give dominance to powerful groups weakens the canons of Western culture. Liberation Pedagogy's attack on the transmission of the heritage weakens the vital role of instruction. Critical Theory's tendency to see society as a set of power relationships based on race, class, and gender weakens the universal mission of family, state, church, and school. It is important, Conservatives argue, that teacher-education programs and American education itself, be restored to their true function of preparing well-educated teachers who identify with the traditional culture and are committed to transmitting its skills, subjects, and values to the young.

Restoring Academic Standards

Conservatives insist on high academic standards and hold schools and teachers account-able for students' academic performance. To those who contend that tests for academic standards are culturally biased, Dinesh D'Souza argues that high standards serve as a "common index for all who seek to improve themselves, regardless of race, sex, or background." They only discriminate against those failing "to meet them."[5] *A Nation at Risk* (1983) launched the major Conservative counterattack against the nonacademic subversion of schools and declining academic standards. This national report called for a curriculum of academic basics—mathematics, science, language, social studies and history, and computer literacy. The Reagan administration developed a strategy that encouraged the states to enact legislation that added requirements in the basics, especially in English, mathematics, and science. It also encouraged them to use stan-dardized testing to determine students' academic competency at specific grade levels. The initiative stimulated by *A Nation at Risk* led to the standards movement in educa-tion that asserts that schools need to be held accountable for the academic instruction they are supposed to provide. The only way to determine academic competency is to require standardized testing that measures students' academic achievement, especially in the key areas of reading and mathematics. The Education Act of 2001, the No Child Left Behind Act sponsored by the George W. Bush administration, requires states to implement standardized testing in reading and mathematics in grades three through eight in order to receive federal funds. The intent of this educational policy is:

> Schools must have clear, measurable goals focused on basic skills and essential knowl-edge. Requiring annual state assessments in math and reading in grades 3–8 will ensure that the goals are being met for every child, every year. Annual testing in every grade gives teachers, parents and policymakers the information they need to ensure that chil-dren will reach academic success.[6]

■ ■ ■ ■ ■ ▬▬▬▬▬▬▬▬▬▬▬▬▬▬▬▬▬▬▬▬

WILLIAM J. BENNETT, THE CONSERVATIVE CASE IN THE CULTURE WARS

William Bennett is a former Secretary of Education and a defender of Conservative principles in American society, politics, and education. His approach to Conservatism as an ideology is included because Bennett integrates Conservatism with Perennialist values based on the Aristotelian-Thomist philosophical tradition. As you read the selection, you might wish to consider the following focusing questions:

1. How does Bennett define "Conservatism?"

2. Do you agree or disagree with Bennett's endorsement of education for a "common culture"?

3. Do you agree or disagree with Bennett's description of what constitutes a sound program of character education? What contemporary American social and educational trends work for or against such a program?

4. Can you identify any common themes in Bennett's philosophy of education with those developed in Chapter 3 on Realism and Chapter 4 on Theistic Realism.

. . .

No man is a good citizen alone, Plato teaches us in his dialogue *Gorgias*. And so individuals and families need support, their values need nourishment, in the common culture, in the public arena. Our common culture is not something manufactured by the upper stratum of society in the elegant salons of Washington, New York, or Cambridge. Rather, it embodies truths that most Americans can recognize and examine for themselves. These truths are passed down from generation to generation, transmitted in the family, in the classroom, and in our churches and synagogues. They reside in what Burke called the "moral imagination" of the nation. And today, the moral imagination of most Americans is, I believe, sound.

But far too many decent Americans still remain, in effect, on the moral defensive before their own social and cultural institutions. We cannot hope to reclaim our culture until we reclaim these institutions. . . .

Can Americans be confident that their children are going to inherit the habits and values they themselves honor? Are we confident they will be raised in an environment that properly nurtures their moral and intellectual qualities? Can we have confidence in the cultural signals our children receive from our educational institutions, from the media, from the world of the arts, even from our churches? Are we confident that our society is transmitting to our young the right messages, teaching them the right lessons, about the family, drug use, respect for religious beliefs, and our meaning as a nation and our responsibilities as individuals? Is the public air conducive to moral and intellectual health? I believe that most Americans would still answer "no" to these questions.

Even social scientists now recognize the importance of sound values and moral norms in the upbringing of children. Empirical studies confirm what most people, because of their basic common sense, already know. What determines a young person's behavior in academic, sexual, and social life are his deeply held convictions and beliefs. They determine behavior far more than race, class, economic background, or ethnicity. Nature abhors a vacuum; so does a child's soul. If that soul is not filled with noble sentiments, with virtue, if we do not attend to the "better angels of our nature," it will be filled by something else. These matters are of overwhelming importance to our children. As the Roman scholar Pliny the Elder put it, "What we do to our children, they will do to society." Looking today at what we see many kids doing to themselves, to others, and to society at large, we need to reflect on what society collectively is doing to them in the critical task of inculcation, the passing on of our values, in an often hostile atmosphere.

From William J. Bennett, *The De-Valuing of America: The Fight for Our Culture and Our Children*. New York: Simon & Schuster, 1992, pp. 34–35, 56, 58–60, 255. Reprinted with the permission of Simon & Schuster from *The De-Valuing of America* by William J. Bennett. Copyright © by William J. Bennett.

I started my career in government as a philosophical conservative. Conservativism as I understand it is not essentially theoretical or ideological, but rather a practical matter of experience. It seeks to conserve the best elements of the past. ("What is conservatism?" Lincoln once asked. "Is it not adherence to the old and tried, against the new and untried?") It understands the important role that traditions, institutions, habits and authority have in our social life together, and recognizes many of our national institutions as products of principles developed over time by custom, the lessons of experience, and consensus. Conservatives are interested in pursuing policies that will better reinforce and encourage the best of our people's common culture, habits, and beliefs. Conservatism, too, is based on the belief that the social order rests upon a moral base, and that what ties us together as a people—the *unum* in *e pluribus unum*—is in constant need of support.

. . .

Improving American education requires not doing new things but doing (and remembering) some good old things. At the time of our nation's founding, Thomas Jefferson listed the requirements for a sound education in the Report of the Commissioners for the University of Virginia. In this landmark statement on American education, Jefferson wrote of the importance of calculation and writing, and of reading, history, and geography. But he also emphasized the need "to instruct the mass of our citizens in these, their rights, interests, and duties, as men and citizens." Jefferson believed education should aim at the improvement of both one's "morals" and "faculties." That has been the dominant view of the aims of American education for over two centuries. But a number of changes, most of them unsound, have diverted schools from these great pursuits. And the story of the loss of the school's original moral mission explains a great deal.

Starting in the early seventies, "values clarification" programs started turning up in schools all over America. According to this phi-

losophy, the schools were not to take part in their time-honored task of transmitting sound moral values; rather, they were to allow the child to "clarify" his own values (which adults, including parents, had no "right" to criticize). The "values clarification" movement didn't clarify values, it clarified wants and desires. This form of moral relativism said, in effect, that no set of values was right or wrong; everybody had an equal right to his own values; and all values were subjective, relative, personal. This destructive view took hold with a vengeance.

. . .

The leaders of the common school movement were mainly citizens who were prominent in their communities—businessmen, ministers, local civic and government officials. These people saw the schools as upholders of standards of individual morality and small incubators of civic and personal virtue; the founders of the public schools had faith that public education could teach good moral and civic character from a common ground of American values.

But in the past quarter century or so, some of the so-called experts became experts of value neutrality, and moral education was increasingly left in their hands. The common-sense view of parents and the public, that schools should reinforce rather than undermine the values of home, family, and country, was increasingly rejected.

There are those today still who claim we are now too diverse a nation, that we consist of too many competing convictions and interests to instill common values. They are wrong. Of course we are a diverse people. We have always been a diverse people. And as Madison wrote in *Federalist* No. 10, the competing, balancing interests of a diverse people can help ensure the survival of liberty. But there are values that all American citizens share and that we should want all American students to know and to make their own: honesty, fairness, self-discipline, fidelity to task, friends, and family, personal responsibility, love of country, and belief in the principles of liberty, equality, and the freedom to practice one's faith. The explicit teaching of these values is the legacy of the common school, and it is a legacy to which we must return.

People often say, "Yes, we *should* teach these values, but *how* do we teach them?" This question deserves a candid response, one that isn't given often enough. It is by exposing our children to good character and inviting its imitation that we will transmit to them a moral foundation. This happens when teachers and principals, by their words and actions, embody sound convictions. As Oxford's Mary Warnock has written, "You cannot teach morality without being committed to morality yourself; and you cannot be committed to morality yourself without holding that some things are right and others wrong." The theologian Martin Buber wrote that the educator is distinguished from all other influences "by his *will* to take part in the stamping of character and by his *consciousness* that he represents in the eyes of the growing person a certain *selection* of what is, the selection of what is 'right,' of what *should* be." It is in this will, Buber says, in this clear standing for something, that the "vocation as an educator finds its fundamental expression."

There is no escaping the fact that young people need as examples principals and teachers who know the difference between right and wrong, good and bad, and who themselves exemplify high moral purpose.

As Education Secretary, I visited a class at Waterbury Elementary School in Waterbury, Vermont, and asked the students, "Is this a good school?" They answered, "Yes, this is a good school." I asked them, "Why?" Among other things, one eight-year-old said, "The principal, Mr. Riegel, makes good rules and everybody obeys them." So I said, "Give me an example." And another answered, "You can't climb on the pipes in the bathroom. We don't climb on the pipes and the principal doesn't either."

This example is probably too simple to please a lot of people who want to make the topic of moral education difficult, but there is something profound in the answer of those chil-dren, something educators should pay more attention to. You can't expect children to take messages about rules or morality seriously unless they see adults taking those rules seriously in their day-to-day affairs. Certain things must be said, certain limits laid down, and certain examples set. There is no other way.

We should also do a better job at curriculum selection. The research shows that most "values education" exercises and separate courses in "moral reasoning" tend not to affect children's behavior; if anything, they may leave children morally adrift. Where to turn? I believe our literature and our history are a rich quarry of moral literacy. We should mine that quarry. Children should have at their disposal a stock of examples illustrating what we believe to be right and wrong, good and bad—examples illustrating that what is morally right and wrong can indeed be known and that there is a difference.

What kind of stories, historical events, and famous lives am I talking about? If we want our children to know about honesty, we should teach them about Abe Lincoln walking three miles to return six cents and, conversely, about Aesop's shepherd boy who cried wolf. If we want them to know about courage, we should teach them about Joan of Arc, Horatius at the bridge, and Harriet Tubman and the Underground Railroad. If we want them to know about persistence in the face of adversity, they should know about the voyages of Columbus, and the character of Washington during the Revolution and Lincoln during the Civil War. And our youngest should be told about the Little Engine That Could. If we want them to know about respect for the law, they should understand why Socrates told Crito: "No, I must submit to the decree of Athens." If we want our children to respect the rights of others, they should read the Declaration of Independence, the Bill of Rights, the Gettysburg Address, and Martin Luther King, Jr.'s "Letter from Birmingham Jail." From the Bible they should know about Ruth's loyalty to Naomi, Joseph's forgiveness of his brothers, Jonathan's friendship with David, the Good Samaritan's kindness toward a stranger, and David's cleverness and courage in facing Goliath.

These are only a few of the hundreds of examples we can call on. And we need not get into issues like nuclear war, abortion, creationism, or euthanasia. This may come as a disappointment to some people, but the fact is that the formation of character in young people is educationally a task different from, and prior to, the discussion of the great, difficult controversies of the day. First things first. We should teach values the same way we teach other things: one step at a time. We should not use the fact that there are many difficult and controversial moral questions as an argument against basic instruction in the subject. After all, we do not argue against teaching physics because laser physics is difficult, against teaching biology or chemistry because gene splicing and cloning are complex and controversial, against teaching American history because there are heated disputes about the Founders' intent. Every field has its complexities and its controversies. And every field has its basics, its fundamentals. So too with forming character and achieving moral literacy. As any parent knows, teaching character is a difficult task. But it is a crucial task, because we want our children to be not only

healthy, happy, and successful but decent, strong, and good. None of this happens automatically; there is no genetic transmission of virtue. It takes the conscious, committed efforts of adults. It takes careful attention.

. . .

Nothing more powerfully determines a child's behavior than his internal compass, his beliefs, his sense of right and wrong. If a child firmly believes, if he has been taught and guided to believe, that drugs, promiscuity, and assaulting other people are wrong things to do, this will contribute to his own well-being and to the well-being of others. And if this lesson is multiplied a million times—that is, taught a million times—we will have greater and broader well-being, fewer personal catastrophes, less social violence, and fewer wasted and lost lives. The character of a society is determined by how well it transmits true and time-honored values from generation to generation. Cultural matters, then, are not simply an add-on or an afterthought to the quality of life of a country; they determine the character and essence of the country itself. Private belief is a condition of public spirit; personal responsibility a condition of public well-being. The investment in private belief must be constantly renewed.

. . .

CONCLUSION

In this chapter we defined and analyzed Conservatism in terms of its historical antecedents, its key principles, and its educational implications. Conservatives see education as the transmission of the cultural heritage to the young in order to preserve and maintain it. The principles enunciated by Edmund Burke were identified as a fountainhead of Conservative ideology. We pointed out that in the American experience, Conservatism has embraced some economic ideas of Classical Liberalism. The rise of neo-Conservatism as a major force in American politics and education was examined in terms of the Conservative agenda, the demand for restoring an academic curriculum, and for establishing standards verified by standardized testing.

DISCUSSION QUESTIONS

1. Identify and describe the basic principles of Conservatism.
2. Why was Burke so troubled by the French Revolution?
3. Why has there been a revival of Conservatism in contemporary American politics, society, and education?
4. Analyze the Conservative belief that education should transmit the cultural heritage and stable values.
5. Do you think the mood on your campus is Liberal or Conservative? Why?

INQUIRY AND RESEARCH PROJECTS

1. Listen to several "talk shows" on radio and television. Determine whether they reflect the Conservative viewpoint. What are the major messages of Conservatives on these programs?
2. With the permission of your instructor, prepare a questionnaire to be administered to the members of your class. Ask a series of questions based on Conservative principles to elicit whether the members of the class agree or disagree with these principles.
3. Compile a clippings file of articles from newspapers and magazines about current controversies in education such as the standards movement, zero-tolerance policies in schools, school prayer, creationism versus evolutionism, and school uniforms. What is the Conservative position on these issues?
4. Organize a debate on the proposition: Public schools should transmit the cultural heritage, require a common core based on Western culture, and emphasize traditional values.

INTERNET RESOURCES

For a discussion of the ideas of Russell Kirk, a leading American conservative, consult
www.townhall.com/hall_of_fame/kirk/kirkhome.html

For a discussion and an essay on Conservatism, consult
www.xrefer.com/entry/552667.html

SUGGESTIONS FOR FURTHER READING

Abbott, Pamela, and Wallace, Claire. *The Family and the New Right*. London and Boulder, CO: Pluto Press, 1992.

Bennett, William J. *The De-Valuing of America: The Fight for Our Culture and Our Children*. New York: Simon & Schuster, 1992.

Bredvold, Louis I., and Ross, Ralph G. *The Philosophy of Edmund Burke: A Selection from His Speeches and Writings*. Ann Arbor: University of Michigan Press, 1960.

Burke, Edmund. *Further Reflections on the Revolution in France*. Ed. Daniel E. Ritchie. Indianapolis, IN: Liberty Fund Books, 1992.

Burke, Edmund. *On Revolution.* Robert A. Smith, ed. New York: Harper & Row, 1968.

Cheney, Lynne V. *Telling the Truth: Why Our Culture and Our Country Have Stopped Making Sense—and What We Can Do About It.* New York: Simon & Schuster, 1995.

Devigne, Robert. *Recasting Conservatism: Oakeshott, Strauss, and the Response to Postmodernism.* New Haven, CT: Yale University Press, 1994.

D'Souza, Dinesh. *Illiberal Education: The Politics of Race and Sex on Campus.* New York: The Free Press, A Division of Macmillan, 1991.

Frohnen, Bruce. *Virtue and the Promise of Conservatism: The Legacy of Burke and Tocqueville.* Lawrence: University Press of Kansas, 1993.

Gottfried, Paul. *The Conservative Movement.* New York: Twayne Publishers, 1993.

Honderich, Ted. *Conservatism.* Boulder, CO: Westview Press, 1991.

Kirk, Russell. *Academic Freedom.* Chicago: Henry Regnery Co., 1995.

Phillips, Norman R. *The Quest for Excellence: The Neo-Conservative Critique of Educational Mediocrity.* New York: Philosophical Library, 1978.

U.S. Department of Education, Office of the Secretary. *No Child Left Behind.* Washington, DC: Education Publications Center, 2001.

NOTES

1. Edmund Burke, *Reflections on the Revolution in France* (London: Rivingtons, 1868), pp. 459–460.

2. James Davison Hunter, *Culture Wars: The Struggle to Define America* (New York: Basic Books, 1991), pp. 197–204.

3. Lynne V. Cheney, *Telling the Truth: Why Our Culture and Our Country Have Stopped Making Sense—and What We Can Do About It* (New York: Simon and Schuster, 1995), p. 24.

4. Dinesh D'Souza, *Illiberal Education: The Politics of Race and Sex on Campus* (New York: The Free Press, A Division of Macmillan, 1991), pp. 249–252.

5. Ibid, pp. 249–251.

6. U.S. Department of Education, Office of the Secretary, *No Child Left Behind* (Washington, DC: Education Publications Center, 2001), p. 7.

CHAPTER THIRTEEN

MARXISM

In this chapter we will examine Marxism, an ideology that became an important revolutionary doctrine in the twentieth century. Marxism, also known as Scientific Socialism, shaped the revolutionary doctrines Lenin used to establish the Soviet Union. With the demise of the Soviet Union, it continues to be the official ideology in the People's Republic of China and Cuba. Today, Marxism is used as a tool of social, economic, political, and educational analysis for those who are critical of capitalism and seek to bring about socioeconomic change. In this chapter we will define Marxism, situate it in the work of Karl Marx, identify and examine its major ideas, and draw forth its implications for education.

DEFINING MARXISM

To define Marxism, we must begin with a discussion of Karl Marx (1818–1883), the founder of the ideology that bears his name. Marx, a German philosopher, economist, and journalist, created a synthesis of revolutionary ideas in his *The Communist Manifesto*, written with Friedrich Engels to rally their followers during the European revolutions of 1848. His most detailed socioeconomic analysis was *Das Kapital*, a multivolume work published in 1867, 1885, and 1894.[1] **Marxism** can be defined as the social, political, and economic theories of Marx, which interpreted Western history as class struggle. Marxism is also referred to as Scientific Socialism by those who subscribe to the ideology to distinguish it from non-Marxist varieties of socialism such as Utopian and Democratic Parliamentary Socialism. The designation, *Scientific Socialism*, rests on Marx's claim that, unlike philosophies such as Idealism that assert that reality is spiritual or supernatural, Marxism bases reality on materialism, matter that can be examined scientifically.

SITUATING MARXISM

As a university student, Marx studied Hegelian Idealism, the philosophy that dominated German intellectual life in the nineteenth century. Hegel believed human history was the dialectical unfolding of the ideas contained in the Absolute, the highest and most comprehensive form and source of all ideas. Each idea contained its opposite. From this clash of ideas, a higher-order, more comprehensive idea would result. The process would continue until it culminated in the Absolute Idea. (For a discussion of Hegel, see Chapter 2.)

Marx abandoned Hegelian Idealism and argued instead that reality was material, not spiritual. However, he made use of Hegel's dialectic, which he reformulated as class conflict—the struggle of competing socioeconomic classes to control the material foundations of life, the means and modes of production. Thus, in Marx's ideology, dialectical materialism, matter, the primary reality, follows the law of the dialectic as struggle occurs between conflicting classes. In the final struggle, the proletariat, the working class, will inevitably triumph over its adversaries, the capitalists. A supporting corollary of dialectical materialism is economic determinism, which asserts that society's base is economic and whoever controls the economic foundation controls the superstructure of the society. Marx believed that human behavior is determined by economic forces.

In political ideology, Marxism is associated with Communism and some varieties of Socialism. The Communists proclaimed themselves to be Marx's true disciples. Marxism was a highly significant ideology in the twentieth century. From 1917 to 1989, Marxist-Leninism, or Communism, was the official ideology of the Communist Party that ruled the Soviet Union and the Soviet-controlled satellite countries in eastern Europe. Soviet Communism, under Lenin and Stalin, created a ruthless authoritarian police state. With the demise of the Soviet system, Communism lost its official status and is in general disrepute in the former Soviet Union and in eastern Europe. The People's Republic of China was established as a Marxist nation in 1949, where Mao ZeDong was the chief interpreter of Marxism. Today, Communism remains the official ideology in China but there, too, Marxism is being diluted and revised as the private sector grows as part of that country's modernization process. Fidel Castro's Cuba remains a nation in which Marxism is the official state ideology.

The critics of Marxism contend that it is a failed, discredited, and totalitarian ideology. Arguing that it has never really been implemented, Marxism's defenders say that the Soviet version of Communism was really authoritarian statism rather than the true implementation of Marx's ideas.

Some but not all Socialists rely on Marxist doctrines. Democratic Socialists, who use the parliamentary process, believe they can succeed through political and educational means rather than by violent revolution. Generally, Socialists work for the reduction of class privileges and a more egalitarian society, with greater equity in the distribution of social, health, and educational services. They favor some degree of public ownership of basic services, and in some cases, of basic industries. For example, they would favor government-owned, rather than private, energy production, health care, and transportation. The European social democratic parties and the social welfare states in Scandinavia represent Democratic Socialist ideology put into policy and practice.

While Marxism has suffered serious reversals as a political ideology, it remains an important theoretical perspective in philosophy, especially in educational philoso-

■ ■ ■ ■ ■

MAJOR WORKING ASSUMPTIONS IN MARXISM:

1. Reality is material.
2. History is the record of class conflicts for economic control.
3. The class that controls the economy also controls the superstructure of society—the state, education, the law, media, and so forth.
4. In the final struggle, the proletariat (the working classes) will triumph over the capitalists.
5. After the overthrow of capitalism, a fair and equitable society will be created.

phy. Allan Block, arguing that Marxism should not be equated with the failure of governments that have styled themselves as Marxist, says Marxism's continuing importance lies in the way it views society.[2] Educators such as Bowles and Gintis use Marxism as a means of analyzing education in a capitalist society. Marxism has influenced Postmodernism, Liberation Pedagogy, and Critical Theory.[3] (Postmodernism is discussed in Chapter 8, Liberation Pedagogy in Chapter 14, and Critical Theory in Chapter 19.)

WHY STUDY MARXISM?

Despite its downfall in the Soviet Union, there is another dimension to Marxism that needs to involve us as educators. From the time when Marx wrote *Das Kapital* and *The Communist Manifesto*, Marxism has been a powerful ideological force and a significant tool in political and economic analysis. Whether or not we reject Marxism, we have to recognize that the power Marx gave to economic factors as a force in shaping society, politics, and education has profoundly influenced how we think about the world. In the field of education, especially in the foundations of education, varieties of Marxism and neo-Marxism exert a significant influence on educational analysis. The study of Marxism also is useful in understanding Postmodernism, an important contemporary movement in philosophy and literature. There are also elements of Marxism in Paulo Freire's Liberation Pedagogy and in Critical Theory.

MARXISM'S BASIC DOCTRINES

In this section, we identify and comment on some of Marx's basic doctrines and then indicate how they have been revised by contemporary neo-Marxists. The term **neo-Marxist** refers to new or contemporary Marxists, who, while keeping Marx's basic doctrines, have revised them in terms of the modern situation.

Matter in Dialectical Motion

The basic dynamic in Marx's theory is matter in dialectical motion. As a university student, Marx studied Hegel's Idealism, in which all ideas came forth from the mind of the Absolute Idea, the universal idea that contained all other subordinate ideas. History was the unfolding of these ideas on earth and change resulted from conflicts in the realm of ideas. Every idea stated a thesis that embodied a partial truth but also contained its contradiction. From the conflict of thesis and antithesis emerged a newer and higher idea, a synthesis, that was also an idea that generated a new conflict. Although Hegel's dialectic was rooted in his Idealist spiritual metaphysics, Marx borrowed the concept of the dialectical process, which he transferred to his own version of reality that was strictly material or physical. Marx believed that the ideas and perceptions of human consciousness arise from human activity, with economic production and control of the material as the base of society. Our ideas about reality and how we perceive social relations are determined by the material conditions, the economic foundations, of society. Instead of a conflict of ideas, Marx saw human history as a ceaseless struggle between economic classes which were, in turn, based on control of the material conditions of society. Thus, historical and social change is a process of conflict and resolution between opposing economic forces in society.

Marx's dialectic is a way of thinking, an epistemology, that sees the human situation as immersed in a process of conflict and struggle. In the dialectical mode of thought, there are always two opposing sides and two sets of arguments. These opposites are contradictory stages that will be reconciled in a synthesis, a new thesis. Dialectical reasoning continues to be used by neo-Marxists who analyze social and education issues in terms of contradictions or conflicts to be resolved. Although they are less certain that history is determined, they continue to find the dialectic a useful form of social and educational analysis.

The Material Conditions of Society and Class Conflict

Two important and related ideas in Marxism are the material conditions of society and class conflict. For Marx, who said that matter is what is real, the human being is a physical being, with physiological needs and drives, and with a brain that enables him or her to think. In this physical reality, humans work, produce goods or commodities, and live. How the goods are produced and distributed are the means and modes of production and are the economic foundation upon which rests the social structure—the family, state, church, school, law court, police force, and army, for example. Whoever controls the means and modes of production will also control these social institutions. To understand how society, politics, and education really work requires us to examine the economic base—the means and modes of production that support them.

Throughout much of history, people survived by working the land, growing crops, and raising livestock. Land was the material condition upon which society depended throughout much of history—during the Greek and Roman, classical, and medieval periods. A strong group of warriors, the medieval knights, created a feudal system in which they owned the land and forced others, the serfs, to work for them. In addition to using brute physical force to oppress the agricultural workers, the land-lords used the church as an agency of social control to convince the oppressed that life on earth was fated to be this way and the after-life in heaven would be better.

Agricultural production eventually created a surplus of wealth. This surplus led to the formation of a new class, the bourgeoisie, or middle class, that left agriculture and took up other economic pursuits such as trade, banking, and other professions. In the industrial revolution of the early nineteenth century, machines were invented that produced goods on a massive scale. Some of the middle class invested in the new industries and created the factory system of mass production and mass consumption. Industrialism, allied with corporate financing and banking, created the economic system known as Capitalism, which was at first allied with laissez-faire liberalism and later with neo-Conservatism. (See Chapter 11 on Liberalism and Chapter 12 on Conservatism for a discussion of capitalism in relation to these ideologies.) The term *capitalism* derives from the use of capital (money or credit) to purchase the machinery and technology needed to produce goods.[4] Defenders of capitalism, such as Adam Smith and Herbert Spencer, in the eighteenth and nineteenth centuries, claimed the competition of economic forces in the free market would result in greater efficiency and productivity. Economists such as Milton Friedman make a similar argument for capitalism today. Modern industrial society is composed of two classes: the capitalists, who own the factories (the means and modes of production) and the proletariat, the workers who produce goods but who do not own the machines with which they work.

Marx believed that economic class is our primary identification. Our social interactions are based on our relationship to the economy—the means and modes of production. The economic class that controls the economy also controls society's institutional superstructure. Among these institutions are the state (the government), the church (organized religion), the courts (the legal system), the police and military (the arms of state power), the media (agencies of information), and the school (the agency of organized education). The exploiting class also has created a false ideology, designed to mislead and miseducate the workers so they are not conscious of their true situation as victims of exploitation. Marx predicted that the workers, as a result of their exploitation and repression, would organize, arise, revolt, and overthrow their capitalist exploiters.

Neo-Marxists continue to see control of the economy as the real source of power in modern society. They call for a critical examination of the economy to reveal who owns much of the resources, the means of production, and the networks of consumption. They undertake to establish how large modern corporations, the capitalist successors of the older industrialists, control politicians through campaign contributions, manipulate the media through paid advertising, and use the courts to legitimize their exploitation. Modern society, for them, remains an arena of conflicting economic interests. They broaden the contours of class struggle to enlarge Marx's proletariat to include oppressed racial and ethnic groups, women, the homeless, and the poor. It is the ownership and exploitation of the economy, the material conditions of society, that cause racism, sexism, and other forms of discrimination. Unless a deep and thoroughgoing radical restructuring of the economic foundations of modern society occurs, piecemeal reforms to bring about greater equality will be delusions. The continuation of capitalism will ensure continuing inequities, poverty, and injustices in society and education.

Neo-Marxist educators call for a thorough and critical examination of the nature and conditions of economic control in a capitalist-dominated society. They urge teachers to examine critically the material conditions in which schools function—the surrounding neighborhood and its conditions of unemployment, lack of health care, and lack of hope. This kind of critical examination will work to combat and correct the false ideology of consumerism, promoted by capitalists, and raise the consciousness of students about the true nature of the conditions that lead to their exploitation.

Vanguard of the Proletariat

Karl Marx and his chief associate, Friedrich Engels, were not members of the proletariat; they were not factory workers. Marx, a university graduate, had earned a doctorate in philosophy and worked as a journalist. If it is our economic class that defines us, how could Marx, himself, have escaped the thinking that goes with being middle class? Marx reasoned that a small intellectual elite of dedicated revolutionaries, who knew the true course of history, would lead the working class revolution. Because they were removed from the actual means of production, this group of intellectual ideologists could escape and rise above their economically determined class position. This vanguard of the proletariat would: (1) study the true course of history as a process generated by economic class conflict; (2) organize the workers and raise their consciousness about the true conditions of their exploitation; (3) lead the revolution at the correct moment; (4) organize the new classless society that is destined to replace the capitalist economic order. It is important to note that the vanguard engages not only in theorizing but is also activist.

In contemporary neo-Marxist thought, the idea of the vanguard has been revised. In the older Marxist ideology, the vanguard, a secretive group of conspirators, governed by rigid ideological constraints, was an elite. Neo-Marxists are more likely to favor a broad-based form of organization and activism that is more populist than elitist. The revised vanguard does not necessarily refer to intellectuals or intelligentsia. Coming from the grass roots, from the oppressed themselves, the new vanguard is those who are conscious of the conditions of exploitation and can articulate the needs of the oppressed.

Marxist thinking significantly influences those who belong to current academic movements such as Liberation Pedagogy and Critical Theory. In some respects, the ideologues of contemporary neo-Marxism resemble a vanguard movement in education. However, their goal is to build a broad-based coalition for change rather than to operate as an elite.

Contemporary neo-Marxist educators reject new forms of modern capitalism like the international business corporation, economic globalism, and the ethics of a consumer-driven society as the old exploitative capitalism in modern guise. They see the international business corporation as a capitalist invention that on a global scale is allowing a small elite to oppress a mass force of workers. Multinational corporations, have located factories in third-world countries in Africa, South America, and Asia, where workers, often including children, work at a near-poverty level. Agribusinesses, too, have displaced small family farms with huge single-crop agricultural estates that produce food for export while many of the residents of the country in which they operate are ill-nourished.

In a capitalist society and educational system, students of the oppressed groups are indoctrinated into a "false ideology" that denies them the opportunity to study and critically examine the social, political, and economic conditions that contribute to their subjugation. The imposition of the official ideology denies students a critical understanding of their reality. The Neo-Marxist task is to raise the revolutionary consciousness of the masses, the proletariat, through propaganda, informal education, and formal education.

Historical Inevitability

In Marxist thought, the march of history is inevitable and inexorable. In an ideological form of predestination, past, present, and future are the products of the workings of the dialectical process—the struggle of contending classes to control the means and modes of production.[5] The dialectical process follows a predetermined pattern that relentlessly builds new syntheses from the clash of thesis and antithesis. At the current moment of history, Marx wrote, the conflict is between the capitalists and the proletariat, with inevitable victory going to the working classes.

Capitalism, with its never-satisfied appetite for profits, is destined to sow the seeds of its own destruction. Its demands for more markets and more consumer goods will lead to spirals of overproduction that will lead to recurring economic crises, recession, and depression. Capitalists will be forced to reinvest profits to increase production without being able to guarantee the consumption of commodities produced. As the ranks of unemployed grow because of "economic restructuring," more people will need goods and services but will be unable to purchase them. Imperialist wars would result between capitalist nations that seek mastery over colonial sources of raw material and markets. Unemployment, once periodic, will become chronic, and conditions grow ripe for revolution.

After the revolution, all instruments of production will be centralized in the proletarian state created by the victorious workers. The dictatorship of the proletariat will be established to bring about the reforms needed in a classless society. The state apparatus will be taken over and redirected to ensure the working class consolidation of power and control. When the remnants of the old capitalist regime have been obliterated, a classless society will appear, in utopian fashion, in which there is no repression. When everyone is a member of one class, the working class, the state, as an instrument of the domination of one class over another, will wither away.

Contemporary neo-Marxists are most likely to reject or seriously revise Marx's original premise of historical inevitability. While they may still think in dialectical terms that involve the clash of opposing classes and see society as an arena of competing class interests, they are unlikely to accept the idea that victory is inevitable. Events are not just going to take place because of the workings of a fated dialectical process. The struggle will be long, with many temporary setbacks along the way.

Class Conflict

Historical economic change is caused by the struggle to control production. The origin of new classes and the resulting class conflict are determined by the economy. Social class divisions are determined by the classes' relationship to the means, modes, and ownership of production. The ideological rationales used to legitimize class domination rest on an economic base.

Over time, developments in economic production destroyed the feudal system. Modern capitalism brought into existence its own antithesis, the opposing proletarian class. The exploitative methods of capitalism brought into existence and increased the numbers of exploited, property-less laborers.

The proletariat, dependent on selling their labor for their livelihood, were forced to give up any claim to the products of their labor. As factory workers, the proletariat were denied ownership of the means of production. However, they created wealth by laboring on the machines and using the materials owned by their exploiters, the capitalists.

Marx saw modern society grouped into two great opposing camps: capitalist and proletariat. Subgroups that could not be easily classified within either of the two major conflicting classes were really satellites of the major contenders for power. The capitalists were the owners of the resources and employed the proletariat. The capitalists lived on surplus value, which Marx defined as a fund arising from the exploitation of the labor force that made economic profits for them. The lower-middle class of small businessmen, shopkeepers, artisans, and small land-holding peasants would see their economic enterprises absorbed by the large capitalist corporations. This lower strata of the middle class was destined to sink gradually into the proletariat because their capital was insufficient for the scale required by modern industry.

In the final struggle, the capitalists would face the proletariat, their economically determined successors. Although it was history's unalterable course that the proletariat would gain control of the means of production, the capitalists would unsuccessfully attempt to resist. As a result of the proletarian revolution, the capitalist system would be overthrown violently.

Although neo-Marxists may temper Marx's sense of inevitability, they still retain a commitment to viewing society in terms of contending classes. Truly progressive and democratic educators, they argue, would encourage students to identify with the working classes and to work for endemic structural change in the economy and society.

The Superstructure of Society and False Ideology

As stated earlier, it is matter—the material conditions or economic factors—that are at the base of all societies. Upon this economic foundation, social institutions are created. Remember that social institutions are not independent entities; they are dependent on the economic foundation or base upon which they are erected for their existence. Also, recall that whoever controls the material conditions, the economy, will also control the superstructure.[6] The term *superstructure* refers to the body of legal, political, religious, aesthetic, and educational ideas, principles, and institutions in a society. In a modern society, it also would include the sources of information, the media, and entertainment industries. The use of the word *industry* here implies that the press, radio, television, motion pictures, and other producers of information and entertainment are manufacturing and selling a product.

The modern nation–state is the principal agency in the social superstructure. The nation–state, under capitalist control, has military and police forces, a legal system, and prisons to protect it, especially from dissenters and, of course, from Marxist revolutionaries. The church, an agency in the superstructure, gives religious sanction to the status quo that protects capitalism. Further, the national school systems are agencies that indoctrinate the young to accept the status quo by transmitting a false ideology to them. The public school system in the United States is part of the superstructure of society. It is designed to reproduce the ideas, the ideology, and the social and economic relationships that sustain a capitalist, and inherently unequal, society.

In both informal education via the media, and in schooling, the role played by false ideology is important in defending a capitalist society. Although the dominant classes will proclaim their ideology to be true, Marxists label it false. A *false ideology* is one that purports that the agencies in the superstructure have a life of their own and are not dependent on control of the economic base. For example, religion, dealing with the human relationship to God, seeks to create a separate realm of thought, theology, to explain this relationship. The religious emphasis on a heaven and an afterlife, Marx felt, was the opiate of the masses, which deluded them from understanding their true economic condition.

Another example of false ideology can be found in education and other academic areas, especially in Liberals who claim that they can be objective and not take a position on social and political issues. Marxists claim that objectivity is not possible: you are either on the side of the oppressors or on the side of the oppressed.

Contemporary neo-Marxist educators continue to pay great attention to who controls the economic foundation upon which the superstructure rests. They point out that the schools are controlled by the capitalists and often serve the interests of the modern business corporation. They believe it is necessary to examine the actual economic conditions in which an institution functions.[7] If you want to cut through the sentimental fog of the false ideology that proclaims the public school to be the agency of equality of opportunity, you have to go to schools and their neighborhoods. You have to study the material conditions of schools in the inner cities and analyze the impact that poverty, homelessness, unemployment, gang violence, and drugs have on education. This kind of analysis will replace false ideology with true ideological consciousness, which will demonstrate the importance of economic domination on society and culture.

Value and Alienation

Wealth in a capitalistic society is based on the production and sale of an immense accumulation of commodities, manufactured goods, for which there is a market. Some of these commodities—food, clothing, fuel, medicine—satisfy human needs. If the product does not satisfy a human need, the capitalists will use an advertising campaign to convince people that they need the product and should buy it. Because the product either satisfies or is perceived to satisfy a human need, it has a price on the market, what Marx called a *use value*. For Marx, the value is determined by the amount of necessary labor needed to produce the commodity. Labor power, the work needed to make some product, is also a commodity that can be sold. In exchange for their labor, workers receive a wage that sustains them for further production. Because labor creates more exchange value than the cost of working, surplus value is built up. It is surplus value, a price higher than the cost of production, that provides the capitalist with profit. This profit is used by the capitalist to make more profit. As a result, the worker is exploited in that the products of his or her labor are used for the capitalists' wealth and power.

On the modern factory assembly line, the worker performs a small part of the total production of a commodity. The worker's role in production is partial rather than holistic. Further, the value based on the workers' efforts is appropriated by a nonworking capitalist. As a result of partial production and exploitation, workers become alienated from their work. They no longer take pride in what they are making; they work to earn enough to survive. Work becomes wage slavery and drudgery. The Marxist seeks to restore wholeness to work and to emphasize the socially useful nature of productive work. Work then takes on a social value when the products are shared fairly with other workers.

MARXISM'S EDUCATIONAL IMPLICATIONS

Marx concerned himself more with economic and political themes than with education. Marx saw formal education or schooling as the content and exercises that led to intellectual, social, and physical development. He emphasized the importance of polytechnical training in the vocations and occupations of modern society, with an emphasis on the values of socially useful labor. Polytechnical education was a generalized preparation for the world of work that combined the theory of scientific socialism with the knowledge and skills needed in an industrial society.

Marxism's importance lies mainly in its implications for educational analysis. These implications are based on Marx's interpretation of education in a capitalist soci-

■ ■ ■ ■ ■

MARXISM'S BASIC DOCTRINES

1. Matter is in dialectical motion.
2. Struggle for control of the material conditions of society causes class conflicts.
3. The vanguard of the proletariat will raise the consciousness of the exploited class.
4. The eventual triumph of the proletariat over the capitalists is historically determined.
5. The social superstructure rests on an economic base.
6. In a capitalist economy, workers are alienated from their work.

ety. Especially relevant is Marx's view that education needs to be interpreted as arising from the relationship of economic power to control. In Marx's view, the dominant class in society, the class that controls the means and modes of production, will define what constitutes legitimate knowledge, the curriculum, found in the schools. It will determine appropriate subjects and establish the definitions and boundaries between them. In a capitalist society, in which wealth and power are unequally distributed, educational resources, expectations, and opportunities will also be unequal.[8] The driving goal of a Marxist-inspired education is to bring about fundamental economic change and restructuring so that ownership of the means and modes of production passes to dispossessed groups. This major Marxist implication drives neo-Marxist educational theory. It is also a powerful tool of analysis for Liberation Pedagogy and Critical Theory.

Schools in a Capitalist Economy

Neo-Marxists see schools in a capitalist society as agencies used by the dominant class to reproduce the existing class structure that favors their interests.[9] The concept of "reproduction" of existing structures and power relationships is an important tool used by Marxists; it is also a key tool of analysis in Liberation Pedagogy and Critical Theory. Schooling, in a capitalist society, reproduces the ideological, social, political, and economic relationships that are based on dominant class interests. The school's location reflects the material conditions of the society. If it is located in a predominantly white, affluent, upper-middle-class district, with a high tax base and a low crime rate, the climate within the school will reflect these materials conditions. However, if it is located in a predominantly minority, lower-income district, with a high rate of unemployment, the school, too, will reflect these material conditions.

The school's curriculum will reflect how the dominant class conceives of and uses knowledge. What is selected to be part of the curriculum will reinforce existing beliefs and values for the children of the dominant class and will be used to convince children of subordinate classes that this curriculum is also valid for them. Administrators, employed by the dominant group, will claim that they are using standardized tests as an objective measure of students' academic achievement. However, neo-Marxists allege that these so-called objective instruments are framed in class-referenced ways that work to the benefit of the dominant class. Students then will be grouped according to test results. What really is happening, however, is that the tests are used as a sorting device to arrange groups in the school that mirror and reproduce the class situation that exists outside of the school.

Rather than being the institutions that they claim to be in a capitalist society, schools are agencies that reproduce, ensure, and perpetuate the control of the dominant group. They do not practice the theory of equality of opportunity, but rather reinforce inequalities. They educate those who are in a favored position to stay in that position by preparing them for prestigious colleges and universities so that they can take their parents' places in the corporate sector. Simultaneously, the children of the less-favored, dominated classes are also prepared to stay in their places at the bottom of the social and economic scale.

In addition to the content of the curriculum, Marxists argue that the way schools are governed, organized, and operate is based on the ideology of the dominant group. In a capitalist system, an effective school operates like a business, where economic efficiency is the reigning principle. How many students can be educated at the least possible cost? Superintendents are regarded, like their corporate counterparts, as educational CEOs, who seek to maximize outcomes while limiting expenditures. Principals are regarded as middle managers who implement directives issued to them from officials higher in the school bureaucracy. Teachers are regarded as educational functionaries who carry on the processes of instruction with efficient precision, and students are human commodities to be processed through the school's machinery.

Educational reforms in a capitalist society aim to develop new ways of doing more with less expenditure of funds. Educational results are measured by fixed standards that are somewhat like the quality control measures used in mass production.

Education and Schools as a Tool for Raising Consciousness

Marx believed that a genuine education, as opposed to capitalist indoctrination, aimed to develop a critical consciousness in students that would enable them to penetrate the intellectual fog, the rationales of those who controlled the means and modes of production. False consciousness, the ideology of the dominant ruling class, is a strategy used in schools to confuse the children of marginalized groups about the conditions that exploit them and to indoctrinate them in ideology that oppresses them.

Contemporary neo-Marxists, like Marx, call for an education that encourages students to develop a critical consciousness about reality, about the economic factors that govern society, and the class structure that arises from it. They argue that the dominant class, the capitalists, in their modern corporate form, control schools as well as other institutions, and use them for their own economic profit and social aggrandizement at the expense of the oppressed classes. Neo-Marxists, today, undertake a broader and more comprehensive examination of the causes of class domination that extends beyond Marx's original economic factors.[10] Marxist teachers should raise their students' critical consciousness by examining the real economic, political, and social conditions that impact their lives. Much of the examination focuses on classism, the control of one class by another, on racism, discrimination and oppression because of one's race, and sexism, the oppression of women in a male-dominated patriarchal society. Development of critical consciousness requires: (1) a realistic examination of the economic factors that lead to exploitation in modern society; (2) an exposure of the "false ideology" into which students are indoctrinated in a capitalist consumer-driven society; (3) a discussion of what can be done to organize oppressed groups in order to improve their economic, political, and society situation; (4) strategies for taking action in order to transform the society and economy.

Schools as Arenas of Conflict

Using conflict theory derived from Marx's idea of class conflict, neo-Marxists argue that schools, like other social institutions, are places where opposing groups struggle for power and control. The essential struggle is between the dominant groups—the white upper and middle classes who enjoy a favored economic status—and the dominated, oppressed groups—racial and ethnic minorities, the unemployed and underemployed, and women.

To understand group dominance and subordination and to raise students' critical consciousness, neo-Marxist educators seek to: (1) examine the nature of class and class culture; (2) determine how power is distributed between the classes; (3) examine the social control mechanisms that the dominant class has developed to subordinate the dominated class; (4) examine how the dominant class uses schools as agencies of social control.

■ ■ ■ ■ ■

SAMUEL BOWLES AND HERBERT GINTIS, A MARXIST ANALYSIS OF SCHOOLING IN A CAPITALIST SOCIETY

In *Schooling in Capitalist America*, Bowles and Gintis use Marxist concepts to analyze how capitalism, as the dominant economic system in the United States, causes inequalities and contradictions in society and education. They contend that public schools, as educational agencies of capitalism, work to reproduce these contradictions. As you read the selection, you might wish to reflect on the following focusing questions:

1. Can you identify the Marxist tools of analysis that Bowles and Gintis use in their commentary on education and schooling in the United States?

2. How do Bowles and Gintis define "the hierarchical division of labor," "bureaucratic authority of corporate enterprise," and "stratification by race, sex, education, and social class." How do these concepts function in a capitalist society?

3. How and why do public schools legitimize economic and social inequalities?

4. How and why do public schools encourage a technocratic-meritocratic ideology?

The halting contribution of U.S. education to equality and full human development appears intimately related to the nature of the economic structures into which the schools must integrate each new generation of youth. We have seen both liberal educational reform and the social theories on which reform is based flounder on an incomplete understanding of the economic system. We do not intend to repeat these mistakes. We must devote enough attention to the nature of U.S. economic institutions to securely base a realistic alternative educational theory. No facile or superficial snapshot of the U.S. economy will do. We do not wish to

From Samuel Bowles and Herbert Gintis, *Schooling in Capitalist America: Education Reform and the Contradictions of Economic Life*. New York: Basic Books, 1976, pp. 53–56, 102–105, 125–126, 131–133. Credit: *Schooling in Capitalist America* by Samuel Bowles and Herbert Gintis. Copyright © 1976 by Basic Books, Inc. Reprinted by permission of Basic Books, a member of Perseus Books, L.L.C.

hide the fact that our analysis of U.S. capitalism will require attention to some difficult problems in economic theory. Indeed this substantive excursion into economics on which we now embark may seem to the reader out of place in a book on education. Yet only through such a study, we believe, can one understand the workings of the U.S. educational system and the means to change it.

The economy produces people. The production of commodities may be considered of quite minor importance except as a necessary input into people production. Our critique of the capitalist economy is simple enough: the people production process—in the workplace and in schools—is dominated by the imperatives of profit and domination rather than by human need. The unavoidable necessity of growing up and getting a job in the United States forces us all to become less than we could be: less free, less secure, in short less happy. The U.S. economy is a formally totalitarian system in which the actions of the vast majority (workers) are controlled by a small minority (owners and managers). Yet this totalitarian system is embedded in a formally democratic political system which promotes the norms—if not the practice—of equality, justice, and reciprocity. The strongly contrasting nature of the economic and political systems can be illustrated by the diametrically opposed problems faced in maintaining their proper functioning. For the political system, the central problems of democracy are: insuring the maximal participation of the majority in decision-making; protecting minorities against the prejudices of the majority; and protecting the majority from any undue influence on the part of an unrepresentative minority. These problems of "making democracy work" are discussed at length in any high school textbook on government.

For the economic system, these central problems are nearly exactly reversed. Making U.S. capitalism work involves: insuring the minimal participation in decision-making by the majority (the workers); protecting a single minority (capitalists and managers) against the wills of a majority; and subjecting the majority to the maximal influence of this single unrepresentative minority. A more dramatic contrast one would be hard pressed to discover. High school textbooks do not dwell on the discrepancy.

The undemocratic structure of economic life in the United States may be traced directly to the moving force in the capitalist system: the quest for profits. Capitalists make profits by eliciting a high level of output from a generally recalcitrant work force. The critical process of exacting from labor as much work as possible in return for the lowest possible wages is marked by antagonistic conflict, in contract bargaining and equally in daily hassles over the intensity and conditions of work. The totalitarian structure of the capitalist enterprise is a mechanism used by employers to control the work force in the interests of profits and stability. . . .

Our first step is to analyse the market and property relations of capitalism, for it is here that formal political equality, legal reciprocity, and voluntary free market exchange are translated into economic domination. Of prime importance is the severely unequal ownership of productive and financial resources. Were these more or less equally distributed, economic life might not be undemocratic. The concentration of control of these resources, however, means the majority must exchange their only productive property (their capacity to labor) for a wage or salary, thereby agreeing to give formal jurisdiction over their economic activities to owners and managers. Thus formal equality in the political sphere and equal exchange in competitive markets give rise to relationships of dominance and subordinacy within the confines of the capitalist enterprise.

But these power relationships are still only formal. Once within the *formally* totalitarian factory or office, what prevents workers from wresting control of their activities from their employers? What prevents workers, through the combined power of their potential unity, from altering the terms of their contract with employers toward satisfying their own needs? Part of the answer lies again in market and property relations: the employer has the formal right to hire and fire. This right is effective, however, only when the cost to workers is high; that is, when there is a large pool of labor with the appropriate skills available in the larger society, into which workers are threatened to be pushed. Indeed, we shall suggest that the maintenance of such a "reserve army" of skilled labor has been a major, and not unintended, effect of U.S. education through the years.

Part of the answer to maintaining the dominance of the employer over workers lies in the direct application of force: the passage of antilabor laws and the use of the police power of the state. It is precisely against this "solution" that workers have fought their major battles and won some significant victories over the past century. The direct application of force by no means insures the maintenance of capitalist power relations, however, in part because its unlimited and undisguised use may be counterproductive, and in part because the labor-capital contract cannot stipulate all, or even most, of the requirements to insure the profitability and stability of the enterprise.

We shall argue that a major instrument wielded by owners and managers in stabilizing a totalitarian system of economic power is the organization of the production process itself. The long run success of any totalitarian system requires a widely accepted ideology justifying the social order and a structure of social relationships which both validates this ideology through everyday experience, and fragments the ruled into mutually indifferent or antagonistic subgroups.

The capitalist enterprise is no exception to this pattern. . . . The chosen structure of social relationships is the hierarchical division of labor and bureaucratic authority of corporate enterprise. The system of stratification is by race, sex, education, and social class, which often succeeds admirably in reducing the creative power and solidarity of workers.

. . . We suggest that the quality of work life is inimical to healthy personal development and indeed, the structure of power in the economy would be threatened by institutions (such as liberated education) which promote full human development. Moreover, we argue that the alienated character of work as a social activity cannot be ascribed to the nature of "modern technology," but is, rather, a product of the class and power relations of economic life. Though the structural changes required are far-reaching, unalienated work can be achieved without sacrificing the material conveniences of modern life. Similarly, we suggest that economic inequality is a structural aspect of the capitalist economy and does not derive from individual differences in skills and competencies. While the extent of inequality is subject to change through changes in the structure of the economy, it is hardly susceptible to amelioration through educational policy. . . .

The humanity of a nation, it is said, can be gauged by the character of its prisons. No less can its humanity be inferred from the quality of its educational processes. In the initiation of youth, a society reveals its highest aspirations, tempered less by the weight of tradition than by the limits to which the social relationships of adult life can be pushed. We believe that in the contemporary United States, these limits are sufficiently narrow to preclude the educational system from simultaneously integrating youth into adult society and contributing significantly to economic equality. In promoting what John Dewey once called the "social continuity of life," by integrating new generations into the social order, the schools are constrained to justify and reproduce inequality rather than correct it.

. . . The pattern of economic inequality is predominantly "set" in the economy itself—via market and property institutions which dictate wide inequalities in income from property, in the basic social relations of corporate enterprises, and in the tendency toward uneven development, which leads to regional, sectional, racial, sexual, and ethnic disparities. But the "legitimation hypothesis" . . . goes considerably beyond this level of analysis. For it suggests that a major element in the integrative function of education is the legitimation of preexisting economic disparities. Thus efforts to realize egalitarian objectives are not simply weak; they are also, as we shall demonstrate, in substantial conflict with the integrative function of education.

The educational system legitimates economic inequality by providing an open, objective, and ostensibly meritocratic mechanism for assigning individuals to unequal economic positions. The educational system fosters and reinforces the belief that economic success depends essentially on the possession of technical and cognitive skills—skills which it is organized to provide in an efficient, equitable, and unbiased manner on the basis of meritocratic principle.

Of course the use of the educational system to legitimize inequality is not without its own problems. Ideologies and structures which serve to hide and preserve one form of injustice often provide the basis of an assault on another. The ideology of equal educational opportunity and meritocracy is precisely such a contradictory mechanism.

We shall argue that beneath the facade of meritocracy lies the reality of an educational system geared toward the reproduction of economic relations only partially explicable in terms of technical requirements and efficiency standards. Thus we shall first suggest that educational tracking based on competitive grading and objective test scores is only tangentially related to social efficiency. Then we shall confront the technocratic-meritocratic ideology head on by showing that the association between length of education and economic success cannot be accounted for in terms of the cognitive achievements of students. Thus the yardstick of the educational meritocracy—test scores—contribute surprisingly little to individual economic success. The educational meritocracy is largely symbolic.

Clearly, though, this symbolism is deeply etched in the American consciousness. Nothing exhibits this more clearly than the recent "IQ debate," where it has been generally assumed that IQ and other measures of cognitive performance are important indicators of economic success. Only the genetic or environmental determinants of IQ have been questioned. Yet we will argue that social class or racial differences in IQ are nearly irrelevant to the process of intergenerational status transmission.

Throughout history, patterns of privilege have been justified by elaborate facades. Dominant classes seeking a stable social order have consistently nurtured and underwritten these ideological facades and, insofar as their power permitted, blocked the emergence of alternatives. This is what we mean by "legitimation": the fostering of a generalized consciousness among individuals which prevents the formation of the social bonds and critical understanding whereby existing social conditions might be transformed. Legitimation may be based on feelings of inevitability ("death and taxes") or moral desirability ("everyone gets what they deserve"). When the issue is that of social justice, these feelings are both present, with a dose of "custom" and "resignation" as well.

In U.S. economic life, legitimation has been intimately bound up with the technocratic-meritocratic ideology. . . . Several related aspects of the social relations of production are legitimized, in part, by the meritocratic ideology. To begin with, there are the overall characteristics of work in advanced U.S. capitalism: bureaucratic organization, hierarchical lines of authority, job fragmentation, and unequal pay. It is essential that the individual accept and, indeed, come to see as natural these undemocratic and unequal aspects of the workaday world. Moreover, the staffing of these positions must appear egalitarian in process and just in outcome, parallel to the formal principle of "equality of all before the law" in a liberal democracy.

This legitimation of capitalism as a social system has its counterpart in the individual's personal life. Thus, just as individuals must come to accept the overall social relations of production, so workers must respect the authority and competence of their own "supervisors" to direct their activities, and justify their own authority (however extensive or minimal) over others. That workers be resigned to their position in production is perhaps sufficient; that they be reconciled to their fate is even preferable.

The hallmark of the meritocratic perspective is its reduction of a complex web of social relationships in production to a few rules of technological efficiency. In this view, the hierarchical division of labor arises from its natural superiority as a device to coordinate collective activity and nurture expertise. To motivate the most able individuals to undertake the necessary training and preparation for occupational roles, salaries and status must be clearly associated with level in the work hierarchy. . . .

This meritocratic ideology has remained a dominant theme of the mainstream of social science since the rise of the factory system in the United States. The robustness of this perspective (even those who reject it have nagging doubts) is due, in no small part, to its incorporation in major social institutions—factories, offices, government bureaus, and schools. For the technocratic justification of the hierarchical division of labor leads smoothly to a meritocratic view of the process whereby individuals are matched to jobs. An efficient and impersonal bureaucracy, so the story goes, assesses the individual purely in terms of his or her expected contribution to production. And the main determinants of job fitness are seen to be those cognitive and psychomotor capacities relevant to the worker's technical ability to do the job. The technocratic view of production, together with the meritocratic view of hiring, provides the strongest form of legitimation of alienated work and social stratification in capitalist society. Not only does it strongly reinforce the notion that the hierarchical division of labor is

technically necessary (albeit politically totalitarian), but it also justifies the view that job assignment is objective and efficient and, therefore, just and egalitarian (albeit severely unequal). Moreover, the individual is resigned to, if not satisfied with, his or her own position in the hierarchy of production. The legitimacy of the authority of superiors flows not from social contrivance but from Science and Reason.

. . .

. . . We must consider schools in the light of the social relationships of economic life. . . . We suggest that major aspects of educational organization replicate the relationships of dominance and subordinancy in the economic sphere. The correspondence between the social relation of schooling and work accounts for the ability of the educational system to produce an amenable and fragmented labor force. The experience of schooling, and not merely the content of formal learning, is central to this process. In our view, it is pointless to ask if the net effect of U.S. education is to promote equality or inequality, repression or liberation. These issues pale into insignificance before the major fact: The educational system is an integral element in the reproduction of the prevailing class structure of society. The educational system certainly has a life of its own, but the experience of work and the nature of the class structure are the bases upon which educational values are formed, social justice assessed, the realm of the possible delineated in people's consciousness, and the social relations of the educational encounter historically transformed. . . .

Economic life exhibits a complex and relatively stable pattern of power and property relationships. The perpetuation of these social relationships, even over relatively short periods, is by no means automatic. As with a living organism, stability in the economic sphere is the result of explicit mechanisms constituted to maintain and extend the dominant patterns of power and privilege. We call the sum total of these mechanisms and their actions the reproduction process.

Amidst the sundry social relations experienced in daily life, a few stand out as central to our analysis of education. These are precisely the social relationships which are necessary to the security of capitalist profits and the stability of the capitalist division of labor. They include the patterns of dominance and subordinacy in the production process, the distribution of ownership of productive resources, and the degrees of social distance and solidarity among various fragments of the working population—men and women, blacks and whites, and white- and blue-collar workers, to mention some of the most salient.

. . .

The educational system helps integrate youth into the economic system, we believe, through a structural correspondence between its social relations and those of production. The structure of social relations in education not only inures the student to the discipline of the work place, but develops the types of personal demeanor, modes of self-presentation, self-image, and social-class identifications which are the crucial ingredients of job adequacy. Specifically, the social relationships of education—the relationships between administrators and teachers, teachers and students, students and students, and students and their work—replicate the hierarchical division of labor. Hierarchical relations are reflected in the vertical authority lines from administrators to teachers to students. Alienated labor is reflected in the student's lack of control over his or her education, the alienation of the student from the curriculum content, and the motivation of school work through a system of grades and other external rewards rather than the student's integration with either the process (learning) or the outcome (knowledge) of the educational "production process." Fragmentation in work is reflected in the institutionalized and often destructive competition among students through continual and ostensibly meritocratic ranking and evaluation. By attuning young people to a set of social relationships similar to those of the work place, schooling attempts to gear the development of personal needs to its requirements.

But the correspondence of schooling with the social relations of production goes beyond this aggregate level. Different levels of education feed workers into different levels within the occupational structure and, correspondingly, tend toward an internal organization comparable to levels in the hierarchical division of labor. As we have seen, the lowest levels in the hierarchy of the enterprise emphasize rule-following, middle levels, dependability and the capacity to operate without direct and continuous supervision, while the higher levels stress the internalization of the norms of the enterprise. Similarly, in education, lower levels (junior and senior high school) tend to severely limit and channel the activities of students. Somewhat higher up the educational ladder, teacher and community colleges allow for more independent activity and less overall supervision. At the top, the elite four-year colleges emphasize social relationships conformable with the higher levels in the production hierarchy. Thus schools continually maintain their hold on students. As they "master" one type of behavioral regulation, they are either allowed to progress to the next or are channeled into the corresponding level in the hierarchy of production. Even within a single school, the social relationships of different tracks tend to conform to different behavioral norms. Thus in high school, vocational and general tracks emphasize rule-following and close supervision, while the college track tends toward a more open atmosphere emphasizing the internalization of norms.

These differences in the social relationships among and within schools, in part, reflect both the social backgrounds of the student body and their likely future economic positions. Thus blacks and other minorities are concentrated in schools whose repressive, arbitrary, generally chaotic internal order, coercive authority structures, and minimal possibilities for advancement mirror the characteristics of inferior job situations. Similarly, predominantly working-class schools tend to emphasize behavioral control and rule-following, while schools in well-to-do suburbs employ relatively open systems that favor greater student participation, less direct supervision, more student electives, and, in general, a value system stressing internalized standards of control.

The differential socialization patterns of schools attended by students of different social classes do not arise by accident. Rather, they reflect the fact that the educational objectives and expectations of administrators, teachers, and parents (as well as the responsiveness of students to various patterns of teaching and control) differ for students of different social classes. At crucial turning points in the history of U.S. education, changes in the social relations of schooling have been dictated in the interests of a more harmonious reproduction of the class structure. But in the day-to-day operation of the schools, the consciousness of different occupational strata, derived from their cultural milieu and work experience, is crucial to the maintenance of the correspondences we have described. That working-class parents seem to favor stricter educational methods is a reflection of their own work experiences, which have demonstrated that submission to authority is an essential ingredient in one's ability to get and hold a steady, well-paying job. That professional and self-employed parents prefer a more open atmosphere and a greater emphasis on motivational control is similarly a reflection of their position in the social division of labor. When given the opportunity, higher-status parents are far more likely than their lower-status neighbors to choose "open classrooms" for their children.

Differences in the social relationships of schooling are further reinforced by inequalities in financial resources. The paucity of financial support for the education of children from minority groups and low-income families leaves more resources to be devoted to the children of those with more commanding roles in the economy; it also forces upon the teachers and school administrators in the working-class schools a type of social relationships that fairly closely mirrors that of the factory. Financial considerations in poorly supported schools militate against small intimate classes, multiple elective courses, and specialized teachers (except for disciplinary personnel). They preclude the amounts of free time for teachers and free space required for a more open, flexible educational environment. The well-financed schools attended by the children of the rich can offer much greater opportunities for the development of the capacity for sustained independent work and all the other characteristics required for adequate job performance in the upper levels of the occupational hierarchy.

CONCLUSION

Marxism, the ideology developed by Karl Marx, emphasizes that the material base of society, the economic means and modes of production, determine social structures and our relationship to them. In this chapter we presented the basic Marxist critique of capitalist society and institutions and discussed the fact that Marxism has provided some of the tools of analysis found in influential contemporary ideologies such as Liberation Pedagogy and Critical Theory.

DISCUSSION QUESTIONS

1. Do you think that Marxism, as the official ideology in the former Soviet Union, the People's Republic of China, and Cuba, is relevant or irrelevant to Marxism as an ideological tool to analyze education in the United States?

2. How does the economy shape educational policy and practices in the United States?
3. Do you think public schooling reinforces or diminishes class, race, and gender differences in the United States?
4. Why has neo-Marxism exerted considerable influence in contemporary movements in educational theory, especially on Postmodernism and Critical Theory?
5. Do you agree or disagree with the Marxist interpretation of the current socioeconomic and educational situation in the United States?
6. Marx argued that for capitalism to work, larger and more efficient means of production must be developed and markets must be expanded throughout the world. Apply this form of Marxist analysis to the process of globalization by multinational corporations. Do you agree or disagree with the Marxist analysis?

INQUIRY AND RESEARCH PROJECTS

1. Research how public education is funded. Do you think current funding promotes equality or inequality in educational opportunities?
2. Examine some of the programs used for conflict resolution in education. Then, do a Marxist analysis of these programs.
3. Interview several public school teachers. Do you find that they exhibit career satisfaction or alienation in their work? Then, do a Marxist analysis of your findings.
4. In your clinical experience in schools, do you find evidence of stratification and reproduction of existing socioeconomic classes? If so, do a Marxist analysis of your findings.
5. Read and review a book on education written by a Critical Theorist. (See the chapter on Critical Theory that appears later in the book.) Do you find evidence of class conflict, similar to that developed by Marx, in the book?

INTERNET RESOURCES

Selected works of Marx and Engels can be accessed from the Marx/Engels Library at **www.marxists.org/archive/marx/works.html**

For an essay on Marxism, consult **www.xrefer.com/entry/552725**

SUGGESTIONS FOR FURTHER READING

Apple, Michael W. *Ideology and Curriculum*. London: Routledge, 1990.
Bowles, Samuel, and Gintis, Herbert. *Schooling in Capitalist America*. New York: Basic Books, 1975.
Brosio, Richard A. *A Radical Democratic Critique of Capitalist Education*. New York: Peter Lang, 1994.
Churchich, Nicholas. *Marxism and Alienation*. Rutherford, NJ: Fairleigh Dickinson University Press, 1990.
Churchich, Nicholas. *Marxism and Morality: A Critical Examination of Marxist Ethics*. Cambridge: James Clarke, 1994.

Cohen, G.A. *Karl Marx's Theory of History: A Defense*. Princeton, NJ: Princeton University Press, 2000.

Femia, Joseph V. *Marxism and Democracy*. New York: Oxford University Press, 1993.

Gottlieb, Roger S. *Marxism, 1844–1990: Origins, Betrayal, Rebirth*. New York: Routledge, 1992.

Torrance, John. *Karl Marx's Theory of Ideas*. New York: Cambridge University Press, 1995.

Wheen, Francis. *Karl Marx: A Life*. New York: W.W. Norton & Co, 1999.

Wood, Ellen M. *Democracy Against Capitalism: Renewing Historical Materialism*. New York: Cambridge University Press, 1995.

NOTES

1. Biographies of Marx are Francis Wheen, *Karl Marx: A Life* (New York: Norton, 2000) and David McLellan, *Karl Marx: His Life and Thought* (New York: Harper and Row, 1973).

2. Alan A. Block, "Marxism and Education," in Rebecca A. Martusewicz and William M. Reynolds, eds., *Inside/Out: Contemporary Critical Perspectives in Education* (New York: St. Martin's Press, 1994), p. 62.

3. For the relationship of Marxism to Critical Theory, see Douglas Kellner, *Critical Theory, Marxism, and Modernity* (Cambridge, MA and Baltimore, MD: Polity and Johns Hopkins University Press, 1989).

4. Block, p. 65.

5. G. A. Cohen, *Karl Marx's Theory of History: A Defense* (Princeton, NJ: Princeton University Press, 2000).

6. Block, p. 66.

7. Michael W. Apple, "Education, Culture, and Class Power: Basil Bernstien and the Neo-Marxist Sociology of Education," *Educational Theory*, 42, no. 2 (Spring 1992), pp. 127–128.

8. Block, pp. 65–66, 70.

9. Samuel Bowles and Herbert Gintis, *Schooling in Capitalist America* (New York: Basic Books, 1975).

10. Frank Margonis, "Marxism, Liberalism, and Educational Theory," *Educational Theory*, 43, No. 4 (Fall 1993), p. 449.

CHAPTER FOURTEEN

LIBERATION PEDAGOGY

In Chapter 14 we will examine Liberation Pedagogy, which is primarily associated with Paulo Freire (1921–1997), a Brazilian educator who developed his educational ideas by working to bring literacy—the power of reading and writing—to impoverished, illiterate peasants and the urban poor. The ideology of Liberation Pedagogy originated when Freire recognized that literacy brought much more to the individual than simply learning the skills needed to read and write. Acquiring literacy marked the beginning of their consciousness about the conditions that marginalized them, and it stimulated their desire to liberate themselves from their oppressors.

Freire recognized that ignorance and poverty were not simply conditions that victimized the illiterate and unschooled, but were caused by interrelated contexts of economic, social, and political domination. Liberation Pedagogy created a new and powerful self-awareness in individuals who began to examine critically the social situation in which they lived and worked.[1] It often empowered them to take the initiative to change the conditions that oppressed them.

DEFINING LIBERATION PEDAGOGY

To define Liberation Pedagogy, we begin with the words, *liberation* and *pedagogy*. Liberation is derived from *liberate*, which means to release from restraint or bondage or to set free from domination or control. It is important to distinguish Freire's concept of Liberation from that held by Liberals, especially the Classical Liberals, of freedom from restraints, particularly economic ones. (For a discussion of Classical Liberalism, see Chapter 11.) For Freire, the Liberal view of economic freedom—the interplay of free-market forces—is one of the tendencies of modernism that leads to the domination and control of oppressed people. The "bondage" to which Freire refers is the social, economic, and political conditions that give a ruling group power over others, especially people at the margins of society.

The term *pedagogy* refers to the art, science, or profession of teaching. Its meaning in ancient Greek as leading one to knowledge is especially appropriate to Freire's ideology. **Liberation Pedagogy** then is that education that frees a person from domination and oppression.

A very important term in Liberation Pedagogy is *conscientização*, a Portuguese word used by Freire that means consciousness raising for a critical awareness of social, political, and economic conditions and contradictions, and a desire to remove or eliminate those that cause oppression. This critical attitude leads to *radicalization*, defined not as "leftist" politics but as a commitment to transform social reality to enable one to reach self-construction.

SITUATING LIBERATION PEDAGOGY

In situating Liberation Pedagogy, Freire's own work as a literacy campaigner and his evolution as an educational theorist is of paramount importance. Since much of this chapter examines Freire's ideology, the theoretical elements in Liberation Pedagogy will be discussed in later sections of the chapter.

Ivan Illich's theory of deinstitutionalizing and deschooling society is related to Freire's Liberation Pedagogy. Illich's hypothesis about deinstitutionalization contains elements that anticipated Postmodernism. Illich believed that technologically advanced, modern nations, such as the United States, were imposing their institutions, technologies, and processes on the people of less technologically developed countries, especially in Latin America, Asia, and Africa.[2] Geared to advancing a consumer-oriented, materialistic, exploitative society and economy that favored those in economic and political control, the Western nations introduced modern institutions—large corporations, agribusinesses, costly health agencies, and complex transportation networks—that served them but ignored local grassroots needs. In other words, modern institutions were being imposed on people who did not need or want them. While these modern institutions were being imposed, local needs, defined by the people at the immediate grassroots level, were neglected. For example, giant agribusinesses took over large tracts of land. Aided by their political allies, these corporate interests expropriated the small farms of peasant families who were displaced and became landless peasants or impoverished urban slum dwellers. The impoverished masses were too poor and uneducated to benefit from the modern institutions—the airports, hospitals, and universities—that served the ruling classes.

Illich believed the process of modernist institutionalization was achieved through schooling. Schools, in the modern sense, are age-specific institutions in which areas of knowledge are packaged like products within a compulsory curriculum. Society implies that a person has to move through this curriculum in order to succeed in the modern world and economy. The more schooling one acquires, the higher the anticipated socioeconomic income and social status. Schooling's outcomes are projected as higher pay, higher social status, and the attainment of more of the good things in life—more consumer goods. The price for this promise of wealth, happiness, and power is more schooling—more certificates, diplomas, and degrees.[3] Along with the formal curriculum, the "hidden curriculum"—the underlying attitudes and values of institutionalized formal education—create an addictive consumerism, leading one to want and desire things one does not really need.

Illich suggested that the way out of the modernist addiction for more unneeded material goods is to deinstitutionalize society by creating friendly, convivial, humane ways to serve human needs.[4] The process of deinstitutionalization must begin with deschooling. Instead of using the formal, imposed curriculum, Illich proposed that local people, in their grassroots settings, should create the educational processes that serve them best. Freire's literacy circles, for example, were grassroots organizations, operating informally at the local level. A literacy circle is composed of individuals who come together voluntarily in a local situation to learn to read and to become literate. The materials that the participants use to learn to read are those that relate closely to their lives and work. Although guided by a literate person, the members of the circle, through their mutual interests and interactions, actually are teaching each other to read. Illich argued that literacy and numeracy should be taught directly, without the need of surmounting the rigid packaging—the sequence and scope—of the formal curriculum. Work skills could be learned through an apprenticeship system. Other kinds of learning—about literature, history, the humanities, and the arts—could be acquired as individuals interested in these areas joined together in voluntary informal discussion groups. Instead of outside officials and experts determining how local people should live, the people, themselves, were to identify their needs, structure solutions, and work together to solve their problems.

Several premises from Freire's and Illich's work that guide Liberation Pedagogy are: (1) modern institutions, by promising to benefit humankind, actually enrich and empower a few, but dehumanize and impoverish many; (2) education and schooling are never really objective and neutral processes, but involve ideological commitment and imposition; (3) it is possible, indeed necessary, to challenge the status quo and bring about humanizing institutional, social, political, economic, and educational change.

WHY STUDY LIBERATION PEDAGOGY?

Liberation Pedagogy is the educational ideology developed by Freire, a pioneering radical but reflective theorist. His ideas have been influential in providing the central ideas of informal education, and education for sustainable development. Many of his ideas run parallel to Postmodern philosophy but tend to restate its principles in more comprehensible language. Freire's Liberation Pedagogy is, in itself, an intrinsically valuable body of educational ideas and is also a bridge between Postmodernism and Critical Theory.

LIBERATION PEDAGOGY AS AN IDEOLOGY

It is difficult to know precisely where to locate Freire's Liberation Pedagogy. It does not fit easily into the organizing divisions of philosophy, ideology, or theory used in this book since it interpenetrates all three. In this book, Liberation Pedagogy is primarily designated as an ideology since it contains the essential defining characteristics of an ideology: (1) an interpretation of the past; (2) an appraisal or assessment of present conditions; (3) a program for change. Although some may question its placement as an ideology, Freire himself urged his readers to recognize how ideology created and shaped educational institutions and pedagogical practices. He contended that all education was conditioned by ideology. The real choice is between the ideology that promotes liberation and the ideology that dehumanizes people. In many ways, Liberation Pedagogy forms an ideological bridge or linkage between Postmodern philosophy and Critical Theory.

A View of the Past

Life and education, according to Freire, take place in a specific historical context because we live in a specific place at a specific time. With this contextual specificity, we should take a look around. What do we see? Who do we see? How are our days shaped? Do we shape them or do others shape them for us? Who are those "others"? Do these same questions apply to our family and friends? How did we arrive at the time and place in which we now live? What is our story?

History, when studied critically and not as a celebration or apology for the status quo, reveals that some groups or classes have taken control of wealth and have used their power to control others. History is not a laissez-faire, anarchistic, impersonal string of events beyond our control that randomly give power to some but not to others. Neither is our history determined for us by inexorable laws of the universe or of society and the economy that are beyond our control. Our history is both personal and social; it is indeterminate rather than determined. We have the power to write our own history if we are willing to seize the moment.

It is through the story of our lives—the events, past and present—that we begin to understand our contexts. The process of consciousness-raising takes place in a concrete historical context, in a given place at a given time. We are born into and live in a specific historical situation; we have shaped some of the events that make up our lives. However, there are important times when others have taken control of the events that have shaped our story. Although others may have been in control, this does not mean that we must abandon our choices to them. Our lives are not necessarily determined by others, and we have the power to take control of them and live them as we would like. Becoming conscious of our historical situation means that we do not accept the status quo—the standing institutions and practices—as givens somehow embedded in reality, to which we must adjust. Rather, these historical products are the situational points of origin from which we can begin our journey to self-definition. We are not merely inheritors of history. We have the power to make history.

Freire's contextualism is similar to that found in Postmodernism, which asserts that all societies include dynamics of power, in which some are empowered and some are disempowered. (Postmodernism is discussed in Chapter 8.) Freire, like the Postmodernists, is most concerned with the marginalized people of the Earth. To truly understand power relationships, it is necessary to examine the immediate situations in which they occur.

Interpretation of the Current Situation

In analyzing the contemporary situation, Freire urges an examination of the material conditions that bear upon a society. It is the examination of the material conditions that Freire borrows from Marx. (For a discussion of Marxism, see Chapter 13.) What are the material conditions of a given society? Who are the owners of property? How did they acquire and how do they maintain their wealth and power? Who is wealthy and who is impoverished? What are the political, social, economic, and educational arrangements that maintain the distribution of wealth and power?[5] These conditions of life and work—cultural, social, political, economic, and educational—are historically derived and constitute the ongoing reality in which people operate. As they become conscious of their social reality, individuals can understand their personal and social situations and the conditions in it that either repress or liberate them.

The Program of Action

In such an ideologically charged situation, Freire maintains that teachers cannot remain neutral or hide behind a veil of objectivity. Teachers cannot escape the ideological issues confronting them. They have to answer the question: Do existing social, economic, and political conditions retard human liberation and freedom, or do they promote self-fulfillment? Claiming or feigning neutrality actually allies the teacher with the oppressors. The teacher either supports the oppressors, who have appropriated the material conditions of life—wealth, land, property—and have constructed a social, cultural, and political system that justifies their exploitation of subordinated groups, or the teacher acts to advance the liberation of the dispossessed.[6]

The goal of Liberation Pedagogy is the creation of a new social order. Creating the new world will come from opening the self and society to new possibilities for leading a richer and fuller life. The new world is not a utopian vision, but the result of a transformation of the social situation into one of more open, enriched, possibilities.

PHILOSOPHICAL AND IDEOLOGICAL RELATIONSHIPS

There are substantial traces of Existentialist philosophy in Freire's Liberation Pedagogy. (Existentialism is discussed in Chapter 6.) Like the Existentialists, he rejects the Idealist and Realist assertion that we are defined a priori as a category in a universal metaphysical system. Freire's rejection of a priori first principles agrees somewhat with Pragmatism. (For Pragmatism, see Chapter 5.) Another similarity is the importance given to the person in interaction with the environment. Like Dewey, Freire holds that individuals are in constant interaction with the world in which they live.

An important difference between Pragmatism, especially Dewey's Experimentalism, and Liberation Pedagogy is that Freire does not see the scientific method as the most accurate and objective way to think. Science and technology are merely one of many kinds of rationality and, indeed, can be used as instruments of oppression.[7]

Freire, though using Marxist concepts, rejects the Marxist determinism that our future, like our past, is a product of historical inevitability. Drawing on Existentialism, he sees the person as an incomplete presence in the world. Once we accept that we are unfinished individuals, we can fully understand that we are free—indeed responsible—to continually define ourselves in what is really an indeterminate situation. The ethical person consciously accepts the responsibility to create a future filled with promise and possibilities.[8]

Where Freire departs from other Existentialist positions is in his insistence that a genuinely ethical person works to become conscious of the conditions in which she or he lives and deliberately works to change those that are unjust or pernicious to human freedom. Other Existentialists would regard Freire's call to commit oneself to social, political, economic, and educational change as another form of imposition that gets in the way of freedom of choice.

The concept of ideology looms very large in Freire's Liberation Pedagogy. As indicated, Freire considers all education to be conditioned by ideology. He distinguishes Liberation Pedagogy, as a radicalizing ideology, from rightist and leftist sectarian ideologies that distort history and rely on myths to create a sense of false consciousness. Freire, in his educational work in Latin America, was most engaged in opposition to rightist ideologies that rationalized the rule of reactionary, oligarchic, militaristic regimes. Freire argues that rightist ideologies, such as Conservatism, fearing change, seek to "slow down the historical process" by constructing a protective historical interpretation that defends the ruling class's privileged position. (Conservatism is discussed in Chapter 12.)

Liberalism, though promising equality of opportunity, establishes institutions and procedures that create new elites, usually bureaucratic and corporate ones, that disempower those not initiated in the intricacies of modernization. (For Liberalism, see Chapter 11.) Liberals tend to display a presumed benevolence toward subordinated groups but fail to acknowledge that they enjoy a privileged status that makes them accomplices in repressive situations. Rather than acting directly to end the repression of marginalized people, Liberals tend to skirt the main issues and instead are content with piecemeal reforms that often secure their own position rather than improve the situation of those they pretend to help. Even the Liberal notion of welfare and assistance, benignly intended to aid the poor, tends to create dependency that locks the dependents into the system rather than liberating them from it.[9] Even more manipulative than Conservatism, Liberalism offers unfulfilled false promises.

Freire, by calling for a radical transformation of society, rejects what he calls leftist sectarianism, similar to Communism, which, adhering to a rigidly doctrinaire Marxism, constructs an ideology of reaction to Conservatism and Liberalism. Leftist sectarian ideology justifies every action that is in line with the inevitability of reaching a predetermined perfect state of society, a utopia. For the leftist sectarian, the future is "inexorably preordained" rather than indeterminate.[10]

PHILOSOPHICAL IMPLICATIONS

As indicated earlier, Freire's Liberation Pedagogy does not lend itself to being neatly categorized as a philosophy, ideology, or theory. It overlaps these distinctions. In this section, we consider some of its philosophical implications.

Freire's philosophical orientation draws heavily from Existentialism, especially his concept of the human being as an "unfinished presence" in the world who is engaged in working out her or his identity and purpose in social reality. The idea of the individual as unfinished or incomplete, however, is not an abstraction. It means the person is engaged in self-identification in a concrete cultural, social, historical, political, and economic context. It is this context that contains the forces that seek to impose a definition, a social construction, that is not of the person's free choosing. The raising of consciousness, through Liberation Pedagogy, means that the person is consciously examining the objective conditions in this context, identifying those that diminish the power of self-fulfillment.[11]

Epistemology

Freire draws an intimate connection between thinking (being conscious) and acting on our thoughts (praxis). To think critically means to be empowered to penetrate through the ideological mists of false consciousness—the myths, theories, and rationales that others, especially the oppressors, have constructed to confuse and indoctrinate dominated groups. These rationales, derived from the oppressor's ideology, are designed to indoctrinate the oppressed to accept blindly the oppressive conditions in the social environment as being "right," "just," "the standard," or "in the nature of things." Thinking critically requires the ability to see these rationales for what they are—the constructions of an oppressive group. Related to critical thinking is engaging in liberating dialogues in which the oppressed voice their ongoing conceptions of social reality. Once this has been done, it becomes possible to reject these constructions and to create true knowledge, a genuine consciousness of social reality. Critical thinking is not merely an academic exercise. It is a call to change things by acting to transform the conditions of oppression. As individuals make these changes in thought and act on them, they are recreating themselves and reconstructing the social environment.

Axiology

In terms of ethics and aesthetics, Freire sees the value conflict between conditions that humanize and those that dehumanize. The question is: Are values freely made and chosen by the person who embraces and is guided by them, or are they prescriptions imposed on the oppressed by their oppressors? According to Freire, prescription "represents the imposition of one man's choice on another." It subverts the consciousness of the subordinated person by imposing the dominant person's values. Prescriptions of oppression—imposed as the "right way" to act—are often indoctrinated into the oppressed and reinforced by sanctions and threats or actual punishments. Thus, the values of the oppressor become internalized and dehumanize the oppressed.[12] To become free to create one's own values, it is necessary to become fully conscious that the choice resides within. The person's awareness of being "unfinished" carries with it a responsibility to actively engage in making the decisions that bring about self-definition and self-fulfillment. This kind of authentic decision making brings forth a sense of ethics. Authentic values come from the individual's critical awareness of what it means to be free to create him or herself. To do so means to have knowledge of the

■ ■ ■ ■ ■

LIBERATION PEDAGOGY'S PHILOSOPHICAL RELATIONSHIPS

1. From Marxism: The analysis of economically based conditions that cause political and social repression
2. From Existentialism: The principle that the human being is an unfinished project
3. From Postmodernism: An emphasis on analysis of the immediate contexts in which oppressive conditions are imposed

conditions that diminish this freedom and to take responsibility for choice. Humanization refers to values that are freely chosen, that enlarge, and liberate.

LIBERATION PEDAGOGY'S EDUCATIONAL IMPLICATIONS

Freire states that educational institutions and processes are never free of the conditions and situations—the contexts—of which they are a part. They are never ideologically neutral or scientifically objective. All educational institutions, like all social, political, and economic systems, are ideologically conditioned. Education either adjusts the younger generation to accept and conform to the power relationships of the existing system or it becomes a pedagogy of liberation. Education, committed to liberation, implies raising people's consciousness, encouraging them to reflect critically on social reality, and empowering them to transform the conditions or contexts that shape their lives.

Struggling Against Miseducation

The raising of consciousness involves exposing situations and actors that miseducate people either unconsciously or deliberately. False consciousness—a failure or unwillingness to recognize historical truth and social reality—is a concept Freire borrows from Marx. Falling into the intellectual and psychological trap of believing in the rhetoric of those who control social institutions, including schools, prevents us from coming to grips with the reality of what has actually happened in our group and personal lives, leading to a falsified history and a faulty self-concept, and often to low self-esteem. For example, a history that celebrates the achievements of the ruling class while ignoring the contributions of those who are marginalized, distorts the truth and provides a falsified record of the past. An education that defines a person's values in terms of wealth and power and sees schooling as a ticket to a place in the corporate system misses the mark of being truly humanizing.[13]

Teaching and Learning

Freire attacks modes and methods of instruction that lead to false, rather than critical, consciousness in students' perceptions of reality. Some of the standard methods of teaching commonly used in schools cause this kind of false consciousness. For example, there is "teacher talk" in which a teacher becomes a kind of "talking text," purporting to possess knowledge and explaining reality by means of indirect descriptions or narratives. Teacher talk implies that students should be attentive listeners who fix on each word spoken by the teacher, take it in, and store it in their minds to be recalled for a test. Teaching–listening as the primary mode of instruction leads to what Freire calls educational "banking."[14] Each bit of information is perceived as a deposit in the mind, a mental bank, where it is stored and supposedly will resurface, to be cashed in, when needed. In traditional schooling, information is often needed to pass some kind of examination. The current standards movement that emphasizes standardized testing is an example of assessment based on the banking model of education. The elaborate testing mechanisms constructed to determine student's academic achievement in mastering externally imposed curricula are used to sort students into groups, reproducing the inequalities of the existing social and economic system.[15] Freire's discussion of subject matter as banking closely resembles Illich's critique of schooling as creating addictive conditions of dependency and consumerism.

Teaching as Committed Partiality

Freire completely rejects the proposition that teachers can and should be neutral or impartial on social, political, and economic issues. Freire says of himself, "I am not impartial or objective; not a fixed observer of facts and happenings."[16] Freire is especially critical of educators, such as Liberals, who claim to be ideologically unbiased and open-minded in their teaching. In Liberation Pedagogy, such claims to objectivity mean the teacher is not conscious of the true conditions that affect education, or is engaged in a pretense that covers up ideological commitments.

Freire believes genuine learning occurs when teachers and students engage in a shared, ongoing dialogue that creates rather than transmits knowledge. Knowledge is created when teachers and students share and critically reflect upon their experiences. An important moment occurs when teachers and students begin to evaluate critically what they know and how they got this knowledge. This kind of consciousness-raising reflection marks the opportunity for examining and transforming life.[17] According to Macedo, a close friend and interpreter of Freire, genuine teaching:

- Recognizes that all social and educational situations are ideological.
- Is ethically committed to fight racial, sexual, and class discrimination.
- Requires a critical capacity, tempered by humility and reflection.[18]

Freire asserts that teachers should have two important traits: a tough, rigorous, critical attitude toward socioeconomic and political reality, as well as a sense of humility (and therefore respect for students). Having a rigorous, critical attitude means that the teacher needs to approach the ideologically framed context of teaching with a full and realistic awareness of conditions that limit the potentialities of human freedom. This may mean going against the grain and against conventional wisdom, and challenging the power structure both inside and outside of the school. At the same time, the teacher needs to remember that she or he does not know everything, but has much to learn from the members of the community—especially the disempowered groups— and from students. This blending of critical awareness and humility will allow teachers to engage in dialogues with students that examine the students' experience of life, and discuss with them how they have felt rejection or suffered from discrimination. This kind of dialogue is intended to bring forth *conscientization* in both teachers and students—an awareness of the impediments to self-fulfillment.

In Freire's view, teaching is not collecting and transmitting knowledge; neither is learning the memorization of information to be retrieved in the future. Teaching and learning require that the teacher and the students be mutually engaged in constructing knowledge through critical dialogue. The participants in the educational dialogue— teacher and students—are reforming themselves. This idea reflects Freire's reliance on the Existentialist theme that the human condition is one of incompleteness in which we act to bring our lives, through our own actions, to wholeness.

PAULO FREIRE, PEDAGOGY OF THE OPPRESSED

Paulo Freire's *Pedagogy of the Oppressed*, his groundbreaking introduction of Liberation Pedagogy, was an influential book that changed thinking in educational philosophy and theory. It transcended the boundaries of philosophy, ideology, and theory to embrace all these areas of discourse. Based on his experiences in literacy campaigns among the rural poor in Brazil, Freire argued that education that raised consciousness could be a genuine instrument of personal and social liberation. As you read the selection, you may wish to consider the following focusing questions:

1. What are Freire's arguments in support of the idea that human beings can achieve their own humanization?

2. Distinguish between "oppressed consciousness" and "oppressor consciousness."

3. What is critical dialogue and why is it so important in Liberation Pedagogy?

4. Analyze Freire's critique of "narration" and the "act of depositing" as methods of teaching. Do you agree or disagree with his critique?

5. How does Freire define "problem posing" teaching?

From Paulo Freire, *Pedagogy of the Oppressed*. Translated by Myra Bergman Ramos. New York: Herder and Herder, 1971, pp. 27–29, 40–41, 52–59, 72, 74. Excerpted from *Pedagogy of the Oppressed* by Paulo Freire, Copyright © 1970, 1993 by Paulo Freire. Reprinted by permission of The Continuum International Publishing Group, Inc.

While the problem of humanization has always, from an axiological point of view, been man's central problem, it now takes on the character of an inescapable concern. Concern for humanization leads at once to the recognition of dehumanization, not only as an ontological possibility but as an historical reality. And as man perceives the extent of dehumanization, he asks himself if humanization is a viable possibility. Within history, in concrete, objective contexts, both humanization and dehumanization are possibilities for man as an uncompleted being conscious of his incompletion.

But while both humanization and dehumanization are real alternatives, only the first is man's vocation. This vocation is constantly negated, yet it is affirmed by that very negation. It is thwarted by injustice, exploitation, oppression, and the violence of the oppressors; it is affirmed by the yearning of the oppressed for freedom and justice, and by their struggle to recover their lost humanity.

Dehumanization, which marks not only those whose humanity has been stolen, but also (though in a different way) those who have stolen it, is a *distortion* of the vocation of becoming more fully human. This distortion occurs within history; but it is not an historical vocation. Indeed, to admit of dehumanization as an historical vocation would lead either to cynicism or total despair. The struggle for humanization, for the emancipation of labor, for the overcoming of alienation, for the affirmation of men as persons would be meaningless. This struggle is possible only because dehumanization, although a concrete historical fact, is *not* a given destiny but the result of an unjust order that engenders violence in the oppressors, which in turn dehumanizes the oppressed.

Because it is a distortion of being more fully human, sooner or later being less human leads the oppressed to struggle against those who made them so. In order for this struggle to have meaning, the oppressed must not, in seeking to regain their humanity (which is a way to create it), become in turn oppressors of the oppressors, but rather restorers of the humanity of both.

This, then, is the great humanistic and historical task of the oppressed: to liberate themselves and their oppressors as well. The oppressors, who oppress, exploit, and rape by virtue of their power, cannot find in this power the strength to liberate either the oppressed or themselves. Only power that springs from the weakness of the oppressed will be sufficiently strong to free both. Any attempt to "soften" the power of the oppressor in deference to the weakness of the oppressed almost always manifests itself in the form of false generosity; indeed, the attempt never goes beyond this. In order to have the continued opportunity to express their "generosity," the oppressors must perpetuate injustice as well. An unjust social order is the permanent fount of this "generosity," which is nourished by death, despair, and poverty. That is why the dispensers of false generosity become desperate at the slightest threat to its source.

True generosity consists precisely in fighting to destroy the causes which nourish false charity. False charity constrains the fearful and subdued, the "rejects of life," to extend their trembling hands. True generosity lies in striving so that these hands—whether of individuals or entire peoples—need be extended less and less in supplication, so that more and more they become human hands which work and, working, transform the world.

This lesson and this apprenticeship must come, however, from the oppressed themselves and from those who are truly solidary with them. As individuals or as peoples, by fighting for the restoration of their humanity they will be attempting the restoration of true generosity. Who are better prepared than the oppressed to understand the terrible significance of an oppressive society? Who suffer the effects of oppression more than the oppressed? Who can better understand the necessity of liberation?

They will not gain this liberation by chance but through the praxis of their quest for it, through their recognition of the necessity to fight for it. And this fight, because of the purpose given it by the oppressed, will actually constitute an act of love opposing the lovelessness which lies at the heart of the oppressors' violence, lovelessness even when clothed in false generosity.

. . .

The pedagogy of the oppressed, as a humanist and libertarian pedagogy, has two distinct stages. In the first, the oppressed unveil the world of oppression and through the praxis commit themselves to its transformation. In the second stage, in which the reality of oppression has already been transformed, this pedagogy ceases to belong to the oppressed and becomes a pedagogy of all men in the process of permanent liberation. In both stages, it is always through action in depth that the culture of domination is culturally confronted. In the first stage this confrontation occurs through the change in the way the oppressed perceive the world of oppression; in the second stage, through the expulsion of the myths created and developed in the old order, which like specters haunt the new structure emerging from the revolutionary transformation.

The pedagogy of the first stage must deal with the problem of the oppressed consciousness and the oppressor consciousness, the problem of men who oppress and men who suffer oppression. It must take into account their behavior, their view of the world, and their ethics. A particular problem is the duality of the oppressed: they are contradictory, divided beings, shaped by and existing in a concrete situation of oppression and violence.

Any situation in which "A" objectively exploits "B" or hinders his pursuit of self-affirmation as a responsible person is one of oppression. Such a situation in itself constitutes violence, even when sweetened by false generosity, because it interferes with man's ontological and historical vocation to be more fully

human. With the establishment of a relationship of oppression, violence has *already* begun. Never in history has violence been initiated by the oppressed. How could they be the initiators, if they themselves are the result of violence? How could they be the sponsors of something whose objective inauguration called forth their existence as oppressed? There would be no oppressed had there been no prior situation of violence to establish their subjugation.

Violence is initiated by those who oppress, who exploit, who fail to recognize others as persons—not by those who are oppressed, exploited, and unrecognized. It is not the unloved who initiate disaffection, but those who cannot love because they love only themselves. It is not the helpless, subject to terror, who initiate terror, but the violent, who with their power create the concrete situation which begets the "rejects of life." It is not the tyrannized who initiate despotism, but the tyrants. It is not the despised who initiate hatred, but those who despise. It is not those whose humanity is denied them who negate man, but those who denied that humanity (thus negating their own as well). Force is used not by those who have become weak under the preponderance of the strong, but by the strong who have emasculated them.

For the oppressors, however, it is always the oppressed (whom they obviously never call "the oppressed" but—depending on whether they are fellow countrymen or not—"those people" or "the blind and envious masses" or "savages" or "natives" or "subversives") who are disaffected, who are "violent," "barbaric," "wicked," or "ferocious" when they react to the violence of the oppressors.

. . .

Critical and liberating dialogue, which presupposes action, must be carried on with the oppressed at whatever the stage of their struggle for liberation. The content of that dialogue can and should vary in accordance with historical conditions and the level at which the oppressed perceive reality. But to substitute monologue, slogans, and communiqués for dialogue is to attempt to liberate the oppressed with the instruments of domestication. Attempting to liberate the oppressed without their reflective participation in the act of liberation is to treat them as objects which must be saved from a burning building; it is to lead them into the populist pitfall and transform them into masses which can be manipulated.

At all stages of their liberation, the oppressed must see themselves as men engaged in the ontological and historical vocation of becoming more fully human. Reflection and action become imperative when one does not erroneously attempt to dichotomize the content of humanity from its historical forms.

The insistence that the oppressed engage in reflection on their concrete situation is not a call to armchair revolution. On the contrary, reflection—true reflection—leads to action. On the other hand, when the situation calls for action, that action will constitute an authentic praxis only if its consequences become the object of critical reflection. In this sense, the praxis is the new *raison d'être* of the oppressed; and the revolution, which inaugurates the historical moment of this *raison d'être*, is not viable apart from their concomitant conscious involvement. Otherwise, action is pure activism.

To achieve this praxis, however, it is necessary to trust in the oppressed and in their ability to reason. Whoever lacks this trust will fail to initiate (or will abandon) dialogue, reflection, and communication, and will fall into using slogans, communiqués, monologues, and instructions. Superficial conversions to the cause of liberation carry this danger.

Political action on the side of the oppressed must be pedagogical action in the authentic sense of the word, and, therefore, action *with* the oppressed. Those who work for liberation must not take advantage of the emotional dependence of the oppressed—dependence that is the fruit of the concrete situation of domination which surrounds them and which engendered their unauthentic view of the world. Using their dependence to create still greater dependence is an oppressor tactic.

Libertarian action must recognize this dependence as a weak point and must attempt through reflection and action to transform it into independence. However, not even the best-intentioned leadership can bestow independence as a gift. The liberation of the oppressed is a liberation of men, not things. Accordingly, while no one liberates himself by his own efforts alone, neither is he liberated by others. Liberation, a human phenomenon, cannot be achieved by semihumans. Any attempt to treat men as semihumans only dehumanizes them. When men are already dehumanized, due to the oppression they suffer, the process of their liberation must not employ the methods of dehumanization.

The correct method for a revolutionary leadership to employ in the task of liberation is, therefore, *not* "libertarian propaganda." Nor can the leadership merely "implant" in the oppressed a belief in freedom, thus thinking to win their trust. The correct method lies in dialogue. The conviction of the oppressed that they must fight for their liberation is not a gift bestowed by the revolutionary leadership, but the result of their own *conscientização*.

The revolutionary leaders must realize that their own conviction of the necessity for struggle (an indispensable dimension of revolutionary wisdom) was not given to them by anyone else—if it is authentic. This conviction cannot be packaged and sold; it is reached, rather, by means of a totality of reflection and action. Only the leaders' own involvement in reality, within an historical situation, led them to criticize this situation and to wish to change it.

Likewise, the oppressed (who do not commit themselves to the struggle unless they are convinced, and who, if they do not make such a commitment, withhold the indispensable conditions for this struggle) must reach this conviction as Subjects, not as objects. They also must intervene critically in the situation which surrounds them and whose mark they bear; propaganda cannot achieve this. While the conviction of the necessity for struggle (without which the struggle is unfeasible) is indispensable to the revolutionary leadership (indeed, it was this conviction which constituted that leadership), it is also necessary for the oppressed. It is necessary, that is, unless one intends to carry out the transformation *for* the oppressed rather than *with* them. It is my belief that only the latter form of transformation is valid.

. . .

The oppressed, who have been shaped by the death-affirming climate of oppression, must find through their struggle the way to life-affirming humanization, which does not lie *simply* in having more to eat (although it does involve having more to eat and cannot fail to include this aspect). The oppressed have been destroyed precisely because their situation has reduced them to things. In order to regain their humanity they must cease to be things and fight as men. This is a radical requirement. They cannot enter the struggle as objects in order *later* to become men.

The struggle begins with men's recognition that they have been destroyed. Propaganda, management, manipulation—all arms of domination—cannot be the instruments of their rehumanization. The only effective instrument is a humanizing pedagogy in which the revolutionary leadership establishes a permanent relationship of dialogue with the oppressed. In a humanizing pedagogy the method ceases to be an instrument by which the teachers (in this instance, the revolutionary leadership) can manipulate students (in this instance, the oppressed), because it expresses the consciousness of the students themselves.

. . .

A revolutionary leadership must accordingly practice *co-intentional* education. Teachers and students (leadership and people), co-intent on reality, are both Subjects, not only in the task of unveiling that reality, and thereby coming to

know it critically, but in the task of re-creating that knowledge. As they attain this knowledge of reality through common reflection and action, they discover themselves as its permanent re-creators. In this way, the presence of the oppressed in the struggle for their liberation will be what it should be: not pseudo-participation, but committed involvement.

. . .

Narration (with the teacher as narrator) leads the students to memorize mechanically the narrated content. Worse yet, it turns them into "containers," into "receptacles" to be "filled" by the teacher. The more completely he fills the receptacles, the better a teacher he is. The more meekly the receptacles permit themselves to be filled, the better students they are.

Education thus becomes an act of depositing, in which the students are the depositories and the teacher is the depositor. Instead of communicating, the teacher issues communiqués and makes deposits which the students patiently receive, memorize, and repeat. This is the "banking" concept of education, in which the scope of action allowed to the students extends only as far as receiving, filing, and storing the deposits. They do, it is true, have the opportunity to become collectors or cataloguers of the things they store. But in the last analysis, it is men themselves who are filed away through the lack of creativity, transformation, and knowledge in this (at best) misguided system. For apart from inquiry, apart from the praxis, men cannot be truly human. Knowledge emerges only through invention and re-invention, through the restless, impatient, continuing, hopeful inquiry men pursue in the world, with the world, and with each other.

In the banking concept of education, knowledge is a gift bestowed by those who consider themselves knowledgeable upon those whom they consider to know nothing. Projecting an absolute ignorance onto others, a characteristic of the ideology of oppression, negates education and knowledge as processes of inquiry. The teacher presents himself to his students as their necessary opposite; by considering their ignorance absolute, he justifies his own existence. The students, alienated like the slave in the Hegelian dialectic, accept their ignorance as justifying the teacher's existence—but, unlike the slave, they never discover that they educate the teacher.

The *raison d'être* of libertarian education, on the other hand, lies in its drive towards reconciliation. Education must begin with the solution of the teacher-student contradiction, by reconciling the poles of the contradiction so that both are simultaneously teachers *and* students.

. . .

Problem-posing education affirms men as beings in the process of *becoming*—as unfinished, uncompleted beings in and with a likewise unfinished reality. Indeed, in contrast to other animals who are unfinished, but not historical, men know themselves to be unfinished; they are aware of their incompletion. In this incompletion and this awareness lie the very roots of education as an exclusively human manifestation. The unfinished character of men and the transformational character of reality necessitate that education be an ongoing activity.

. . .

Problem-posing education is revolutionary futurity. Hence it is prophetic (and, as such, hopeful). Hence, it corresponds to the historical nature of man. Hence, it affirms men as beings who transcend themselves, who move forward and look ahead, for whom immobility represents a fatal threat, for whom looking at the past must only be a means of understanding more clearly what and who they are so that they can more wisely build the future. Hence, it identifies with the movement which engages men as beings aware of their incompletion—an historical movement which has its point of departure, its Subjects and its objective.

. . .

Problem-posing education, as a humanist and liberating praxis, posits as fundamental that men subjected to domination must fight for their emancipation. To that end, it enables teachers and students to become Subjects of the educational process by overcoming authoritarianism and an alienating intellectualism; it also enables men to overcome their false perception of reality. The world—no longer something to be described with deceptive words—becomes the object of that transforming action by men which results in their humanization.

Problem-posing education does not and cannot serve the interests of the oppressor. No oppressive order could permit the oppressed to begin to question: Why? While only a revolutionary society can carry out this education in systematic terms, the revolutionary leaders need not take full power before they can employ the method. In the revolutionary process, the leaders cannot utilize the banking method as an interim measure, justified on grounds of expediency, with the intention of *later* behaving in a genuinely revolutionary fashion. They must be revolutionary—that is to say, dialogical—from the outset.

CONCLUSION

In this chapter, Freire's Liberation Pedagogy was examined as an ideology of education. We explored the influences of Existentialism and Marxism on Freire's ideology of education. We then examined his opposition to false consciousness and his argument that genuine education should lead to the construction of a true consciousness, based on a critical examination of the conditions that empower some and disempower others. Emphasis was placed on the teacher as an ideologically committed person, who, with students, is engaged in mutual learning.

DISCUSSION QUESTIONS

1. How does Freire define the human being?
2. Why does Freire argue that education should stimulate a person's critical consciousness?
3. What does it mean when we say that we are conditioned by the contexts in which we live?
4. What does it mean when we say that we are incomplete individuals? What are the implications of incompleteness for education?
5. Analyze Freire's conception of the teacher and the teacher–student relationship.
6. What does Freire mean by the "banking" approach to education?
7. Why does Freire argue against the proposition that teaching is the transfer of knowledge?

INQUIRY AND RESEARCH PROJECTS

1. Organize a dialogue, modeled on Freire's approach, in your class on the questions: What does it mean to be a teacher? What does it mean to be a student?
2. Review the chapters on Existentialism (Chapter 6) and Marxism (Chapter 13) in this book and then write a paper that identifies and analyzes their elements in Freire's Liberation Pedagogy.
3. In a class discussion, identify what it means to have ideas based on "false consciousness." During your discussion, develop a list of the factors that contribute to false consciousness in American society.
4. In a class discussion, identify those who are empowered and disempowered in American society in general, and in your educational context (your school or college) in particular.

INTERNET RESOURCES

For a discussion of issues related to Freirean education and a glossary of Freire's terms, consult
http://nlu.nl.edu/ace/Resources/Documents/FreireIssues.html

The home of informal education provides a short biography and discussion of Freire's work
www.infed.org

SUGGESTIONS FOR FURTHER READING

Freire, Paulo. *Letters to Cristina. Reflections on My Life and Work.* London: Routledge, 1996.
Freire, Paulo. *Pedagogy of Freedom: Ethics, Democracy, and Civic Courage.* Lanham, MD: Rowman and Littlefield, 1998.
Freire, Paulo. *Pedagogy of Hope, Reliving Pedagogy of the Oppressed.* New York: Continuum, 1995.
Freire, Paulo. *Pedagogy of the Oppressed.* Trans., Myra Bergman Ramos. New York: Continuum, 1984.
Gadotti, M. *Reading Paulo Freire: His Life and Work.* New York: SUNY Press, 1994.

Gartner, Alan, Greer, Colin, and Riessman, Frank. *After Deschooling, What?* New York: Harper and Row, 1973.

Horton, Myles, and Freire, Paulo. *We Make the Road by Walking: Conversations on Education and Social Change.* Philadelphia: Temple University Press, 1990.

Illich, Ivan D. *Celebration of Awareness: A Call for Institutional Revolution.* New York: Doubleday and Co., 1970.

Illich, Ivan D. *Deschooling Society.* New York: Harper and Row, 1971.

Illich, Ivan D. *Tools for Conviviality.* New York: Harper and Row, 1973.

McLaren, Peter, and Leonard, Peter. *Paulo Freire: A Critical Encounter.* New York and London: Routledge, 1993.

Morrow, Raymond A., and Torres, Carlos Alberto. *Reading Freire and Habermas: Critical Pedagogy and Transformative Social Change.* New York: Teachers College Press, Columbia University, 2002.

Reimer, Everett. *School is Dead: Alternatives in Education.* Garden City, NY: Doubleday and Co., 1970.

Shor, Ida, and Freire, Paulo. *A Pedagogy for Liberation: Dialogues on Transforming Education.* Boston: Bergin & Garvey, 1987.

NOTES

1. Richard Shaull, "Preface," in Paulo Freire, *Pedagogy of the Oppressed* (New York: Continuum, 1984), pp. 9–11.

2. Ivan Illich, *Deschooling Society* (New York: Harper and Row, 1971).

3. Ibid, pp. 37–38.

4. Ivan Illich, *Tools for Conviviality* (New York: Harper & Row, 1973), pp. 10–45.

5. Donaldo Macedo, "Foreword," in Paulo Freire, *Pedagogy of Freedom: Ethics, Democracy, and Civic Courage,* translated by Patrick Clarke (Lanham, MD: Rowman & Littlefield, 1998), p. xxiv.

6. Stanley Aronowitz, "Introduction," in Paulo Freire, *Pedagogy of Freedom: Ethics, Democracy, and Civic Courage,* translated by Patrick Clarke (Lanham, MD: Rowman & Littlefield, 1998), p. 11.

7. Paulo Freire, *Pedagogy of the Oppressed,* trans. Myra Bergman Ramos (New York: Continuum, 1984), p. 46.

8. Paulo Freire, *Pedagogy of Freedom, Ethics, Democracy and Civic Courage* (Lanham, MD: Rowman and Littlefield, 1998), pp. 25–26, 54.

9. Macedo, p. xxviii.

10. Freire, *Pedagogy of the Oppressed,* pp. 21–23.

11. Freire, *Pedagogy of Freedom, Ethics, Democracy and Civic Courage,* p. 51.

12. Freire, *Pedagogy of the Oppressed,* p. 31.

13. Aronowitz, p. 4.

14. Freire, *Pedagogy of the Oppressed,* pp. 57–59.

15. Aronowitz, pp. 4–5.

16. Freire, *Pedagogy of Freedom, Ethics, Democracy and Civic Courage,* p. 22.

17. Aronowitz, pp. 8–9.

18. Macedo, p. xiii.

CHAPTER FIFTEEN

THEORY AND EDUCATION

We will examine the relationship between theory and education in this chapter. We often use the word *theory* in our everyday language to mean that we have an idea, an opinion, a conjecture, or a belief about something. We refer to a theory as a related set of ideas about something that is general and abstract rather than concrete and particular. It is a word that is in constant use in education. Although we frequently talk about *theory* and the *theoretical*, the precise meaning of the word is somewhat slippery and elusive. In this chapter, we shall try to clarify how the word *theory* is used in education, schooling, and instruction.

DEFINING THEORY

The word *theory* is derived from the ancient Greek work, *theoria*, which means the mental act of viewing, contemplating, or considering something. The ancient Greeks tended to separate theory from practice. For example, Plato and Aristotle regarded theory—abstract thought about the nature of things—as higher, more elevated, and more important than the concrete or particular. (See Chapter 2 on Idealism and Chapter 3 on Realism for discussions of Plato and Aristotle.) Also, note that John Dewey, in his Experimentalist philosophy, challenged the Greek dualistic way of thinking and argued against separating theory from practice. (See Chapter 5 on Pragmatism.)

At this point, we will consider several meanings of *theory*, each of which has implications for education. As a hypothetical set of ideas or principles that can guide practice, theories can be turned into "if-then" statements. *If* I do this or act in this way, *then* the following is likely to happen. Theorizing can refer to the act of forming generalizations—plans that we can replicate in varying situations—based on how something is done successfully in a given field such as medicine, law, or education. In this instance, theory arises from observing or performing similar actions that cause results which can be anticipated. Here, the process of forming the generalizations is inductive, in that the reasoning and logic used goes from specific to general. For example, a football coach who has had experience in the sport can frame a number of plays or strategies that the team can use successfully in certain situations in a series of games. In education, especially in instruction, a teacher who has had experience teaching reading or mathematics can identify those exercises and activities that have succeeded, and those that have failed to bring about the desired outcomes. The teacher can generalize about those that work and arrive at a set of principles that guide instruction. The guiding principles, derived from a particular experience, can be generalized and applied to other teaching situations. Further, a group of teachers can share their experiences in teaching a particular skill or subject or dealing with a particular issue and problem, and generalize to a set of operating principles—how to do something in a given situation.

Theory can refer to a general abstract conceptual frame of reference that can be used to guide practice. Such a frame of reference includes: (1) a set of generalizations or explanations about the subject or field; (2) strategies for how to apply the generalizations as guiding principles in action; (3) hypotheses, conjectures, or expectations about what is likely to happen when the generalization is applied in a specific instance. A frame of reference can be created in at least two ways: (1) based on experience that arises from practice, as discussed earlier; or (2) deduced from another set of generalizations as in the case of putting a philosophy or an ideology into practice.

In the latter instance, the theory is formed by deductive reasoning, in which the guiding principles are found in some larger and more comprehensive body of thought. For example, a lawyer, using the common law, will look for precedents (earlier decisions) that can be used to support her or his argument in a particular case. A teacher can look to a philosophy, such as Idealism or Realism, or an ideology, such as Liberalism or Conservatism, for goals to be implemented in the classroom. Here, the problem is taking the abstractions, provided by the philosophy or ideology, and implementing them in practice.

Still another meaning of theory is our beliefs, ideas, and concepts about phenomenon—the objects, people, and situations—that we observe and interact with. Kerlinger, for example, defines a theory as "a set of interrelated constructs (concepts, definitions, and propositions) that present a systematic view of phenomena by specifying relations among variables, with the purpose of explaining and predicting the phenomena."[1] It is what we see as the origin and nature of something or actions and reactions that take place. This kind of theorizing occurs when we try to make sense of and give meaning to our situations and the actors, objects, and occurrences in these situations. It is a way of generalizing about our experience so that we construct some explanations about it. An important characteristic of a theory is the interrelationship of its parts and how it is possible to deduce one proposition from another.

In the case of all of these meanings of theory, the important point is that theory is a guide to practice. However, further questions remain: Are the assumptions in the theory valid? If the assumptions are valid, can they be successfully transferred and applied to other situations? Will implementation confirm or invalidate the theory's working generalizations? For example, consider the following assumptions given as a rationale for the No Child Left Behind Act:

> We know from business practices that if we want to boost performance, we must set clear, measurable goals and align our systems to them. In education, academic standards are the foundation of a performance-based system. High standards do not just help teachers; they also encourage children, because children tend to perform to meet

the expectations of adults. If these expectations are low, children can miss their true potential. When expectations are high, progress can be amazing. . . .

Creating clear and rigorous academic standards is an important first step in improving our schools. We will never know, however, if we are reaching those standards unless we measure student performance.[2]

WHY STUDY THEORY AND WHY THEORIZE?

Human beings find themselves in constantly changing situations or events. Each of these situations is unique in that the setting and the actors (the other people) and the issue or problem presented may be different. However, in each situation there are some common elements. The recognition and the clustering together of these common elements is the foundation of theorizing. For example, at the beginning of each school year, a teacher will find that she or he has a class of new and unfamiliar students. However, with experience, the teacher will build up a repertoire of strategies to deal with these students. The teacher can recognize that students' needs and abilities tend to fall into patterns found in each of the different classes. From this recognition, the teacher can generalize about the similarities found in different groups of students and create plans of action—strategies—that can be used in instruction. Further, teachers can collaborate with each other and discuss common successes, weaknesses, and issues and formulate some generalizations about teaching. These generalizations, when clustered and organized together, are the basis of a theory of teaching. Such theoretical underpinnings are the basis of methods.

Theory also relates to the larger issue of teacher professionalization. In contrast to a trade—the mastery of a set of techniques—a profession rests on a theoretical foundation—informed hypotheses, based on knowledge, about why, as well as how, something is done. While there are certain techniques that are followed in teaching, teaching itself implies more than using these techniques. It is informed by concepts from learned disciplines such as philosophy, history, sociology, and psychology that provide a theoretical foundation—an examination of why something is done in its larger contexts.

THEORY AS A BRIDGE BETWEEN PHILOSOPHY AND IDEOLOGY AND PRACTICE

This chapter on theory and education can be thought of as a bridge that carries the reader from the more abstract chapters on philosophies and ideologies to four selected theories of education: Essentialism, Perennialism, Progressivism, and Critical Theory. As indicated in our definitions of theory, each of these four theories: (1) operates from a coherent set of generalizations and explanations about the purpose of education, the organization and structure of schools, and processes of teaching and learning; (2) contains guiding hypotheses or working principles about how curriculum and instruction should be organized and conducted: (3) indicates projected outcomes that will follow if the theoretical assumptions are applied in practice.

In the next sections, we examine theories: (1) as derived from or deduced from other larger and more abstract bodies of thought such as philosophies and ideologies; (2) that develop as educational, or school-centered, responses to larger social, economic, cultural, or political problems and issues; (3) that arise as generalizations or hypotheses from practices with schools and classrooms. It should be pointed out that in some cases a theory may include all three elements: derivations, responses, and generalizations from practice.

THEORY AS DERIVATION

Philosophical Derivation

In Part I of this book we examined the philosophies of Idealism, Realism, Theistic Realism, Pragmatism, Existentialism, Philosophical Analysis, and Postmodernism. Of these, Idealism, Realism, and Theistic Realism are based on a grand metaphysical structure that provides a kind of architecture of the universe and the human being's place in it. These older, more traditional philosophies are systematic in that they expound on what is real (metaphysics), how we know (epistemology), and what is right and beautiful (ethics and aesthetics). Education—especially schooling, curriculum, and instruction—is dealt with in these larger systems and subsumed as areas that are included and explained by the larger and more comprehensive world view. Throughout history, these metaphysically based philosophies have attracted adherents who sought to apply their principles to society, politics, and education. Educators who look to eternal and universal truths seek to apply them to education and to base a curriculum on what they believe is always good, true, and beautiful. For example, Essentialism (discussed in Chapter 16) includes many elements of Idealism and Realism, and Perennialism (in Chapter 17) draws heavily from the Realism of Aristotle and Aquinas.

More modern philosophies such as Pragmatism, Existentialism, Philosophical Analysis, and Postmodernism reject the metaphysical base of the older philosophies as unverifiable speculation and turn their attention to epistemology, meaning, and other issues. Dewey's Experimentalism, a variety of Pragmatism (discussed in Chapter 5), had a strong influence on Progressivism, which seeks to apply the concepts of democracy, community, and the scientific method to education, schooling, and instruction. (See Chapter 18 for a complete discussion of Progressivism.) Postmodernism (discussed in Chapter 8), which borrowed some Existentialist themes, strongly influenced Critical Theory. (See Chapter 19 for a discussion of Critical Theory.)

Ideological Derivation

Theories of education are often also derived from ideologies such as Nationalism, Liberalism, Conservatism, Marxism, and Liberation Pedagogy, all of which were treated in Part II of this book. Schools throughout the world are organized into national systems of education. In these systems, strong elements of Nationalism are always present and are used to shape national identity. For example, public schooling in the United States seeks to create a sense of American identity and citizenship in students. The same is true for other countries. Within a country, competing groups often vie for con-

■ ■ ■ ■ ■

PHILOSOPHICAL AND IDEOLOGICAL DERIVATIONS IN EDUCATIONAL THEORIES

- Essentialism is derived from Idealism, Realism, and Conservatism
- Perennialism is derived from Realism, Theistic Realism, and Conservatism
- Progressivism is derived from Pragmatism and Liberalism
- Critical Theory is derived from Existentialism, Postmodernism, Marxism, and Liberation Pedagogy

trol over schools and curriculum. Liberals, Conservatives, Marxists, and Liberation Pedagogues differ on the goals of education, the purpose and function of schools, the composition and organization of the curriculum, and styles of teaching and learning. Conservatism, with its emphasis on traditional knowledge and values, has influenced Essentialism and Perennialism. Liberalism, with its emphasis on flexibility and innovation, has influenced Progressivism. Themes from Marxism and Liberation Pedagogy such as class domination, control, and conflict are evident in Critical Theory.

THEORY AS A RESPONSE

Theory also develops as a response to social, political, economic, and educational situations, issues, problems, and crises that range from local to national to global. There are many examples of this kind of theorizing.

Since the 1960s, there has been global concern about the degradation of the environment due to industrial and fossil fuel pollution, the depletion of the rain forests, the hunting of endangered animal species, and global warming. This concern led schools to establish courses in environmental education that emphasized conservation of natural resources, the use of alternative energy sources, and recycling of items. These courses also emphasized personal and social responsibilities and ethics regarding protection and respect for the conservation of the natural environment. When environmental issues are scrutinized for their global implications, they are broadened to include questions about the role of industrialized nations, such as the United States, who are major polluters; about the socioeconomic disparities between the generally wealthy nations of the northern hemisphere and the poorer ones of the southern; and about the negative effects of economic globalization by multinational corporations.

Environmental education, which originated as a response to a problem, can also be juxtaposed with other philosophies, ideologies, and educational theories and reformulated. For example, Marxists see the multinational business corporation as a modern form of capitalism that exploits the poor of the less technologically developed nations. Liberation Pedagogues argue that literacy programs tied to small-scale, grassroots, sustainable-development projects will empower the poverty-ridden classes in these countries. These themes of empowerment are also embraced and voiced by Critical Theorists.

In the 1990s, incidences of violence increased in schools in the United States. Some students, in locations across the country, smuggled guns into schools, shooting and killing their classmates and teachers. One of the most tragic cases of in-school violence took place at Columbine High School in Littleton, Colorado, when two male students, using guns and bombs, killed twelve of their classmates and two teachers. These incidents clearly signaled that the nation faced a major problem. Educators responded with programs to create safe schools with zero tolerance for those who endanger the lives of others. Part of the response included programs in conflict resolution, and identifying and providing therapy to bullies, social isolates, and other students with social problems. As a result, a theory of nonviolent safe schools developed. Once again, this theory that arose as a response to a particular problem soon was juxtaposed with other ideological positions. Conservatives claimed that the problem of violence in schools mirrored the moral breakdown in the larger society. Rap music, videos, and games that used violence as a theme had eroded and weakened traditional social morals and engendered a climate that was prone to violence. Permissiveness and values clarification programs in schools had created a climate of ethical relativism that lacked universal moral standards. Perennialists called for a reaffirmation of universal values found in the Judeo–Christian religious tradition and in the Aristotelian philosophical tradition. Conservatives called for a return to strict discipline and moral standards along with zero-tolerance school management. Religious Conservatives called for the posting of the Ten Commandments in the schools as a reminder of universal moral values and responsibility.

THEORY ARISING FROM PRACTICE

Many times, theory arises from practice. In this scenario, a practitioner in a field gains experience from dealing with a number of similar instances. For example, a pediatrician may have treated many ear infections in children and as a result can form generalizations about their cause and treatment. These generalizations provide the physician with a set of hypotheses about the prevention and treatment of these cases. Or, a foreign language teacher who has taught a course in Italian to secondary school students for several years may have identified the situations that facilitate or impede learning the language for most students. She or he can then reflect on these situations and arrive at some generalizations to guide instruction. These generalizations then form a theory that can guide a method of teaching the language.

Another example of theory being generated from practice can be found in the "effective" schools movement. Certain schools, their principals, and teachers, are identified as especially competent educators whose students have demonstrated high levels of academic achievement. After analyzing specific practices that they believe contribute to effective schools, the U.S. Department of Education arrived at the following generalizations, compiled in *What Works: Research About Teaching and Learning:*

- Belief in the value of hard work, the importance of personal responsibility, and the importance of education itself contribute to greater success in school.

- Children learn science best when they are able to do experiments, so they can witness "science in action."

- Teachers who set and communicate high expectations to all their students obtain greater academic performance from those students than teachers who set low expectations.

- The most important characteristics of effective schools are strong instructional leadership, a safe and orderly climate, schoolwide emphasis on basic skills, high teacher expectations for student achievement, and continuous assessment of pupil progress.[3]

The effective schools theory consists of a cluster of related generalizations about school organization and administration, the role of the principal and teachers, the climate of the school, methods of teaching, and student assessment. It is assumed that these generalizations are valid and describe an effective school and can be replicated in other schools. The anticipated result is that if these practices are implemented, they will result in increasing the number of effective schools.

■ ■ ■ ■ ■

JOHN DEWEY, EXPERIENCE IN RELATION TO THEORY AND PRACTICE

In *Experience and Education*, Dewey criticizes the either–or arguments used by some traditionalist and progressive educators and argues for the integration of theory and practice in experience. In the selection, Dewey discusses how intelligent reflection, the origin of theory, arises from experience when we begin to estimate the consequences of our actions. We engage in the process of intelligent reflection when we step back from our activity to determine if it is taking us in the direction in which we wish to go; is it leading to the results that we want? It is from this intelligent reflection that we can begin to estimate what consequences a particular action will have and to make predictions for the future. It is this stepping back from the act itself, and reflecting on how it changes our life and our behavior that is the beginning of theory. The process of reflecting on and judging the consequences of our behavior is part of what Dewey regards to be theory arising from experience. The selection illustrates how theory arises from reflection about practice. As you read the selection, you may wish to consider the following focusing questions:

1. For Dewey, how does "intellectual organization" arise from and function in experience?

2. How does theory arise from generalizations about cause and effect in our experiences?

3. What does Dewey see as the relationship between theory and practice?

From John Dewey, *Experience and Education*. New York: Collier Books, 1963, pp. 82–85. Permission to print excerpts from John Dewey, *Experience and Education*, 1938, by Kappa Delta Pi.

When a moment ago I called this organization an *ideal*, I meant, on the negative side, that the educator cannot start with knowledge already organized and proceed to ladle it out in doses. But as an ideal the active process of organizing facts and ideas is an ever-present educational process. No experience is educative that does not tend both to knowledge of more facts and entertaining of more ideas and to a better, a more orderly, arrangement of them. It is not true that organization is a principle foreign to experience. Otherwise experience would be so dispersive as to be chaotic. The experience of young children centers about persons and the home. Disturbance of the normal order of relationships in the family is now known by psychiatrists to be a fertile source of later mental and emotional troubles—a fact which testifies to the reality of this kind of organization. One of the great advances in early school education, in the kindergarten and early grades, is that it preserves the social and human center of the organization of experience, instead of the older violent shift of the center of gravity. But one of the outstanding problems of education, as of music, is modulation. In the case of education, modulation means movement from a social and human center toward a more objective intellectual scheme of organization, always bearing in mind, however, that intellectual organization is not an end in itself but is the means by which social relations, distinctively human ties and bonds, may be understood and more intelligently ordered.

When education is based in theory and practice upon experience, it goes without saying that the organized subject-matter of the adult and the specialist cannot provide the starting point. Nevertheless, it represents the goal toward which education should continuously move. It is hardly necessary to say that one of the most fundamental principles of the scientific organization of knowledge is the principle of cause-and-effect. The way in which this principle is grasped and formulated by the scientific specialist is certainly very different from the way in which it can be approached in the experience of the young. But neither the relation nor grasp of its meaning is foreign to the experience of even the young child. When a child two or three years of age learns not to approach a flame too closely and yet to draw near enough a stove to get its warmth he is grasping and using the causal relation. There is no intelligent activity that does not conform to the requirements of the relation, and it is intelligent in the degree in which it is not only conformed to but consciously borne in mind.

In the earlier forms of experience the causal relation does not offer itself in the abstract but in the form of the relation of means employed to ends attained; of the relation of means and consequences. Growth in judgment and understanding is essentially growth in ability to form purposes and to select and arrange means for their realization. The most elementary experiences of the young are filled with cases of the means-consequence relation. There is not a meal cooked nor a source of illumination employed that does not exemplify this relation. The trouble with education is not the absence of situations in which the causal relation is exemplified in the relation of means and consequences. Failure to utilize the situations so as to lead the learner on to grasp the relation in the given cases of experience is, however, only too common. The logician gives the names "analysis and synthesis" to the operations by which means are selected and organized in relation to a purpose.

This principle determines the ultimate foundation for the utilization of *activities* in school. Nothing can be more absurd educationally than to make a plea for a variety of active occupations in the school while decrying the need for progressive organization of information and ideas. Intelligent activity is distinguished from aimless activity by the fact that it involves selection of means—analysis—out of the variety of conditions that are present, and their arrangement—synthesis—to reach an intended aim or purpose. That the more immature the learner is, the simpler must be the ends held in view and the more rudimentary the means employed, is obvious. But the principle of organization of activity in terms of some perception of the relation of consequences to means applies even with the very young. Otherwise an activity ceases to be educative because it is blind. With increased maturity, the problem of interrelation of means becomes more urgent. In the degree in which intelligent observation is transferred from the relation of means to ends to the more complex question of the relation of means to one another, the idea of cause and effect becomes prominent and elicit. The final justification of shops, kitchens, and so on in the school is not just that they afford opportunity for activity, but that they provide opportunity for the *kind* of activity or for the acquisition of mechanical skills which leads students to attend to the relation of means and ends, and then to consideration of the way things interact with one another to produce definite effects. It is the same in principle as the ground for laboratories in scientific research.

Unless the problem of intellectual organization can be worked out on the ground of experience, reaction is sure to occur toward externally imposed methods of organization. There are signs of this reaction already in evidence. We are told that our schools, old and new, are failing in the main task. They do not develop, it is said, the capacity for critical discrimination and the ability to reason. The ability to think is smothered, we are told, by accumulation of miscellaneous ill-digested information, and by the attempt to acquire forms of skill which will be immediately useful in the business and commercial world. We are told that these evils spring from the influence of science and from the magnification of present requirements at the expense of the tested cultural heritage from the past. It is argued that science and its method must be subordinated; that we must return to the logic of ultimate first principles expressed in the logic of Aristotle and St. Thomas, in order that the young may have sure anchorage in their intellectual and moral life, and not be at the mercy of every passing breeze that blows. . . .

CONCLUSION

In this chapter we examined the relationships between theory and education. Theory was defined as a set of ideas or principles that are derived from a larger body of thought such as a philosophy or an ideology, are responses to issues, or are generalized from experience. We emphasized that teachers, as they reflect on their experiences and use them to create teaching strategies, are theory builders.

In the following chapters, we shall examine four theories of education—Essentialism, Perennialism, Progressivism, and Critical Theory—in greater depth.

DISCUSSION QUESTIONS

1. How would you define an educational theory? Using your definition, determine if you have any theories about education.
2. What expectations do you have about teaching as a career? Do you have an underlying theory about teaching?
3. In your opinion, what constitutes a competent teacher? Do your generalizations about teacher competency constitute a theory of education?

INQUIRY AND RESEARCH PROJECTS

1. Examine your college catalogue. Is there an underlying theory of education?
2. Interview several experienced teachers. After completing your interviews, see if you can construct a theory of education based on your findings.
3. Analyze the teacher education program at your college or university. What are its essential elements? Do they constitute a theory of teacher education?
4. Obtain a copy of your state's guidelines for the approval of teacher education programs. Analyze the guidelines and determine if they reflect an underlying theory of education.
5. Research a recent movement in education, such as the standards movement, authentic assessment, or constructivism. Determine if these movements rest on a theory of education.

INTERNET RESOURCES

For educational systems theory, consult
http://education.indiana.edu/~frick/edusys.html

For links to philosophy, theory, and education, consult Educational Policy Studies at the University of Illinois, Urbana, at
http://w3.eduiuc.edu/EPS/category.asp?-token-phil-n-phil-of-ed&site=Res

SUGGESTIONS FOR FURTHER READING

Archer, Margaret S. *Realist Social Theory: The Morphonetic Approach*. New York: Cambridge University Press, 1995.

Chambliss, J. J. *Educational Theory as Theory of Conduct*. Albany: State University of New York Press, 1987.

Collins, Randall. *The Sociology of Philosophies: A Global Theory of Intellectual Change*. Cambridge, MA: Harvard University Press, 1998.

Feinberg, Walter. *Understanding Education: Toward a Reconstruction of Educational Inquiry*. New York: Cambridge University Press, 1983.

Jackson, Philip. *Life in Classrooms*. New York: Teachers College Press, 1993.

Phillips, D. C. *Philosophy, Science, and Social Inquiry*. New York: Pergamon Press, 1987.

Silver, Harold. *Good Schools, Effective Schools: Judgments and Their Histories*. New York: Cassell, 1995.

NOTES

1. Fred N. Kerlinger, *Foundations of Behavioral Research* (New York: Holt, Rhinehart, and Winston, 1973), p. 9.

2. U. S. Department of Education, Office of the Secretary, *Back to School, Moving Forward, What No Child Left Behind Means for America's Communities* (Washington, DC: U. S. Department of Education, 2001), pp. 6–7.

3. *What Works: Research About Teaching and Learning* (Washington, DC: U. S. Department of Education, 1986), pp. 7, 17, 23, 45.

CHAPTER SIXTEEN

ESSENTIALISM, BASIC EDUCATION, AND STANDARDS

In this chapter we will examine Essentialism, an educational theory that emphasizes fundamental, or basic, skills and subjects, as the components of the curriculum. We will define Essentialism, situate it in recent American history of education, discuss its major principles, and examine its relevance for contemporary education.

DEFINING ESSENTIALISM

How many times have you heard the phrase, "Let's get back to basics"? Getting back to basics means stripping away the nonessentials, distractions, trivialities, and digressions and identifying what is fundamental to a discussion, an argument, or a position. Often in unfocused discussions it is necessary to keep "returning to the subject" so that the participants don't get lost in irrelevant issues. As an educational theory, Essentialism asserts that schooling, instruction, teaching, and learning need to focus on the basics—on what is really necessary to become an educated, productive, effective, and capable individual and citizen in American society.

In working toward a definition of Essentialism, we begin with its root, *essence*, which refers to what is necessary to and indispensable about something—an object, a discipline, or a subject, for example. Essence relates to the intrinsic or fundamental character or nature of something rather than its accidental or incidental features. What is it that you must know to understand something? What is it that is most basic, fundamental, or necessary? What is unnecessary or incidental?

As an educational theory, **Essentialism** asserts that certain basic ideas, skills, and bodies of knowledge are essential to human culture and civilization. Because Essentialists are convinced that these basics are indispensable, necessary to, and fundamental in education, their position is often called *Basic Education*. Basic skills and certain bodies of knowledge can be formulated and organized into subjects that can and should be taught by adults to the young. These fundamentals or essentials are the skills of literacy (reading and writing) and computation (arithmetic), and the subjects of history, mathematics, science, languages, and literature. (A more extensive discussion of the

Essentialist curriculum follows later in the chapter.) Deliberate instruction that transmits the basic skills and knowledge areas from one generation to the next guarantees the survival of the civilization. To disengage from this necessary and essential cultural transmission places civilization in peril.

Essentialists further insist that this transmission of basic skills takes place more efficiently and effectively through methods that have stood the test of time. Since there is much to learn and a limited time in which to learn it, instruction should be planned, deliberate, and efficient. It is important to learn from the past rather than trying to keep reinventing the wheel. Schools, then, are academic agencies established by society to transmit basic skills and knowledge to its children and youth.

SITUATING ESSENTIALISM

Essentialism has shown great staying power in education. Despite many challenges from various reformers—Pragmatists, Postmodernists, Liberals, Progressives, and Critical Theorists—Essentialism, in its various forms, has been present and has exerted considerable influence over schools for many years. In the nineteenth century, Essentialism took the form of the "three R's" (reading, writing, and 'rithmetic) and mental discipline (the theory that certain subjects trained or disciplined the mind). In the 1930s, a group of educators who opposed progressive education, coined the term *Essentialism*. In the 1950s, Essentialism was voiced by educational theorists such as Arthur E. Bestor, Jr., who called for a return to the teaching of fundamental intellectual disciplines. In the 1970s and 1980s, there was another revival of basic education during which the U. S. Commission on Excellence in Education's *A Nation at Risk* asserted basic educational themes. In 2000, the standards movement began making an impact throughout the United States as states enacted legislation requiring standardized testing in basic subjects. In 2001, the Education Act "No Child Left Behind" mandated standardized testing in reading as a requirement for federal aid to local school districts. To illustrate the persistence of Essentialism, we briefly examine these reoccurring calls for a return to basic education.

Essentialism

Though not articulated as a philosophy of education, Essentialism has existed for a long time as an informal expression of what schooling should be, emphasizing that the curriculum should consist of traditional skills and subjects. This traditional structure was challenged by Pragmatist educators such as John Dewey and Progressive educators. (See Chapter 5 for a discussion of Pragmatism and Chapter 18 for Progressivism.) The Essentialists, challenged by Progressivism, formally articulated their position.

Led by William Chandler Bagley (1874–1946), a professor of education at Columbia University's Teachers College, the Essentialist educators proclaimed their platform in 1938. The Essentialists' platform established a rationale that would be followed by advocates of Essentialism and basic education in later years. Their position included: (1) stating the purpose of education by defining the role of schools in strictly academic terms and expectations; (2) identifying deficiencies that were allegedly consequences of failing to follow a basic education orientation; (3) calling for a remedy to restore schools to their proper role and function.

The Essentialists' goal for education is to transmit and preserve the crucial elements of human culture. The school, as an institution, has the special and well-defined task of transmitting the essential skills and subjects to the young so that cultural continuity is maintained and preserved.

As later critics such as the Commission on Excellence would do, the Essentialists listed the deficiencies they found in American education. (1) U. S. elementary students were failing to meet the "standards of achievement" in the basics—reading, arithmetic, geography—that students in other countries met; (2) U. S. high school students were academically deficient in comparison to secondary students in other countries, especially in reading, language skills, and mathematics; (3) despite its large expenditures on education, the United States had a considerable increase in serious crime rates.[1]

The Essentialists blamed Progressivism and other "essentially enfeebling" educational theories for weakening discipline and eroding high academic standards in the schools. After describing American education's weaknesses, the Essentialists asked: "Should not our public schools prepare boys and girls for adult responsibility through systematic training in such subjects as reading, writing, arithmetic, history, and English, requiring mastery of such subjects, and, when necessary, stressing discipline and obedience?"[2]

Answering their own question with a strong "yes," the Essentialists proposed that the problems of American education could be solved by:

- Keeping schools on task; teaching essential skills and subjects and avoiding diversion by incidentals.
- Teaching skills and subjects systematically and sequentially in an orderly and cumulative manner.
- Insisting on high standards of academic achievement for promotion and graduation.
- Emphasizing that learning requires discipline, effort, and hard work.

Fundamental Intellectual Disciplines

The next strong argument for Essentialism or basic education was made by Arthur E. Bestor, Jr., an American historian who argued that schools, particularly secondary institutions, should teach the fundamental "intellectual disciplines" that cultivated "disciplined intelligence."[3] While earlier Essentialists such as Bagley had reacted against Progressivism, Bestor was reacting against "life-adjustment education," an educational theory that emphasized students' personal, social, civic, and economic interests and needs as well as academic subjects. Life-adjustment educators devised a new curriculum that focused on these need-based skills and experiences; they revised, and often de-emphasized, the academic subjects to highlight students' everyday needs and issues rather than intellectual disciplines. For example, skills for maintaining effective interpersonal relations, managing money, and using leisure time for fulfilling recreational pursuits were infused into the curriculum. Bestor accused the life-adjustment educators of foisting an anti-intellectual theory of education on the schools, with diluting the basic curriculum by introducing trivialities, and with lowering academic standards.

Bestor, like the earlier Essentialists, argued that education should provide, "sound training in the fundamental ways of thinking represented by history, science, mathematics, literature, language, art and other disciplines evolved in the course of mankind's long quest for usable knowledge, cultural understanding, and intellectual power."[4] He asserted that the role of schools and the function of teaching and learning was to cultivate intellectual disciplines. Based on the liberal arts and sciences, the fundamental intellectual disciplines, organized into a required curriculum of skills and subjects, represented the best means of educating people to lead intelligent, purposeful, civilized, and productive lives within civil societies. The elementary school curriculum was to stress the fundamentals of literacy (reading and writing) and arithmetic; provide an introduction to the natural sciences, geography, history, and library and research skills; and elicit the behaviors conducive to democratic citizenship and civility. These basics would provide the necessary foundation for the skills needed for further education and for later life. The secondary school's curriculum was to consist of a core of five intellectual disciplines—sciences (chemistry, physics, biology), mathematics (algebra, plane geometry, trigonometry, analytical geometry, and calculus), history, English, and foreign languages. These fundamental skills and subjects should be required as the essential core and standard for all students. Bestor argued that a differentiated curriculum in which able students took the academic subjects and the students with less academic ability enrolled in life-adjustment programs was inherently undemocratic.

Neo-Essentialism and *A Nation at Risk*

In the late 1970s and throughout the 1980s, a pronounced revival of basic education occurred and a new Essentialism resurfaced. The neo-Essentialists, often allied with political and cultural conservatives, developed a critique of existing schools and proposed a reform program to remediate perceived deficiencies in the educational system, especially in public schools. In several respects, the neo-Essentialist revival of Basic Education echoed the earlier Essentialist platform of the 1930s. It is important to recognize this ongoing theoretical lineage of Essentialism to understand why it has stayed in American educational history. The neo-Essentialists developed a list of weaknesses in America's public schools and stated the following:

- Permissive, open, and progressive education had neglected systematic instruction in basic skills of reading, writing, and computation and had caused a decline in the standards of literacy.
- Supposedly innovative and experimental programs such as the "new" math, social studies, and science had sacrificed subject matter competencies in the name of ill-defined process learning such as the "discovery method," "critical thinking," "whole language learning,"and "constructivism."

- Character and value education had degenerated into morally permissive programs of "values clarification" that undermined the fundamental values of industriousness, responsibility, and patriotism.
- Radical multicultural programs were creating ethnic and racial isolation and eroding a common American core of values.
- Social promotion policies in public schools had eroded academic standards and produced a notable decline in scores on standardized tests such as the SAT and ACT.

Neo-Essentialism, supported by a revived neo-Conservatism, received a major boost with the election of Ronald Reagan as President in 1980. Terrel Bell, Secretary of Education in the Reagan administration, appointed the Commission on Excellence in Education. In *A Nation at Risk*, a highly publicized report, the Commission claimed the United States was facing an educational crisis caused by secondary curricula that had been "homogenized, diluted and diffused to the point that they no longer have a central purpose." Using dramatic war-time rhetoric, the Commission warned Americans that "the educational foundations of our society are presently being eroded by a rising tide of mediocrity that threatens our very future as a Nation and a people."[5] The Commission recommended that all high school students be required to complete a curriculum of "Five New Basics" consisting of:

1. Four years of English;
2. Three years of mathematics;
3. Three years of science;
4. Three years of social studies;
5. One-half year of computer science.[6]

A Nation at Risk, extensively covered in the media, gained a national audience. President Reagan and Secretary Bell urged the governors of each state to take a leadership role to bring about a more academically focused curriculum, high standards of academic achievement, and improved classroom discipline. The states heeded the call and the standards movement was born.

The Standards Movement

The essential theme of the standards movement is that American education will be improved by creating high academic standards, or benchmarks, to measure student achievement. For example, an empirical, measurable, predetermined goal should be set that will indicate if a student is reading at grade level or has acquired a specific level of achievement in mathematics and science. Students could then be examined by standardized tests to determine if they are achieving at the set standard in the subject or if they are below or above it. Using statistics based on the performance of students in a given school, that school could be judged to be performing at, above, or below the set standard. Advocates of setting standards and measuring them using standardized tests argue that student performance in a particular school could be used to determine the competency of the teachers and administrators in that school. In a counterargument, critics contend that using standardized tests encourages teachers to "teach for the test" rather than providing a general and well-rounded education to students. They argue that social, economic, and other variables have a powerful impact on student achievement that cannot be measured by standardized tests. Although these arguments resound throughout the educational community, the standards movement has gained a strong foothold in various states. A pronounced endorsement of standards came with the enactment of the federal Education Act of 2001, No Child Left Behind.

No Child Left Behind

The No Child Left Behind Act, strongly promoted by President George W. Bush, was based on the premise running through the standards movement that academic achievement could be measured with standardized tests. Schools in which large numbers of students failed to perform at the set standard of achievement could be identified and given remediation designed to improve performance. If this comparative identification of school performance was left undone, children in low-performing schools would be left behind academically. The rationale for the act followed the usual Essentialist argument of identifying weaknesses and then specifying corrective procedures. Deficiencies noted included the following:

> Today, nearly 70 percent of inner city fourth graders are unable to read at a basic level on national reading tests. Our high school seniors trail students in Cyprus and South Africa in international math tests. And nearly a third of our college freshmen find they must take a remedial course before they are able to even begin regular college level courses.[7]

Although the act is comprehensive legislation that deals with many areas of education, certain key features, reflecting the standards movement, reinforce an Essentialist basic education approach. The act identifies the key basics as reading and mathematics and requires that standardized tests be used to determine students' achievement in these essential subjects. The act mandates that in order for school districts to qualify for federal aid, they must establish annual assessments in reading and mathematics for every student in grades three through eight. It holds school districts accountable for improving the performance of *all* students, not just those that perform poorly on the tests. Schools and districts failing to make adequate yearly progress are to be identified and remediated. If the schools fail to meet standards for three years, their students may then transfer to a higher-performing public or private school.[8]

RECURRING MOVEMENTS IN ESSENTIALISM

- Traditional Reading, Writing, and Arithmetic
- Essentialist Platform
- Intellectual Disciplines Movement
- Basic Education Movement
- *A Nation at Risk*
- Standards Movement

ESSENTIALISM'S PHILOSOPHICAL AND IDEOLOGICAL RELATIONSHIPS

We encountered the word *essence* in our earlier discussions about the metaphysics of Idealism, Realism, and Thomism that assert the existence of an underlying ultimate and universal being or nature in reality. (See Chapters 2, 3, and 4.) These traditional philosophies, based on a belief in universal essence, are congenial to Essentialism. Although similarities exist between Essentialism and Perennialism (discussed in the following chapter), there are some important differences. Perennialism, which asserts that truth and values are eternal and universal, is derived largely from Aristotelian Realism and Thomism. Both Essentialism and Perennialism assert that the school's primary function is academic and intellectual, and that the curriculum should focus on basic skills and subjects. However, an important difference is that while Perennialists base their arguments on the Aristotelian-Thomistic concept of a rational human nature, Essentialism is more historically than metaphysically grounded, in that it looks to the past, rather than to human nature, to identify the skills and subjects that have contributed to human survival and civilization.

Essentialism, especially the current basic education and standards version, has become increasingly aligned with the neo-Conservative ideology. (See Chapter 12.) Neo-Conservatives and neo-Essentialists agree that schools should:

- Be academic institutions that have a well-defined curriculum of basic skills and subjects.
- Inculcate traditional values of patriotism, hard work, effort, punctuality, respect for authority, and civility.
- Emphasize a core based on Western civilization and traditional American values.
- Operate efficiently and effectively and be places of discipline and order.
- Promote students on the basis of academic achievement.

In addition to agreeing on traditional educational principles, neo-Essentialists and neo-Conservatives also concur that schools have an important role to play in enhancing U. S. economic productivity in the competitive global economy.

Essentialism meets strong opposition from philosophies such as Pragmatism, Existentialism, and Postmodernism, from ideologies such as Marxism, and from theories such as Progressivism and Critical Theory. Liberals, depending on their view, tend to be somewhat critical of neo-Essentialism, particularly when it is associated with religious fundamentalism. (For a discussion of Liberalism, see Chapter 11.) Pragmatists oppose the Essentialist assumption that the curriculum can be defined a priori to the students' needs and experiences and separated by contemporary social issues. (For Pragmatism, see Chapter 5.) Postmodernists see Essentialism's claims of perpetuating civilization via a required curriculum to actually be a dated historical rationale that once ensured the education of favored socioeconomic groups and classes. (See Chapter 8 for Postmodernism.) Existentialists oppose Essentialism for imposing an other-defined, rather than self-constructed, identity on students. (For Existentialism, see Chapter 6.) Modern Liberals oppose the Essentialist curriculum as being too rigid and lacking relevance to contemporary issues and problems. Marxists find Essentialism to be a defense of the existing capitalist status quo. Progressives find Essentialism to be too formal, too lockstep, and not open to the varieties of human experience. Critical Theorists, similar to Marxists and Existentialists, find the Essentialist mandate for basic skills and subjects to actually be a guise for reproducing the socioeconomic status quo and locking students into predetermined class-based situations. (Critical Theory is discussed in Chapter 19.)

WHY STUDY ESSENTIALISM?

Essentialism is worth studying because of its persistence and frequent reappearance. During these various appearances, and under such titles as the "three R's," the Essentialist platform, intellectual disciplines, basic education, and the standards movement, Essentialists have been very consistent in defining schools as primarily academic institutions. They have been equally consistent in defining the curriculum as basic skills and subjects. It is important to focus on the core features of this recurring educational theory and to recognize that Essentialists, in their educational constancy and commitment, see this approach to education as being the most certain path to human survival and civility. Although the social, economic, and political problems may change, the best response for schools, say Essentialists, is to reaffirm and rely on the tried, true, and tested curriculum of basic skills and subjects.

ESSENTIALISM AS AN EDUCATIONAL THEORY

As indicated earlier, Essentialism is a theory of education that tends to focus on specifics. It defines the school as a sociocultural agency whose primary role is the formal and academic education of students in prescribed essential skills and subjects. The school, in particular, is an agency of cultural transmission that passes these essential skills and subjects on as an inheritance from one generation to the next, thereby perpetuating civilization. Essentialism rejects the Liberal and Progressive orientation that the school is a multifunctional institution that performs a variety of social, political, economic, and psychologically therapeutic roles. For the Essentialist, the more schools and teachers are diverted into nonacademic pursuits, the less time, money, and resources will be available for them to perform their primary academic function.

A Subject Matter Curriculum

Essentialists resolutely endorse the subject matter curriculum in which subjects are differentiated and organized according to their own internal logical or chronological principles. They are suspicious of so-called "innovative" or process learning approaches, such as Constructivism, in which students construct or create their own knowledge in a collaborative fashion. Essentialists argue that civilized people learn effectively and efficiently by using the knowledge that has been developed and organized by scientists, scholars, and other experts. There is no need to waste time and resources "discovering" what is already known. There is no need to continually re-invent the wheel. Curriculum that ignores the past, rejects subject matter boundaries, and prides itself on being interdisciplinary or transdisciplinary often, in reality, causes educational confusion. Based on the concept that the school has a primary function, the curriculum, too, is very specific to instruction in what is termed the basic skills and subjects. These skills and subjects should be well-defined as to scope, have a sequence, be cumulative, and prepare students for the future.

Specific Scope

Essentialists are suspicious of educational theories and methods that do not have a particular scope and are not defined by borders. For them, reading and arithmetic are skills to be taught in a specific way at a particular time in a child's life. History, as an academic subject, is defined as a chronological description and interpretation of the human past. Essentialists are suspicious of interdisciplinary methods such as whole language learning and constructivism, and broad-area studies like language arts and social studies. They believe that for something to be learned it has to be taught. Children will not simply acquire knowledge of arithmetic, history, and geography as concomitant learnings, as some Progressives claim.

Specific Sequence

Essentialists believe that instruction in particular skills and subjects is determined largely by the internal logical of that skill or subject. In other words, there is an order to be observed in teaching something. For example, the teaching of American history follows a definite chronological order, such as (1) encounter of the Native Americans and Europeans; (2) European settlement; (3) the Revolutionary War and struggle for independence; (4) the early national period; (5) the westward-moving frontier; (6) the Civil War and Reconstruction: (7) industrialization and immigration; (8) the Progressive movement; (9) World War I; (10) the Depression; (11) World War II; (12) the Cold War; (13) the post–Cold War world. Sequence also means that instruction in a particular subject area is organized according to its order of complexity, abstraction, and difficulty. For example, mathematics instruction begins with basic arithmetical computation and operations, moves to algebra, then to geometry, and on to calculus and trigonometry. The principle of sequence means that skills and subjects are to be taught according to a definite procedure and not necessarily according to what may currently interest students.

Cumulative

For Essentialists, progressing through the curriculum is a cumulative process. Initially, foundational or basic skills—such as reading, writing, and computing—are mastered. These basic skills are seen as having generative power in that they are generic and can be used in many other operations. Based on these foundations, students advance to other subjects that have a greater complexity and require higher-order thinking. This cumulative effect allows the student to acquire a body of knowledge that will be needed for further education, for work, and for life in general.

Preparation

Essentialists see the benchmarks of schooling—progress through the curriculum and promotion to higher grade levels—not as ends in themselves but as an educational ladder that prepares one for more advanced education, the world of work, citizenship, and effective social and political participation. Education is a process of climbing the educational ladder rung by rung to prepare for the future. Preschool prepares children for elementary school, elementary school prepares them for secondary school, and so on. Since schooling is seen as leading a person to another institution and another set of goals, it is important that the network of institutions, the educational ladder, be articulated in terms of its core—the essential curriculum. In such an arrangement, the higher institution sets many of the goals of the lower ones, in that it has expectations and entry requirements.

Critics say that such a closely ordered and sequential pattern tends to become a rigidly prescribed lockstep in which students must march to the beat of the same drummer. John Dewey, the Pragmatist philosopher and Progressive educator, attacked the doctrine of preparation on the grounds that the future for which we are preparing will be radically different from the present in which the preparation takes place. Education that is so tightly geared to preparation, rather than to experience in the immediate situation, becomes quickly obsolete. Better, said Dewey, was to have a flexible method of intelligence that could be applied to solving problems and an ever-changing world. In response, Essentialists contend that the basic skills and subjects have worked in the past and are most likely to work in the future.

Staying on Task

Essentialists also argue that schools and teachers need to stay with their primary task and not be diverted into nonacademic areas. While Essentialists have their own political and economic beliefs, they tend to believe that schools should not be used to solve social and economic problems. While these problems can be explored in terms of subjects that are relevant to them, schools should not endorse particular political, social, and economic ideologies and agendas. They should not be used as agencies of political indoctrination. Further, Essentialists do not believe that schools have the power to solve society's problems and ills. What schools can do is teach students the basic skills and subjects that will prepare them to deal with social, political, and economic problems in the future. Essentialist critics, such as Critical Theorists, contend that the Essentialist claim to political impartiality is a sham. The curriculum itself, they say, is ideologically and politically determined. The real question is not impartiality but who will control the creation of the curriculum.

■ ■ ■ ■ ■ ▬▬▬▬▬▬▬▬▬▬▬▬▬▬▬▬▬▬▬▬▬▬▬▬▬▬▬▬▬▬▬▬▬▬▬▬▬▬

DIANE RAVITCH, THE ACADEMIC CURRICULUM AND SCHOOLS

In *Left Back*, Diane Ravitch argues that the failure of many of the educational reforms of the twentieth century can be attributed to Progressive educators who weakened the academic function of the schools. As they created different programs for different students, the Progressives jeopardized and weakened the schools' defining academic character. For her, the true leaders in American education were the earlier, but often neglected Essentialist educators William C. Bagley and Isaac Kandel, rather than Progressives such as William H. Kilpatrick and George S. Counts. As you read the selection, you may wish to consider the following focusing questions:

1. According to Ravitch, how does curriculum differentiation cause social and racial stratification?

2. How does Ravitch define an academic curriculum? Who should enroll in such a curriculum? Do you agree or disagree with her?

3. According to Ravitch, how did Progressivism contribute to anti-intellectualism in American education?

4. How does Ravitch define a school? Do you agree or disagree? Why?

As enrollments, in school increased in the early twentieth century, there was a decided split between those who believed that a liberal education (that is, an academic curriculum) should be given to all students and those who wanted such studies taught only to the college-bound elite. The latter group, based primarily in the schools of education, identified itself with the new progressive education movement and dominated the education profession in its formative years.

Thinking they could bridge the gap between school and society and make the schools socially useful, pedagogical theorists sought alternatives to the academic curriculum for non-college-bound students. Curricular differentiation meant an academic education for some, a nonacademic education for others; this approach affected those children—mainly the poor, immigrants, and racial minorities—who were pushed into undemanding vocational, industrial, or general programs by bureaucrats and guidance counselors who thought they were incapable of learning much more. Such policies, packaged in rhetoric about democracy and "meeting the needs of the individual child," encouraged racial and social stratification in American schools. This book will argue that this stratification not only was profoundly undemocratic but was harmful, both to the children involved and to American society.

As used in this book, the term "academic curriculum" does not refer to the formalistic methods, rote recitations, and student passivity about which all reasonable educators and parents have justly complained. Nor does it refer only to teaching basic skills. It refers instead to the systematic study of language and literature, science and mathematics, history, the arts, and foreign languages; these studies, commonly described today as a "liberal education," convey important knowledge and skills, cultivate aesthetic imagination, and teach students to think critically and reflectively about the world in which they live.

Certainly the college-bound need these studies. But so too do those who do not plan to go to college, for they may never have another chance to get instruction about the organizing principles of society and nature, about the varieties of human experience. Even if they choose not to enroll in a university, they too need the knowledge and skills that will enrich their lives as citizens, individuals, and members of a community.

The conventional story of the twentieth century told by historians of education is about the heroic advance of the progressive education movement, how it vanquished oppressive traditionalism in the classroom, briefly dominated American schools, then lost its vitality and withered away in the mid-1950s. The paradigm for this telling of the story is Lawrence A. Cremin's magisterial work *The Transformation of the School: Progressivism in American Education, 1876–1957*. This is not the story told in this book. The progressive education movement did not disappear in the 1950s; at the very time Cremin thought he was writing its obituary, the movement was at a low ebb, but it sprang back to life in the early 1960s. More troubling, it sprang back to life with anti-intellectualism at the forefront.

In Cremin's important book, anti-intellectualism appears as an occasional, unfortunate by-product of the progressive education movement for much of the century. However, this book argues that anti-intellectualism was an inescapable consequence of important strains of educational progressivism, particularly the versions of progressivism that had the most influence on American public education. Cremin and other historians of progressivism give short shrift to the movement's critics, such as William Torrey Harris, William Chandler Bagley, and Isaac Kandel; in this book they are treated as major figures in American education whose ideas were balanced and sound, if not often heeded, and whose philosophy remains central to the reconstruction of American education today.

Why does this argument about the past

matter today? As we shall see, whenever the academic curriculum was diluted or minimized, large numbers of children were pushed through the school system without benefit of a genuine education. As the academic curriculum lost its importance as the central focus of the public school system, the schools lost their anchor, their sense of mission, their intense moral commitment to the intellectual development of each child. Once that happened, education reform movements would come and go with surprising rapidity, almost randomly, each leaving its mark behind in the schools. Over time, as this happened, educators forgot how to say "no," even to the loopier notions of what schools were for. Every perceived need, interest, concern, problem, or issue found a place in the curriculum or provided a rationale for adding new specialists to the school's staff. Once the hierarchy of educational values was shattered, once schools lost their compass, hawkers of new wares could market their stock to the schools. Every purveyor of social reform could find a willing customer in the schools because all needs were presumed equal in importance, and there was no longer any general consensus on the central purpose of schooling.

Today, as the schools compete for children's time and attention with television, movies, the Internet, and other mass media, those who run them must know what schools alone can do. The schools must reassert their primary responsibility for the development of young people's intelligence and character. Schools must do far more than teach children "how to learn" and "how to look things up"; they must teach them what knowledge has most value, how to use that knowledge, how to organize what they know, how to understand the relationship between past and present, how to tell the difference between accurate information and propaganda, and how to turn information into understanding. If youngsters are set free from serious studies, unencumbered by the significant ideas and controversies of American and world history, untouched by the great poets and novelists of the world, unaware of the workings of science, they will turn to other sources for information and stimulation. Children today swim in a sea of images shaped by the popular culture, electronic media, and commercial advertising. Everything becomes trivia, everything is packaged to fit the terms of celebrity and sensationalism, famous for a minute or two, then gone.

If we are to have a chance of reclaiming our schools as centers of learning, we must understand how they came to be the way they are. At the opening of the twenty-first century, Americans find themselves in search of traditions that nourish and ideas that make sense of a world that is changing swiftly. One of the great virtues of the academic tradition is that it organizes human knowledge and makes it comprehensible to the learner. It aims to make a chaotic world coherent. It gives intellectual strength to those who want to understand social experience and the nature of the physical world. Despite sustained efforts to diminish it, the academic tradition survives; it survives because knowledge builds on knowledge, and we cannot dispense with the systematic study of human knowledge without risking mass ignorance. It survives because it retains the power to enlighten and liberate those who seek knowledge. Now, as parents, educators, policy makers, and other citizens seek high standards, it is time to renew the academic tradition for the children of the twenty-first century.

. . .

Large social organizations cannot succeed unless they focus on what they do best. The same is true for schools. What is it that schools and only schools can and must do? They cannot be successful as schools unless nearly all of their pupils gain literacy and numeracy, as well as a good understanding of history and the sciences, literature, and a foreign language. They cannot be successful unless they teach children the importance of honesty, personal responsibility, intellectual curiosity, industry, kindness, empathy, and courage.

Schools must prepare youngsters to have the "versatile intelligence" of which William T. Harris wrote, the intelligence that allows individuals to learn new tasks and take charge of their lives. They must teach them to use symbolic language and abstract ideas. They must teach youngsters about the culture and world in which they live and about cultures that existed long ago and far away.

If schools know and affirm what they do well, they can liberate themselves from the fads and panaceas that have often been inflicted on them by pressure groups, legislators, and well-meaning enthusiasts. Schools cannot compete with the visual drama of television, the Internet, and the movies. But the mass media, random and impersonal as they are, cannot compete with teachers, who have the capacity to get to know youngsters, inspire them, and guide them to responsible maturity.

The three great errors demonstrated in these pages are, first, the belief that schools should be expected to solve all of society's problems; second, the belief that only a portion of children need access to a high-quality academic education; and third, the belief that schools should emphasize students' immediate experiences and minimize (or even ignore) the transmission of knowledge. The first of these assumptions leads to a loss of focus, diverting the schools from their most basic mission; the second contributes to low achievement and antidemocratic policies; the third deprives youngsters of the intellectual power that derives from learning about the experiences of others and prevents them from standing on the shoulders of giants in every field of thought and action.

Perhaps in the past it was possible to undereducate a significant portion of the population without causing serious harm to the nation. No longer. Education, today more than at any time in the past, is the key to successful participation in society. A boy or girl who cannot read, write, or use mathematics is locked out of every sort of educational opportunity. A man or woman without a good elementary and sec-

ondary education is virtually precluded from higher education, from many desirable careers, from full participation in our political system, and from enjoyment of civilization's great aesthetic treasures. The society that allows large numbers of its citizens to remain uneducated, ignorant, or semiliterate squanders its greatest asset, the intelligence of its people.

The disciplines taught in school are uniquely valuable, both for individuals and for society. A society that does not teach science to the general public fosters the proliferation of irrational claims and antiscientific belief systems. A society that turns its back on the teaching of history encourages mass amnesia, leaving the public ignorant of the important events and ideas of the human past and eroding the civic intelligence needed for the future. A democratic society that fails to teach the younger generation its principles of self-government puts these principles at risk. A society that does not teach youngsters to appreciate great works of literature and art permits a coarsening and degradation of its popular culture. A society that is racially and ethnically diverse requires, more than other societies, a conscious effort to build shared values and ideals among its citizenry. A society that tolerates anti-intellectualism in its schools can expect to have a dumbed-down culture that honors celebrity and sensation rather than knowledge and wisdom.

Schools will not be rendered obsolete by new technologies because their role as learning institutions has become even more important than in the past. Technology can supplement schooling but not replace it; even the most advanced electronic technologies are incapable of turning their worlds of information into mature knowledge, a form of intellectual magic that requires skilled and educated teachers.

To be effective, schools must concentrate on their fundamental mission of teaching and learning. And they must do it for all children. That must be the overarching goal of schools in the twenty-first century.

CONCLUSION

Essentialism, or Basic Education, is an educational theory that has been around for a long time. It has demonstrated great longevity in actual school practice. It sees the school's primary function to be the preservation and transmission of the basic elements of human civilization. It emphasizes: (1) a curriculum of basic skills and subjects; (2) learning as the mastery of these skills and subjects according to high and verifiable standards; (3) schools as places of order, discipline, and efficient and effective instruction; (4) that the goal of organized education is to prepare people to be productive, civil, and patriotic individuals. Currently, the standards movement and the use of standardized tests to measure student academic achievement reflect the continuing influence of Essentialism on educational policy making.

DISCUSSION QUESTIONS

1. Define Essentialism and indicate how it applies to the contemporary school and curriculum.
2. Reflect on your own educational experience. Do you find evidence of an Essentialist or Basic Education orientation?
3. Of the philosophies and ideologies examined in this book, which is most, and which is least, compatible with Essentialism?
4. How much of your formal education has been based on the doctrine of preparation?
5. Do you think that the contemporary standards movement and the use of standardized tests resonates well with Essentialism?

INQUIRY AND RESEARCH PROJECTS

1. Maintain a clipping file of articles about education that appear in the popular (non-professional) press. Analyze the articles and determine if they represent an Essentialist orientation.
2. Make a list of the skills and subjects that you think are essential or necessary to a sound education. Does your list agree with the Essentialist position?
3. Debate the proposition: True equality requires all students to enroll in the same curriculum.
4. Create a curricular core based on Essentialist assumptions.
5. Conduct a survey of the members of your class on how they define the role and function of the school; determine if these opinions represent an Essentialist orientation.
6. Review several textbooks used in courses in professional teacher education. Determine if these books reflect an orientation that is for or against Essentialism.

INTERNET RESOURCES

For the Council for Basic Education, access
http//www.c-b-e.org

For standards and accountability in the No Child Left Behind Act, contact the U. S. Department of Education at
www.ed.gov/inits/nclb/part3.html

SUGGESTIONS FOR FURTHER READING

Bestor, Arthur E., Jr., *Educational Wastelands: Retreat from Learning in Our Public Schools.* Urbana: University of Illinois Press, 1953.

Bestor, Arthur E., Jr. *The Restoration of Learning: A Program for Redeeming the Unfulfilled Promise of American Education.* New York: Alfred A. Knopf, 1956.

Bunzel, John H., ed. *Challenge to American Schools: The Case for Standards and Values.* New York: Oxford University Press, 1985.

Hirsch, E. D., Jr. *Cultural Literacy: What Every American Needs to Know.* Boston: Houghton Mifflin, 1987.

National Commission on Excellence in Education. *A Nation at Risk: The Imperative for Educational Reform.* Washington, DC: U. S. Government Printing Office, 1983.

Ravitch, Diane. *Left Back: A Century of Failed School Reform.* New York: Simon and Schuster, 2000.

Ravitch, Diane, and Finn, Chester E., Jr. *What Do Our 17-Year-Olds Know? A Report on the First National Assessment of History and Literature.* New York: Harper & Row, 1987.

NOTES

1. William C. Bagley, "An Essentialist's Platform for the Advancement of American Education," *Educational Administration and Supervision,* XXIV (April 1938), pp. 241–256.

2. Adolphe E. Meyer, *The Development of Education in the Twentieth Century* (Englewood Cliffs, NJ: Prentice Hall, 1949), p. 149.

3. Arthur E. Bestor, Jr., *The Restoration of Learning: A Program for Redeeming the Unfulfilled Promise of American Education* (New York: Alfred A. Knopf, 1956), p. 4.

4. Ibid, p. 7.

5. National Commission on Excellence in Education, *A Nation at Risk: The Imperative for Educational Reform* (Washington, DC: U. S. Department of Education, 1983), p. 5.

6. Ibid, p. 24.

7. *No Child Left Behind* (Washington, DC: U. S. Printing Office, 2001), p. 1.

8. Ibid, pp. 8–9.

CHAPTER SEVENTEEN

PERENNIALISM

.

In Chapter 17 we will examine the educational theory of Perennialism, which asserts that education is universal, as is human nature itself. Stressing universal knowledge and values, Perennialists look to the reoccurring patterns of human life to set the foundations for education and schooling. We will define Perennialism's approach to education and schooling, situate it, identify its major principles, and its implications for education.

DEFINING PERENNIALISM

I am an amateur gardener and I have a perennial garden made up of plants that come up each spring, bloom for their particular season in the summer, die in the fall, are dormant in the winter, and return again each spring to repeat their life cycle. Unlike annual plants, which live for one season, perennials return and repeat their cycle of growth each year.

In philosophy and in educational theory, Perennialism flows from the tradition of the great founders of Western philosophy, especially from Aristotle, the Realist, and Aquinas, the Thomist. (Realism was discussed in Chapter 3 and Theistic Realism in Chapter 4.) These philosophers were concerned with metaphysical questions about ultimate reality. **Perennialism** can be defined as an educational theory that proclaims that people possess and share a common nature that defines them as human beings. This common human nature, in the Aristotelian tradition, is grounded in rationality and is the same at all times and in all places. Possession of this commonly shared rationality makes it possible for individuals to search for and find universal truth and live the values based on it. Like the seasons of the perennial plants, this human rational nature is a possession of all generations—past, present, and future. It enables each generation to find the great universal commonalities that transcend time, place, situation, and circumstance. It makes it possible to read, understand, and be guided by the great thinkers of the past, such as Plato, Aristotle, and Aquinas. We can also read the great writers, listen to the classics in music, appreciate the great works of art and be guided by their wisdom and enjoy their beauty.

Impressed by the recurring features of human experience across time and space, the Perennialists are concerned with what they call the search for enduring truths and values. Certain philosophers, writers of literature, artists, poets, and musicians, with their insights and styles, have captured a glimpse of that truth and value, as did the prisoner in Plato's cave who finally saw the light rather than shadows and distorted images of reality. (Refer to Plato's Allegory of the Cave in Chapter 2.) Their insights are embodied in philosophy, literature, art, and music. Some of these works, having survived the test of time, become classics that appeal to people of all generations. For example, Plato's *Republic*, Aristotle's *Nichomachean Ethics*, Rousseau's *Social Contract*, Tolstoy's *War and Peace*, and other great writings have been read by women and men at different times and in different places. Perennialist educators seek to bring the young of each generation into contact and understanding with these classics.

SITUATING PERENNIALISM

Perennialism has had a long history, though not a fashionable one, in modern times. In most cultures, there is literature that is considered sacred, or at least deeply philosophical, and is regarded as a font of wisdom in that particular culture. In Chinese and Japanese cultures this reverence is given to the Confucian classics; in India to the Bhagavad Ghita; in Islamic cultures to the Koran; and in Judaic and Christian cultures to the Bible. These sacred texts are considered repositories of perennial truths and values, and education has been focused on studying and learning from them.

In Western civilization, Perennialism has been heavily influenced by Aristotle's Realism, especially his assumptions that the human being is rational and that happiness consists of actions that conform to reason. Aristotle's assumptions became part of Western history when Thomas Aquinas incorporated them into Christian doctrine.

For a very long period in Western civilization—from the Greek and Roman Classical Period to the nineteenth century—Greek and Latin were regarded as the languages of the educated person. The works of Greek and Roman writers were considered classics and used as texts in schools. To these Greek and Latin classics were added the great works of the Medieval, Reformation, Renaissance, Enlightenment, and modern eras. In many ways, these secular texts were held in almost the same regard as the religious texts. Esteemed as the best that civilization has produced, they often formed the core subjects to be studied by the educated person.

In the modern era, especially in the twentieth century and today, Perennialism has been in retreat, fighting a rear-guard defensive action against Pragmatists, Postmodernists, Progressives, and Critical Theorists. While these more modern philosophies and theories challenge Perennialism, the greatest threat has come from the modern society and economy's emphasis on specialization, and from educational programs designed to prepare specialists rather than generalists.

Although they might not always identify themselves as Perennialists, the Perennialist position has been ably defended by educational theorists such as Robert Maynard Hutchins, Mortimer Adler, Allan Bloom, and William Bennett. Hutchins, a former president of the University of Chicago, argued for a general education grounded in the study of the great books of Western civilization.[1] Hutchins's associate, Mortimer Adler, drafted the Paidea Proposal, which called for the same general education for all students.[2] Allan Bloom attacked ethical relativism in higher education.[3] William Bennett, a former Secretary of Education, looked to universal moral values as a way to renew society and education.[4]

WHY STUDY PERENNIALISM?

Perennialism merits study as an educational theory because it reflects an important world tradition in education; that is, the great works or sacred texts convey wisdom based on universal and recurrent truths. In Western civilization, Perennialism translates Aristotelian and Thomist metaphysics and epistemology into educational theory. Although eclipsed by the more modern theories of education such as Progressivism and Critical Theory, Perennialism remains a significant theory.

PERENNIALISM'S PHILOSOPHICAL AND IDEOLOGICAL RELATIONSHIPS

Perennialism derives its basic principles from the Realist and Thomist philosophies, especially their metaphysics. The Universe is seen as purposeful and operating according to a rational design. Humans are defined as rational beings who, possessing the power of free will, can use their rationality to frame alternatives and choose among them. When functioning properly, human beings will act rationally and make rational choices. The traditional philosophies believe that a major purpose of education is to cultivate and exercise rationality. Perennialism's ideological derivations are not that obvious. Some Perennialists such as Robert Hutchins were in many ways civil libertarians. However, Perennialism also has an affinity with Conservatism, especially with the older European statement of Burkean principles—the need for an intellectual elite.

Often Perennialism and Essentialism, treated in the previous chapter, are equated as traditional theories that agree on the emphasis given to such shared features as: (1) the school's primary purpose as an intellectual and academic agency; (2) the organization of the curriculum into discrete subject matters; (3) the importance of structure, order, and sequence in curriculum and instruction. However, there is a significant difference in the foundational beliefs of the two theories. The Essentialists argue that the school's purpose and its curriculum is largely a product of history in that it emphasizes the skills and subjects that have contributed to human survival, productivity, and civility. Perennialists look to metaphysics, especially to human nature, so they see the purpose of education, the role of the school, and the organization of the curriculum as coming from humanity's enduring and universal characteristics.

The Perennialist theory of education is opposed by Pragmatists who see reality as being in constant flux. It is also opposed by Existentialists who argue that the Perennialist theory of education is based on prior definitions of human nature and education that are established prior to the individual's personal existence and choice. Philosophical Analysts would contend that Perennialism's basic propositions are empirically nonverifiable. Postmodernists and Critical Theorists would dismiss Perennialism's claims to universality and timelessness as masking a metanarrative once used to rationalize the control of favored classes, namely intellectual elites, at a particular period in history.

PERENNIALISM AS A THEORY OF EDUCATION

A Metaphysically Derived Theory

While many influential contemporary theories, especially Critical Theory, reject metaphysically based claims to universal truth as metanarratives that mask a once-favored elite's claims to power and control, Perennialism exalts metaphysics as the source of universal truth. While Critical Theorists reject universal justifications, Perennialism builds its case on eternal and universal principles. Like Aristotle and Thomas Aquinas, Perennialists assert that the universe itself is governed by rational and spiritual principles. Like Aquinas, who defined humans as rational beings, endowed with intellect and free will, Perennialists see education as a means of cultivating human reason. They define the school as an intellectual agency that has the primary purpose of developing human reason. Based on these metaphysical principles, Perennialists assert:

- Human beings, everywhere and at all times, are endowed with the power of reason.
- The possession of rationality enables humans to express their ideas in symbolic systems and language patterns, that enable them to communicate with each other.
- Human beings have free will in that they can construct and choose between alternative patterns of action.
- Behavior is most humane and civil when it is based on knowledge and reason.

Affirming Aristotle's premise that human beings are rational and that their greatest happiness comes from exercising and applying reason, Perennialists also assert that we inhabit a purposeful, intelligible, and orderly universe. This rationality, order, and purpose is the source of universal and eternal truths and values.

Perennialists reject the propositions of those who assert that the universe is an accident and that we are accidental beings. While they recognize that some things appear to change over time, they insist that the most important aspects of human life—the search for truth and beauty and the mysteries of love and death—do not change and are universal.

Perennialists also reject the proposition that human beings are defined by heredity, environment, race, ethnicity, gender, and class. While specific geographical, historical, political, and economic situations condition human society and institutions, there is something about human beings that transcends these factors. It is this common humanity that makes it possible to communicate with and share the hopes and fears of people everywhere in the world. It is this universality of human nature that makes it possible to recognize human rights.

An Epistemology Based on Reason

Perennialists rely on a Realist (Aristotelian) epistemology, namely that human beings, through sensation and abstraction, can construct concepts that correspond to the objects found in reality. All people—regardless of time or place, race or ethnicity, gender or class—possess the same intellectual power to grasp the truth and use it to guide their behavior. What is true is always universally valid. There are not different truths for different people; they are the same for all people. Using syllogistic reasoning, the Perennialists assert that: (1) the truth is eternal, universal, and the same for all people; (2) education is about the truth; (3) therefore, education, too, should be universal and the same for all people.[5]

A General Curriculum Based on Universals

Perennialists move their argument from the metaphysical claim that we live in a purposeful and rational universe to a consideration of human beings. What is it that makes a being human? They find their answer in a universal human nature. Regardless of the accident of place and time of birth and regardless of race, gender, and class, all human beings are endowed with the power of thought. They can create intellectual constructs, or concepts, and can represent these ideas in the form of symbols. Whether they speak Arabic, English, Spanish, or Swahili, all people are language creators and users. Therefore, language is one of the universals, rooted in our common human nature, that can be found everywhere at every time and is a perennial subject in the curriculum. Each individual has a personal history and as a member of society, they also have a remembered past, a collective history of their own human group. History, too, as the collective memory of the human race, has a place in the curriculum. In every culture, people use mathematics, from simple counting to complex systems of geometry, algebra, and calculus and so mathematics, too, has earned a place in the curriculum. People have sought to explain the biological and physical world in which they live through the natural and physical sciences, which are also included in the Perennialist curriculum. People live in civil societies and produce and consume goods; therefore, civics, political science, and economics merit a place in the curriculum. Human beings have always sought to concretize and portray their profoundest experiences into works of art, literature, and music. These fine arts, too, are worthy of a place in the curriculum.

Religious Perennialists, such as those influenced by Thomism, also contend that human beings have always worshipped God and have sought to explain the relationship between God and humanity in systems of theology. Judaism, Christianity, Buddhism, Hinduism, and Islam are the major world religions that have exemplified the human search for the divine. The study of religion, as a universal experience, should have a place in the curriculum. Indeed, religious Perennialists would place study of human spirituality and religion at education's core.

Like Idealists, Realists, Thomists, and Essentialists, Perennialists endorse a skill- and subject-matter-based curriculum. As a principle of curriculum organization, they look for guidance to those skills which civilized people have used to cultivate literacy and numeracy and to those subjects which represent the accumulated knowledge of the human race—language and literature, mathematics, science, history and humanities, and philosophy and religion. The distinctive emphasis of the Perennialists that sets them off from other educational theories, is their emphasis on the great books and the classics of art, music, and literature. A classic is a work that has captured the essence of the human search for what is true, good, and beautiful. The author of a classic has provided a window that enables others—from different times and places—to share her or his insights. For example, the philosophers Plato and Aristotle, though living in ancient Greece, in their search for truth and beauty, have continued to engage the attention of modern people. John Stuart Mill, writing on liberty, and Karl Marx on economics, remain relevant. Tolstoy's *War and Peace*, though written in the nineteenth century, still elicits a profound response in modern readers. Alexis de Tocqueville's insights about Americans remain an enduring, but also prophetic, analysis of the American character.

Though oriented mainly to subject matter, the Perennialist, in the later years of schooling, especially at the college and university level, seeks to develop a sense of the integration of the fields of knowledge into large-scale generalizations with great explanatory power. These generalizations provide perspective into the principles that organize and govern the universe and explain the commonality of the human family. Based on their allegiance to metaphysics, Perennialists orient their approach to education in the great classics, the metanarratives of philosophy, theology, history, literature, and science. It is at this point of great generalizations—metanarratives—that an important theoretical clash occurs between Perennialists and Postmodernists and Critical Theorists. For the Perennialists, the great classics provide the "mystic chords" of insight into the universe and the human condition, which generates wisdom. Critics, such as Postmodernists and Critical Theorists, contend that these metanarratives, elevated as classics, are really time-bound, historically generated justifications for one class to have power over another. Multiculturalist critics also argue that the so-called great classics of Western civilization are based on a Eurocentric, patriarchal, elitist view of education.

A Universal Value Core

Just as human nature itself, in its world experience, has provided general answers to what should be found in the curriculum, this same nature is also the source of moral, ethical, and aesthetic values—what is good and right and beautiful. Perennialists are fond of referring to the enduring virtues as the consistent values that form the axiological core of education. Such virtues cluster around Aristotle's golden mean, a balanced and moderate position that avoids excesses of extreme inhibition and repression on the one hand and extreme exhibition and indulgence on the other. Reason comes into play to guide people in finding the mean of moderation.

Regardless of their ethnicity, gender, race, or class, individuals have the right to enjoy their humanity, to exercise their rationality, and to enjoy the Earth's good things. In other words, human beings have primary, inherent, universal rights that are not given by governments, societies, or classes. They question those, especially Postmodernists and Critical Theorists, who contend that the most important aspects of individuals are based on race, ethnicity, or socioeconomic class. Human rights, say Perennialists, are not determined by gender, class, race, or ethnicity but by humanity itself. In reply, Critical Theorists contend that to speak of general human rights in the abstract is misleading; in most cases, human rights are violated because of economic, sexual, and racial discrimination and exploitation.

PERENNIALISM'S CRITIQUE OF MODERN EDUCATION

As mentioned earlier, Perennialists have been fighting a rear-guard defense against many features of modern education. Although all educational theorists look for flaws in positions they oppose, this kind of critique has been especially important for Perennialists such as Hutchins, Adler, Bloom, and Bennett. Based on their grounding in Aristotelian philosophy and the classics, the Perennialists have strong views on what has caused weaknesses in modern education. As they see it, among the ills of contemporary American education are: presentism and too-early specialization.

Presentism

Presentism is a belief that everything of significance, relevance, and importance is happening at the present time—right here and now. It tends to reject the past as antiquarian and largely irrelevant. It is focused instead on the immediate happening. When it looks to the past, it explains it almost exclusively in terms of the present. Presentism is characterized by looking to public opinion polls to discover what people feel about an issue; it is characterized by turning quickly to the Internet and the World Wide Web to find information about a subject. It is characterized by the "talking heads," the "experts," who give an instantaneous, quick, and capsule analysis of difficult issues. The quickness, immediacy, and superficiality associated with presentism has resulted in a lack of perspective that would come from careful research, standing back a bit, and reflecting on a theme, issue, or topic. The world's great books, the classics, provide the perspective needed by the truly educated person—a view of how things and situations truly relate to each other.

Too-Early Specialization

Perennialists contend that individuals should first be educated as human beings before being trained as specialists. Every human being should enjoy a general liberal education geared to the cultivation of reason. Students should not be sorted out and placed in different educational tracks, such as general, vocational, and technical. This kind of sorting is not only undemocratic but it is illiberal. Note that the Perennialist use of "liberal education" refers to the liberal arts and sciences and not to the Liberal ideology. Perennialists recognize that people have different ability levels. However, differences in academic ability do not mean that able students should enjoy a general education while less academically able ones are assigned to vocational programs. While all students should have a general liberal education, curriculum subjects may be prepared in a graded manner so students can approach them at their level of ability.

Technical and vocational education should be deferred until after the completion of a general liberal education. Some Perennialists, such as Hutchins, argued that vocational and technical education should not take place in schools at all. It is more efficient, argued Hutchins, if this kind of training takes place in apprenticeship or training programs located in industries and businesses.

Perennialists are concerned that presentism and specialization have seriously eroded the necessary general knowledge and value core that sustains civilized society. Such a core is rooted in the cultural heritage, the past of a people, and is recorded in its enduring works of art, literature, philosophy, and politics. This core is eroded by the sensationalist attention given to works of popular culture that enjoy acclaim for a fleeting moment in time and then are forgotten. Specialization also undermines a tenable knowledge core when specialists use an exclusive language, a "jargon," with which they speak only to each other, rather than to the general public. Premature specialization in the education of the young means that they are programmed to learn the specialty and its terminology before acquiring the needed knowledge and value base.

THE NEED FOR A STABLE CULTURAL CORE

Recent decades have seen considerable struggle over the core of the curriculum. Although there are many positions on the content that should be included in this core, three main camps can be identified: (1) those who see it rooted in Western culture; (2) those who see it in global, often Third World terms; (3) and those who reject the idea of a general core and see it in specific gender, ethnic, or racial terms.

Perennialists argue that civilized society needs to rest on a well-defined core of generally accepted knowledge and values. They believe this core is rooted in the recurring aspects of human life, especially in Aristotelian metaphysics and the classics of Western civilization. In addition, they point to the important principles, traditions, and classics found in the American experience.

Critics argue that the traditional Perennialist core is culturally biased in favor of Western culture and is therefore insufficiently multicultural. They argue that the Western value core, reflecting the historically based views of white European males, neglects the broader global experience. It needs to include material from hitherto underrepresented groups, such as Asians, Africans, African Americans, women, and gays and lesbians. These critics argue that it is important to include the voices of those who have been marginalized due to race, gender, class, and ethnicity. It is also important to include the voices of people who live in less technologically developed regions.

A second group of critics, often influenced by Postmodernism and Critical Theory, argues that attempts to impose a general core, allegedly based on universal truth and value, is either a delusion or a deliberate misrepresentation. Claims of universality and timelessness are false; the so-called general universal value core really represents the economic and political interests of a particular group at a specific time in history. Rather than seeking a universal knowledge and value, educators should look to their immediate situation and to the people who interact in them. These people—often the marginalized and exploited—have their own stories to tell. It is more important to listen to these unique voices than to search for universals.

ROBERT M. HUTCHINS, GENERAL EDUCATION

Robert Hutchins's argument for general education in his *The Higher Learning in America* is included here because of the clarity and directness of his theoretical position. In his discussion, Hutchins makes the classic argument for Perennialism, namely that a general education is the same for all people, regardless of time or place. Hutchins's emphasis on the intellectual virtues is derived from the Aristotelian and Thomist philosophies examined in Chapters 3 and 4. As you read the selection, you may wish to consider the following focusing questions:

1. Why does Hutchins argue that a person must first be educated as a generalist before being trained as a specialist? Do you agree or disagree with Hutchins?

2. What are Hutchins's views of human nature, truth, and knowledge? Contrast his views with those of the Pragmatists, Postmodernists, and Critical Theorists. (See discussions in Chapters 5, 8, and 19.)

3. For Hutchins, what is the primary purpose of schools and colleges? Compare his view with that of Broudy in Chapter 3.

4. Why does Hutchins argue for a curriculum based on the great books?

. . .
We may take it for granted that we shall always have specialists; yet neither the world nor knowledge of it is arbitrarily divided up as universities are. Everybody cannot be a specialist in every field. He must therefore be cut off from every field but his own unless he has the same basic education that other specialists have.

From Robert M. Hutchins, *The Higher Learning in America.* New Haven, CT: Yale University Press, 1936 (Yale Paperbound, 1962), pp. 59–81. Used with permission of Yale University Press.

This means more than having the same language and the same general interest in advancing knowledge. It means having a common stock of fundamental ideas. This becomes more important as empirical science advances and accumulates more and more data. The specialist in a narrow field has all he can do to keep up with the latest discoveries in it. Other men, even in his own department, struggling to stay abreast of what is happening in their own segments of the subject, cannot hope to keep up with what is happening in his. They may now expect to have some general understanding of what he is doing because they all have something in common; they are in the same department. But the day will shortly be upon us when even this degree of comprehension will be impossible, because of the infinite splitting of subject matters and the progressive submergence of any ideas by our insistence on information as the content of education.

. . .

. . . I should like to talk about content, not about method. I concede the great difficulty of communicating the kind of education I favor to those who are unable or unwilling to get their education from books. I insist, however, that the education I shall outline is the kind that everybody should have, that the answer to it is not that some people should not have it, but that we should find out how to give it to those whom we do not know how to teach at present. You cannot say my content is wrong because you do not know the method of transmitting it. Let us agree upon content if we can and have faith that the technological genius of America will solve the problem of communication.

Economic conditions require us to provide some kind of education for the young, and for all the young, up to about their twentieth year. Probably one-third of them cannot learn from books. This is no reason why we should not try to work out a better course of study for the other two-thirds. At the same time we should continue our efforts and experiments to find out how to give a general education to the hand-minded and the functionally illiterate. Even these attempts may be somewhat simplified if we know what a general education is.

. . . The scheme that I advance is based on the notion that general education is education for everybody, whether he goes on to the university or not. It will be useful to him in the university; it will be equally useful if he never goes there. I will admit that it will not be useful to him outside the university in the popular sense of utility. It may not assist him to make money or to get ahead. It may not in any obvious fashion adjust him to his environment or fit him for the contemporary scene. It will, however, have a deeper, wider utility: it will cultivate the intellectual virtues.

The trouble with the popular notion of utility is that it confuses immediate and final ends. Material prosperity and adjustment to the environment are good more or less, but they are not good in themselves and there are other goods beyond them. The intellectual virtues, however, are good in themselves and good as means to happiness. By the intellectual virtues I mean good intellectual habits. The ancients distinguish five intellectual virtues: the three speculative virtues of intuitive knowledge, which is the habit of induction; of scientific knowledge, which is the habit of demonstration; and of philosophical wisdom, which is scientific knowledge, combined with intuitive reason, of things highest by nature, first principles and first causes. To these they add the two virtues of the practical intellect: art, the capacity to make according to a true course of reasoning, and prudence, which is right reason with respect to action.

In short the intellectual virtues are habits resulting from the training of the intellectual powers. An intellect properly disciplined, an intellect properly habituated, is an intellect able to operate well in all fields. An education that consists of the cultivation of the intellectual virtues, therefore, is the most useful education, whether the student is destined for a life of contemplation or a life of action. . . .

One purpose of education is to draw out the elements of our common human nature. These elements are the same in any time or place. The notion of educating a man to live in any particular time or place, to adjust him to any particular environment, is therefore foreign to a true conception of education.

Education implies teaching. Teaching implies knowledge. Knowledge is truth. The truth is everywhere the same. Hence education should be everywhere the same. I do not overlook the possibilities of differences in organization, in administration, in local habits and customs. These are details. I suggest that the heart of any course of study designed for the whole people will be, if education is rightly understood, the same at any time, in any place, under any political, social, or economic conditions. Even the administrative details are likely to be similar because all societies have generic similarity.

If education is rightly understood, it will be understood as the cultivation of the intellect. The cultivation of the intellect is the same good for all men in all societies. It is, moreover, the good for which all other goods are only means. Material prosperity, peace and civil order, justice and the moral virtues are means to the cultivation of the intellect. So Aristotle says in the *Politics:* "Now, in men reason and mind are the end towards which nature strives, so that the generation and moral discipline of the citizens ought to be ordered with a view to them." An education which served the means rather than their end would be misguided.

I agree, of course, that any plan of general education must be such as to educate the student for intelligent action. It must, therefore, start him on the road toward practical wisdom. But the question is what is the best way for education to start him and how far can it carry him. Prudence or practical wisdom selects the means toward the ends that we desire. It is acquired partly from intellectual operations and partly from experience. But the chief requirement for it is correctness in thinking. Since education cannot duplicate the experiences which the student will have when he graduates, it should devote itself to developing correctness in thinking as a means to practical wisdom, that is, to intelligent action.

As Aristotle put it in the *Ethics*, ". . . while young men become geometricians and mathematicians and wise in matters like these, it is thought that a young man of practical wisdom cannot be found. The cause is that such wisdom is concerned not only with universals, but with particulars, but a young man has no experience, for it is length of time that gives experience." Since practical wisdom is "a true and reasoned capacity to act with regard to the things that are good or bad for man," it would seem that education can make its best contribution to the development of practical wisdom by concentrating on the reasoning essential to it.

A modern heresy is that all education is formal education and that formal education must assume the total responsibility for the full development of the individual. The Greek notion that the city educates the man has been forgotten. Everything that educated the man in the city has to be imported into our schools, colleges, and universities. We are beginning to behave as though the home, the church, the state, the newspaper, the radio, the movies, the neighborhood club, and the boy next door did not exist. All the experience that is daily and hourly acquired from these sources is overlooked, and we set out to supply imitations of it in educational institutions. The experience once provided by some of these agencies may be attenuated now; but it would be a bold man who would assert that the young person today lived a life less full of experience than the youth of yesterday. Today as yesterday we may leave experience to other institutions and influences and emphasize in education the contribution that it is supremely fitted to make, the intellectual training of the young. The life they lead when they are out of our hands will give them experience enough. We cannot try to give it to them and at the same time perform the task that is ours and ours alone.

Young people do not spend all their time in school. Their elders commonly spend none of it there. Yet their elders are, we hope, constantly growing in practical wisdom. They are, at least, having experience. If we can teach them while they are being educated how to reason, they may be able to comprehend and assimilate their experience. It is a good principle of educational administration that a college or university should do nothing that another agency can do as well. This is a good principle because a college or university has a vast and complicated job if it does what only it can do. In general education, therefore, we may wisely leave experience to life and set about our job of intellectual training.

If there are permanent studies which every person who wishes to call himself educated should master; if those studies constitute our intellectual inheritance, then those studies should be the center of a general education. They cannot be ignored because they are difficult, or unpleasant, or because they are almost totally missing from our curriculum today. The child-centered school may be attractive to the child, and no doubt is useful as a place in which the little ones may release their inhibitions and hence behave better at home. But educators cannot permit the students to dictate the course of study unless they are prepared to confess that they are nothing but chaperons, supervising an aimless, trial-and-error process which is chiefly valuable because it keeps young people from doing something worse. The free elective system as Mr. Eliot introduced it at Harvard and as Progressive Education adapted it to lower age levels amounted to a denial that there was content to education. Since there was no content to education, we might as well let students follow their own bent. They would at least be inter-

ested and pleased and would be as well educated as if they had pursued a prescribed course of study. This overlooks the fact that the aim of education is to connect man with man, to connect the present with the past, and to advance the thinking of the race. If this is the aim of education, it cannot be left to the sporadic, spontaneous interests of children or even of undergraduates.

. . .

By insisting on the permanent studies as the heart of a general education I do not mean to insist that they are the whole of it. We do not know enough to know whether certain technological work, for example, may not have a certain subsidiary value in general education for some students. Nor do I overlook the fact that since by hypothesis general education may be terminal for most students, it must connect them with the present and future as well as with the past. It is as important for them to know that thinking is still going on as it is for them to know what has been thought before.

The question whether certain technical work shall be allowed to be a part of general education is rather a question of method than of content, a question how to teach rather than what. Technology as such has no place in general education. If it can be justified at all, it can only be because we discover that certain principles can best be communicated through technical work. The question of present thought is largely answered by saying that it is impossible to think of a teacher who contented himself with elucidating the thought of the past without intimating that these ideas have a history running to the present day.

. . .

They are in the first place those books which have through the centuries attained to the dimensions of classics. Many such books, I am afraid, are in the ancient and medieval period. But even these are contemporary. A classic is a book that is contemporary in every age. That is why it is a classic. The conversations of Socrates raise questions that are as urgent today as they were when Plato wrote. In fact they are more so, because the society in which Plato lived did not need to have them raised as much as we do. We have forgotten how important they are.

Such books are then a part, and a large part, of the permanent studies. They are so in the first place because they are the best books we know. How can we call a man educated who has never read any of the great books in the western world? Yet today it is entirely possible for a student to graduate from the finest American colleges without having read any of them, except possibly Shakespeare. Of course, the student may have heard of these books, or at least of their authors. But this knowledge is gained in general through textbooks, and textbooks have probably done as much to degrade the American intelligence as any single force. If the student should know about Cicero, Milton, Galileo, or Adam Smith, why should he not read what they wrote? Ordinarily what he knows about them he learns from texts which must be at best second-hand versions of their thought.

In the second place these books are an essential part of general education because it is impossible to understand any subject or to comprehend the contemporary world without them. If we read Newton's *Principia*, we see a great genius in action; we make the acquaintance of a work of unexampled simplicity and elegance. We understand, too, the basis of modern science. The false starts, the backing and filling, the wildness, the hysteria, the confusion of modern thought and the modern world result from the loss of what has been thought and done by earlier ages. The Industrial Revolution begins our study of history and the social sciences. Philosophy begins with Descartes and Locke and psychology with Wundt and William James. Natural science originates with the great experimenters of the nineteenth century. If anything prior is mentioned, it is only as a reminder that our recent great achievements in these fields must, of course, have had some primitive beginnings in the dark earlier centuries. The classics, if presented at all, are offered in excerpts out of context, and for the most part for the sake of showing the student how far we have progressed beyond our primitive beginnings.

. . .

. . . Every educated person should know the colossal triumph of the Greeks and Romans and the great thinkers of the Middle Ages. If every man were educated—and why should he not be?—our people would not fall so easily a prey to the latest nostrums in economics, in politics, and, I may add, in education.

You will observe that the great books of the western world cover every department of knowledge. The *Republic* of Plato is basic to an understanding of the law; it is equally important as education for what is known as citizenship. The *Physics* of Aristotle, which deals with change and motion in nature, is fundamental to the natural sciences and medicine, and is equally important to all those who confront change and motion in nature, that is, to everybody. Four years spent partly in reading, discussing, and digesting books of such importance would, therefore, contribute equally to preparation for specialized study and to general education of a terminal variety. Certainly four years is none too long for this experience. It is an experience which will, as I have said, serve as preparation for advanced study and as general education designed to help the student understand the world. It will also develop habits of reading and standards of taste and criticism that will enable the adult, after his formal education is over, to think and act intelligently about the thought and movements of contemporary life. It will help him to share in the intellectual activity of his time.

CONCLUSION

Perennialism represents an educational theory that rests on a metaphysical foundation of Aristotelianism. It emphasizes that recurrent universal and timeless truths and values are the cultural property of all people, regardless of race, gender, ethnicity, or class. It calls for a general value core and curriculum for all. Perennialists stress the world's great works of art and literature, especially those of Western civilization, as the core of studies in the curriculum. They oppose the trends to presentism, specialization, and fragmentation that they believe are weakening American education.

DISCUSSION QUESTIONS

1. Do you find the theory of Perennialism to be meaningful in contemporary education? Explain your answer.
2. Although Essentialists and Perennialists agree on many points, what are the major distinctions between the two theories?
3. Do you think American education is over- or under-specialized?
4. Should American education have a general knowledge and value core that is the same for all students? Why?

INQUIRY AND RESEARCH PROJECTS

1. Review your program of teacher education. Do you find any evidence of Perennialism?
2. Read and review a book by a Perennialist theorist such as Allan Bloom, Mortimer Adler, Robert Hutchins, or William Bennett.
3. Prepare an outline of what should be included in a Perennialist core curriculum for elementary, secondary, or higher education.

INTERNET RESOURCES

For the educational theory of Robert Hutchins, consult
www.newfoundations.com/GALLERY/Hutchins.html

For a biography, essays, and bibliography of Mortimer Adler, consult the Mortimer J. Adler Archives at the Radical Academy at
http://radicalacademy.com/adlerdirectory.htm

SUGGESTIONS FOR FURTHER READING

Adler, Mortimer J. *Paideia Problems and Possibilities: A Consideration of Questions Raised by the Paideia Proposal.* New York: Macmillan, 1983.

Adler, Mortimer J. *The Paideia Program: An Educational Syllabus.* New York: Macmillan, 1984.

Adler, Mortimer J. *The Paideia Proposal: An Educational Manifesto.* New York: Macmillan, 1982.

Ashmore, Harry S. *Unseasonable Truths: The Life of Robert Maynard Hutchins.* Boston: Little, Brown, and Co., 1991.

Bennett, William J. *The De-Valuing of America: The Fight for Our Culture and Our Children.* New York: Simon and Schuster, 1992.

Bloom, Allan. *The Closing of the American Mind.* New York: Simon and Schuster, 1987.

Dzuback, Mary Ann. *Robert M. Hutchins: Portrait of an Educator.* Chicago: University of Chicago Press, 1991.

Hutchins, Robert M. *The Higher Learning in America.* New Haven, CT: Yale University Press, 1961.

NOTES

1. For Hutchins at the University of Chicago, see William H. McNeill, *Hutchins's University: A Memoir of the University of Chicago, 1929–1950* (Chicago: University of Chicago Press, 1991).

2. Mortimer J. Adler, *The Paideia Proposal: An Educational Manifesto* (New York: Macmillan, 1982).

3. Allan Bloom, *The Closing of the American Mind* (New York: Simon and Schuster, 1987).

4. William J. Bennett, *The De-Valuing of America: The Fight for Our Culture and Our Children* (New York: Simon and Schuster, 1992).

5. Robert M. Hutchins, *The Higher Learning in America* (New Haven, CT: Yale University Press, 1936), p 63. Also see Hutchins, *A Conversation on Education* (Santa Barbara, CA: Center for the Study of Democratic Institutions, 1963).

CHAPTER EIGHTEEN

PROGRESSIVISM

In this chapter we will examine Progressivism, a theory that has had ramifications for politics, society, and education. In particular, we examine such varieties of Progressivism as the child-centered and socially oriented positions. Inclined to innovation and change, Progressivism has been a theory of reform in both American society and education. We will define Progressivism, situate it by tracing its origins, identify its key principles, and examine its educational implications.

DEFINING PROGRESSIVISM

To define Progressivism, we must go to its root, *progress*, a word that proclaims the possibility of improving something. For Progressives, it is the human situation—society, politics, the economy, and education—that can be improved. As a verb, *to progress* refers to actions that are ongoing or onward. For Progressives, such actions should be nonviolent and follow known and fair procedures in order to bring about gradual, related, serial, and cumulative reforms. *Progression* means to move forward by a series of related steps, a series of ends-in-view rather than utopian leaps into the future.

Progressivism, which has been shaped by Liberalism, is committed to using public, rather than secret, procedures. (See Chapter 11 on Liberalism.) Fairness results from using agreed-upon processes to identify and solve problems and to adjudicate disputes. All participants in the process share a commitment to respecting and using the same rules. To achieve this commitment, Progressives, like Liberals, emphasize the importance of creating a broad, general consensus or agreement on the rules. Education is seen as a consensus builder in which people learn procedures, practice them, and become committed to using them.

The kinds of reforms or improvements envisioned by Progressives are proximate, that is they begin with where we are right now and arise from existing conditions. If schools are to be reformed, the process of reform starts with existing problems and situations, rather than with utopian proposals such as that advanced by Ivan Illich to "deschool society." Each reform becomes part of a related series of reforms that

PROGRESSIVE REFORMS:

- Are nonviolent
- Follow known and accepted procedures
- Begin with existing situations
- Are gradual, serial, and cumulative

leads to still more reforms. The anticipated result is that these reforms will have the cumulative effect of generally improving society.

Progressives believe in the possibility of gradually improving or reforming the human situation over time. In politics, Progressives advocate social, economic, political, or educational change by gradual internal reforms that take place within the system.

In education, Progressives advocate allowing children to express themselves freely and creatively and they also endorse general social reforms discussed above. This dual advocacy has sometimes produced tension among educational Progressives, especially when they unite to organize reform organizations or movements. Many educational Progressives prefer using informal, less structured, and open methods of instruction that they believe allow children to follow their interests and use their creativity. They stress encouraging children's self-expression in informal classroom environments that satisfy individual interests and needs, and also result in collaborative group learning. While recognizing the importance of children's individual needs, Progressives inclined to use schools for social reform emphasize that schools and teachers have a role in introducing controversial issues; in examining important social, political, and economic problems; and in seeking to solve them.

At times, the emphasis on children's interests and needs and on social issues and reforms have generated tension within the ranks of Progressive educators. Some child-centered Progressives fear that the emphasis on social and political problems can result in politicizing the educational process by imposing goals that are outside of children's needs and interests. Social-reform Progressives, in contrast, believe that following children's interests as the sole criterion of curriculum and instruction retreats into laissez-faire romanticism, which reinforces the status quo rather than reforming it.

SITUATING PROGRESSIVISM

Progressivism's beginnings can be traced back to the Eighteenth-Century Enlightenment, also known as the Age of Reason. The Enlightenment philosophers rejected the belief inherited from the Medieval and Reformation periods, that human beings are, innately, ethically depraved or spiritually deprived. In contrast, French philosophes such as Condillac, Diderot, and Rousseau conjectured that human beings are inherently noble beings who have tremendous possibilities for improving their situation on earth. Their strategy for improving the human situation was to use science to discover the truths or general principles about how the universe functioned, and to reform social, political, economic, and educational institutions to conform to those natural laws. The Enlightenment theorists embraced the ideal of progress as a guiding principle. They reasoned that the future could be better than the past if the human power to reason was unshackled and given free rein. In order for this to occur, the power to reason had to be freed from arbitrary, authoritarian, and absolutist controls by the church and the state. It also had to be strengthened by an education that was based on nature and science.

In Europe, noted forerunners of Progressivism were Jean-Jacques Rousseau, whose romantic naturalism emphasized educating children according to the principles of nature, liberating them from artificial social restraints, and educating them in an open, unstructured, informal environment. Johann Heinrich Pestalozzi, influenced by Rousseau, redefined Rousseau's method into school-based instruction. Pestalozzi emphasized simultaneous instruction in group settings, graduated learning through the use of objects, and field trips into the natural environment.[1] These European educational ideas influenced American Progressives such as Colonel Francis Parker, who introduced them into teacher education programs in the United States.

Progressive education converged with the more general Progressive movement that took place in the United States from 1900 to 1920. Progressives in politics, such as Theodore Roosevelt, Woodrow Wilson, and Robert LaFollette, although differing on many issues, agreed on the need to reform the American political system. Political Progressives sought to regulate business corporations so they could not monopolize the economy, free government from the control of corrupt politicians, and conserve environmental resources. Political Progressives also sought to reform the system by enacting regulatory legislation to curb monopolies, create more direct political processes, ensure the safety of food and drugs, and safeguard natural resources. Progressives believed these reforms could take place within the Constitutional framework by using established electoral and legislative processes. Generally, the Progressive reform process involved: (1) identifying the problem and investigating it in a public and scientific way; (2) informing and educating the public, often through investigative journalism; (3) discussing and structuring possible ways to resolve the problem; (4) proposing and enacting legislation to remedy and reform the situation; (5) establishing regulations to ensure the reforms were implemented and followed.

Although they had multiple goals, Progressive educators followed a three-pronged agenda: (1) remove the formalism, routine, and bureaucracy that devitalized learning in many schools; (2) devise and implement innovative methods of instruction that focus on children's needs and interests; (3) professionalize teaching and school administration. Progressive educators pioneered the development of new methods of education, such as "learning by doing," activity-based learning, group projects, and problem solving. Marietta Johnson (1864–1938), the founder of the Organic Philosophy of Education, epitomized child-centered Progressive education. At her School of Organic Education in Fairhope, Alabama, Johnson shaped the curriculum around children's needs, interests, and experiences. Creative activities such as dancing, drawing, singing, and weaving took center stage, while reading and writing were delayed until the child was nine or ten years old.[2]

The Pragmatist philosopher John Dewey was a key figure in the development of Progressive educational theory. Dewey, at his own Laboratory School at the University of Chicago, tested many experimental ideas about education. Emphasizing the importance of experience in education, Dewey was a pioneer in developing activity-based instruction and the use of problem solving by the scientific method. Dewey's innovative ideas were embraced by many Progressive educators.

Progressive education gained the spotlight in the United States with the founding of the Progressive Education Association in 1919. The Association joined innovative public and private school educators and reform-minded professors of education into one large organization. The Association journal, *Progressive Education*, disseminated articles about educational reforms and innovative programs across the country. John Dewey served as the Association's honorary President.[3]

Although united in opposing traditional schooling, Progressive educators came to be divided into two groups: Child-Centered and Social-Reconstructionist. Child-Centered Progressivism looked to the child as education's vital source. They believed that the curriculum grew out of the individual child's interests and needs, rather than being imposed as the prescribed, preestablished skills and subjects of the traditional curriculum so prized by Essentialists, Perennialists, and Conservatives. Child-Centered Progressives believed that children should be at liberty to pursue their own interests, without arbitrary rules. Through their own self-initiated activity, children, guided by permissive and encouraging teachers, were to explore their environment and thereby enlarge their horizons. Working together in cooperative and collaborative groups, children would learn how to participate as members of a democratic society. If children were free to learn without the imposition of adult-imposed external aims, they would become the builders of a new and better world.

Like the Child-Pentered Progressives, the Social Reconstructionists opposed traditional schooling's authoritarianism and formalism. However, the Reconstructionists were more inclined to see education as a politically charged process.[4] In some ways, they anticipated the Critical Theorists, who see education, especially schools, as places of ideological conflict between competing groups and classes. While many Social Reconstructionists were modern Liberals and anti-Communists, some were Marxists. The Reconstructionists believed that education should be used as a deliberate agency of social, political, and economic reform. Reconstructionists such as George Counts, Harold Rugg, and Theodore Brameld argued that education is a highly charged social and political activity. While not neglecting children's interests, schools and teachers needed to face and deal with important contemporary issues, no matter how controversial. Counts argued that schools and teachers should work to build a new, better, and more equitable society.[5]

The Child-Centered and Reconstructionist Progressives disagree on the degree to which schools and teachers should deliberately attempt to direct social and political change. Some child-centered educators feared the Reconstructionist agenda was so politically motivated that it would lead to students' indoctrination. The Reconstructionists, in contrast, argued that schools, by not taking a side on the major political and economic issues, were reinforcing the status quo. Although their theoretical origins are different, contemporary Critical Theorists endorse many of the same ideas about educational reform proclaimed by the earlier Social Reconstructionists.

■ ■ ■ ■ ■

INFLUENCES ON THE DEVELOPMENT OF PROGRESSIVISM

- Eighteenth-Century Enlightenment's faith in progress
- European educational reformers: Rousseau and Pestalozzi
- Progressive movement in the United States
- John Dewey's Pragmatic Experimentalism
- Progressive Education Association

PROGRESSIVISM'S PHILOSOPHICAL AND IDEOLOGICAL RELATIONSHIPS

Progressivism's philosophical source is Pragmatism, especially Dewey's Experimentalism. Its ideological source is modern Liberalism. (See Chapter 5 on Pragmatism and Chapter 11 on Liberalism.) Naturalism, especially Rousseau's version, inspired the Child-Centered Progressive orientation that children were naturally good or, at least morally neutral, in their early years. Like Rousseau, Progressives agreed that children's nurturing and education should be free from artificial restraints and they accentuated the educational efficacy of activities and excursions taking place in the natural environment.

Progressivism, like Pragmatism, rejects many philosophical principles associated with Idealism, Realism, and Thomism. These more traditional philosophies were based on metaphysical principles that asserted that reality already exists and the purpose of education is to aid human reason in realizing this antecedent, or prior knowledge. For the Progressives, knowledge is not a ready-made given. Children construct their own knowledge and beliefs through interaction with the environment. Further, the Thomist emphasis on ultimate goals, realized in the afterlife, is judged by Progressives as not only unverifiable in experience but too remote to direct the activities of everyday life.

Ideologically, Progressivism and Liberalism share many common themes. The Liberal commitment to reform through gradual processes of change; to the following of shared procedures to adjudicate differences of opinion; to open discussion and debate; and to the freedom to express ideas are all viewed favorably by Progressives. Indeed, the distinctions between Liberals and Progressives are often blurred by their shared interests and commitments.

While there is a strong Naturalist resonance in the child-centered strains of Progressivism, John Dewey's Pragmatism, too, exerts a strong influence. Dewey's belief that the sole purpose of education was growth for the sake of further growth corresponds nicely to the Progressive's call for children's freedom to explore and learn from activities in the environment. His concept of experience as the interaction of the person with the environment corresponds well with the Progressive emphasis on process, "learning by doing," projects, and activities. Dewey's Complete Act of Thought, or problem solving according to the scientific method, corresponds to the Progressive orientation that children learn best by reflecting on past actions and validating those actions in terms of the consequences they produced. His emphasis on shared human experience, or associative

PROGRESSIVISM'S PHILOSOPHICAL AND IDEOLOGICAL ROOTS

- Pragmatism
- Naturalism
- Liberalism

living and learning, corresponds well with the Progressive emphasis on collaborative group projects. While Dewey and the Progressive educators had much in common, the Pragmatic philosopher warned Progressives against taking an "either–or" stance that ignored the importance of past experience in education. In *Experience and Education*, Dewey advised them to develop a philosophy of education based on the ongoing experience that created a continuum uniting past, present, and future.[6]

Conservatives, Essentialists, and Perennialists regard Progressive education with disdain and suspicion. Conservatives believe Progressivism's failure to emphasize the past weakens transmission of the traditional cultural heritage from generation to generation. Further, Progressivism's tendency to ethical relativism weakens traditional values of patriotism, religion, and respect for authority. Essentialists charge that Progressives have abandoned the tried-and-true skills and subjects—the basics of literacy, numeracy, and civility—that perpetuate a civilized society. Perennialists, who often stress that the classics and the great books of Western culture should be at the curriculum core, find Progressivism intellectually inadequate. They charge Progressives with foisting anti-intellectualism upon schools, teachers, and students.

WHY STUDY PROGRESSIVISM?

Progressivism has been and continues to be an important reform tendency in American education. The dominant trends in curriculum have alternated between neo-Essentialism (Basic Education) with its emphasis on academic skills and subjects, and Progressivism with its emphasis on open education, inquiry-based learning, collaborative learning, projects, process learning, authentic assessment, and constructivism. It is useful for contemporary educators to recognize how these innovations in education are both reactions against the status quo and also assertions of new approaches to education. Progressivism, as a theory of education, is directly linked to curricular reform and innovation. However, it also has broader implications because of its assumptions about children's growth and development and because of its idea that schools can be instruments of social, political, and educational change.

PROGRESSIVE PRINCIPLES OF EDUCATION

Since Progressive education is characterized by variety rather than uniformity, it is difficult to generate a list of principles.[7] Progressives often find it easier to agree on what they are against than what they favor. Progressives generally oppose:

1. Formal types of instruction that feature routine over spontaneity.
2. A prescribed curriculum that emphasizes subject matter over children's interests and needs.
3. Competitive situations that pit children against each other.
4. Instruction geared to test preparation.
5. External incentives, such as rewards and punishments, that are extrinsic rather than intrinsic to learning.

Progressive educators generally favor:

1. Stimulating children's growth and development through activities that encourage initiative, creativity, and self-expression.
2. An experience-referenced curriculum that features activities, process learning, inquiry, and problem solving.
3. Collaborative learning that features group cooperation.
4. Teachers who act as facilitators of learning rather than as task masters.
5. Education that is multifunctional and geared to the whole child—emotionally, physically, socially, and intellectually—rather than exclusively academic.

PROGRESSIVISM AS A THEORY OF EDUCATION

Based on the principles enumerated above, it is possible to comment on various features of Progressivism as a theory of education. Like Pragmatism and Liberalism from which it draws, Progressivism is not concerned with metaphysics, with ultimate questions of being. It takes for granted that we live in a natural world that can be explained scientifically. Though we can never really have certain knowledge, science has generated a long list of probabilities and tentative assertions about knowledge that provide reliable but revisable guides to practice. It is up to the individual to work out social, political, economic, and cultural relationships in ways that are most satisfying for growth and development. Indeed, social knowledge and values are relational—arrived at by participating in satisfying interactions—rather than based on immutable universal beliefs.

Since they regard metaphysical questions as unanswerable in terms of public and scientific verification, Progressives are more concerned with epistemological questions such as: How do we know? What is the most accurate way of knowing? True to the belief in Progress asserted in the Enlightenment, Progressives turn to science—the investigation and verification of natural phenomena—and our experience with it to provide answers to our questions. The Progressive version of knowing was reshaped by Pragmatist emphasis on the theory of relativity. The scientific method provides the most accurate way of knowing; findings, however, are always subject to further research, experimentation, revision, and reinterpretation.

In terms of values—ethics and aesthetics—Progressives discount claims of universally based standards as being without a real-life basis in human experience. Instead of accepting moral absolutes, associated with metaphysically based philosophies, they look to human interactions and relationships. Their approach to ethics and morals is relational—those interactions that work best in interpersonal situations. "Working best" is not an easy term to define. For Progressives, working best occurs in a free and democratic society, where individuals are free to relate to each other. Relationships are judged on what they contribute to human growth, development, culture, and satisfaction. Often, these relationships are grounded in the particular environmental situations—the time and place—in which people live and are relative to what is taking place in these particular cultural situations. It is at this point that Conservatives, Essentialists, and Perennialists accuse Progressives of encouraging ethical relativism—a theory that holds that right and wrong, good and bad, are defined culturally rather than universally. These critics of Progressivism charge that ethical relativism has weakened moral character and created a code of ethics in which "anything goes."

The logic that Progressives tend to use is inductive. They believe that logic is a way of making sense of experience, the interactions with the environment. The scientific method is prized for its adherence to inductive logic. Progressives favor learning that is process-oriented and allows children to create their own beliefs and values through reflection on their interactions with the environment.

Progressives take a large view of education that extends beyond intellectual development defined in academic terms. Their version of the school is that of a multi-functional institution that serves a broad range of individual and social needs. Concerned with the education of the whole person, the school's aims are intellectual, psychological, moral, social, civic, and economic. Progressives warn against the "four walls" philosophy of education that separates schools from their society and the community they serve. Conservatives, Essentialists, and Perennialists, in contrast, say that the Progressive proclivity to try to do everything weakens the school's primary function as an academic institution.

Based on its multiple goals, Progressive curriculum and instruction reject the more traditional Essentialist and Perennialist reliance on predetermined discrete skills and subjects. Rather, Progressives contend that the curriculum should come from children's interests and needs and their exploration of the environment. For Child-Centered Progressives, the exploration of the environment leads to opportunities to stimulate creativity through expressive activities. It also presents occasions in which children can encounter problem-solving situations, work out solutions, and construct their concepts of reality.

Just as the goals of the Progressive school are multifunctional, the instructional repertoire of Progressive teachers needs to be versatile. They need to have informed insight into children's cognitive and emotional growth and development; they need to have a wide range of skill and subject knowledge as a background for teaching; and they need to be skilled in using group dynamics for cooperative learning.

MARIETTA JOHNSON, CHILD-CENTERED PROGRESSIVE EDUCATION

Marietta Johnson, the founder of the School of Organic Education in Fairhope, Alabama , developed the theory of Organic Education that emphasized the principles of Child-Centered Progressivism. The term "organic" came from her idea that the child was a living organism who learned by having the freedom to interact with the environment. Johnson called for child-focused schools that educated the whole child—mentally, physically, socially, and emotionally—in a permissive environment. As you read the selection, you might wish to consider the following focusing questions:

1. How does Johnson define "organic education"? Do you agree or disagree with her approach to education? Why?

2. What is Johnson's view of grouping children for instruction? Do you agree or disagree? Why?

3. How do you think Johnson would react to the contemporary standards and constructivist movements in education?

4. In what way is Johnson's educational theory an example of Child-Centered Progressivism?

. . .

The aim of the school is to study to know and meet the needs of the growing organism; that is, to conduct a school program which will preserve the sincerity and unself-consciousness of the emotional life—provide for the finest, keenest intellectual activity, and minister to the all-round development of the nervous system. Ministering to growth, meeting the needs of the organism, is the sole function of the educational process—hence the term "organic." The child is a reaching organism and the test of the environment is his reaction. A bad child may not come from a good home. However good the home is, it is bad for him or he would be good! Parents and teachers often protest that they treat the children "all alike!" thinking that this is impartial. The only way to be truly impartial is to secure the right reaction! We must constantly bear in mind that we are dealing with a unit organism. As Henderson says, it is impossible to have good health in one part of the organism and ill health in another! It is either good or ill for the entire organism always!

No one knows exactly the needs of childhood, or just how to supply these, but even though the ideal may not be realized at once it is still the high privilege and duty of the adult to try to know. *The* way has not yet been found—the last word has not been spoken. Skeptics sometimes ask, "Will it fit my child?" There is no "it"—but an effort to furnish the best conditions for every child. What those needs are and how they are to be met may never be agreed upon, but we must continue to "reason together" and to study with an open mind. We do not present our program as final. The youngest teacher may find a better way. But we offer the following program as the best we have at this time.

We group the children according to chronological age; this is really the only age of which we may be certain. We think this prevents self-consciousness and we believe the first condition of growth is unself-consciousness.

From Marietta Johnson, *Thirty Years with an Idea*. Tuscaloosa, AL: University of Alabama Press, 1974, pp. 52–55, 62–63, 86–87, 95. Marietta Johnson Museum.

Grouping children according to attainment or achievement gives a wrong conception of education. It gives the child the idea that education consists in meeting the demands of the adult. This self-consciousness may arrest development. Children should grow mentally as they do physically—without effort or strain. Grading makes the child think that an educated person is one who knows a great deal, or has unusual skill, or one who has met the requirements of the system and perhaps has received honors. Isn't it strange that we should feel it right and proper to reward people for learning? Some of the leaders in the progressive schools still contend that an external standard is necessary. Even in religion we constantly hear of a "crown" as the reward of faith or a good life, never realizing that the thought of the *reward* weakens the faith and disfigures the good life!

Learning is merely satisfying mental hunger. If society ever has rewards to offer they should be in recognition of a real contribution in actual service! And this is unnecessary, however, for whole-hearted, disinterested service is always its own reward! Therefore, it seems perfectly logical to eliminate the "reward" idea entirely. We shall never know how much real happiness and joy—yes, power—in the present has been lost, by this subtle fear of the future! This preparation idea!! Adults may fail to minister to growth but a child *cannot* fail. Even the idea of "measuring progress" may develop self-consciousness and be inhibiting—and furthermore, we all know that the *essential* in all progress is immeasurable!

The child should never feel that he must "keep up" with others mentally, any more than he should be stimulated to "keep up" in height or weight. When young children are grouped with older children they often feel superior to those of their own age and the child who is grouped with children much younger may acquire an inferiority complex. Still, it is always better for a child to be a little older than a little younger than his group. In the former case, he is more relaxed and gains poise and confidence.

In the latter, he often suffers strain, which is especially undesirable for the growing child. The child who is fully the age of his group or a trifle older gets more out of his experience—is staying young—while the child grouped with older children is unable to benefit as fully from the experience and is *growing* old!

When the adolescent period is reached there is danger of forcing of the sex and social consciousness. As society becomes more complex, the period of childhood should be prolonged to preserve the power to adjust. The prolonging of childhood is the hope of the race—the longer the time from birth to maturity, the higher the organism. This is true individually as well as biologically. No parent should be proud of a precocious child. Intellectual "brilliance" in the very young may not be the promise of the finest maturity. Henderson says, "Children should be ignorant." This must be a great comfort to parents and teachers!

Children should not strive to get into a higher *grade*. Why should we subject the mental power of the child to measurements and external stimulation more than the physical or spiritual powers? If the body were subjected to the same conscious striving to meet external ends as those for which the mind is stimulated, all real physical vigor would be destroyed and such a process for the spirit would develop the most objectionable hypocrisy. When one sees children trying to "show off" their knowledge or skill, or insisting that certain children do not belong in their class, the elders are to be blamed, not the children. Sometimes children and even parents have complained because others who do not know as much or who have not done as fine work are promoted with them! We are hoping to forget the word "promoted." Education is the process of meeting the needs of children.

The teacher endeavors to provide activities and exercises which are adapted to the stage of development of the group, giving special attention to any individual child. This individual attention should never be of the kind that stimulates a child to "catch up" or "keep up" with the class—nor to "get ahead" or "keep ahead" of anyone—but merely to see that he clearly understands what he is doing. Not so much what one does, as the effect of the work on the pupil.

A college professor tells the story of a student coming to him one day and saying, "I know I am not doing very much this class and I know that you know I am not a good student; but I want you to know I am *getting more* out of this work than I ever did before."

All zest in learning depends upon mental grasp. If the work secures the best mental activity, it is educational. The observing eye of the teacher is necessary to discover when children are using their mental endowment to highest advantage. This is evidenced by eager and sustained interest and resulting satisfactions. It requires no test or examination to discover when children do their best at play. Neither should it be difficult to know when they are doing their best in school work.

. . .

The child who reads early learns to rely upon the printed page for authority and may fail lamentably to understand the meaning of his experiences! The entire race seems quite unable to learn from experience! Isn't it strange that so many people feel there is little or no *learning* except from books? In fact, they often speak of the "tools of learning," meaning symbols. When one considers the immense amount of learning that takes place before the child reaches school age, it is surprising that such emphasis is placed upon books as *tools* of *learning!*

Reading should be postponed until ten years of age. If children were allowed to think through experience, a tendency to wait for data, to search for truth and use it for authority, might be developed. Children tend to act on thinking. This is intelligence. Excessive or too early use of books may interfere. The use of books too early often develops an unsocial attitude. Children are entertained by reading stories when they should be working creatively or playing with others. Many children become quite unfit to live with others as a result of sitting for hours in a bad light, bad position, passively being entertained by a book! The bragging, bossy, irritable, unhappy, self-centered child is quite apt to be the child who reads excessively. We have had children whose behavior was positively subnormal caused by too constant use of books—utterly lacking in ability to meet situations. "My child cannot do anything with his hands, and he enjoys being with adults much more than playing with children," says a perplexed mother.

While information is not the aim in nature study, at this age children are interested to know many things that might escape the notice of younger children. Snakes and toads and all animals are attractive to children if the observation is not pressed upon them. The living creature is studied through actual contact, rather than lessons about them. Gardens are very interesting and excursions and walks and all-day picnics are popular. Our bay is a never-exhausted attraction. Here they may dig in the sand to their hearts content, wade and sail their little boats, build dams, make lakes, waterfalls, islands, and all forms of land and water. The gullies are always stimulating to dramatic or investigating impulses. "Let's play the gods! I'm Jupiter—I'm Juno—I'm Minerva!" shout the children as they troop to the gully. Many happy hours have been spent in the gully dramatizing the old Greek myths and other stories, while the teacher lazily sits on a log in the sun.

Handwork holds a very prominent place on the program, being almost wholly self-prompted and self-directed. Work in color is very fascinating for these children. They love to illustrate poems or stories, using large sheets of paper, large brushes and vivid water colors. Much work in clay is also done quite independently, though the teacher's help is sometimes solicited. But the great joy of children of this age is wood-working. They never tire of the jigsaw, plane, hammer and nails, and sometimes the lathe, and many happy and profitable hours are spent using tools and soft wood. What do they make and how well is the work done? They make many objects for use and some things are well done, but the work is successful if the children enjoy the activity and experience real satisfaction. "Just think, Mother," exclaims a new boy, "You can make what you want, and you can take it home!" They sometimes need help to persist until an object is finished, and occasionally articles begun may be abandoned. . . .

Teachers often take themselves too seriously, they take the work too seriously, they are too conscious of standards of work and behavior. "They've just got to do a month's work in a month," exclaimed an irritable teacher who found it difficult to hold attention without pressure. It is true that an indifferent teacher is always deplorable, but a teacher may be jolly and free and human—and should really *enjoy* his work. "I like Miss K outside school," cried a child. "She is fun at a party—but oh, how strict and sober she is in school!!"

Of course, many children are weak in power of concentration, and assistance may be needed at times to prevent trifling and fooling; but given work suited to their development and an earnest teacher understanding children, as well as the subject, we find that they do concentrate and acquire information and skill without recourse to external goals of accomplishment—passing—or threats of failure!

The situation is sufficient to secure good work and the satisfaction in the activity is sufficient reward! A little girl from another school constantly called attention to herself and her work, and sometimes was guilty of glaring falsehoods, so anxious was she to secure the favorable attention of the adults! Such a spirit could never have developed without the external standard in the minds of both teacher and pupil!

We believe even more is accomplished in the so-called subject matter when enjoying it from day to day without any thought of require-ments, than could possibly be done under pressure—and we believe that the absence of pressure is absolutely essential to growth. We do not encourage children to measure themselves. This is apt to develop self-consciousness which must dull the edge of real learning. "I often talk over the work with the children helping them to compare today's results with former work," said an earnest though mistaken teacher. When one is thinking of his rate of intellectual progress or increase in skill, his mind is divided. He should be able to concentrate utterly upon the activity. Learning is satisfying mental hunger as eating is satisfying physical hunger. If we were obliged to keep track of their learning, nausea and indigestion would certainly result. I wonder if children's withdrawal from the learning program of the schools may not be due to this mental indigestion which may follow the conscious effort of learning.

If they have enjoyed facts and have thought through cause and effect with concentration and with resulting satisfaction—they are growing, being educated, and to measure that experience would be to weaken it.

. . .

There are no special methods of discipline throughout the school. The children must do as they are told because of their unformed condition, but the school is careful what it tells. Throughout the years we have been accused of conducting a "do as you please school" in spite of the fact that I have repeatedly denied this. Children do not know what is best for them. They have no basis for judgment. They need guidance, control, but this must really be for their good, not merely for the convenience of the adult! Every effort is made to have this conformity merge into and become obedience. That is, to get the child's *will* to act in harmony with the adult will. The fundamental condition for securing the cooperation of the child is to cooperate *with* the child. The teacher, therefore, instinctively grants every request that the children make if it is wholesome and possible to do so. Children should *know* that their wishes are respected by the adult!

Not only is this cooperation with the expressed desire of the child important, but the school endeavors to cooperate in a deeper way with the needs of the child's nature; that is, it aims to anticipate his desires by providing activities and exercises which are in harmony with his stage of development and which will secure the sincerest response.

CONCLUSION

Progressivism has often asserted and reasserted itself in American education. Drawing inspiration from the European reformers such as Rousseau and Pestalozzi, American Progressives fashioned their own variety of educational innovation. At times, the Progressive stance rejected the formalism, routine, and bureaucracy found in traditional schools. It rejected conventional subject matter, textbooks, memorization, and competition for grades. With their rejection of traditional schooling, Progressives became proactive agents of educational change.

Progressives see schools as educational laboratories for the testing of new ideas. Envisioning the curriculum as open-ended rather than closed, they see it evolving conjointly from the interests of children and from the guidance of teachers. Rather than relying on prescribed subject matter, they see learning flowing out of experiences and activities. The contemporary innovations of process learning, projects, collaborative learning, and authentic assessment all resonate well with Progressives. Many Progressives see schooling as a process with broad cultural, social, political, and economic implications.

DISCUSSION QUESTIONS

1. Do you believe that most Americans believe in the concept of Progress; that the future will be better than the past?
2. Identify the philosophies and ideologies that have shaped Progressive thinking.
3. Identify the similarities and differences between Child-Centered and Social Reconstructionist Progressivism. Do you believe that these differences can be resolved and compromised in one theory of education?
4. Compare and contrast how Progressives, Essentialists, and Perennialists define education and conceive of the role and function of schools.
5. Do you agree with the broad Progressive view of the school as a multifunctional institution?
6. Do you think that the ethical relativism associated with Progressive education is compatible with the current moral climate in the United States?

INQUIRY AND RESEARCH PROJECTS

1. Do you see evidence of Progressivism in classroom situations that you have observed as part of your professional clinical experience? If so, in a log, record and analyze those examples of Progressivism.

2. Write a position paper in which you describe how Progressives might react to the standards movement and the use of standardized tests to measure student achievement.

3. Devise a lesson plan in which you outline a learning situation based on the Progressive theory of education.

4. Write a position paper in which you describe how Progressives might react to constructivism and to portfolio assessment.

5. Organize a debate on the subject: American public schools should follow Progressive principles of curriculum and instruction.

INTERNET RESOURCES

For recent developments and an active voice for Progressive education, contact the John Dewey Project on Progressive Education at the University of Vermont at
www.uvm.edu/dewey/

For a biography of Jane Addams, contact Women in History at
www.Lkwdpl.org/wihohio/adda-jan.htm

SUGGESTIONS FOR FURTHER READING

Carlson, Dennis. *Making Progress: Education and Culture in New Times.* New York: Teachers College Press, 1996.

Cremin, Lawrence A. *The Transformation of the School: Progressivism in American Education, 1876–1957.* New York: Alfred A. Knopf, 1961.

Dennis, Lawrence J., and Eaton, William E. *George S. Counts: Educator for a New Age.* Carbondale and Edwardsville: Southern Illinois University Press, 1980.

Dewey, John. *Experience and Education: The 60th Anniversary Edition.* West Lafayette, IN: Kappa Delta Pi, 1998.

Graham, Patricia A. *Progressive Education: From Arcady to Academe: A History of the Progressive Education Association, 1919–1955.* New York: Teachers College Press, 1967.

Kliebard, Herbert M. *The Struggle for the American Curriculum, 1893–1958.* Boston: Routledge & Kegan Paul, 1986.

Reese, William J. *Power and Promise of School Reform: Grassroots Movements During the Progressive Era.* Boston: Routledge & Kegan Paul, 1986.

Tanner, Daniel. *Crusade for Democracy: Progressive Education at the Crossroads.* Albany: State University of New York Press, 1991.

Zilversmit, Arthur. *Changing Schools: Progressive Education Theory and Practice, 1930–1960.* Chicago: University of Chicago Press, 1993.

NOTES

1. Gerald L. Gutek, *Pestalozzi and Education* (Prospect Heights, IL: Waveland Press, 1999), pp. ix–xiv, 165–170.

2. Marietta Johnson, *Thirty Years with an Idea* (Tuscaloosa: University of Alabama Press, 1974), pp. 52–55, 62–63, 86–95.

3. The definitive history of the Progressive Education Association is by Patricia Albjerg Graham, *Progressive Education: From Arcady to Academe—A History of the Progressive Education Association, 1919–1955* (New York: Teachers College Press, Columbia University, 1967).

4. For the history of Social Reconstructionism, see Michael E. James, *Social Reconstructionism Through Education: The Philosophy, History, and Curricula of a Radical Ideal* (Norwood, NJ: Ablex, 1995).

5. George S. Counts, *Dare the School Build a New Social Order?* (New York: John Day, 1932), pp. 17–18.

6. John Dewey, *Experience and Education: The 60th Anniversary Edition* (West Lafayette, IN: Kappa Delta Pi, 1998).

7. This list of Progressive educational principles is devised by the author. It borrows from the list of principles stated by the Progressive Education Association. For a discussion of Progressive principles, see Patricia Albjerg Graham, *Progressive Education: From Arcady to Academe—A History of the Progressive Education Association, 1919–1955* (New York: Teachers College Press, Columbia University, 1967).

CHAPTER NINETEEN

CRITICAL THEORY

In this chapter we will examine Critical Theory, one of the leading contemporary educational theories. Critical Theory commands a position among many educators in the Foundations of Education, especially in the social and philosophical areas. As a theory, it is opposed to the trend to neo-Conservatism and the resurgence of Essentialism.

DEFINING CRITICAL THEORY

Critical Theory can be defined as a complex set of working assumptions about society, education, and schooling that question and analyze educational aims, institutions, curriculum, instruction, and relationships in order to raise consciousness and bring about transformative change in society and education. Critical Theory assumptions, derived from Postmodernism and Liberation Pedagogy, argue that society, education, and schooling are arenas in which groups contend for power and control. In particular, Critical Theorists see schools as places of contestation between rival ideologies. Critical Theorists are not neutral in this struggle but are committed advocates of advancing the cause of disempowered and subordinate groups. They use these assumptions to raise questions about who controls educational institutions and determines the content of the curriculum and the methods by which students are instructed. Their goal is to raise the consciousness of teachers and the oppressed members of society about the conditions of exploitation and how they can liberate and empower themselves to take control of their own lives and shape their own future. Transformative change refers to sweeping reforms to the entire social structure as opposed to the small-scale, incremental reforms advocated by Liberals.

Critical Theory's assumptions and working generalizations are based on a philosophical and ideological orientation shaped by Postmodernist and Existentialist philosophies, Liberation ideology, feminist theory, and multiculturalism. The word *critical* refers to engaging in a rigorous probing and analytical investigation of social and educational conditions in schools and society that aims to uncover exploitative power relationships and bring about reforms that will produce equity, fairness, and justice.

The anticipated consequence of this analysis is the empowerment of subordinate classes and groups so that they can determine their own futures in an equitable society.

Critical Theorists believe that many institutions, especially political, economic, and educational ones, maintain and reproduce inequitable and exploitative conditions that favor one group or class, the dominant one, over subordinate groups and classes. They believe people have the right to be self-determined, or empowered, rather than be controlled by those who hold power in institutional life. Self-determination is possible if people become conscious of and overthrow the forces that cause their exploitation.

THE CRITICAL THEORIST STRATEGY

To understand the Critical Theorist approach to the problems of education and schooling we will look at its: (1) theoretical core of guiding principles or assumptions; (2) critique of existing institutions; (3) agenda for deliberate change or reform.

Theoretical Guiding Principles or Assumptions

Critical Theorists approach education, especially schools, as agencies in need of far-reaching reforms. They begin with an allegiance to several important theoretical principles or assumptions. Institutions, including schools, are controlled by the dominant classes and groups and are centers of conflict between competing classes and groups. An individual's social status, including educational and economic expectations and opportunities, are largely conditioned by how a society constructs the meaning of race, ethnicity, gender, and class. The dominant, higher socioeconomic class controls social, political, economic, and educational institutions, including schools. The dominant class uses their control to maintain, or reproduce, their favored position and to subordinate socially and economically disadvantaged classes. Schools, through both the official and hidden curriculum, are used by the dominant class to reproduce the status quo that ensures their dominance.

Critical Theorists believe that it is possible, through a critical education, for the subordinated classes and groups to become conscious of their exploitation, to resist domination, to overturn the pattern of domination, and to determine their own futures through their self-empowerment. In the United States, the historically marginalized groups are the urban and rural poor, African, Hispanic, and Native Americans, women, and gays and lesbians. The conditions of marginality in the larger society are reinforced by the school's organization and curriculum.[1] Educational policy and practice, informed by Critical Theory, can become a force to empower these marginalized groups and to secure greater equity, fairness, and justice throughout the United States and other countries.

The Critique

Much of the Critical Theorist approach is devoted to developing a critique of existing institutions. The critique is conducted both at the micro level, investigating the forces operating internally within schools, and at the broader macro level, which includes the historical, social, political, and economic conditions in the larger society.[2] Guided by their working assumptions, Critical Theorists ask such questions as: Who controls the schools and what are their motives? How are educational resources allocated and who benefits from this allocation? Who makes the policies that govern schools and who benefits from these policies? Who determines the goals and expectations of schools? Who establishes the curriculum? What is the nature of the curriculum in terms of race, ethnicity, language, class, and gender? What power do teachers really have over the educational process? How and why are students grouped? How is student academic achievement assessed and measured?

Critical Theorists answer these questions by referring to their theoretical assumptions and then examining schools in specific communities. They begin their critique at the micro level—in the particular school—by assembling statistics, case studies, and the stories of those who teach in, and attend, them. This examination leads to the following findings. Schools in economically disadvantaged urban and declining rural areas are attended predominately by the poor, by African Americans and Hispanic Americans, and are typically old, deteriorating, under-financed and lacking adequate resources.

Still using microanalysis, the Critical Theorist turns to an examination of conditions within the school. They are likely to find that the typical inner-city school is enmeshed in a large educational bureaucracy that operates in a hierarchical, top-down style. With orders coming down from the higher levels, there is little opportunity for local governance or teacher decision making. The curriculum, too, is determined by and handed down from higher-level administrators, with little room for local initiatives that could relate to the life experiences of students in the school or people in the community. Teachers within the school tend to be isolated from each other, teaching in self-contained, insulated classrooms. They tend to have little or no power in setting goals or in making decisions about curriculum and instruction. Further, parents and others in the local community are kept at a distance, with little involvement or interaction allowed with the school.

After the microanalysis, the Critical Theorist critique broadens its scope and moves to the communities the schools serve. The inner city or isolated rural community, like the school, is beleaguered by endemic social, economic, and political problems. It is often physically and socially isolated from the health, recreational, and cultural resources of the larger society. There is often a high unemployment rate among adults in the community. The community is likely to be ineffectively organized to secure greater political representation. There is likely to be a high incidence of street gangs, and drug and alcohol abuse.

Next, the micro critique is connected to the larger social, political, and economic analysis of the Critical Theorist theoretical perspective. The immediate problems faced by local schools mirror those faced in the larger state, regional, and national contexts. Society is controlled by the affluent, who exercise enormous influence on politicians and the media. Often living in gated residential areas in the large cities or comfortable wealthy suburbs, the affluent have isolated themselves from the problems in the inner cities and declining rural areas. Nevertheless, they control institutions, including schools, throughout the country. Following a neo-Marxist mode of analysis, Critical Theorists contend that the power of the affluent governing class comes from their control of the capitalist corporate economy.[3] (See the chapter on Marxism for a

■ ■ ■ ■ ■

THE CRITICAL THEORY STRATEGY

- Use guiding theoretical assumptions from Postmodernism, neo-Marxism, Liberation Pedagogy, Feminist Theory, and Multiculturalism
- Conduct a rigorous microanalysis of conditions and relationships within schools
- Connect the microanalysis to a larger macroanalysis of historical, economic, political, and social forces
- Develop an agenda to raise the consciousness of, and to empower, members of marginalized groups

further discussion.) The members of the favored class use schools to maintain their power by educating their children in well-financed schools that prepare them for entry to prestigious colleges and universities and for positions of importance within the corporate and government structures. Invested in keeping things as they are, they use their power and influence to reproduce the system that gives them control. Children of the less economically favored classes, indoctrinated in the approved official curriculum constructed by the powerful class, are conditioned to accept subordinate roles at the margins of the existing society.

Education for Empowerment

For Critical Theorists, their critique of society and schools is not merely an academic exercise but is an attempt to create a real agenda for deliberate transformative change. Influenced by Freire's Liberation Pedagogy, they argue that the genuine role of education is to raise the consciousness of dispossessed, marginalized groups.[4] As they learn about the real causes of their subordinate situation, the marginalized will find the courage to work toward their own empowerment.

Critical Theorists, using a Freirean mode of dialogue, urge teachers to begin raising the consciousness of the students in their classes with an examination of the conditions in their communities. (Freire is discussed in Chapter 14.) Each student has her or his own life story to share; these autobiographies can form a collective story that describes what they are experiencing in school, in their homes, and in their neighborhood. These life stories can be connected with the larger histories of the economic classes and the racial, ethnic, and language groups of which they are members. After exploring their own identities and meanings, students, guided by teachers, can work to develop ways to recognize stereotyping and misrepresentation and to resist indoctrination both in and out of school. They can learn how to take control of their own lives and shape their own futures. This kind of micro-level change can be the base from which larger macro reforms can take place.

SITUATING CRITICAL THEORY

Critical Theory gained a major foothold during the 1960s, a period of intense social change marked by the civil rights movement, a concerted effort by African, Hispanic, and Native Americans to organize for increased political, economic, and educational representation and opportunities. During the 1960s, the women's rights movement began a renewed effort to secure equal rights, employment opportunities, and compensation for women. Environmentalist groups campaigned against the degradation of the natural environment and for greater conservation of natural resources. Gays and lesbians went public with their demands for recognition of their right to an alternative lifestyle and against discriminatory practices in education and employment. The period was also a time of protests, mainly by disaffected students and intellectuals, against the American corporate structure and its political allies. The flash point that galvanized much of the protests was the United States' role and involvement in the war in Vietnam.[5]

While these events were taking place nationally and globally, American education was responding to the challenge of ending racial segregation and achieving racial integration. As part of President Lyndon Johnson's War on Poverty, schools were enlisted as socioeducational agencies to develop programs to educate the urban and rural poor. Johnson's efforts were largely undone, however, by his leadership role in involving the United States in the morass in Vietnam.

In educational philosophy and theory, several trends converged in the late 1960s that paved the way for Critical Theory to emerge as one of the leading theories of education. Liberals were under attack as major contributors to the control of the United States by what was called the "military-industrial complex" and Liberal ideology was increasingly challenged by more radical theorists. At the same time, Philosophical or Language Analysis was beginning to weaken as the dominant philosophy among educational theorists. More radical theorists were attracted to the Frankfurt School of sociology and philosophy associated with Jürgen Habermas and with the Liberation Pedagogy of Ivan Illich and Paulo Freire.[6] Postmodernism came on the scene with work by the prominent French philosophers Jacques Derrida and Michel Foucault. (See the chapter on Postmodernism for more information.)

While certain strong voices in educational theory were moving to the left in social and political thinking, a very strong neo-Conservative movement came to power with the election of Ronald Reagan in 1980. Margaret Thatcher was also leading a strong Conservative renaissance in the United Kingdom. The Soviet Union and its satellites collapsed in eastern Europe and the Cold War ended after more than fifty years. With the Soviet Union's demise, state socialism, or Marxism-Leninism, was discredited. The world economy, led by the United States, began to follow the principles of free-market theory, reduced government controls, and economic deregulation. In American education, the neo-Conservative political ascendancy was marked by the resurgence of a new Essentialism, called Basic Education, the emergence of the standards movement, a greater association of schooling with economic training, and mandated achievement testing.[7] (See Chapter 12 for a discussion of Conservatism and Chapter 16 for Essentialism.)

Critical Theorists, already subscribing to Postmodernism and Liberation Pedagogy, voiced strong opposition to the neo-Conservative and neo-Essentialist ascendancy in education. They challenged what they considered to be the stratagems of the political right with a counterattack led by Henry Giroux and Peter McLaren. Their theory contains significant elements from Marxism but without Marx's metanarrative worldview and determinism. Giroux credits Samuel Bowles and Herbert Gintis for their Marxist interpretation of education in a capitalist society. (For a discussion of Bowles and Gintis, see Chapter 13 on Marxism.)

CRITICAL THEORY'S PHILOSOPHICAL AND IDEOLOGICAL RELATIONSHIPS

Critical theory has been influenced by Marxism, much of which came by way of theoreticians associated with the Frankfurt School of sociology in Germany, especially the ideas of Jürgen Habermas. Certain Marxist concepts such as the central role of economics in social change, class struggle for control of the means and modes of production, and alienation have influenced Critical Theorists. Critical Theorists have modified and revised these Marxist concepts in order to reduce their ideological rigidity, making them more flexible tools for social and educational analysis. They use these concepts as analytical tools in studying society, education, and schools, rather than as specific dialectical recipes for creating a revolutionary society. For example, Critical Theorists, like Marx, argue that social institutions, including schools, are strongly influenced by economic forces, especially by those who control the means and modes of production. For Marx, however, this control was determined by inexorable dialectical forces. While Marxist revolutionaries could identify and join these forces, the course of historical events that would lead to the overthrow of capitalism was historically destined to occur. Revising the Marxist view of historical inevitability, Critical Theorists believe that education can play a much larger role in bringing about social, political, and economic change.

Critical Theorists have also been influenced by the Marxist concept that history is the record of the struggle for ownership and control of the means and modes of production. Marx believed that the inevitable struggle was between the proletariat (the working class) and the capitalists. The proletariat, predicted Marx, was destined to triumph and would establish a classless society. Critical Theorists agree with Marx on the importance of class struggle and control. Focusing on schools as social institutions, they argue that in contemporary America, educational institutions are controlled by the powerful economic classes—the wealthy who are invested in the corporate economy. The educational needs of less-favored economic groups are subordinated to those of the rich and powerful. The struggle for control in schools takes the form of domination of the curriculum. It is through the control of governance of schools and the curriculum that the upper classes subordinate the lower classes.

The Critical Theorists also make use of the Marxist concept of alienation. In a capitalist society, the workers are exploited by those who control the means and modes of production—the industries, businesses, and corporations. They do not receive the benefits of their labor; instead, the value that they create through their work is expropriated by the capitalists as profits. As a result, workers in a capitalist society face social and psychological alienation from their work and from the products or commodities they are making. Critical Theorists use the concept of alienation in broader terms to refer to the social and psychological state of people who have been driven to the peripheries of society—the homeless and those who live in poverty. In addition to the economically destitute, others have been alienated or marginalized in modern society—African Americans, Hispanics, women, and gays and lesbians, for example. The educational struggle, according to Critical Theorists, takes place in the immediate situation and condition of schools, where they are right now. The struggle takes the form of raising the consciousness of the alienated so that they can empower themselves and take their rightful place in society.

Critical Theory has also been influenced by Liberation Pedagogy, especially by the ideas of Ivan Illich and Paulo Freire, two educators who worked in Latin America. (See Chapter 14 for a discussion of Liberation Pedagogy.) Both of these educators, while concerned with education worldwide, developed many of their ideas by working with economically disadvantaged people in less technologically developed societies. Illich worked mostly in Mexico and Freire in Brazil. Illich, in *Deschooling Society*, argued that Western schooling was an instrument of neocolonialist exploitation and repression of the people in less technologically developed societies in Asia, Africa, and South America. Schooling had become a great "sales pitch" in that it imposed capitalist, consumerist ideas on the children of the working class and peasantry, conditioning them to want products that they shouldn't have and didn't need. It also conditioned people to believe that all learning had to take place in institutions, rather than in voluntary associations.[8] Critical Theorists tend to reject Illich's call for the elimination of schools. Rather, they believe that it is possible to change and reform schools so that they are not agencies designed to create a great mass of like-minded people, driven by the appetite to consume. Illich's work, however, has influenced Critical Theorists to think of the struggle to empower the dispossessed in global terms, in which the marginalized groups in the United States are connected to the oppressed in less technologically developed societies.

Paulo Freire has been an inspiration for many Critical Theorists. In *The Pedagogy of the Oppressed*, Freire called for education that would raise peoples' consciousness about the reality of their economic and social condition and encourage them to take the necessary steps for their own empowerment. Freire was especially concerned with helping the poor, landless farmers and the urban slum dwellers to become literate so that they could better understand their situation and the causes of their exploitation. Freire, himself, borrowed some Marxist concepts, such as economic condition and class conflict, as do the Critical Theorists. However, he adamantly rejected Marxist and other forms of determinism. He insisted that the human project was not finished and that each person, especially the dispossessed, needed to be empowered to undertake their own self-determined project.[9] Freire's strong admonition that education should lead to consciousness raising and self-determination have been themes embraced by many Critical Theorists.

Critical Theory also includes some crucial themes from Postmodern philosophy. It rejects the metaphysical structures of the more traditional philosophies such as Idealism and Realism. It opposes the modernist claims, arising from the Enlightenment, that it is possible to use science and the social sciences to generate objective knowledge claims. Like Postmodernists, Critical Theorists are suspicious of metanarratives that claim universal validity. As is the case with Derrida, Foucault, and other Postmodernists, Critical Theorists are concerned with the critical analysis, or deconstruction, of the texts and dialogues used to generalize about the human social experience. They see these texts as statements justifying the domination, or hegemony, of powerful groups and classes at a given time in history. Thus, Philosophical Analysis, or Language Analysis, if it is used critically, can be a useful tool. Critical analysis of language, however, is not simply clarifying language statements, but rather tracing their origin and examining how different groups, at different times, have constructed and used words as instruments of power.[10]

Critical Theory has a tenuous and sometimes strained relationship with Pragmatism and Progressivism. Critical Theorists value the Pragmatist contention that our conceptions of social reality are constructions arising from the relationships we have with other individuals in a shared environment. However, they question the emphasis that Dewey and other Pragmatists give to the use of the scientific method as a complete act of thought. For them, the scientific method, as an extension of modernist Enlightenment ideology in education, is just another historically generated construction favored by a certain group.

Some Critical Theorists might find a relationship to Progressivism's emphasis on reform. However, they would question the Child-Centered Progressives' antagonism to espousing particular political, social, and economic goals as a failure to recognize the ideological nature of education. They would find more compatibility with Social Reconstructionists who argue that schools should be agencies for creating a new social order.

THE CHALLENGE OF EDUCATIONAL THEORY

For Critical Theorists, the challenge of educational theory is to redefine the purpose and meaning of education, schooling, curriculum, and instruction in terms that accurately describe social reality. To do this requires an exposure to the body of ideas derived from metaphysics and metanarratives, especially those that originated in the Enlightenment and espouse modernism. Critical Theorists see their challenge as not engaging in mere academic exercises, but using theory to effect a program of profound social change.

CRITICAL THEORY AND EDUCATION AND SCHOOLING

Aims of Education

Critical Theorists believe that the aims of education are related to larger social, political, and economic goals of establishing greater equality and equity for people. In particular, education should aim to raise the consciousness of those who have been consigned to lesser, marginal, and subordinate positions in society due to their membership in a particular racial, ethnic, language, class, or gender group. Such consciousness raising is necessary as a first step to empowerment.

Schools

The Critical Theorist view of schools is ideological and political in that they are seen as places in which groups vie for power and control. They tend to view schools in a historical perspective and as places of possibility for human liberation. Often relying on interpretations from revisionist history, Critical Theorists contend that schools have been controlled and used by the economically, politically, and socially dominant classes for purposes of social maintenance and control. To maintain the status quo that allows them to keep their commanding position, the children of the dominant classes are provided with the kind of education that enables them to attend prestigious schools and colleges that will prepare them for high-level careers in business, industry, and government. Children of subordinate groups and classes are indoctrinated to accept the conditions that disempower them. The curriculum is used to confirm or legitimatize and transmit the dominant class's construction of reality. Schools, thus, are not ideologically neutral institutions but rather are used to empower some and disempower others.

While the powerful classes have dominated schools historically, Critical Theorists do not believe this domination is inevitable. They challenge the ideology that justifies and rationalizes control of schools by the favored classes and they seek to break the cycle of domination. They believe it is possible to raise the consciousness of the exploited, to deconstruct the texts that support domination, to expose the conditions of domination, and to organize and empower the dispossessed. Schools can become truly democratic public spheres in which young people learn to live a life of equality.

Values

Unlike the Idealists, Realists, Thomists, and Perennialists, who see values as arising from universal rational or spiritual principles, Critical Theorists see values—ethics and aesthetics—as resulting from informed public discourse and from putting equity and equality into practice. Using their own lives as an initial point of discussion, every person can enter into the discourse about what is right or wrong, beautiful or ugly. Genuine values, say Critical Theorists, are not imposed by those in power but result from the communal interface and sharing by individuals whose voices have an equal right to be heard.

Teachers should encourage students to voice their beliefs and concerns about what they hold to be correct conduct and what they prize. This helps students understand how their peers feel about what is right and wrong. Hearing the different voices raised in the shared discourse, they will come to value the idea that there is a pluralism of values, not just the officially imposed set of values. Such ethical discourse aims to help students find their voice, learn how to articulate their beliefs and feelings, learn to value the opinions of other, and become aware of those who would interfere with or close off the dialogue. Beginning with the individual's lone voice, the goal is to build the volume of voices, like a chorus, to incorporate many melodies and tones. Teachers should guide the ethical discussion so that it gradually enlarges so that students see the injustice of the silencing of those who are at the margins.

Empowering Teachers

As they do with education and schooling, Critical Theorists critique the situation of teachers in the United States and present an agenda for teacher empowerment. Historically, they find that elementary- and secondary-school teachers have been severely limited in determining their own professional life. The majority of elementary school teachers, since the late nineteenth century, have been women who are underpaid in contrast to males in the general workforce. Although they are considered professionals, their generally lower salaries place them in the lower-middle classes. Entry requirements for teaching are established by state authorities rather than by the body of teachers themselves. The schools are governed by boards of education that typically represent the favored socioeconomic classes. The administration of schools is controlled by educational bureaucrats who see to it that the knowledge, beliefs, and values of the ruling classes are imposed on subordinate groups.

Along with the long-standing historical features that have disempowered teachers, several contemporary trends add to weakening of teacher power. The school effectiveness movement, as determined by the Conservative neo-Essentialist agenda, defines student achievement and teacher competency in terms of results on standardized tests. Teachers and schools are judged by how well students score on these tests, which are mandated by state legislators and prepared by those outside of the particular school. Thus, an external system has been imposed on teachers that orients instruction to the tests rather than to teachers' educational aims.

Endorsing consciousness raising by critical dialogue, Critical Theorists urge teachers to take on a deep and far-reaching examination of the conditions in and out of schools that have caused their disempowerment and the miseducation of their students. In addition to critiquing the system of bureaucratically controlled schools, they need to be aware of the broader socioeconomic and political factors that have disempowered the poor, racial and ethnic minorities, and women in the United States. Rather than reacting to change from above, they need to become agents for real and deep social and educational change. They need to:

- Find their true allies in the struggle for control of schools.
- Learn who their students are by helping them to achieve their own identity.
- Interact with the people in the local communities to work for community improvement.
- Join like-minded teachers in collegial organizations that are controlled by teachers and work for real educational reform.
- Participate in a larger critical dialogue about the political, social, economic, and educational issues confronting American society.[11]

Curriculum and Instruction

As with the other areas of education and schooling, Critical Theorists approach curriculum first with a critique of the existing situation and then with a program for reform. Curriculum is seen as existing in two dimensions or layers: the overt, formal, official curriculum and the "hidden" curriculum. The official curriculum includes the skills and the subjects—the prescribed approved program imposed on students. The "hidden" curriculum refers to those values, behaviors, and attitudes conveyed to and imposed on students through the milieu and practices of the school in a capitalist consumer-oriented society. Both the official and the "hidden" curriculum represent the knowledge claims and value preferences of the dominant group or class that controls the school system.

The dominant classes use the official curriculum to reinforce the status quo that gives them power, wealth, and status. They use it to present their particular beliefs and values as the legitimate version of knowledge for all students. For example, they have constructed a version of history that portrays the American experience as a largely European American series of triumphs in settling and industrializing the nation. The heroes in this version of history are typically white males of northern European ethnicity. African, Hispanic, and Native Americans are relegated to the margins of historical narratives. Industrial capitalism is favorably presented, with little discussion about the exploitation of workers or environmental pollution. The American role in foreign affairs is generally presented as altruistic. Bilingual and multicultural education is viewed with suspicion as a challenge to the dominance of English as the semiofficial national language.

The favored method of instruction is using textbooks to transmit information to students. This process of transmission, instead of encouraging critical thinking and analysis, tends to reproduce the approved text—the officially constructed version of knowledge.

A key element in social control via the school is lodged in the hidden curriculum. It is called hidden because it does not appear in published state mandates or local school policies; however, it permeates the ideology and milieu of the public school. The early emphasis on "this is mine and that is yours" developed in early-childhood education begins to build an attitude supportive of the capitalist consumer-driven mentality. The sexist attitude that males are better in mathematics and science courses than females builds a gender-specific attitude that affects subsequent education and careers.

The way students are arranged, scheduled, and grouped in school tends to stream similar students together. Homogeneous grouping, although justified in terms of academic ability, actually reproduces and perpetuates socioeconomic stratification in schools. It tends to reproduce the classism, racism, and sexism of the larger society.

After exposing how the dominant class uses the curriculum and school structure to reproduce itself, Critical Theorists turn to strategies that can change the socioeducational situation so that it empowers those who are currently disadvantaged by the status quo. Just as the metanarratives purporting to stand for universal knowledge are deconstructed, so are the texts that support the traditional curriculum. The subject areas that reinforce the beliefs of the dominant group can be scrutinized, dissected, analyzed, and deconstructed. While these fields were constructed by the dominant group, they can be deconstructed by those who are disempowered. This analysis can raise the consciousness of both teachers and students about claims to legitimate knowledge and can dissolve artificially constructed boundaries between subjects.

Critical Theorists believe that the knowledge and values that are truly legitimate in schools and curriculum arise in the local context and the immediate situation in which students live, and in the school they attend. The Critical Theorist curriculum would begin with the students' own life stories, which they tell to each other. In the multicultural U. S. society, there would be many versions of the story of the American experience, rather than a single, officially approved one. Members of each race, ethnic, and language group would give voice to their own story. A convergence of life stories is likely to take place as similarities and differences are found. It is from these autobiographical beginnings that a historical mosaic of the United States as a multicultural society could arise.

Critical Theorists emphasize that life is lived in a context and that the community in which the school is located is a microcosm of the larger society. The place to begin the study of science, social studies, the working world, and the environment is with the context in which students live. The issues and the problems of the community are those that can be examined in terms of who holds power and who does not; in terms of who is at the center of American political, economic, and social life and who is at the margins. Based on an ethics of equity and equality, the aim of a critical education is to identify the causes of marginality, to challenge them, and to bring the marginalized into control of their own destinies.

Critical Theorists assert that the purpose of instruction through dialogue is to create, rather than transmit or force-feed, knowledge. Students' autobiographies, images, reflections, and interactions create their own knowledge and values rather than imposing other-constructed versions through the official curriculum.

Given the kind of far-ranging dialogue that Critical Theorists advocate, the boundaries that separate one subject from another are deliberately dissolved. They regard subject matter boundaries as human constructions, often defined by academic elites. This approach to curriculum organization is diametrically opposed to the Aristotelian idea that the concepts found in different subjects are naturally related. Rather than being subject-specific, as advocated by Essentialists and Perennialists, the curriculum is interdisciplinary and transdisciplinary. Critical Theorists also reject the concept of a hierarchy of knowledge that judges some subjects to be more important than others. Dialogue is not limited by being located in literature, science, and history, for example, but uses all these disciplines and moves from one to another, depending on what needs to be said and examined. Moving from one discipline to another leads to education that cuts across them all and becomes transdisciplinary.

■ ■ ■ ■ ■

HENRY A. GIROUX, SCHOOLING AND CULTURAL POLITICS

In this selection, Henry A. Giroux, a leading advocate of Critical Theory, argues that schools must be seen as places of conflict between dominant and subordinate groups. He calls for teachers to be students of the cultural politics, especially the discourses, that shape schools, curriculum, and instruction either into agencies of reproducing the patterns of domination and subordination found in the larger society, or as places of liberation. As you read the selection, you may wish to consider the following focusing questions:

1. What does Giroux mean when he refers to schools as "socially constructed sites of contestation"? Do you accept or reject his definition? Why?

2. How are self-images organized around constructions of gender, race, class, ethnicity, and age? How do these constructions influence curriculum and instruction?

3. What is the meaning of Giroux's concept of a "pedagogy of difference"? What are the implications of this pedagogy for teachers?

4. Why is the analysis of language so important for Giroux?

5. How do teachers and students construct different forms of knowledge?

To view schooling as a form of cultural politics suggests that teachers can both elaborate and implement empowering pedagogical practices, and it is to this issue that I will now turn. The search for a radical pedagogy informed by a cultural politics involves the task of creating theoretical models that provide a critical discourse for analyzing schools as socially constructed sites of contestation actively involved in the production of knowledge, skills, and lived experiences. Central to this approach is the need to understand how pedagogical practice represents a particular politics of experience, or, in more exact terms, a cultural field where knowledge, discourse, and power intersect so as to produce historically specific modes of authority and forms of moral and social regulation.

Such an approach makes central the need to analyze how human experiences are produced, contested, and legitimated within the dynamics of everyday classroom life. The theoretical importance of this type of analysis is linked directly to the need for teachers to fashion a language in which a comprehensive politics of culture, voice, and experience can be developed. At issue here is the recognition that schools are historical and cultural institutions that always embody ideological and political interests and that signify reality in ways that are often actively named and contested by various individuals and groups. Schools in this sense are ideological and political spheres in which more often than not the dominant culture attempts to produce knowledge and subjectivities consistent with its own interests; but it is important to stress that schools cannot be reduced to a mirror image of the dominant society. They are also places where dominant and subordinate groups define and constrain each other through an ongoing battle and exchange in response to the sociohistorical conditions "carried" in the institutional, textual, and lived practices that define school culture and teacher and student experience within a particular specificity of time, space, and place. In other words, schools are anything but ideologically innocent; nor are they simply reproductive of dominant social relations and interests. At the same time, as previously mentioned, schools do exercise forms of political and moral regulation intimately connected with technologies of power that "produce asymmetries in the abilities of individuals and groups to define and realize their needs."

More specifically, schools establish the conditions under which some individuals and groups define the terms by which others live, resist, affirm, and participate in the construction of their own identities and subjectivities. Central to recognizing the insight that schools are agencies of moral and political regulation is the notion that power is productive of knowledge, meaning, and values. But, as Teresa de Lauretis points out, "We have to make distinctions between the positive effects and the oppressive effects of such production." In pedagogical terms, this means being able to identify the ways in which the complex associations of habits, relations, meanings, desires, representations, and self-images are organized around the construction of gender, race, class, ethnicity, and age considerations in the production of different forms of subjectivity and ways of life. Again, as Lauretis argues, it is imperative that educators and others come to understand how subjectivity, experience, and desire interrelate within specific technologies of power that name and legitimate differences that both enable and limit or punish differentially empowered groups in this society.

Lauretis's work suggests the need to develop what I will call a *pedagogy of difference* and a *pedagogy for difference*. In the first instance, it is important that educators come to understand theoretically how difference is constructed through various representations and practices that name, legitimate, marginalize, and exclude the cultural capital and voices of various groups in American society; similarly, a pedagogy *of* difference needs to address the important question of how the representations and practices of difference are actively learned, internalized, challenged, or transformed. For it is only through such an understanding that teachers can develop a pedagogy *for* difference, one which is characterized by "an ongoing effort to create new spaces of discourse, to rewrite cultural narratives, and to define the terms of another perspective—a view from 'elsewhere.'" This

suggests a critical pedagogy in which there is a critical interrogation of the silences and tensions that exist between the master narratives and hegemonic discourses that make up the official curriculum of the school and the self-representations of subordinate groups as they might appear in "forgotten" histories, texts, memories, experiences, and community narratives. A pedagogy *for* difference not only seeks to understand how difference is constructed in the intersection of the official curriculum of the school and the various voices of students from subordinate groups; it also brings into play all of the contradictions within the multiple subject positions that characterize the subjectivities of the students themselves. The voices that characterize various groups of students are not of one piece, reducible merely to the categories of class, race, or gender; they are produced within cultural formations that create historically constituted subject-positions which are often shifting and multiple. These subject-positions are constructed within horizons of meaning, habit, and practice that are available in ways both determined and limited by the discourse, cultural context, and historically specific relations that constitute the conditions and parameters of student voice. Not only do these historically specific associations and positions construct students in gendered, racial, and class-specific terms, but they also provide the basis for making the practices of subjectification problematic and the object of political and theoretical reflection.

A pedagogy of and for difference does not merely illuminate the welter of conflicting ideologies and social relations that operate within the public and private spheres of students' lives; it also attempts to have students engage their experiences through "political, theoretical, self analyzing practice by which the relations of the subject in social reality can be rearticulated from the historical experience of women [or from the historical experiences of blacks, Latinos, poor working-class males, etc.]." This approach to the related issues of subjectivity and difference further suggests that the issues of language and experience need to become central categories in a theory of schooling as a form of cultural politics. It is to these issues that I will now turn.

By defining schools as sites of contestation and cultural production, it becomes possible to engage forms of self- and social representations, along with the practices and interests they articulate, as historically specific cultural practices that construct as well as block the exercise of human agency among students. This becomes clearer by recognizing that one of the most important elements at work in the construction of experience and subjectivity in schools is language. In this case, language intersects with power in the way particular linguistic forms structure and legitimate the ideologies of specific groups. Intimately related to power, language functions to both position and constitute the way that teachers and students define, mediate, and understand their relation to each other, school knowledge, the institution of schooling, and the larger society. The notion that meaning is constituted in language is a crucial insight, but it is equally important to recognize that what is actually chosen as meaningful within a range of historically constituted meanings is what gives cultural and political substance to the pedagogical practice of agency and identity formation. Students make choices, not as autonomous, free-floating "subjects" in the manner argued by liberal humanism, but within a range of historically constituted conditions and discursive boundaries. However, it needs to be stressed that students are not merely positioned into discovering meanings; they also actively construct meaning by analyzing the "real practices and events" that constitute their everyday lives. The main point here is that although language constitutes meaning, it is not, as Linda Alcoff points out, "the sole source and locus of meaning, [and] that habits and practices are crucial to the construction of meaning, and that through self-

analyzing practices we can rearticulate. . . [the] matrix of habits, practices, and discourses" that constitute our subjectivity. In this case, language *and* practice provide the intersecting constructions that make the notion of 'choice' an element of lived experience that both constitutes the basis for theorizing a notion of subjectivity and simultaneously makes it the object of pedagogical inquiry. As part of a wider pedagogical task, this suggests making the notion of subjectivity not merely problematic but also the point of a political inquiry regarding how the particulars of human will, identity formation, investments of meaning, and desire are implicated and constructed regarding how people learn to consent, resist, negotiate, and live out their lives within a wide range of signifying practices and meanings.

As a form of cultural politics, a radical pedagogy must insist upon analyzing language as a central force in carrying the historical weight of already constituted meanings as well as a major force in the production of meanings that are constantly being generated as part of the discourse of opposition and affirmation. Discourse in this sense is not merely a meaning system over which one struggles, that is, not simply a system of signification whose real meanings need to be uncovered and demystified. Such an approach to language is important but insufficient for a radical pedagogy. Foucault illuminates a broader approach in his claim that "discourse in not simply that which expresses struggles or systems of domination, but that for which, and by which one struggles; it is the power which one is striving to seize." In this sense, the relationship between language and power is not reduced solely to its oppressive, hegemonic functions. On the contrary, language is viewed more dialectically to include its productive, positive moments as part of the wider issue of voice, as a discourse that produces and confirms particular ways of life. This position represents one of the most important pedagogical tenets of a cultural politics: the necessity for teachers to work with the knowledge that students actually use to give meaning to the truth of their often difficult lives, to construct meaning out of their own narratives: in other words, knowledge that is often derived within the context of the intersection of mass and popular cultures, neighborhood life, family experiences, and the historical memories and contradictory narratives that define one's sense of identity and place.

With the above theoretical assumptions in mind, I want to argue in more specific terms for the development of curricula that embody a form of cultural politics. In effect, I want to present the case for constructing a pedagogy of cultural politics around a critically affirmative language that allows teachers to understand how subjectivities are produced within those social forms in which people move but which are often only partially understood. Such a pedagogy makes problematic how teachers and students sustain, resist, or accommodate those languages, ideologies, social processes, and myths that position them within existing relations of power and dependency. Moreover, it points to the need to develop a theory of politics and culture that analyzes discourse and voice as a continually shifting balance of resources and practices in the struggle for privileging specific ways of naming, organizing, and experiencing social reality. Discourse in this case can be recognized as a form of cultural production, linking "agency" and "structure" through the ways in which public and private representations are concretely organized and mediated within schools. Furthermore, discourse can be acknowledged as a diverse and fractured set of experiences that are lived, enjoyed, and suffered by individuals and groups within specific contexts and settings. In this perspective, the relationship between language and experience is governed by social practices and power relations operating within historically specific contexts. . . .

. . .

In this view the concept of experience is

linked to the broader issue of how subjectivities are inscribed and taken up within cultural processes and power relations that develop with regard to the social and cultural dynamics of production, transformation, and struggle. Understood in these terms, a pedagogy of cultural politics presents a twofold task for teachers. First, they need to analyze how cultural production is organized, within asymmetrical relations of power, through the knowledge, codes, competencies, values, and social relations that constitute the totality of schooling as a lived experience. Second, teachers need to construct political strategies for participating both in and out of schools in social struggles designed to fight for schools as democratic public spheres, that is, as places where students are educated to be active, critical citizens willing to struggle for the imperatives and principles of a meaningful and substantive democracy.

In order to make these tasks realizable, it is necessary to understand classroom social relations as historically constructed cultural forms that produce and legitimate particular experiences that should be the object of inquiry rather than merely the starting points for a theory of schooling. For example, teachers need to be able to examine critically how subjectivities are schooled and what the codes are that govern and give meaning to specific forms of moral and political regulation. But teachers need to do more than provide a critical reading of the cultural forms that structure classroom life; they also need to admit social relations and classroom practices in which needs and ideologies can be experienced and subjectively felt and that legitimate progressive values and democratic forms of sociality. In this case, knowledge, power, and desire provide central categories for understanding how experiences are constructed and reconstructed across social relations that embody varying forms of inequality, dependence, and resistance. As mentioned previously, I take as a starting point here a view of cultural politics that first confirms the lived experience and cultural capital of students so that the latter can then be analyzed more critically as part of a wider set of cultural processes. In this case, student experience has to first be understood and recognized as the accumulation of collective memories and stories that provide students with a sense of familiarity, identity, and practical knowledge. Furthermore, it is imperative to extend the possibilities of such cultural capital both by making it the object of critical inquiry and by appropriating in a similarly critical fashion the codes and knowledge that constitute broader and less familiar historical and cultural traditions. To empower students means more than simply affirming and analyzing the stories, histories, and experiences that are in place in their neighborhoods, that provide an organic connection to the web of relations that immediately shape their lives; it also means making them citizens of a much wider community. A critical pedagogy in this case addresses, affirms, and critically analyzes the experiences, histories, and categories of meaning that shape the immediate reality of students' lives, but it does not limit itself to these categories.

. . .

Central to this view is the need to develop an analysis of how teachers and students give meaning to their lives through the complex historical, cultural, and political forms they both embody and produce. This suggests the need for incorporating into a critical theory of schooling an analysis of those social practices that both organize systems of inequality and that assign meaning to individuals through the self- and social representations that define the dominant categories for ordering social life in any given society. Developing a theory of schooling as a form of cultural politics means analyzing how social power organizes the basic categories of class, race, gender, and ethnicity as a set of ideologies and practices that constitute specific configurations of power and politics. This points to the need for teachers to develop a deconstructive practice that uncovers rather

than suppresses the complex histories, interests, and experiences that make up the diverse voices that construct student subject positions. This is not merely a discourse of pluralism; it is a discourse of irruption, one that pushes history against the grain by challenging those forces within existing configurations of power that sustain themselves by a spurious appeal to objectivity, science, truth, universality, and the suppression of difference. The discourse of student experience is not respectful of abstract, universal claims to the truth. . . .

The discourse of student experience supports a view of pedagogy and empowerment that allows students to draw upon their own experiences and cultural resources and that also enables them to play a self-consciously active role as producers of knowledge within the teaching and learning process. This is a pedagogy in which students get the knowledge and skills that allow them to ascertain how the multiple interests that constitute their individual and collective voices are implicated, produced, affirmed, or marginalized within the texts, institutional practices, and social structures that both shape and give meaning to their lives. Such a pedagogical practice would draw attention to the processes through which knowledge is produced within the ongoing relations in which teachers, students, and texts and knowledge interact. Within these relations teachers and students produce knowledge through their own particular readings of the codes that structure and give meaning to texts.

The type of pedagogy for which I am arguing is not concerned simply with creating classroom knowledge produced through individual oppositional readings of a text, but also with a recognition of the importance of understanding the various ways in which teachers and students produce different forms of knowledge through the complex patterns of exchange they have in their interactions with each other over what constitutes dialogue, meaning, and learning itself. In other words, pedagogy itself represents an act of production. For example, both teachers and students produce knowledge in their interaction with a text by attempting to understand and reproduce the codes and assumptions that inform an author's particular writing; knowledge is also produced in an interpretative practice that reads texts as part of a wider set of cultural and historical experiences and thus produces knowledge that goes beyond the said, stated, and obvious. . . .

At issue here is the development of a pedagogy that provides the foundation for developing curriculum models that replace the authoritative language of recitation and imposition with an approach that allows students to speak from their own histories and voices while simultaneously challenging the very grounds on which knowledge and power are constructed and legitimated. Such a pedagogy makes possible a variety of human capacities which expand

the range of social identities that students may become. Such a pedagogy articulates not only a respect for a diversity of student voices; it also provides a fundamental referent for legitimizing the principle of democratic tolerance as an essential condition for forms of solidarity rooted in the virtue of trust, sharing, and a commitment to improving the quality of human life. Schools need to incorporate the diverse and contradictory stories that construct the interplay of experience, identity, and possibility that students bring to the classroom. For too many students, schools are places of "dead time," that is, holding centers that have little or nothing to do with either their lives or their dreams. Reversing that experience for students must be a central issue in reconstructing a theory of schooling as a form of cultural politics.

. . .

CONCLUSION

In this chapter we examined Critical Theory, one of the leading contemporary positions in educational foundations. We emphasized that Critical Theorists have used themes and terms from Marxism, Postmodernism, and Liberation Pedagogy. Part of Critical Theory involves a critical analysis of existing educational institutions and processes. Based on their critical analyses, Critical Theorists allege that dominant groups control schools and use them to maintain and reproduce the conditions that keep them in power. Subordinate groups are disempowered by the constructions and barriers created by those in control. Critical Theorists seek to raise the consciousness of the marginalized groups and to give them the tools needed for their own empowerment.

DISCUSSION QUESTIONS

1. Reflect on the concept of "marginality." Have you ever felt that you were at the margin rather than in the center of your school experiences? Identify groups that you believe are marginalized in existing school situations.
2. Identify the key knowledge areas and values that were considered important by teachers in your school experience. Do you believe that these knowledge areas and values were genuinely important to you as a person?
3. Compare and contrast the Critical Theorist view of the purpose of the school with that of Essentialists and Perennialists.
4. Reflect on the concepts of "empowerment" and "disempowerment." How are schools agencies of empowerment and disempowerment?

5. Why do Critical Theorists give a high degree of attention to how race, class, ethnicity, and gender are constructed in society and schools?

INQUIRY AND RESEARCH PROJECTS

1. Do an analysis of your teacher education program from a Critical Theorist perspective. Do you find any evidence of class or gender bias?
2. In a dialogue with other students, reflect on how you learned to think about race, class, ethnicity and gender.
3. Interview several experienced teachers about the implications of race, class, ethnicity, and gender for teaching and learning in schools. Report your findings to the class.
4. In your classroom experience, do you find evidence of the existence of a "hidden curriculum"? Write a paper that gives a personal account of the impact of the "hidden curriculum."

INTERNET RESOURCES

For an overview and identification of leaders in Critical Theory, contact Rage and Hope—Critical Theory at
www.perfectfit.org/CT/index2.html

An essay, "Ethics and the Critical Theory of Education," by Benjamin J. Endres can be accessed at
www.ed.uiuc.edu/EPS/PES-yearbook/97-docs/endres.html

SUGGESTIONS FOR FURTHER READING

Aronowitz, Stanley, and Giroux, Henry A. *Postmodern Education: Politics, Culture, and Social Criticism.* Minneapolis, MN: University of Minnesota Press, 1991.

Bailey, Leon. *Critical Theory and the Sociology of Knowledge: A Comparative Study in the Theory of Ideology.* New York: Peter Lang, 1994.

Calhoun, Craig J. *Critical Social Theory: Culture, History, and the Challenge of Difference.* Cambridge, MA: Blackwell, 1995.

Freire, Paulo. *Pedagogy of Freedom: Ethics, Democracy, and Civic Culture.* New York: Rowman & Littlefield, 1998.

Freire, Paulo. *Pedagogy of the Oppressed.* New York: Continuum, 1984.

Forester, John, ed. *Critical Theory and Public Life.* Cambridge, MA: MIT Press, 1985.

Giroux, Henry A. *Border Crossings: Cultural Workers and the Politics of Education.* New York: Routledge, 1992.

Giroux, Henry A. *Ideology, Culture, and the Process of Schooling.* Philadelphia, PA: Temple University Press, 1981.

Giroux, Henry A. *Teachers as Intellectuals: Toward a Critical Pedagogy of Learning.* Granby, MA: Bergin & Garvey, 1988.

Giroux, Henry A. *Theory and Resistance: A Pedagogy for the Opposition.* South Hadley, MA: J. F. Bergin, 1983.

Giroux, Henry A., and McLaren, Peter L. *Between Borders: Pedagogy and the Politics of Cultural Studies.* New York: Routledge, 1993.

Gore, J. M. *The Struggle for Pedagogies: Critical and Feminist Discourses as Regimes of Truth.* New York: Routledge, 1993.

Held, David. *Introduction to Critical Theory: Horkheimer to Habermas.* Berkeley: University of California Press, 1980.

Hoy, David C., and McCarthy, Thomas. *Critical Theory.* Oxford, UK: Blackwell, 1994.

Kincheloe, Joe I. *Toward a Critical Politics of Teacher Thinking: Mapping the Postmodern.* Westport, CT: Bergin & Garvey, 1993.

Martusewicz, Rebecca A., and Reynolds, William M., eds. *Inside/Out: Contemporary Critical Perspectives in Education.* New York: St. Martin's Press, 1994.

NOTES

1. Angeline Martel and Linda Peterat, "Margins of Exclusion, Margins of Transformation: The Place of Women in Education," in Rebecca A. Martusewicz and William Reynolds, eds. *Inside/Out: Contemporary Critical Perspectives in Education* (New York: St. Martin's Press, 1994), pp. 151–154.

2. Rebecca A. Martusewicz and William Reynolds, eds. *Inside/Out: Contemporary Critical Perspectives in Education* (New York: St. Martin's Press, 1994), p. v.

3. The relationship between Marxism and Critical Theory is discussed in Douglas Kellner, *Critical Theory, Marxism and Modernity* (Baltimore, MD: Johns Hopkins Press, 1989).

4. Freire's most influential statement of Liberation Pedagogy can be found in Paulo Freire, *Pedagogy of the Oppressed* (New York: Continuum, 1984); his most recent book, *Pedagogy of Freedom: Ethics, Democracy, and Civic Courage* (New York: Rowman & Littlefield, 2001) was published after his death in 1997.

5. Gerald L. Gutek, *American Education 1945–2000: A History and Commentary* (Prospect Heights, IL: Waveland Press, 2000), pp. 219–245.

6. For works on Habermas and the Frankfurt School, see Thomas McCarthy, *The Critical Theory of Jürgen Habermas* (Cambridge, MA: MIT Press, 1989); Robert E. Young, *A Critical Theory of Education: Habermas and Our Children's Future* (New York: Teachers College Press, 1990); Richard Wolin, *The Terms of Cultural Criticism: The Frankfurt School, Existentialism, Poststructuralism* (New York: Columbia University Press, 1992).

7. Gutek, pp. 270–289.

8. Ivan Illich, *Deschooling Society* (New York: Harper & Row, 1970); also see Illich, *Tools for Conviviality* (New York: Harper & Row, 1973).

9. Paulo Freire, *Pedagogy of Freedom: Ethics, Democracy, and Civic Courage.* Translated by Patrick Clarke (New York: Rowman & Littlefield, 2001) pp. 51–54.

10. Henry A. Giroux and Peter McLaren, eds. *Critical Pedagogy, the State, and Cultural Struggle* (Albany: State University of New York Press, 1989), pp. xi–xiii.

11. Ibid, pp. xxi–xxiii.

INDEX